"God on the cross": Till now there was never and nowhere such an audacity in reversal, something so fearful, questioning and questionable as this formula: It promised a transvaluation of all ancient values.

Nietzsche, *Beyond Good and Evil*

FRACTURE

*The Cross as Irreconcilable
in the Language and Thought
of the Biblical Writers*

Roy A. Harrisville

William B. Eerdmans Publishing Company
Grand Rapids, Michigan / Cambridge, U.K.

© 2006 Wm. B. Eerdmans Publishing Co.

Wm. B. Eerdmans Publishing Co.
255 Jefferson Ave. S.E., Grand Rapids, Michigan 49503 /
P.O. Box 163, Cambridge CB3 9PU U.K.

Printed in the United States of America

11 10 09 08 07 06   7 6 5 4 3 2 1

Library of Congress Cataloging-in-Publication Data

Harrisville, Roy A.
Fracture: the cross as irreconcilable in the language and thought
of the biblical writers / Roy A. Harrisville.
p.   cm.
ISBN-10: 0-8028-3308-X / ISBN-13: 978-0-8028-3308-2 (pbk.: alk. paper)
1. Jesus Christ — Crucifixion. 2. Bible. N.T. —
Criticism, interpretation, etc. I. Title.

BT450.H37   2006

232′.4 — dc22

2006003739

www.eerdmans.com

Contents

Contents

Preface

This book assumes that a discontinuity exists between the New Testament message and its religious environment. The thesis of this book is that the discontinuity between the New Testament and its rivals is created by the crucifixion of Jesus of Nazareth, who was witnessed to in the New Testament as risen and exalted Lord. And the method I have used here clearly serves that thesis: it seeks to uncover from the internal evidence of a given biblical author's work the "mental furniture" he may have brought with him to his encounter with the Crucified Christ — and whatever change or alteration may have resulted from it. This approach has lost much of its attraction because of the mushrooming of semantic-aesthetic research among the "word-helots" and their love of indeterminacy.

A majority of scholars and authors cited in this book are of the persuasion that a method oriented to the historical-theological deserves existence alongside the other, newer techniques; for this reason there is a minimum of references to contemporary scholars who are out of patience with such an approach. The reader will also note the geographical distribution of those who share this persuasion: many are transatlantic, those for whom the historical and theological questions still dominate. Among the European references, there are many to Ferdinand Christian Baur (1792-1860), the celebrated historical-critical pioneer. The influence of Baur on contemporary biblical scholarship is nothing short of staggering; his ghost lurks everywhere. The book also contains frequent references to Rudolf Bultmann, the only twentieth-century New Testament theologian whose work could match Baur's. It was the opinion of Bultmann's student Ernst Käsemann (likewise often quoted here) that Baur's work exceeded that of Bultmann. If the reader should have the feeling, now and then, of having suddenly dropped into a curiosity shop, I happily take responsibility for it — for "there were giants in the earth in those days." Where possible, I have supplied the birth and death years of the principal scholars.

Following the introductory chapter, which deals with the death of Jesus as initiating discontinuity, each subsequent chapter sketches the link between the New Testament author's language- and thought-forms and his perceived or imagined religious past, whether in Judaism or Hellenistic thought. At the outset, I have lifted out the references to Jesus' death in a given biblical author and book and have outlined whatever debate may have arisen over its significance. From that point I have indicated the continuity between the author's language and conceptuality and his religious past, and under the rubric of "fracture" I have shown the discontinuity with his past registered in the death of the Messiah. The study is limited to the investigation of Paul, the Synoptic Gospels, the Gospel of John, plus a briefer review of the Epistle to the Hebrews and the First Epistle of Peter, all of which give sole attention to the subject — and from a variety of perspectives.

As the number of footnotes attests, the locating of links and disconnects between a given biblical author and his religious environment or rivals I have assigned to a host of biblical interpreters. Thus the listing of similarities and differences remains a largely descriptive task; in the last analysis, even giving focus to the scholars' conclusions regarding continuity and discontinuity remains descriptive. Where the bias or prejudice of this book lies is in its appetite for emphasizing discontinuity.

To what extent the historical event of Jesus' death as initiating discontinuity between the New Testament writer's past and present may be used in the service of a system is not the concern of this book. It has been argued that, in the Pauline view, other factors alongside or tethered to the death of Jesus (the resurrection, for example) account for the *diastasis* between his past and present, for which reason the cross cannot be made a formal principle. One scholar says that, in the New Testament, the theology of the cross often proves to be secondary, and asks whether the understanding of the cross belongs to the basic constituents of Christian identity or constitutes an addition.[1] It is true, in fact,

---

1. Ulrich Luz, "Theologia crucis als Mitte der Theologie im Neuen Testament," *Evangelische Theologie* 34 (1974), 140.

that Paul's references to the cross occur exclusively in polemical contexts, a feature recurring in later authors who set the cross in defense against Gnosis. Another scholar inquires whether the cross, weakness, and suffering are so one-sidedly emphasized that other aspects of the Pauline view are disparaged; he concludes that a theology of the cross has such an exclusive character that it cannot be maintained without modification.[2] There has always been impatience with the death of Jesus as basis for a hard-and-fast, enclosed theological system, to say nothing of concentration on his death as such. Few things irritated Goethe (1749-1832) more than poison, snakes, tobacco smoke, bugs, garlic, and the cross.[3] The purpose of this study is simply to focus on an encounter with the death of Jesus as evoking a fracture in or a qualification of the "mental furniture" of an apostle or evangelist — and without attention to whatever else might have done the same.

Finally, a word regarding the readership. The reader I have in mind is anyone interested in reviewing the New Testament's witness to what lies at the heart of earliest Christian confession and what evoked its first and bitterest conflict with neighbors and foes.

This piece is dedicated to my wife, Norma, whose care for me through the years has been far more illustrative of unconditional and unmerited grace than that of anyone else. I cannot imagine what life without her would have been. And I am not unmindful of the infuence of Ernst Käsemann (1906-1998), the often choleric and frequently embattled professor of New Testament at the University of Tübingen, whose friendship I enjoyed for over thirty years, whose robust confession of the Crucified gave me assurance and comfort, and whose scholarship gave me taste for my work. Once again, I owe two of my younger colleagues, Todd Nichol, King Olav V Professor of Scandinavian Studies at St. Olaf College, and Walter Sundberg, Professor of Church History at Luther Seminary, a huge debt of gratitude for advice, and for reading and reviewing the manuscript. And my thanks are due once more to librarian Bruce Eldevik for assistance with technical details.

---

2. Helge Kjaer Nielsen, "Paulus' Verwending des Begriffes *Dynamis,*" in *Die Paulinische Literatur und Theologie,* ed. Sigfred Pedersen (Göttingen: Vandenhoeck & Ruprecht, 1980), pp. 139, 143, 147.

3. "Venetian Epigram No. 67," in *Goethes sämmtliche Werke* (Stuttgart: Verlag der J. G. Cotta'schen Buchhandlung, 1868), I, 209.

Abbreviations

BLiTEc	*Bulletin de Littérature Ecclésiastique*
ChW	*Christliche Welt*
HTR	*The Harvard Theological Review*
JBL	*Journal of Biblical Literature*
JTHS	*Journal of Theological Studies*
LW	*Luther's Works, American Edition*
NRSV	*The New Revised Standard Version of the Bible*
NTS	*New Testament Studies*
ScotJT	*The Scottish Journal of Theology*
ThR	*Theologische Rundschau*
ThLZ	*Theologische Literaturzeitung*
WA	*Luthers Werke, Weimar Ausgabe*
ZNTW	*Zeitschrift für die neutestamentliche Wissenschaft*
ZThK	*Zeitschrift für Theologie und Kirche*

CHAPTER ONE

Introduction

Textbook History without Breaks

The notion of continuous development underlies much of biblical interpretation. Since the nineteenth century, many scholars have regarded the New Testament as a stage — final or intermediate — in a more or less continuous process. Over a hundred years ago, the celebrated historian of theology Ernst Troeltsch (1865-1923) said that whatever breaks may have occurred with Christianity's emergence from its Jewish or Hellenistic matrix were far outweighed by all those forces in history striving toward a single goal.[1] Twenty years ago, in a text written for students of theology, Dieter Lührmann referred to the "link" between early Christianity, Judaism, and Hellenistic thought, declaring that this link comprises the point of departure for New Testament interpretation.[2] Another scholar describes the history of biblical tradition as a coherent process in which the interplay of reception and innovation allows us to observe a gradual progression in the development of ideas.[3] According to the interpretation of yet another biblical scholar, the era of prophecy — within the history of biblical tradition — lays the groundwork for history, the period of the exile weds history to apocalyptic, the postexilic pe-

---

1. Ernst Troeltsch quoted in Robert Morgan, *Biblical Interpretation* (New York: Oxford University Press, 1988), p. 126.

2. Dieter Lührmann, *Auslegung des Neuen Testament* (Zürich: Theologischer Verlag, 1984), pp. 58, 62.

3. Karl Theodor Kleinknecht, *Der leidende Gerechtfertigte* (Tübingen: J. C. B. Mohr, 1984), p. 387.

riod unites apocalyptic and law, to which wisdom is then added — all of which culminates in Jesus' announcement of salvation as present in the here and now. A "process of revelation" thus sets in motion "an ontological process," which is completed in the death and resurrection of Jesus.[4]

This notion of the linear development of religion or New Testament faith has clear illustration in Pauline studies. Rudolf Bultmann may not have been the first of his generation to use the term "call" or "calling" when referring to Paul's Damascus experience, but he was certainly the most widely read. Anxious over the possibility of construing the Damascus event in a psychological way, Bultmann grew more and more wary of referring to it in terms of a break, or "conversion." He finally came to say that "his was not a conversion of repentance" but the "obedient submission to the judgment of God, made known in the cross of Christ."[5] Echoing Bultmann's position, Krister Stendahl says that a closer reading of the accounts in Acts reveals a "greater continuity between 'before' and 'after,'" and he argues that Paul was not converted but merely received a new and special calling in God's service. Thus, Stendahl concludes, Paul remained a Jew while fulfilling his role as apostle to the gentiles.[6] Similarly, E. P. Sanders says that the point at which many have seen a break or gulf between Paul and Judaism is actually the point at which Paul and Judaism connect — the point of grace and works.[7] In concert with Bultmann, Stendahl, and Sanders, Gerd Lüdemann says that the term "conversion" only imperfectly expresses Paul's experience, that is, that Paul did not change his religion at Damascus: there Paul recognized the Christ-event as the eschatological event promised in Scripture, together with his commission to bear the gospel to the gentile world.[8] A Jewish scholar says that, whatever Paul was con-

4. Hartmut Gese in Hans Hübner, *Biblische Theologie des Neuen Testament* (Göttingen: Vandenhoeck & Ruprecht, 1990), pp. 16, 162-163.

5. Rudolf Bultmann, *Theology of the New Testament,* trans. Kendrick Grobel (New York: Charles Scribner's Sons, 1951), I, 188. Cf. Peter Stuhlmacher's reference to Bultmann's "reserve" in "Das Ende des Gesetzes," *Zeitschrift für Theologie und Kirche,* 67 (1970), 20.

6. Krister Stendahl, *Paul among Jews and Gentiles* (Philadelphia: Fortress, 1977), pp. 7, 11.

7. E. P. Sanders, *Paul and Palestinian Judaism* (Philadelphia: Fortress, 1977), pp. 297, 422, 543; cf. p. 513.

8. Gerd Lüdemann, "Paulus und das Judentum," *Theologische Existenz Heute,* Nr. 215 (1983), 21-22, 24.

verted *to,* he never felt he had left Judaism. Like the rabbis, he understood that the truths inherent in the Bible are manifold, complex, and sometimes contradictory, that Scripture is a "gem that gives off a different glint each time it is turned in the light of analysis."[9] The extent to which Old Testament faith may be argued as existing on a continuum — commencing with pre- or post-Israelite worship and culminating in the New Testament cultus — can be seen in Jon Levenson's provocative and fascinating book *The Death and Resurrection of the Beloved Son.*[10]

While it is true that the apparatus of the method, language, and concepts that Paul uses to proclaim his gospel are not at all unique to him, and that he scarcely uses a single device in argument or interpretation that has not already been used by others who never shared his faith,[11] the focus — the concentration — of everything in his possession, whether of method, language, or conceptuality, on a single theme, a single event, a single person, represents a challenge to the application of the linear or cumulative notion to his experience.[12] He says: "May I never boast of anything except the cross of our Lord Jesus Christ, by which the world has been crucified to me, and I to the world" (Gal. 6:14). According to Paul Minear, only when we give proper weight to the revolution that occurs in Paul's own religious world does this "triple crucifixion" of Christ, the world, and Paul make sense. Although the expression is clearly metaphorical, Paul was not playing with trivial figures of speech. The experience was so overwhelming that he was impelled to use figurative language to do it justice. First of all, that world that had

9. Alan Segal, *Paul the Convert* (New Haven, CT: Yale University Press, 1990), pp. 283-284. Cf. Leo Baeck, *Paulus, Die Pharisäer und das Neue Testament* (Frankfurt: Ner-Tamid Verlag, 1961).

10. New Haven, CT: Yale University Press, 1993. Levenson says: "It is the basic thesis of this study that a basic element of the self-understanding of both Jewry and of the Church lies in stories that are the narrative equivalent of these ritual substitutions — narratives, that is, in which the first-born or beloved son undergoes a symbolic death" (p. 59). By "ritual substitutions" Levenson means the use of animal sacrifice as substituting for, but not replacing, child sacrifice.

11. Cf. Roy A. Harrisville, "Paul and the Psalms," *Word and World* 5 (Spring, 1985), 178-179.

12. Hoskyns-Davey say that, whereas the Old Testament provides Paul with his vocabulary, thus with a framework of thought and expression, it is his portrait of Jesus that brings all the scattered fragments together (see *Crucifixion-Resurrection: The Pattern of the Theology and Ethics of the New Testament* [London: S.P.C.K., 1981], p. 188).

been "crucified" to Paul was not a world he had hated. Its crucifixion assumed his prior intimate attachment to it: "He had been as far from hating this cosmos as he had been from hating himself as a son of Abraham." Second, in speaking of himself as crucified to the world, Paul signaled an event with cosmic, ontological proportions, something that was a world away from subjective experience; for, of whatever sort the world or existence might be, it was now all subordinated to the event that had effected the double crucifixion of the world to Paul and Paul to the world — "the cross of our Lord Jesus Christ."

However strange the Pauline "cosmology" or "anthropology" was, it was made to do service to something higher, superior — "a new creation is everything!" — and attests to a revolution, not merely an alteration, in Paul's thought and life.[13] Again, Paul says:

> This one thing I do: forgetting what lies behind and straining forward to what lies ahead, I press on toward the goal for the prize of the heavenly call of God in Christ Jesus. (Phil. 3:13-14)

If these sentences do not reflect a radical break with an earlier existence — if they suggest a mere reorientation, a "calling," or another "glint" seen from the same gem — then the attempts made on Paul's life cannot be interpreted as measures taken by those who saw a quite different "glint": "Five times I have received from the Jews the forty lashes minus one. Three times I was beaten with rods. Once I received a stoning" (II Cor. 11:24-25). Whether or not one may proceed to generalize from the particular of the apostle's "conversion" and assert that the New Testament faith as a whole does not emerge with any kind of necessity from Old Testament–Jewish or pre-Israelite tradition is a question to be raised later.[14]

Where Revolutions Begin

Revolutions begin with "anomalies," with problems subverting existing practice, problems that refuse to be assimilated into the reigning

13. Paul Minear, "The Crucified World: The Enigma of Galatians 6: 14," in *Theologia Crucis — Signum Crucis: Festschrift für Erich Dinkler zum 70 Geburtstag*, ed. Carl Andresen und Günter Klein (Tübingen: J. C. B. Mohr, 1979), pp. 399-401.

14. Cf. Kleinknecht, *Der leidende Gerechtfertigte*, p. 389.

models that control research. There is a perception that something has gone wrong, a growing sense that an existing model no longer functions adequately in exploring an aspect of life or nature toward which that model had once led the way. A period of acute sense of failure results; previous practice had given every reason for confidence in the reigning model.[15]

If we look at the New Testament authors, the preponderance of the evidence is not with those who argue that what mattered was that Jesus was believed to have risen — and not the circumstance of his death. The evidence is rather with those who contend for the "abnormality" of a faith for which the death of a man executed as a criminal, and yet as the Messiah, assumes the center.[16] The entire New Testament speaks of this death, though the one family of texts (the Gospels and Acts) deals with its narration, while the other (the Epistles and the Apocalypse) deals with its representation. In the face of this unconditionally established historical fact, all the religious concepts and practices that once had served were rendered obsolete. The result was a crisis that could be gotten through only by drastically revising or abandoning the traditional models and methods.

At the same time, however anomalous or revolutionary the death of Jesus as Messiah was perceived to be, and however great its demand for a total alteration of the ways people looked at the world, themselves, and God, the biblical writers give little or no attention to the actual mode by which that death occurred. Mark, the earliest Gospel, contains but a single reference to the mode of Jesus' death, in the word of the angel to the women at the tomb: "Do not be amazed; you seek Jesus of Nazareth, *who was crucified*" (Mark 16:6). In the three so-called "passion predictions" of the Synoptic Gospels (cf. Mark 8:31; 9:31; 10:32-34), there is no mention of the precise nature of Jesus' death. In addition, the reader gains nothing from other sources, particularly Jewish ones, to indicate the nature of the accusations or of the order, time, methods, or place of Jesus' trial. If we apply the criterion of a *theological* relationship to the specific type of execution Jesus underwent, the majority of New Testa-

15. Thomas Kuhn, *The Structure of Scientific Revolutions* (Chicago: University of Chicago Press, 1962), pp. 6, 57, 67-68, 75, 92, 97.

16. Gerhard Ebeling, "Der Sühnetod Christi als Glaubensaussage: Eine hermeneutische Rechenschaft," *ZThK,* Supplement 8 (1990), p. 15.

ment authors fall short of it. Up to the middle of the second century
C.E., only Ignatius (ca. 35-107 C.E.), John, and Paul refer to the particular
mode of Jesus' execution, while a depiction of Jesus on the cross can be
documented only after the year 400.[17]

In all probability, Jesus was executed at the site of the present
Church of the Holy Sepulchre, since the tradition fixing this site as near
or outside the city (John 19:20; Heb. 13:13) is older than the layout of
Constantine the Great (274-337 C.E.) or of the British general Charles
George Gordon (1833-1885). Despite the paucity of information about
the precise mode of Jesus' death, we gain some description of it from
other sources. The "cross" *(stauros)*, originally denoting a pole or pali-
sade for fencing areas in,[18] became the all-but-exclusive method the
Romans used for execution for political crimes, a method they presumably adopted from the Carthaginians during the first Punic War (264-
241 B.C.E.). The only evidence of Jewish use of crucifixion as punishment is contained in Josephus's account of the execution of eight hundred rebels by zealots and Idumeans under the command of the Seleucid
Alexander Jannai (103-76 B.C.E.) in approximately 90 B.C.E.[19] On the
other hand, there is ample evidence of the crucifixion of Jews on the part
of their conquerors.[20] Following scourging — a fixed component be-

---

17. Cf. Heinz-Wolfgang Kuhn, "Jesus als Gekreuzigter in der frühchristlichen
Verkündigung bis zur Mitte des 2. Jahrhunderts," *ZThK* 72 (1975), 10-11, 20-22, 26, 29; Da-
vid Flusser, *Die letzten Tage Jesu in Jerusalem: Das Passionsgeschehen aus jüdischer Sicht,
Bericht über neueste Forschungsergebnisse* (Stuttgart: Calwer Verlag, 1982), p. 93; Egon
Brandenburger, "*Stauros*, Kreuzigung Jesu und Kreuzestheologie," *Wort und Dienst,*
Verlagshandlung der Anstalt Bethel, n.s., 10 (1969), 40.

18. Cf. Homer, *Iliad*, trans. A. T. Murray, rev. by Wm. F. Wyatt, The Loeb Library of
Classics (Cambridge, MA: Harvard University Press, 1999), pp. 24, 453, 596, in which
the hut of Achilles, to whom Priam goes to beg the body of Hector, is squared with a
court made of thick-set stakes *(staurousin)*; see also Homer, *Odyssey,* trans. A. T. Murray,
rev. George E. Dimock (Cambridge, MA: Harvard University Press, 1995), pp. 14, 11, 36,
in which Odysseus's swineherd, who cares for his master's property, has built a court set
off with stakes. For the reference, cf. Georg Friedrich, *Die Verkündigung des Todes Jesu im
Neuen Testament* (Neukirchen-Vluyn: Neukirchener Verlag, 1982), p. 134.

19. Cf. Josephus, *The Jewish War,* trans. H. St. J. Thackeray, The Loeb Library of
Classics (Cambridge, MA: Harvard University Press, 1968), Vol. IV, paras. 326-333, pp.
98-99.

20. For example, in 3 B.C.E., Publius Quintilius Varus, governor of Syria, allowed
two thousand Jews to be crucified around Jerusalem; cf. Josephus, *The Jewish War,* Vol. II,
para. 75, p. 351. Further, in his description of the investing of the Jewish trans-Jordan for-

tween judgment and execution — the subject's arms were affixed to a horizontal beam *(patibulum),* which may have lain on his neck and shoulders. The vertical beam, the portion of the cross set in the earth, may have been provided with a *sedile,* or seat, to furnish support; the wrists and feet were then fixed to either beam by ropes or nails. In the Fourth Gospel, the risen Christ displays the print of nails in his hands (John 20:25, 27), while in Luke he displays wounds in his feet as well as his hands (Luke 24:39) — a medical conundrum, since the victim's palms would scarcely support the weight of his body.

In 1968, during reconstruction after the Six-Day War, workers discovered the remains of a crucified man from the time of Jesus at Giv'at ha-Mivtar, in northeast Jerusalem. The victim's ankles appear to have been penetrated from the side by nails. Between the head of the nail and the right anklebone are remnants of a piece of wood that may have been used to extend the head of the nail. The feet seem to have been hacked off after the body's removal from the cross. The two shin bones and left calf bone are broken. Finally, the victim's underarms appear to have been bound to the cross since there is no trace of damage to hands or wrists. These remains are the sole evidence in all of Hellenistic-Roman antiquity of a crucified man, dating approximately from the first half of the first century C.E.[21]

The hearing before Pilate, the crucifixion, and the superscription on Jesus' cross have encouraged many in the opinion that he was executed by the Romans as a political revolutionary. His crucifixion between two thieves, allowing us to infer their involvement in an anti-Roman rebellion (cf. Mark 15:27 and John 19:18), suggests that his punishment was a civil action.[22] If this is true, Pilate must have been personally involved as prefect, having arrived at his decision on the basis of legitimate executive powers, whether or not a formal process or an

---

tress Machaerus, and the crucifixion of the revolutionary leader Eleazar in 71 C.E., Josephus says that "those in the fortress were seized with deeper dismay and with piercing shrieks exclaimed that the tragedy was intolerable" *(The Jewish War,* VII, 202, 563).

21. For a discussion of this find and its relevance to the New Testament narrative, see Heinz-Wolfgang Kuhn, "Zum Gekreuzigten von Giv'at ha-Mivtar," *Miszellen, ZNTW* 69 (1978), 118-122; see also Kuhn, "Kreuz," in *Theologische Realenzyklopädie* (Berlin: Walter de Gruyter, 1990), XIX, 714-717.

22. Dieter Sänger, *Die Verkündigung des Gekreuzigten und Israel,* WUNT (Tübingen: J. C. B. Mohr, 1994), pp. 210-211.

"extraordinary criminal procedure" resulted.[23] On the basis of the oldest pagan reference, one writer invests the sole and exclusive responsibility of Jesus' death with Pilate, who did not declare him innocent at all, as the Gospels record.[24] Hans Conzelmann (1915-1989) says that it can be confidently maintained that not only did Pilate issue the command that a death sentence be handed down by a Jewish court, but also that he sentenced Jesus.[25]

The precise role of the Jewish authorities in Jesus' crucifixion has long been a matter of debate. One side says that the practice of crucifixion was not alien to Jewish judges, that it had been decreed by Jewish courts since the second century B.C.E., and that only later was it characterized as Roman and disqualified.[26] Luke's Gospel describes Jesus' being handed over to the Jews as the result of Pilate's crumpling before Jewish pressure (Luke 23:23-24), for which reason Jesus' death is interpreted as an altogether Jewish deed; that is, in Luke there is no hint of cooperation between two parties in Jesus' crucifixion.[27] The other side

23. Heinz-Wolfgang Kuhn, "Kreuz," p. 718.

24. Cf. Wolfgang Reinbold, *Der älteste Bericht über den Tod Jesu* (Berlin: Walter de Gruyter, 1994), pp. 304, 309-310. Cf. the notice of the Roman historian Tacitus in *Ann.* 15, 44, 3, composed in or around 120-125 C.E.: *Tibero imperitante per procuratorem Pontium Pilatum supplicio adfectus erat* ("who suffered the extreme penalty during the reign of Tiberius at the hands of one of our procurators, Pontius Pilatus") (*The Complete Works of Tacitus,* trans. Alfred John Church and William Jackson Brodribb [New York: The Modern Library, 1942], p. 380). The term *supplicio adfectus* denotes mere execution, not crucifixion. Martin Kähler wrote that "the tenacious tradition" of Jesus' death on the cross was the point for which posterity retains an extrabiblical witness, that of the famous Tacitus ("Das Kreuz. Grund und Mass der Christologie," in *Schriften zu Christologie und Mission,* ed. Heinzgünter Frohnes [Munich: Christian Kaiser Verlag, 1971], p. 303). Cf. also the notice of Josephus in his *Antiquities of the Jews,* the reliability of which is in dispute. In Book XVIII, 3, the notice reads: "Pilate, upon hearing him accused by men of the highest standing amongst us, had condemned [Jesus] to be crucified" (*Antiquities of the Jews,* trans. Louis H. Feldmann [Cambridge, MA: Harvard University Press, 1981], XVIII, 64, 51).

25. Hans Conzelmann, "Die Historie und Theologie in den synoptischen Passionsberichten," in *Zur Bedeutung des Todes Jesu: Exegetische Beiträge* (Gütersloh: Gütersloher Verlagshaus Gerd Mohn, 1967), p. 47, n. 21.

26. Cf. Ernst Bammel, "Crucifixion as a Punishment in Palestine," in *The Trial of Jesus, Cambridge Studies in Honor of C. F. D. Moule* (London: SCM Press, 1970), pp. 162-165.

27. Ulrich Wilckens, *Die Missionsreden der Apostelgeschichte* (Neukirchen-Vluyn: Neukirchener Verlag, 1961), p. 128.

says that in Israel there was no execution by crucifixion, merely the order for hanging a corpse after stoning, and that the Septuagint subsequently confused this usage with the non-Jewish "hanging on wood" as execution.[28] The debate has been further complicated with the 1977 publication by Yigael Yadin (1917-1984) of the so-called Temple Scroll, longest of the scrolls of Qumran. In column 64:7-12, the passage in Deuteronomy 21 is expanded to refer to crucifixion, and the curse is widened to read that those who are crucified are cursed by God *and* men:

> If a man passes on information about his people and betrays his people to a foreign people and does evil to his people, then you shall hang him on the wood, so that he dies. On the strength of two witnesses or on the strength of three witnesses he shall be killed and they shall hang him on the wood. If a man has committed a capital offence and flees to the nations and curses his people, the Israelites, then you shall also hang him on the wood, so that he dies. Yet they shall not let his corpse hang on the wood, but must bury it on the same day, for cursed by God and men are those who are hanged on the wood, and you shall not pollute the earth. . . .[29]

To conclude from this passage that the Jews actually had the power to carry out the death sentence may assign it a weight it cannot bear. After

---

28. Cf. Gert Jeremias, *Der Lehrer der Gerechtigkeit* (Göttingen: Vandenhoeck & Ruprecht, 1963), pp. 131-132. In addition, Jeremias believes that the emphatic position of terms in the Qumran *pesher* on Nahum, which refer to the Lion of Wrath's hanging "men alive" *(thalah anoshim hayyom),* implies a type of execution counter to Jewish usage (p. 133); cf. Florentino Garcia Martinez and Eibert J. C. Tigchelaar, eds., *The Dead Sea Scrolls Study Edition,* 4Q169 (Grand Rapids: Eerdmans, 2000), p. 337. It is possible that Jeremias's argument had less to do with syntactical considerations than with opposition to John Allegro's fanciful opinion that the *pesher* refers to the crucifixion of the Righteous Teacher. The entire reference is absent from Vermes's edition of 4Q169, *The Dead Sea Scrolls in English* (Sheffield, UK: Sheffield Academic Press, 4th edition, 1995), p. 336.

29. Johann Maier, *The Temple Scroll,* trans. Richard T. White (Sheffield: JSOT Press, 1985), p. 55. Peter Stuhlmacher ("Achtzehn Thesen zur paulinischen Kreuzestheologie," in *Versöhnung, Gesetz und Gerechtigkeit* [Göttingen: Vandenhoeck & Ruprecht, 1981], p. 196) says that the extracts published by Yadin indicate that pre-Christian Judaism referred the command in Deuteronomy 21 to the crucifixion of transgressors. Heinz-Wolfgang Kuhn had already noted that Paul's argument in Galatians 3 involved a contemporary Jewish view that related Deuteronomy 21 to a crucified man ("Jesus als Gekreuzigter," pp. 33-34).

Yadin's publication — as well as before it — some have insisted that the power of execution had been taken from the Jews, for which reason their authorities denounced Jesus before Pilate.[30] Referring to the passage in John's passion narrative in which Pilate says to those clamoring for Jesus' death, "Take him yourselves and judge him according to your law," a number of commentators insist that only the procurator had the *ius gladii,* and that thus the Jews' response ("We are not permitted to put anyone to death") reflects totally reliable tradition.[31]

The oldest extant passion narrative notes that Jesus was not crucified *by* but rather *under* Pontius Pilate (lst century C.E.), which would indicate that, by laying claim to the power of the Roman prefect, the Jews brought Jesus to his cross on the basis of his messiahship.[32] In response to what he terms a "hermeneutics of suspicion," which "loses the soil of historical reality under its feet" — thus making the real event of the passion all but inaccessible — Gerhard Lohfink proposes the following sequence: the Sanhedrin clearly recognizes that no Roman judge may sen-

---

30. Cf. Eduard Lohse, "Die alttestamentlichen Bezüge im neutestamentlichen Zeugnis vom Tode Jesu Christi," in *Zur Bedeutung des Todes Jesu,* and Peter Stuhlmacher, *Was geschah auf Golgotha?* (Stuttgart: Calwer Verlag, 1998), pp. 11, 22. In his Göttingen lectures on Matthew in 1957, Ernst Käsemann described the reference to crucifixion in Jesus' attack on the scribes and Pharisees ("I send you prophets, sages, and scribes, some of whom you will kill and crucify" [Matt. 23:34]) as "unfortunate, since the Jews neither had the right to punishment by crucifixion nor made use of it" (*Matthäusevangelium,* II, 137).

31. Cf. Alois Stöger, "Das Christusbild im Johanneischen Schrifttum," in *Der historische Jesus und der Christus unseres Glaubens: Eine Katholische Auseinandersetzung mit den Folgen der Entmythologisierungstheorie* (Vienna, Freiburg, Basel: Herder, 1962), p. 142. Stöger refers to an article by Joachim Jeremias in which the latter states that John 18:31 is completely correct, and that the report in Mark 14:55–15:15 is unimpeachable "on the face of the assumed facts of civil relationships" (see Jeremias, "Zur Geschichtlichkeit des Verhörs vor dem Hohen Rat," *ZNTW* 43 (1950/51), 150.

32. Cf. T. A. Burkill, "St. Mark's Philosophy of the Passion," *Novum Testamentum,* Vol. II (1958), 249; see also Nils Alstrup Dahl, *The Crucified Messiah and Other Essays* (Minneapolis: Augsburg Publishing House, 1974), p. 31. In *Der älteste Bericht über den Tod Jesu,* Wolfgang Reinbold says that this narrative forced the process of separation between church and synagogue (pp. 97, 197-199). Cf. Gerhard Lohfink, *Der letzte Tag Jesu: Die Ereignisse der Passion* (Freiburg: Herder, 1981): "Whoever denies to Jesus the confession of his Messiahship before Caiaphas, does not clarify but rather obscures the course of events of the passion and the interweaving of the [Roman and Jewish judicial] process" (p. 39).

tence a Jew to death for transgressing intra-Jewish laws. Accordingly, it brings Jesus to Pilate for indictment under another consideration, that of Jesus as political instigator. Pilate, eager for a juridical evaluation by a Jewish authority, sends Jesus to Herod, who mocks and scorns him, throws an outer garment around him, and sends him back to Pilate. The symbolism is not lost on Pilate: the man from Nazareth is a laughable figure, politically harmless. For this reason the procurator proposes him as a Passover amnesty, but by doing so unwittingly attests to his guilt. The crowd demands Jesus' death.[33] A variant of this view reads that, inasmuch as the trial before the Sanhedrin in the oldest narrative (Mark 14:55-65) bears all the earmarks of an insertion, and since the parallel in John (18:19-24) mentions two high priests, any official Sanhedrin setting may be regarded as suspicious.[34]

One Jewish author says that, if in fact the Sanhedrin held such a trial as Mark or Matthew describes, it would have involved an illegality without parallel in Jewish history. He adds that, since some Sadducean aristocrats friendly to Rome were wiped out in the war of liberation in 70 C.E., they had to be in mortal fear of such reprisals in the preceding years and must have, in the interest of self-preservation, protected themselves from possible messianic revolts. Accordingly, from an understandable feeling of political responsibility and fearful of another Roman bloodbath — and not from hate or envy — "a few Sadducees" delivered Jesus up to the Romans.[35] Albert Schweitzer (1875-1965) was of another opinion. In a footnote contained in his *Quest of the Historical Jesus,* he concedes the illegality of the Sanhedrin session on Passover eve or the night before and its levying of the death sentence — that is, provided Mishnaic rules attaching to such procedure were already in force.

33. Lohfink, *Der letzte Tag Jesu,* pp. 44, 46-47. Albert Vanhoye ("Struktur und Theologie der Passionsberichte in den Synoptischen Evangelien," in *Redaktion und Theologie des Passionsberichtes nach den Synoptikern* [Darmstadt: Wissenschaftliche Buchgesellschaft, 1981], p. 238) says that, according to Matthew, the trial was an unjust procedure, evidenced by the betrayal for silver and Judas' admission of guilt (cf. Matt. 26:14-16; 27:3-10).

34. Heinz-Wolfgang Kuhn, "Kreuz," p. 719.

35. Pinchas Lapide, *Wer war schuldig an Jesu Tod?* (Gütersloh: Gütersloher Verlagshaus, Gerd Mohn, 1987), pp. 64-65, 102, 104-105. Egon Brandenburger says that, though Jesus was judged and executed by the Romans according to their criteria and legal practices, cooperation on the part of the Jewish authority should not be excluded (cf. "*Stauros,* Kreuzigung Jesu und Kreuzestheologie," p. 30).

But, he adds, one may not on this account impugn the historicity of the biblical narrative. Church authorities, imagining their authority or religion to be in danger, can quite easily set themselves above legal regulations.[36]

However suspect the Gospels' report of the Sanhedrin hearing may appear, according to Kurt Schubert,[37] attention to the religious-historical milieu lends support to its historicity. Schubert refers to apocalyptic groups of the early second century B.C.E. who believed that the temple in Jerusalem had been so desecrated that it had to be replaced by a new, heavenly temple. To illustrate, he cites Ethiopic Enoch, a second-century text emerging from a circle that held to a view of history as leading inevitably to the Rule of God of the end-time:

> I stood still, looking at that ancient house being transformed: All the pillars and all the columns were pulled out, and the ornaments of that house were packed and taken out together with them and abandoned in a certain place in the South of the land. I went on seeing until the Lord of the sheep brought about a new house, greater and loftier than the first one, and set it up in the first location which had been covered up — all its pillars were new, the columns new; and the ornaments new as well as greater than those of the first, [that is] the old [house] which was gone (90:28-29).[38]

Such an expectation, Schubert argues, might have combined with Jesus' prediction of the temple's ruin. As a result, the temple priesthood, suspicious of Jesus' prediction as screening actual participation, would have haled him before its court to determine his guilt. Since Jesus gave no response to the charge against him (cf. Mark 14:58; Matt. 26:61), nothing remained but to put the messianic question: "Are you the Mes-

36. Albert Schweitzer, *The Quest of the Historical Jesus,* ed. John Bowden (Minneapolis: Fortress Press, 2001), p. 526, n. 31 (originally published in 1906 and titled *Von Reimarus zu Wrede*).

37. "Kritik der Bibelkritik," in *Redaktion und Theologie des Passionsberichtes nach den Synoptikern,* pp. 329, 331, 334-335; see also Schubert's "Die jüdischen Religionsparteien im Zeitalter Jesu," in *Der historische Jesus und der Christus unseres Glaubens* (Basel: Herder, 1962), pp. 28, 86, n. 47.

38. 1 (Ethiopic Apocalypse of) Enoch, *The Old Testament Pseudepigrapha,* ed. James H. Charlesworth (New York: Doubleday, 1983-1985), Vol. I, *Apocalyptic Literature and Testaments,* p. 71.

siah, the Son of the Blessed One?" (Mark 14:61). If Jesus' followers, whatever their misconceptions, interpreted his activity messianically, the hearing before the high priest might in fact have involved the messianic question. This reading, Schubert contends, suits the religious-historical picture of Judaism during the time of Jesus.[39] As for the reference to the two high priests in John 18, it could be interpreted to read that Annas, as head of the high priestly clan, constructed his own picture of the affair, then handed Jesus over to his son-in-law, Caiaphas, who actually held the high priestly office and in the meantime had summoned members of the Jewish court to his palace.[40] Similarly, Gerard Sloyan says that the current high priest and his father-in-law, Annas, despised by the people as agents of the Caesars, and acting through the prefects since the death of Herod the Great, seem to have brought on Jesus' execution, and that Jesus' words about the temple were the sole reason for his death.[41]

Jesus' cleansing of the temple, which resulted in the authorities' plot to kill him (Mark 11:15-18; Luke 19:45-48), or at least initiated the conflict between him and "the Jews" (John 2:13-16), has equal right to furnishing the occasion for his arraignment. S. G. F. Brandon (1907-1971) says that Jesus' activities in the last few days, especially his attack on the temple establishment, convinced the authorities that he was a subversive force, for the suppression of which the Romans would hold them responsible.[42] Joachim Gnilka suggests that the temple logion (Mark 11:17) furnishes the background foil for the entire narrative of the Sanhedrin action, but that at the same time it assigns interest in such historical details as the assembly of the Sanhedrin and Jesus' arrest to a "second stage of the tradition."[43] Jostein Ädna adds that, with his interference at the temple market, Jesus symbolically marked the end of the sacrificial cult, thus assuring a violent outcome. In support of his hypothesis, he quotes the Jewish scholar Jacob Neusner:

39. Cf. Schubert, "Kritik der Bibelkritik," pp. 320-323, 327, 331-332, 334.

40. Cf. Stuhlmacher, *Was geschah auf Golgotha?*, pp. 21-22.

41. Sloyan, *The Crucifixion of Jesus* (Minneapolis: Fortress, 1995), pp. 27, 39.

42. S. G. F. Brandon, *The Trial of Jesus of Nazareth* (New York: Stein and Day, 1968), pp. 81-92.

43. Joachim Gnilka, "Die Verhandlungen vor dem Synhedrion und vor Pilatus nach Markus 14:53–15:5," in *Redaktion und Theologie des Passionsberichtes nach den Synoptikern*, pp. 297, 303-310.

The overturning of the moneychangers' tables represents an act of the rejection of the most important rite of the Israelite cult, the daily whole-offering, and, therefore, a statement that there is a means of atonement other than the daily whole offering, which now is null.[44]

As to the occasion for Jesus' arraignment, Wolfgang Reinbold says that "in actuality we are stumbling around in the dark."[45] Nevertheless, there is general consensus that the Jewish authorities, together with the Romans, prepared a violent end for Jesus. There is nothing in the Gospel accounts, however, to suggest a judicial murder. In the eyes of Jesus' opponents, he was justly accused, condemned, and suffered death as a false prophet and seducer of the people — a view echoed in later rabbinic sources.[46] For example, there was nothing illegal attaching to the counsel recounted at the conclusion of the conflict-speeches in Mark's Gospel (2:1–3:6). Leviticus 24:16 had required the punishment of death for the blasphemy of which Jesus was accused:

> Now some of the scribes were sitting there, questioning in their hearts, "Why does this fellow speak in this way? It is blasphemy! Who can forgive sins but God alone?" (Mark 2:6-7)

And Numbers 15:32-36 had required the sentence of death for the transgression of the Sabbath, of which he was likewise accused:

---

44. Jostein Ädna, "Jesus' Symbolic Act in the Temple (Mark 11:15-17): The Replacement of the Sacrificial Cult by His Atoning Death," in *Gemeinde ohne Temple/Community without Temple* (Tübingen: J. C. B. Mohr, 1999), pp. 461-473; and Jacob Neusner, "Money-Changer in the Temple: The Mishnah's Explanation," *NTS* 35 (1989), 290.

45. Cf. Wolfgang Reinbold, *Der älteste Bericht über den Tod Jesu,* p. 313.

46. Cf. Jürgen Moltmann, *The Crucified God,* trans. R. A. Wilson and John Bowden (Minneapolis: Fortress, 1993), p. 1765; Dieter Sänger, "Verflucht ist jeder, der am Holze Hängt (Gal. 3:13b.)," *ZNTW* 85 (1994), 284-285. Cf. Deut. 13; 17:2-7; 18:9-13, 20-22; Lev. 24:16; Num. 15:30-31. The Babylonian Talmud, which contains the earliest rabbinic reference to Jesus' death and says that Jesus was executed by stoning and subsequently hanged, is of only minimal historical value. Cf. R. Travers Herford, *Christianity in Talmud and Midrash,* Library of Religious and Philosophical Thought (Clifton, NJ: Reference Book Publishers, Inc., 1966), pp. 83-84; see also the Tosephta reference in Herford, pp. 86-87. Birger Gerhardsson says that the rabbinic rejection of Jesus applied without exception, and he adds that the situation would have been otherwise if Jesus had been executed solely on the order of the Roman authorities; see "Jesus, Ausgeliefert und Verlassen — Nach dem Passionsbericht des Matthäusevangeliums," in *Redaktion und Theologie,* p. 265.

One Sabbath he was going through the grainfields; and as they made their way his disciples began to pick heads of grain. The Pharisees said to him, "Look, why are they doing what is not lawful on the Sabbath?" (Mark 2:23-24)

Whether or not Mark's version of the second passion prediction (Mark 9:30-32) is colored by a concern to describe Jesus' death as benefiting all humankind,[47] it does not separate Jewish from Roman responsibility for it. It rather describes Jesus' betrayal "into human hands," not into the hands of the Jews. To what extent Jesus' crucifixion helped to stabilize normally tense relations between Jews and Romans until the first rebellion can only be surmised.[48]

In the context of Roman rule, the duration of death by torture was constitutive of crucifixion. In the Gospel of Mark, Pilate expresses surprise that Jesus has died so soon after his crucifixion (not more than six hours later; see Mark 15:25, 34-37). The procurator's reaction suits the brutal, sadistic kind of execution, since the one executed hung alive on the cross for hours, even days, his body prey to carrion, which obviated burial (and thus renders the 1968 discovery an unusual find). As for the actual site of crucifixion, whether or not Golgotha was regularly used or was especially chosen for Jesus' execution, it was plainly visible from far off, and the execution was calculated to serve as a warning to potential evildoers.

Whatever the role of the Roman or Jewish authorities in Jesus' death,[49] however little or much the manner of his death furnished occasion for reflection — and whether or not Jesus himself saw any significance in it — the New Testament testifies to a convergence on that event that effected a revolution in language and thought. So-called liberal nineteenth-century theology restricted the convergence, or at least reflection on it, to the Pauline and post-Pauline tradition. Today the tendency is to disallow that restriction.[50] Nils Dahl (1911-2001) contends that, whether or not Jesus laid claim to the title, his crucifixion as Mes-

47. Cf. Gottfried Schille, *Offen für alle Menschen: Redaktionsgeschichtliche Beobachtungen zur Theologie des Markusevangeliums* (Stuttgart: Calwer Verlag, 1974), p. 79.

48. Cf. Stuhlmacher, *Was geschah auf Golgotha?*, p. 23.

49. In Sänger's opinion, nothing certain can be said of the role of the Pharisees — in whatever direction; see Sänger, *Die Verkündigung des Gekreuzigten*, pp. 210-211, n. 68.

50. Cf. Fritz Viering, *Der Kreuzestod Jesu: Interpretation eines theologischen Gutachtens* (Gütersloh: Gütersloher Verlagshaus, Gerd Mohn, 1969), p. 24.

siah has become the content of the gospel par excellence, for which reason inquiry into his preaching as well as his life demands that historical research begin with that death as the "axis" on which everything turns.[51] Gerhard Ebeling says that, though the convergence of the biblical authors regarding Jesus' death cannot be fixed in a formula, the New Testament in its entirety is nonetheless oriented to it.[52]

According to Luke, in Paul's defense before Herod Agrippa II (ca. 27-93 C.E.) at Caesarea, he witnessed to the revolution the death of Jesus had effected in his own case:

> I stand here, testifying to both small and great, saying nothing but what the prophets and Moses said would take place: that the Messiah must suffer. (Acts 26:22-23).

"That the Messiah must suffer" — this was the new model, the new paradigm that had resulted from the crisis. Just as Paul did, the Synoptists leave no doubt regarding the paradigm they have come to embrace. Three times Mark, Matthew, and Luke attach the prediction of the passion to a signal event in Jesus' career: to the confession of Peter at Caesarea Philippi, to the Transfiguration, and to the triumphal entry into Jerusalem:

> Then he began to teach them that the Son of Man must undergo great suffering, and be rejected by the elders, the chief priests, and the scribes, and be killed, and after three days rise again. (Mark 8:31; Matt. 16:21; Luke 9:22)

> He was teaching his disciples, saying to them, "The Son of Man is to be betrayed into human hands, and they will kill him, and three days after being killed, he will rise again." (Mark 9:31; Matt. 17:22-23; Luke 9:44)

> The Son of Man will be handed over to the chief priests and the scribes, and they will condemn him to death; then they will hand him over to the Gentiles; they will mock him, and spit upon him, and flog him, and kill him; and after three days he will rise again. (Mark 10:33-34; Matt. 20:18-19; Luke 18:31-33)

51. Nils Dahl, "The Crucified Messiah," and "The Problem of the Historical Jesus," in *The Crucified Messiah and Other Essays,* pp. 34, 72.

52. Gerhard Ebeling, "Der Sühnetod Christi als Glaubensaussage," p. 9.

Polarization

The "anomaly" of the death of Messiah had its consequence in a polarization that resisted recourse to politics. Paul said: "Jews demand signs and Greeks desire wisdom, but we proclaim Christ crucified, a stumbling block to Jews and foolishness to Gentiles" (I Cor. 1:22-23).

"Jews Demand Signs . . ."

First of all, a crucified and dead Messiah represented for Judaism an impossibility in the face of the conviction that *Sheol* ("the pit"), the realm of the dead, was outside Yahweh's rule. Aside from whether or not that conviction derived from a nomadic past — in which migration spelled separation from the ancestral grave — the God of Israel was conceived as totally removed from death.[53] The God of the Old Testament does not remember the dead; they are bereft of his help. He does no wonders for them, and they can no longer praise him:

> In death there is no remembrance of you; in Sheol who can give you praise? (Ps. 6:5)

> What profit is there in my death, if I go down to the Pit? Will the dust praise you? Will it tell of your faithfulness? (Ps. 30:9)

> Do you work wonders for the dead? Do the shades rise up to praise you? Is your steadfast love declared in the grave . . . ? (Ps. 88:10-11)

> The dead do not praise the Lord, nor do any that go down into silence. (Ps. 115:17)

> For Sheol cannot thank you, death cannot praise you; those who go down to the Pit cannot hope for your faithfulness. (Isa. 38:18f.)

---

53. Gottfried Quell, *Die Auffassung des Todes in Israel* (Erlangen: A. Deichertsche Verlagsbuchhandlung, 1925), pp. 31, 33; Victor Maag, "Tod und Jenseits nach dem Alten Testament," *Schweizerische Theologische Rundschau* 34 (1964), 17, 20; Eberhard Jüngel, *Death: The Riddle and the Mystery,* trans. Iain and Ute Nicol (Philadelphia: Westminster, 1974), p. 109.

The theme is reiterated in the intertestamental, apocryphal literature:

> Who will sing praises to the Most High in Hades in place of the living who give thanks? From the dead, as from one who does not exist, thanksgiving has ceased; those who are alive and well sing the Lord's praises. (Sirach 17:27)

> Open your eyes, O Lord, and see, for the dead who are in Hades, whose spirit has been taken from their bodies, will not ascribe glory or justice to the Lord. (Baruch 2:17)

The subject is also present in a Qumran prayer for deliverance:

> For no worm thanks Thee, nor a maggot recounts Thy loving-kindness. Only the living thank Thee, all they whose feet totter, thank Thee, when Thou makest known to them Thy loving-kindness, and causest them to understand Thy righteousness. For the soul of the living is in Thy hand. . . . (11QPsa XIX)[54]

Thus *Sheol*, Hades, the realm of the dead is totally inaccessible to the creature; it is a realm from which no one returns. Of his dead child born to Bathsheba, David says, "I shall go to him, but he will not return to me" (II Sam. 12:23). And Job cries: "He no longer returns who has gone down into *Sheol*," a realm "as gloomy as the dark night" with "no midday," and where deep sleep has gotten the upper hand (Job 7:9; 10:21; 14:12). In Job, whether or not Yahweh can actually break into *Sheol* is an open question:

> Oh that you would hide me in Sheol, that you would conceal me until your wrath is past, that you would appoint me a set time, and remember me! (Job 14:13)

In the Thanksgiving Psalm, the singer can report his rescue from *Sheol* ("The Lord has heard my supplication; the Lord accepts my prayer," Ps. 6:9), but it is rescue *this side of* "the Pit." For the rest, death means silence on everything heard in the world (Ps. 94:17; 115:17). According to Koheleth, death is totally senseless. The preacher laments: "There is no work or thought or knowledge or wis-

---

54. Geza Vermes, *The Dead Sea Scrolls in English*, p. 240.

dom in *Sheol*" (Eccles. 9:10), for which reason "a living dog is better than a dead lion" (9:4).[55]

For the Old Testament authors, existence beyond the grave can be secured only through God's remembrance, through the memory of the clan or tribe, or, in later postexilic thought, through the memory of the community of those true to the Torah. For all its hope in a conquest of death, or in fellowship with Yahweh after death (cf. Ps. 16:9ff.; Isa. 25:7-8; 26:19; Ezek. 37:3; Ps. 73:23-24, 26), the horror never recedes. It is reflected in Israel's funeral customs and their cultic significance: death and everything connected with it is unclean; it also renders living people unclean, and since the uncleanness threatens to pass over to those still living, great care must be given to the burial of the dead.[56]

If in the postexilic period Greek ideas of immortality began to penetrate Israelite religion, they were hotly contested rather than universally received. Only at the edge of the Old Testament or in the Greco-Roman period do apocalyptic ideas appear of God's swallowing up death and decay (cf. Isa. 25:8; 26:19; Dan. 12:2; the so-called Diptychon in Wisdom 2:12-20; 5:1-7).[57] Second, throughout the history of Judaism, the idea of a suffering Messiah appears in such pale fashion as to allow us to infer an accidental rather than a dogmatic occurrence.[58] In pre-Christian Judaism, the Song of the Servant in Isaiah 52:13–53:12 was interpreted messianically,[59] but largely exclusive of those verses that deal with the Servant's sufferings and death. In his major work, *Kyrios Christos,* Wilhelm Bousset (1865-1920) says that it was doubtful whether it would

55. Maag, *Tod und Jenseits nach dem Alten Testament,* p. 22; Christof Hardmeier, "'Denn im Tod ist kein Gedenken an dich . . .' (Ps. 6:6): Der Tod des Menschen-Gottes Tod?" *Evangelische Theologie,* 48 (Jahrgang No. 4, 1988), 300; Ulrich Kellermann, "Überwindung des Todesgeschicks in der alttestamentlichen Frömmigkeit vor und neben dem Auferstehungsglauben," *ZThK* 73, No. 3 (1976), 264, 274.

56. Kellermann, "Überwindung des Todesgeschicks," 266, 268, 271-272; Quell, *Die Auffassung des Todes in Israel,* pp. 11-12, 22-25, 40-42.

57. Kellermann, pp. 271, 278-279; Maag, *Tod und Jenseits,* pp. 28, 31; Hardmeier, "Denn im Tod," p. 301, n. 39.

58. Cf. Christian Maurer, "Knecht Gottes und Sohn Gottes im Passionsbericht des Markusevangelium," in *Redaktion und Theologie,* p. 116.

59. Hans-Joachim Schoeps writes that in Judaism the Servant was "probably at an early period understood and personified as the Messiah" (*Paul: The Theology of the Apostle in the Light of Jewish Religious History,* trans. Harold Knight [Philadelphia: Westminster, 1961], p. 135).

have been possible, in view of Jewish messianic belief, to interpret Isaiah 53 in terms of a *suffering* Messiah.[60] The contemporaries of Deutero-Isaiah could not accept the idea that God's beloved should die. Nor could the participants at the feast of Purim, which commemorated the deliverance of the exiles from the massacre plotted by Haman, the highest official of the Persian king. At Purim the Book of Esther was read, and each time Haman's name was reached, the audience cried, "Let his name be blotted out," or "The name of the wicked shall rot." In the Septuagint, the term for crucifixion *(stauroō)* is used twice to describe Haman's execution. It was inconceivable that the Messiah should suffer the same fate.[61]

It may be incorrect to declare that the Jews in Jesus' time had forgotten the ideas in Isaiah 53, but it was difficult for the Jews to apply such ideas to the Messiah.[62] The Fourth Book of Maccabees supports the view that, in Palestinian-oriented Judaism of the New Testament period, a man's death could be understood as substitution,[63] but the death of Messiah construed as ransom was a step it probably did not take. As for Jesus, the curse in Deuteronomy 21:22-23 will at least have summarized

60. Wilhelm Bousset, *Kyrios Christos,* trans. John E. Steely (Nashville: Abingdon Press, 1970), pp. 111-114.

61. Franz-Joseph Ortkemper, *Das Kreuz in der Verkündigung des Apostels Paulus* (Stuttgart: Katholisches Bibelwerk, 1968), p. 50; Dieter Sänger, *Die Verkündigung des Gekreuzigten und Israel,* p. 215; T. C. G. Thornton, "The Crucifixion of Haman and the Scandal of the Cross," *JThS* 37 (1986), 421-426.

62. Strack-Billerbeck state that, in the (extant) rabbinic literature, the application of Isaiah 53 to the Messiah does not appear before 200 C.E., and that its application to "the righteous" or the nation of Israel (the now dominant interpretation) occurs later (H. L. Strack and Paul Billerbeck, *Das Evangelium nach Matthäus erläutert aus Talmud und Midrasch* [Munich: C. H. Beck'sche Verlagsbuchhandlung, 1922], p. 481). Cf. Birger Gerhardsson, "Jesus, Ausgeliefert und Verlassen — nach dem Passionsbericht des Matthäusevangeliums," p. 263.

63. When thrown into the fire by his torturers, Eleazar prayed, "Be merciful to your people and let our punishment be a satisfaction on their behalf. Make my blood their purification and take my life as a ransom for theirs" (IV Macc. 6:28-29); and of Eleazar and others who suffered martyrdom under Antiochus, it says that "they became, as it were, a ransom for the sin of our nation. Through the blood of these righteous ones and through the propitiation of their death the divine providence rescued Israel" (17:21-22). See Levenson, *The Death and Resurrection of the Beloved Son,* p. 3, n. 12; see also Jürgen Becker, "Die neutestamentliche Rede vom Sühnetod Jesu," *ZThK,* Supp. 8 (1990), 39.

Jewish reservations if it did not in fact comprise a direct polemic against his messiahship:[64]

> When someone is convicted of a crime punishable by death and is executed, and you hang him on a tree, his corpse must not remain all night upon the tree; you shall bury him that same day, for anyone hung on a tree is under God's curse. You must not defile the land that the Lord your God is giving you for possession.

Paul's argument in Galatians 3, which reads that "Christ redeemed us from the curse of the law by becoming a curse for us" (v. 13), has all the earmarks of a synagogal argument that he himself may once have helped to shape. It may be that Paul's once having forced Christians to blaspheme (see Acts 26:11) involved the application of Deuteronomy 21:23 to Jesus' crucifixion, an application that may be reflected in the response to his preaching at Pisidian Antioch and at Corinth (Acts 13:45; 18:6). Paul may not have been the first to connect the curse threatened in the Torah with the punishment of crucifixion. A passage from the Temple Scroll of Qumran reads: "If a man is guilty of a capital crime and he flees (abroad) to the Gentiles, and curses his people, and the sons of Israel, you shall hang him also on the tree, and he shall die."[65] At any rate, the expletive referred to in I Corinthians 12:3 ("Jesus be cursed" [*anathema Iēsous*]) is exclusively Jewish; if it was not invented by Paul, it was shared with those of his persuasion. In the opinion of one writer, the formulae of faith in Acts point to a debate harking back to the earliest period of Christian faith (cf. Acts 3:13, 15; 4:10; 5:30; 7:52; 10:39; 13:28f.).[66] How better to reject Jesus' claim to messiahship than to refer to a word of the Torah that Christians also accepted? The third-century apologist Tertullian (ca. 220

64. Peter Stuhlmacher, in "Achtzehn Thesen zur paulinischen Kreuzestheologie" (p. 196), notes that extracts published by Yigael Yadin from the Temple Scroll (Col. 64: 6-13) indicate that pre-Christian Judaism referred the command in Deuteronomy 21 to the execution of transgressors on the cross. He then refers to John 19:31ff., to the ancient-apologetic "scheme of contrast" in Acts, and to the well-known passage in Justin Martyr as proof that the Jews also interpreted Jesus' crucifixion in this way.

65. 11Q Temple, LXIV, in Geza Vermes, *The Dead Sea Scrolls in English*, p. 251.

66. Dieter Sänger, "Verflucht ist jeder, der am Holze hängt," pp. 281-282; cf. Gerhard Friedrich, *Die Verkündigung des Todes Jesu im Neuen Testament*, p. 122, and Robin S. Barbour, "Wisdom and the Cross in I Corinthians 1 and 2," *Theologia Crucis — Signum Crucis*, p. 57.

C.E.) said specifically that the Jewish-Christian debate over Jesus' messiahship centered on Deuteronomy 21:23. In his attempt to remove the difficulty posed by the text, he referred to its introduction ("when someone is convicted of a crime . . .") and concluded that since "[Jesus] did not suffer for any evil act of his, but that scripture might be fulfilled from the mouth of the prophets," the Deuteronomic law was not applicable to him.[67] The *Didascalia Apostolorum,* a text translated into Syriac between 300 and 330 C.E., described the Deuteronomic passage as belonging to the "Second *(secundatio)* Legislation," a series of punishments meted out to Israel following its worship of the golden calf, calculated to harden it against Christ and blind it to the point of placing him under a curse. Such legislation, the *Didascalia* argued, was abolished with the advent of Christ, who came "that He might affirm the Law, and abolish the Second Legislation, and fulfil the power of men's liberty, and show forth the resurrection of the dead."[68]

In his allusion to Deuteronomy 21, Trypho, the second-century rabbi cited by the apologist Justin Martyr (ca. 100-165 C.E.), read the text to mean that a curse was uttered "by God" over the crucified, a reading identical to that of the Septuagint, and athwart customary Jewish exegesis. Like Paul in Galatians 3:13, Justin omitted the phrase "by God," which, curiously, Trypho left unnoticed. In what amounts to a summary of Judaism's attitude toward a crucified Messiah, the much-quoted Trypho said:

> It has indeed been proved sufficiently by your Scriptural quotations that it was predicted in the Scriptures that Christ should suffer. . . . But what we want you to prove to us is that he was to be crucified and be subjected to so disgraceful and shameful a death. . . . We find it impossible to think that this could be so.[69]

The rabbi had been prepared to yield the idea of a suffering messiah considerable concession, since such an idea had not yet emerged in Juda-

67. Quintus Septimius Florens Tertullianus, *Adversus Judaeos* 10:3, *Opera Omnia,* Pars Secunda, J.-P. Migne, *Patrologia Latina* (Paris: Migne, 1844), II, 626.

68. *Didascalia Apostolorum,* trans. R. Hugh Connolly (Oxford: Clarendon Press, 1929), p. 224.

69. *Saint Justin Martyr, The Fathers of the Church,* trans. Thomas B. Falls (New York: Christian Heritage, Inc., 1949), pp. 208, 291.

ism.[70] But he rejected the identification of the Christ-Messiah with a crucified Jesus.

With the exception of Trypho, the silence of postbiblical Judaism concerning a suffering messiah is unanimous. In the Aramaic version, or Targum, on the Fourth Servant Song, dating perhaps from the fifth century C.E. — though reflecting a much earlier period — everything suited to make a glorious king of the coming messiah is allowed to stand; but as soon as the Servant's humiliation and suffering is mentioned, the text is altered to its opposite. To cite a few examples, the reference to the Servant (in the Hebrew text of verse 3) as despised and rejected is changed to apply to heathen kings and kingdoms; the reference to the Servant in verse 7 as led like a lamb to the slaughter is taken to refer to the mighty who will be delivered to slaughter; and the reference to the Servant in verse 12 as pouring himself out to death is altered to read that he subjected himself to deadly danger. It is clear that the Targumist has seen the messiah in the Servant, but the *Eved*'s suffering is restricted to the despising of his royal appearance (verse 3), which is avenged in the conquest of his despisers. It is also clear that the roots of the doctrine of Jesus' death as atoning or redemptive do not lie in Jewish interpretations of the Isaian Servant nor in the innocent one beleaguered by his oppressors, which is hymned in the literature between the Testaments.[71] Not until the last century B.C.E. does the idea of vicarious suffering emerge in Judaism. In IV Maccabees 6:27-29 and 17:20-22, Eleazar and his fellow martyrs atone for the nation's sins. If the idea derives from the Fourth Servant Song, it is interpreted of a collective, not of an individual. Further, the benefits of the atonement are restricted to the martyrs' compatriots, and among them, only to the righteous. Finally, in the New Testament the intiative for such activity is exclusively with God.[72]

---

70. See the discussion of the debate involving Tertullian, the *Didascalia,* and Trypho in Willem Cornelis van Unnik, "Der Fluch der Gekreuzigten, Deuteronomium 21, 23 in der Deutung Justinus des Märtyrers," in *Theologia Crucis — Signum Crucis,* pp. 483-498.

71. Gustav Dalman, *Der leidende und der sterbende Messias der Synagoge im ersten christlichen Jahrtausend* (Berlin: H. Reuthers Verlagsbuchhandlung, 1888), p. 48; Ortkemper, *Das Kreuz in der Verkündigung des Apostels Paulus,* p. 50; Paul Seidelin, "Der 'Ebed Jahwe' und die Messiasgestalt im Jesajatargum," *ZNTW* 35 (1936), 210-231; Gerhard Behler, "Das Ärgernis des Kreuzes," *Zeitschrift für Askese und Mystik,* III, 2 (1959), 8-9.

72. Morna Hooker, *Jesus and the Servant* (London: S.P.C.K., 1959), p. 54.

In the Talmudic period, perhaps in the second or third century C.E., the idea of a suffering messiah appears in the figure of the Messiah ben Joseph or ben Ephraim. However, this messiah is not the authentic messiah, the king of Israel. His task consists in waging war on Israel's enemies and dying in preparation for the true messiah, the Messiah ben David. This messiah comes into the world unrecognized by his people, is imprisoned by the heathen and threatened with death, but is rescued by God and is finally vested with kingly glory. Toward the end of the Talmudic period (the seventh century C.E.), the Messiah ben David exists only in paradise and suffers painful impatience. Among the rabbis, then, the two messiahs are never connected. It is possible that, in a period marked by polemical strife between church and synagogue, resistance to the idea of the true messiah's death led to the invention of the Messiah ben Joseph, a messiah without a trace in the ancient tradition.[73]

The messiah of Qumran was likewise given dual shape: in the anointed of Aaron and the royal messiah or Davidic king, both preceded by "the prophet." The first, the high priest of the end time, was to cleanse the community in preparation for the royal messiah, who would exercise lordship over the people of God: "Until the coming of the Prophet and of both the priestly and the lay Messiah, these men are not to depart from the clear intent of the Law in any way in the stubbornness of their own hearts."[74] No more than the rabbis could Qumran wed the two concepts of the suffering, dying Servant and the Davidic king. Early attempts at portraying Qumran's Teacher of Righteousness as a prototype of Jesus, his battered body removed from the cross by adherents who believed he would rise and lead them to the new Jerusalem, have long since been discredited.[75]

---

73. Dalman, *Der leidende und der sterbende Messias,* pp. 1, 7, 9-10, 21-22, 36, 65-66, 68, 90-91, 95; Dieter Sänger, *Die Verkündigung,* pp. 213-215; Strack-Billerbeck, *Das Neue Testament aus Talmud und Midrasch,* II, 273-274, 283, 292-293, 297.

74. *The Manual of Discipline* ix, 8-11, *The Dead Sea Scriptures,* trans. Theodor Gaster (New York: Anchor Books, 1976), pp. 63-64. Cf. the Vermes translation: "[The men of holiness] shall be ruled by the primitive precepts in which the men of the Community were first instructed until there shall come the Prophet and the Messiahs of Aaron and Israel" (*The Dead Sea Scrolls in English,* p. 87). Incidentally, for the scribes of the Talmudic period, hope in a messiah tends to disappear behind the expectation of Elijah.

75. Dieter Sänger, *Die Verkündigung,* pp. 208, 215; Gert Jeremias, *Der Lehrer der Gerechtigkeit,* pp. 127, 319-326. Jeremias refers to H. H. Rowley's sharp rejection of the notion of a crucified Teacher of Righteousness entertained by his one-time pupil, John

In the *Toledoth Yeshu,* a pseudo-life-of-Jesus written in perhaps the eighth century, a cabbage stalk is substituted for the cross as the means of execution. The Amsterdam version reads:

> . . . around evening they hanged him on a beam. But the beam did not hold his corpse. Then they fashioned another beam for him, but it [too] did not hold him, for during his lifetime the Detestable One had sworn by God's name that it (i.e. wood) should not hold him for hanging. But Jehuda '[isch] B[artota] gave thought to this, ran quickly to his garden and there cut off a [cabbage-]stalk, [every] bit as thick as a timber. They hanged him on it. The stalk held and bore him, for during his lifetime the Godless One had paid no mind to exorcizing the stalks, since he put no value on them as timber for hanging.[76]

Tertullian may have been familiar with this detail of Jewish folklore in some early, preliterary form, for in his vision of Christ's return, those who are arraigned before the judgment seat hear these words:

> This is he . . . the son of the carpenter or the harlot, the Sabbath-breaker, the Samaritan, who had a devil. This is he whom you bought from Judas; this is he, who was struck with reed and fist, defiled with spittle, given gall and vinegar to drink. This is he whom the disciples secretly stole away, that it might be said he had risen — unless it was the gardener who removed him, lest his lettuces should be trampled by the throng of visitors![77]

One interpreter locates the origin of this bizarre detail in Jewish attempts to link Christian faith to the Adonis cult, with its myth of the god's death in a lettuce patch. Another refers a version of the legend to Jesus' parable of the mustard seed ("when it has grown it is the greatest of shrubs and becomes a tree" [Matt. 13:32]), but prefers to derive the tale

---

Allegro, and to the lack of support for Krister Stendahl's or A. J. B. Higgins' idea of the priestly messiah as the resurrected Teacher (pp. 139, 276, 281, 285, 287, 295).

76. Günter Schlichting, *Ein jüdisches Leben Jesu, die verschollene Toledot-Jeschu-Fassung Tam u-mu'ad* (Tübingen: J. C. B. Mohr, 1982), p. 151.

77. Tertullian, *De Spectaculis,* trans. Gerald H. Rendall, Loeb Library of Classics (New York: G. P. Putnam's Sons, 1931), p. 299. The legend of the gardener is repeated in, e.g., Hugh J. Schonfield's *The Passover Plot* (New York: B. Geis Associates, distributed by Random House, 1966).

from a pun on the Semitic term for a species of tree.[78] In *Targum Sheni,* a collection of Aramaic homilies on the Book of Esther, Jesus is named as the "ancestor" of Haman, from whose execution all the trees excuse themselves, until a cedar proposes he be hanged on the gibbet erected for Mordecai.[79] In whatever form, this piece of folklore served as a weapon in the struggle between Judaism and Christianity in the medieval period.

Though in fact the raw materials for innovation — for combining shameful suffering and exalted status — may have been at hand in Judaism, a combination that Jesus himself may have pioneered,[80] ultimately death was for Israel an unassimilable, indigestible event. This may explain how Israel could develop ideas of the future from which the concept of resurrection emerged, but it also explains Israel's rejection of a crucified Messiah and the polarization resulting from its affirmation by Christian believers, a polarization that persists to this moment:

> That God became Man and offered up His only begotten Son for the sins of the world, is for the Jews, as Paul said, a "scandal," i.e. an impossible faith-idea; for it violates the sovereignty and sheer transcendence of God, and in fact destroys the world.[81]

"Greeks Desire Wisdom"

The polarization that belief in a crucified Savior could evoke among Greco-Roman contemporaries of earliest Christianity is illustrated by a few well-worn examples. The first is the statement of Rome's greatest orator, Marcus Tullius Cicero (106-43 B.C.E.), rival of the notorious Catiline (?-62 B.C.E.) for the consulship; exiled by Caesar (100-44 B.C.E.), recalled by Pompey (106-48 B.C.E.), and reconciled with Caesar; a supporter of Octavian (Augustus, 63 B.C.E.–14 C.E.) in the power

78. Samuel Krauss, *Das Leben Jesu nach Jüdischen Quellen* (Berlin: S. Calvary & Co., 1902), pp. 225-226; H. I. Newman, "The Death of Jesus in the *Toledoth Yeshu* Literature," *Journal of Theological Studies,* NS 50, No. 1 (April 1999), 62, 65, 72, 75-79.

79. Cf. Gustav Dalman, *Jesus Christ in the Talmud, Midrash, Zohar and the Liturgy of the Synagogue,* trans. A. W. Streane (New York: Arno Press, 1973 [1893]), p. 90.

80. Joel B. Green, "The Death of Jesus and the Ways of God," *Interpretation* 52, No. 1 (Jan. 1998), 32-34.

81. Hans-Joachim Schoeps, *Paul,* p. 162.

struggle with Marc Antony (ca. 83-30 B.C.E.); and following their reconciliation, proscribed and murdered. In 63 B.C.E., in midst of his defense
of a certain C. Rabirius, who had been charged with high treason thirty-
seven years earlier and was now facing exile, Cicero described the penalty with which his client had once been threatened:

> How grievous a thing it is to be disgraced by a public court; how
> grievous to suffer a fine, how grievous to suffer banishment; and yet
> in the midst of any such disaster some trace of liberty is left to us.
> Even if we are threatened with death, we may die free men. But the
> executioner, the veiling of the head, and the very word "cross" should
> be far removed not only from the person of a Roman citizen but from
> his thoughts, his eyes and his ears.[82]

This may be the "aesthetic judgment" of a man belonging to the
"knight's estate," far removed from the *hoi polloi;* but for all that, his expression of horror at crucifixion was scarcely unique.

A second example appears in the letter of the younger Pliny (62-113
C.E.) to his emperor Trajan (53?-117 C.E.), requesting advice regarding
the disposition of a sect with a "depraved and excessive superstition"
(superstitio prava immodica) toward a crucified Christ.[83] A third is contained in the dialogues of the Greek satirist Lucian of Samosata (ca. 120-
180 C.E.). In "The Passing of Peregrinus," he writes of the Christians:
"Their first lawgiver persuaded them that they are all brothers of one
another after they have transgressed once for all by denying the Greek

---

82. *Cicero,* trans. H. N. Grose Hodge, Loeb Classical Library (Cambridge, MA:
Harvard University Press, 1979), Vol. IX, Book 5, para. 16, p. 467. The defense includes
other references to crucifixion: in Book 3, para. 10, p. 461; in Book 4, paras. 11 and 13, pp.
463 and 465, it is described as "the tree of shame." Still other references to crucifixion appear in Cicero's second speech against Verres, where the penalty is described as "cruel
and disgusting," "the worst extreme of the torture inflicted upon slaves." See *The Verrine
Orations,* trans. L. H. G. Greenwood (Cambridge: Harvard University Press, 1967), Vol.
II, Book 5, paras. 64, 66, pp. 165, 169. Cf. Jürgen Moltmann, *Der Gekreuzigte Gott* (Munich: Chr. Kaiser, 1972), p. 36; Heinz-Wolfgang Kuhn, "Jesus als Gekreuzigter," pp. 8-9.
Of the period Augustine wrote: "There was nothing more ignominious in that time than
death on a cross" (Aurelius Augustinus, Sermo LXXXVIII, 8, *Opera Omnia,* V, J.-P.
Migne, *Patrologia Latina* [Paris: J.-P. Migne 1841], Tomus XXXVIII, 543).

83. Pliny, *Letters,* trans. William Melmoth (Cambridge: Harvard University Press,
1963), II, 405.

gods and by worshiping that crucified sophist himself and living under his laws."[84]

In his voluminous response to Celsus (1st century C.E.), Origen of Alexandria (185-251 [or 254?] C.E.) quotes the great first-century adversary of Christianity as follows:

> In all [the Christians'] writings [is mention made] of the tree of life, and a resurrection of the flesh by means of the "tree," because, I imagine, their teacher was nailed to a cross, and was a carpenter by craft; so that if he had chanced to have been cast from a precipice . . . there would have been [invented] a precipice of life beyond the heavens. . . . Now what old woman would not be ashamed to utter such things in a whisper, even when making stories to lull an infant to sleep?[85]

Elsewhere Origen quotes Celsus as declaring that it would have helped to manifest Jesus' divinity if he had immediately disappeared from the cross.[86]

To the third illustration may be added that of a crucified ass, scratched on the wall of a structure located at the southwest slope of Rome's Palatine Hill, discovered in 1856 and dating from the third century C.E. To the left of the figure stands a man, who worships it by throwing it a kiss, and beneath appears the legend: "Alexamenos prays to his god." Whether or not the caricature is of the Christian faith, or of some other religious persuasion, the description may be the oldest portrayal of a crucifixion.[87] With reference to Jew or Roman, one author writes that "no man of that time could have arrived at the notion of con-

---

84. *Lucian,* trans. A. M. Harmon, Loeb Classical Library (Cambridge, MA: Harvard University Press, 1962-68), V, para. 13, p. 15.

85. *The Ante-Nicene Fathers,* Vol. IV, *Origen,* trans. Frederick Crombie (Buffalo, NY: The Christian Literature Publishing Co., 1885), Book VI, chap. xxxiv, p. 588. See also chaps. xxxvi-xxxvii, 589.

86. *The Ante-Nicene Fathers,* Vol. IV, *Origen,* Book VI, chap. lxix, 459-460.

87. Cf. Johannes Leipoldt und Walter Grundmann, *Umwelt des Christentums: Bilder zum neutestamentlichen Zeitalter* (Berlin: Evangelische Verlagsanstalt, 1966), p. 49. Leipoldt and Grundmann claim that the caricature could relate to a Sethian Gnosis derived from Egypt. See also August Strobel, "Die Deutung des Todes Jesu im ältesten Evangelium," in *Das Kreuz Jesu* (Göttingen: Vandenhoeck & Ruprecht, 1969), p. 38. For a further discussion of these and other illustrations of crucifixion in the ancient world, see Martin Hengel's study *Crucifixion* (London: SCM Press, 1977).

necting this gallows of shame with a religious idea," and another, that it was a scandal and folly incapable of being philosophically appropriated or of being exploited in a religious-critical way.

The work of Irenaeus of Lyons (ca. 130-200 C.E.) entitled "Against Heresies" contains what may be the first recorded denial of the reality of the crucifixion by a Christian, albeit a Gnostic. Irenaeus cites the second-century Alexandrian Basilides, according to whom Simon of Cyrene was transformed by the "Christ," the Father's "firstborn Mind," so that he was taken for Jesus and crucified, while Jesus assumed Simon's shape and stood by laughing. Basilides concluded that those who are aware of the deceit

> . . . are not obliged to acknowledge him who was crucified, but the one who came in the form of man, and was thought to have been crucified. . . . Therefore . . . anyone [who] acknowledges him who was crucified is still a slave and is under the power of those who made the bodies.[88]

The underlying idea is that corruption is innate to the flesh and the material world — the one persuasion that all Gnostics held in common, despite their differences. From this it was but a short step to believe that the divine Christ assumed flesh not to redeem but to deceive his cosmic opponents. Similarly, according to Ptolemy Valentinus, another second-century Gnostic, Christ's Spirit — impassible and unable to suffer — abandoned Jesus when he was led away to Pilate.[89] In his treatise against heresies, Tertullian cites Marcion of Sinope, likewise from the second century (ca. 154 C.E.), the most celebrated Gnostic of them all and the founder of a sect second in strength only to the primitive church, who argued that "the passion of the cross was never prophesied of the Creator's Christ." For Marcion, Jesus' crucifixion was proof that the messiah who appeared could not have belonged on the side of the God of the Jewish Bible, but on the side of the unknown, good redeemer God, who could never have exposed his Son to a form of death on which he had laid a curse.[90]

---

88. *St. Irenaeus of Lyons against the Heresies,* trans. Dominic J. Unger, rev. John J. Dillon (New York: Paulist Press, 1992), I, 86. Sloyan (*The Crucifixion of Jesus,* p. 198) erroneously attributes the notion to Valentinus.

89. *St. Irenaeus of Lyons against the Heresies,* p. 39.

90. Tertullian, *Adversus Marcionem,* trans. Ernest Evans (Oxford: Clarendon Press,

With the discovery of the Coptic Gnostic Library at the ancient site of Chenoboskion, a collection comprising twelve books of fifty-two tractates, scholars have no longer been restricted to the works of ancient apologists or their interpreters for an understanding of the Gnostic phenomenon. The crucifixion of Jesus is variously treated in the Nag Hammadi library: in some of the tractates, the passion is either omitted or lacks specific reference;[91] in others, there are references to the cross without any reference to its saving significance,[92] as the object of imitation;[93] in still others, only the "corporeal-bodily" is capable of suffering, so that the "Spirit-Christ" merely "seemed" to die;[94] Christ is described as a stranger to suffering,[95] or his crucifixion is assigned an earthly sub-

---

1972), iii. 18, 225. For a discussion of the statements regarding the cross by the Basilidians, Valentinians, and Marcion, see, e.g., Heinz-Wolfgang Kuhn, "Jesus als Gekreuzigter"; Hans-Ruedi Weber, *Kreuz: Überlieferung und Deutung der Kreuzigung Jesu im neutestamentlichen Kulturraum* (Stuttgart: Kreuz Verlag, 1975), p. 27; Sloyan, *The Crucifixion of Jesus,* pp. 83-84, 124, 202.

91. Cf. the Apocryphon of John, the Gospel of Thomas, the Gospel of Philip, the Exegesis on the Soul, the Dialog of the Savior, the Acts of Peter and the Twelve Apostles, and the Teachings of Silvanus in *The Nag-Hammadi Library in English,* trans. members of the Coptic Gnostic Library Project, James M. Robinson, gen. ed., 4th ed. (Leiden: E. J. Brill, 1996), pp. 104-123, 124-138, 139-160, 190-98, 244-255, 287-294, 379-395. There may be a reference to the passion in The Testimony of Truth, pp. 448-459.

92. In speech collections from Syria-Palestine, such as the Gospel of Thomas, Jesus' crucifixion is never assigned saving significance. Cf. Karl-Wolfgang Troeger, *Die Passion Jesu Christi in der Gnosis nach den Schriften von Nag Hammadi* (Th.D diss., Berlin: Humboldt University, 1978), p. 137.

93. Cf., e.g., the Apocryphon of James, the Second Apocalypse of James, the Interpretation of Knowledge, and the Testimony of Truth in *the Nag-Hammadi Library in English,* pp. 29-37, 269-276, 472-480. In the Gospel of Truth, the saving significance of Jesus' death lies in the offer and possibility for those predestined to it; cf., e.g., I,16, 21, 29, p. 42.

94. Cf. the Apocalypse of Peter, VII 70, 81-82, pp. 396-397; the Second Apocalypse of James, especially V 44, 58, 14-17, p. 274; the Second Treatise of the Great Seth, VII 49, 60, 15-19, p. 367; the First Apocalypse of James, V 24, esp. 25, 7-9; 30, 1-6; 37, 17-20, pp. 262, 264, 266. Para. 101 of the apocryphal Acts of John reads: "So then I have suffered none of those things which they will say of me. . . . You hear that I suffered, yet I suffered not; and that I suffered not, yet I did suffer; and that I was pierced, yet I was not lashed; that I was hanged, yet I was not hanged; that blood flowed from me, yet it did not flow; and, in a word, that what they say of me, I did not endure, but what they do not say, those things I did suffer" (*New Testament Apocrypha,* ed. Wilhelm Schneemelcher, trans. R. McL. Wilson [Louisville: John Knox Press, 1992], pp. 185-86).

95. Cf., e.g., the Tripartite Tractate: the Hypostasis of the Archons, the Gospel of

stitute.[96] Kurt Rudolph detects in some sources an ambivalence leading to a positive regard for Jesus' suffering, though, as in the Gospel of Truth (I, 3, esp. 31, 4-6; 30, 12-23, 26-31), a particular kind of body ("flesh," *sarx*) emerges. For this reason, he adds, an intra-Gnostic polemic against "Docetic" views can take place, where they deny that Jesus Christ was not exposed to suffering or raised from the dead. Thus, he concludes, the Gnostic Christology was as pluralistic as the remainder of Christian literature on this theme.[97]

One of the most passionate polemics against the doctrine of a crucified redeemer is contained in the Second Treatise of the Great Seth. In it the "infinite light which is I" declares:

> I did not die in reality but in appearance. . . . For my death which they think happened, [happened] to them in their error and blindness, since they nailed their man unto their death. . . . Yes, they saw me; they punished me. It was another, their father, who drank the gall and the vinegar; it was not I. They struck me with the reed; it was another, Simon, who bore the cross on his shoulder. It was another upon whom they placed the crown of thorns. But I was rejoicing in the height over all the wealth of the archons and the offspring of their error, of their empty glory. And I was laughing at their ignorance.

Echoing the crucifixion narrative in Matthew 27, the tractate continues:

> They nailed him to the tree, and they fixed him with four nails of brass. The veil of his temple he tore with his hands. It was a trembling which seized the chaos of the earth, for the souls which were in the sleep below were released. And they arose. They went about boldly,

---

the Egyptians, and Zostrianos in *The Nag-Hammadi Library,* pp. 58-103, 161-69, 208-219, 402-430. In the Concept of Our Great Power, the Redeemer's suffering is neither contested nor expressly stated (pp. 311-317). Troeger (in *Die Passion Jesu Christi,* pp. 158-159) notes the striking similarity between the credo contained in the Letter of Peter to Philip (139, 12-25) and references to the passion in the canonical Book of Acts. According to this tractate, Jesus actually suffered, though he was "a stranger to this suffering" because he was an alien in this world, just as is whoever believes in him.

96. Cf., e.g., the Second Treatise of the Great Seth, VII, 55, 9-56, 21, in *The Nag-Hammadi Library in English,* p. 365.

97. Kurt Rudolph, *Gnosis und Spätantike Religionsgeschichte: Gesammelte Aufsätze* (Leiden: E. J. Brill, 1996), pp. 271-272.

having shed zealous service of ignorance and unlearnedness beside the dead tombs, having put on the new man, since they have come to know that perfect Blessed One of the eternal and incomprehensible Father and the infinite light, which is I. . . .

The "infinite light" then adds:

It was ludicrous. It is I who bear witness that it is ludicrous, since the archons do not know that it is an ineffable union of undefiled truth, as exists among the sons of light, of which they made an imitation, having proclaimed a doctrine of a dead man . . . [and joining] themselves with their doctrine to fear and slavery. . . .[98]

The Gnostic Gospel of Thomas, found in complete form in Coptic at Nag Hammadi in 1945, has been celebrated by some as a likelier clue to Christian origins than the canonical Gospels.[99] It appears to preserve two sayings regarding Jesus' death, one in Logion 12 and the other in 55:

The disciples said to Jesus, "We know that you will leave us. Who is going to be our leader?" Jesus said to them, "No matter where you are, you are to go to James the Just, for whose sake heaven and earth came into being." . . . Jesus said, "Whoever does not hate father and mother cannot be a disciple of me, and whoever does not hate brothers and sisters and bear the cross as I do, will not be worthy of me."[100]

Beyond these two indirect references, the Gospel of Thomas has little or no interest in Jesus' death. The references do not assign any saving function to it, nor do they hint of any vindication through resurrection. In fact, the identity of Jesus and of his followers is not a chief concern. To the extent that the Gospel of Thomas mentions the cross, it assigns it only metaphorical significance: the disciple, says the Jesus of the Gospel of Thomas, must "bear the cross as I do," that is, must renounce tradi-

---

98. The Second Treatise of the Great Seth, VII 49, 55, 19-56, 19; 58, 24-59, 9; 60, 13-27 (*The Nag Hammadi Library in English,* pp. 365-367).

99. Cf. *The Five Gospels: The Search for the Authentic Words of Jesus,* trans. with commentary by Robert W. Funk, Roy W. Hoover, and the Jesus Seminar (New York: Macmillan and Co., 1993), pp. 15-16, 26.

100. *A Thomas Reader,* ed. John B. Kloppenborg et al. (Sonoma, CA: Polebridge Press, 1990), pp. 132, 142.

tional family ties. Ernst Haenchen has concluded that, due to its Gnostic view of the elect's essential oneness with God, the idea of forgiveness by way of a redeemer made little sense to the Gospel of Thomas. Salvation did not come by way of a cross but via a message of the unity of the self with the divine, spelling deliverance from temporality.[101]

From this lack of attention to Jesus' death in the Gospel of Thomas, which functions for one set of scholars as a control for the analysis of the canonical Gospels, it has been inferred that it was not Jesus' death but the subsequent mythic imagination of his resurrection that gave birth to a new social experiment, that is, that "the language of resurrection took shape in pre-Pauline and Pauline congregations of the Christ as an elaboration of the myth that Jesus' death . . . was the founding event for the community."[102] Without drawing that inference, it is impossible to deny that "the genre, designs, logic, and theology" of the Gospel of Thomas "are incompatible with the dominant paradigm of Christian origins."[103] Whether or not this means that Jesus' death was not "the main point of departure for all the groups claiming allegiance to Jesus"[104] is a matter for debate.

In summary, it may be that only later in the church's life did reflection on the cross of Jesus become an occasion for orthodoxy or heresy, but, as Troeger writes, the Gnostic tendency toward one-sided emphasis on the deity and the unworldliness of the redeemer became a serious competitor for belief in the historicity of Jesus and the soteriological significance of his death.[105] Thus, while most Gnostics did in fact reflect on the cross, for most of them the gulf between the heavenly and the earthly was so wide that the assumption of flesh on the part of the divine Christ, the heavenly *Sōtēr*, they conceived merely as a ruse by which the archons and the world were discomfited and the inner person of the redeemer left untouched. Thus a Docetic tinge clearly attaches itself to many of the tractates, whose authors summon their readers to resist irritation at the sarkic

---

101. Ernst Haenchen, *Das Botschaft des Thomas-Evangeliums* (Berlin: Verlag Alfred Töpelmann, 1961), p. 74.

102. Cf. Ron Cameron, "Ancient Myths and Modern Theories of the Gospel of Thomas and Christian Origins," *Method and Theory in the Study of Religion* 11, No. 3 (1999), 249.

103. Cameron, p. 253.

104. Kloppenborg, *A Thomas Reader*, p. 105.

105. Karl-Wolfgang Troeger, *Die Passion Jesu Christi*, p. 139.

copy of the model of their redeemer, to participate in his crucifixion as a rejection of the material world, and in this fashion to render themselves impervious to its attacks. The common denominator of the soteriological utterances in the tractates is thus not the saving significance of the cross. The cross was rather the consequence of a tragic error on the part of the ignorant, among whom are the representatives and adherents of the Great Church with their false doctrine of a dying redeemer. At issue is the remembrance of the death of Jesus in a sort of mimesis, reflective of the ascetic or ethical-rigoristic stance threading throughout the writings.[106]

In his study of the Manichaean religious system, Ferdinand Christian Baur discusses what must be the most bizarre variation on the theme of Christ's crucifixion, as described by Evodius of Uzala (ca. 424 C.E.), a companion of Augustine (354-430), as well as by the great church father himself in his treatise against Faustus the Manichaean (ca. 400). According to Evodius, the Manichaean *Jesus patibilis* is born daily in every plant producing seed from the dark bosom of the earth: he suffers insofar as the upward striving soul in every plant is imprisoned in the material; he dies when the plant itself withers and decomposes. According to Augustine, Faustus related the suffering of Christ to the suffering of the world-soul bound to the material and held fast in a suffering condition, though he drew no distinction between the two, since the *Jesus patibilis* was merely a fixed point in the representation of the ordinary appearances of nature. This idea of the *Jesus patibilis,* Baur continued, gave Manichaeans an opportunity to appropriate Christian terminology. The crucified Jesus of the Christians now had its true model in the soul imprisoned in every stem of plant and tree. And just as the Christian saw in the suffering and dying Jesus the salvation and life of the world, so did the Manichaean in his *Jesus patibilis.*[107]

The polarization resulting from adherence to a suffering and dying messiah has its analogy in Islam. In Chapter Four, "Al-Nisa," paragraphs 156-162 of the Quran read:

106. For an extended discussion of the passion in the Gnostic library, see, e.g., Troeger, *Die Passion Jesu Christi,* and James Arthur Cozby, Jr., "Gnosis and the Cross: The Passion of Christ in Gnostic Soteriology as Reflected in the Nag Hammadi Tractates" (Ph.D. diss., Duke University, 1985). For brief comments, see also Ulrich Wilckens, "Kreuz und Weisheit," *Kerygma und Dogma* 3 (Jan. 1957), 77-108; and Luke Timothy Johnson, *The Real Jesus* (San Francisco: Harper, 1996), pp. 150-151.

107. Ferdinand Christian Baur, *Das Manichäische Religionssystem* (Göttingen: Vandenhoeck & Ruprecht, 1928), p. 74.

[The Jews say] We did kill the Messiah, Jesus son of Mary, the Messenger of Allah; whereas they slew him not, nor did they compass his death upon the cross, but he was made to appear to them like one crucified to death; and those who have differed in the matter of his having been taken down alive from the cross are certainly in a state of doubt concerning it, they have no definite knowledge about it, but only follow a conjecture; they certainly did not compass his death in the manner they allege; indeed, Allah exalted him to Himself; Allah is Mighty, Wise, and there is none among the People of the Book but will continue to believe till his death that Jesus died on the cross, and on the Day of Judgment Jesus shall bear witness against them.[108]

Whether or not the Quran denies the death of Jesus, for the Muslim the idea of salvation as conditioned on a *crucifixion* in which God allowed one to suffer who had not deserved such punishment is an irrational idea perpetrated by the Jews (the "People of the Book").

The polarization is clearly reflected in the principal text of Christian Science. In strikingly similar fashion to the Gnostic ideas noted above, Mary Baker Eddy (1821-1910) wrote that "the eternal Christ never suffered," and that

... Jesus could give his human life into his enemies' hands in *appearance and to belief....* He knew that matter had no life, and that real Life is God; therefore he could no more be separated from Life, than God could be extinguished.[109]

Eddy could not found her system on death, whose reality she was denying. She spoke of "the life and not death of our Master," for he never died: "The material blood of Jesus was no more efficacious to cleanse from sin when it was shed upon 'the accursed tree' than when it was flowing in his veins as he went daily about his Father's Business."[110] According to one observer, "She wanted 'the spiritual essence of blood' — and of everything else. Like the rationalist celebrants of Jesus, she went

---

108. The Quran, Arabic text with a new translation by Muhammad Zafrulla Khan (London: Curzon Press, 1985), pp. 95-96.

109. Eddy, *Science and Health with Key to the Scriptures* (Boston: Joseph Armstrong, 1901), pp. 343, 356 (italics mine).

110. Eddy, *Science and Health* (Boston: The Writings of Mary Baker Eddy, 2000), p. 25.

to the gospels for an 'earlier' picture of the man Jesus before Paul theologized his life."[111]

In one of the texts of New Age religion, again strikingly similar to the Gnostic tractates, death is an error of the "lower" mind, dubbed "the ego," a mind at home in the body that denies we are of God:

> From the ego came sin and guilt and death, in opposition to life and innocence, and to the Will of God Himself. Where can such opposition lie but in the sick minds of the insane, dedicated to madness and set against the peace of Heaven?[112]

For this offspring of the Gnostics, God's Son did not die. The idea itself is blasphemy:

> Under the dusty edge of its distorted world the ego would lay the Son of God, slain by its orders, proof in his decay that God Himself is powerless before the ego's might, unable to protect the life that He created against the ego's savage wish to kill.[113]

The idea that the deity of the Christ is unaffected by the suffering of the human Jesus is not limited to the more bizarre representations of Gnosis and its congeners. In his treatise against Praxeas,[114] Tertullian said of Paul's statement about Christ's death in I Corinthians 15 that "it is evident in what respect he says he died, namely in that he is flesh and man and Son of Man, not in that he is spirit and Word and Son of God,"[115] adding that the Son is impassible "as regards that state in which he is God."[116] Of Jesus' cry of dereliction from the cross, the apologist said that it was "of flesh and soul (that is, of the manhood), not of the Word and Spirit (that is, not of God)."[117] In his letter to Flavian,

111. Garry Wills, *Certain Trumpets* (New York: Simon and Schuster, 1994), p. 179.

112. *A Course in Miracles* (Los Angeles: Life Action Press, 1986), p. 418.

113. *A Course in Miracles*, p. 419.

114. *Tertullian's Treatise Against Praxeas,* trans. Ernest Evans (London: S.P.C.K., 1948).

115. Tertullian, para. 29, 177: *"Id est qua carnem et hominem et filium hominis, non qua spiritum et sermonem et dei filium."*

116. Tertullian: *"Quam impassibilis etiam filius ex ea condicione qua deus est."*

117. Tertullian, para. 30, 178: *"Sed haec vox carnis et animae, id est hominis, non sermonis nec spiritus, id est non dei."*

bishop of Constantinople, regarding the heretic Eutyches, Leo the Great wrote that Christ did not suffer "in the divinity itself whereby the Only-begotten is co-eternal and consubstantial with the Father, but in the weakness of the human nature."[118] In its "Definition of the Faith," the Council of Chalcedon registered its approval of Leo's letter and expelled from the assembly of the priests "those who dare to say that the divinity of the Only-begotten is passible."[119]

Since Chalcedon, orthodoxy has been measured against this view. It was left to the Reformers to hand it down. For example, in explaining the relationship of the two natures to the person of Christ (the *communicatio idiomatum*) in his exposition of John 14 and 15,[120] Martin Luther (1483-1546) said that "God's Son sits at table with publicans and sinners, washes the disciples' feet — which, of course, he does not do according to his divine nature, but because one and the same person is doing it, it is rightly said that God's Son is doing it."[121] In his *Geneva Catechism* of 1541, John Calvin (1509-1564) said that it was according to his human nature that Christ suffered, and in order to do so his deity was "hidden for a little while."[122] Huldreich Zwingli (1484-1531) said that, in the incarnation of the Logos, the deity of God remained untouched from all becoming and thus from all suffering.[123] David Hollaz, whose

---

118. "The Letter of Pope Leo to Flavian, bishop of Constantinople, about Eutyches," *Decrees of the Ecumenical Councils,* ed. Norman P. Tanner S.J., Vol. I, *Nicaea I to Lateran V* (London and Washington, D.C.: Sheed and Ward and Georgetown University Press, 1990), p. 80.

119. *"Obsistit et illos qui passibilem deitatem Unigeniti ausi sunt dicere":* "Definition of the Faith," *Decrees of the Ecumenical Councils,* I, 85-86.

120. *WA* XLV, 557.

121. "Gottes Son setzet mit den Zoelnern und suendern uber tissch, wesschet den Juengern die fuesse, Das thut er wol nicht nach der Goettlichen nature, aber doch weil die selbige person solchs thut, ist es recht gesagt, das Gottes Son solchs thue" (ibid., 557, 16-19). On the other hand, in his debate with Zwingli, Luther insisted that in Jesus Christ the attributes of the human nature participated in those of the divine, and vice versa: "In the man Jesus God suffered, died, and conquered death." Cf. "That These Words of Christ 'This Is My Body, etc.' Still Stand Firm Against the Fanatics" (1527), and "Confession Concerning Christ's Supper" (1528), in *LW* 37:13-150, and 161-372.

122. *"Paulisper interea delitescebat eius divinitatis" (Corpus Reformatorum Volumen XXIV, Ioannis Calvini Opera Quae Supersunt Omnia* [Brunswick: Apud C. A. Schwetschke et Filium, 1867], VI, 31-32).

123. Cf. the discussion in Eberhard Jüngel, "Vom Tod des lebendigen Gottes," *ZThK* 65 (1968), 101-104.

Examen theologicum acroamaticum has been regarded as a summation of later Lutheran orthodoxy, explained the proposition "God suffered" in this way:

> Just as when a wound is inflicted on Peter's flesh not only is Peter's flesh said to have been wounded, but Peter or the person of Peter has actually been wounded, even though his soul cannot be wounded: thus when the Son of God suffers according to the flesh, not only the flesh or his human nature suffers, but the Son of God or the person of the Son of God actually suffers, though the divine nature is *apathēs*.[124]

The same ambiguity attaches to the Epitome of the Lutheran *Formula of Concord,* according to which characteristics of the human nature "never become characteristics of the divine nature," though "everything human that can be ascribed to and believed about God" flows from the personal union.[125] In attempting to overcome the dilemma posed by the idea of God as impassible, unmoved, and unchangeable,[126] without tumbling into the ditch of Patripassianism or of Eutychianism, which conceived Christ's humanity as altogether absorbed by his deity, the Great Church separated the deity from the humanity of Christ in his suffering and thus approximated views that it had struggled to eschew.[127]

In sum, as Walter Bauer (1877-1960) has argued,[128] the line between

---

124. Quoted in Heinrich Schmid, *Die Dogmatik der Evangelisch-Lutherischen Kirche* (Gütersloh: C. Bertelsmann, 1893), p. 237.

125. *The Book of Concord: The Confessions of the Evangelical Lutheran Church,* ed. Robert Kolb and Timothy J. Wengert (Minneapolis: Fortress, 2000), p. 510.

126. The terms translate those used by the Lutheran dogmatician Johann Gerhard (1582-1637). In reply to the question about whether or not one might say the deity suffered or died, he said such talk should be avoided since the deity is *apathēs, atreptos kai analloiōtos.* Cf. Schmid, *Die Dogmatik der Evangelisch-Lutherischen Kirche,* p. 237.

127. The epistemologist Alvin Plantinga asks, "Can we say that Christ qua human being (according to his human nature) suffered while Christ qua divine (according to his divine nature) did not? . . . I'm inclined to think this suggestion incoherent. . . . [I]f there really were *two* centers of consciousness here, one suffering and the other not, there would be two persons here . . ." (*Warranted Christian Belief* [New York: Oxford University Press, 2000], p. 319).

128. Walter Bauer, *Orthodoxy and Heresy in Earliest Christianity,* trans. Philadelphia Seminar on Christian Origins, ed. Robert A. Kraft and Gerhard Krodel (Philadelphia: Fortress, 1971).

orthodoxy and heresy was fluid in the Christian community's earliest years. Further, its reflection on the dilemma of the impassibility of the deity, begun with the Incarnation, had to end in ambiguity. Even if that reflection had begun with the crucifixion, it would have suffered the same fate. No explanation would have sufficed. The "anomaly," the death of Jesus of Nazareth, heralded as Son of God, was an event that thwarted every attempt to assimilate or absorb it in a scheme. It created a crisis that would everlastingly lead to confusion, revolution, and polarization. What Hans Küng says of that "fracture" awaiting the language and conceptuality of the biblical writers could just as well be said of all who came after:

> One can only assert that the conceptual material of that period does not suffice, but must be continually broken through, if the meaning of the Christ event is to be explained, and that the concepts, metaphors, analogies and comparisons which the New Testament uses are not identical to the Christ event. They prove to be insufficient for grasping the reality created by Christ.[129]

"Conversion" or "Call"

Paul

Thomas Kuhn (1922-1996), historian of science, says that the history of science is not simply linear but is interrupted by breaks or revolutions, and he describes the transfer of allegiance from one model or paradigm to another as a "conversion." Conversion, he says, lies at the heart of the revolutionary process; he adds that this allegiance to a new paradigm may emerge "all at once, sometimes in the middle of the night, in the mind of a man deeply immersed in crisis." A crisis, then, is not terminated by deliberation and interpretation but by a relatively sudden and unstructured event, similar to a "gestalt switch," the optical shift that occurs when, looking at the same configuration of dots or lines, one sees a duck where a moment before one saw a rabbit. Precisely because the transfer of allegiance or transition is between incommensurables or

129. Hans Küng, "Die Religionen als Frage an die Theologie des Kreuzes," *Evangelische Theologie* 33 (1975), 420.

opposites, Kuhn concludes, it cannot be made one step at a time; it must occur once or not at all.[130]

In the second account of Paul's conversion in Acts, the apostle makes this defense before his countrymen:

> While I was on my way and approaching Damascus, about noon a great light from heaven suddenly shone about me. I fell to the ground and heard a voice saying to me, "Saul, Saul, why are you persecuting me?" I answered, "Who are you, Lord?" Then he said to me: "I am Jesus of Nazareth whom you are persecuting." Now those who were with me saw the light but did not hear the voice of the one who was speaking to me. I asked, "What am I to do, Lord?" The Lord said to me, "Get up and go to Damascus; there you will be told everything that has been assigned to you to do." Since I could not see because of the brightness of that light, those who were with me took my hand and led me to Damascus (Acts 22:6-11).

Earlier I noted that, from their perspective of New Testament faith as occurring on a continuum with Old Testament and pre- or post-Israelite belief, a number of scholars consider the term "conversion" inappropriate to the Damascus event, opting rather for the term "call."[131] Such a perspective *could* reflect what William James (1842-1906) once called an aversion to instantaneous conversion among "the more usual sects of Protestantism." Or it could include allegiance to the idea that the subconscious registers forgotten and discarded sense experience, which achieves a maximum no longer at home there and which thrusts itself up into conscious life.[132] In any case, the interpretation of Paul's encounter with Christ as "call" may allow for the factor of inner preparation, whereas its interpretation as a "conversion" may not.

130. Thomas Kuhn, *The Structure of Scientific Revolutions* (Chicago: University of Chicago Press, 1996), pp. 84, 89-90, 150-151, 160.

131. To the list of scholars named in footnotes 4-12, add Leo Baeck (*Paulus, die Pharisäer und das Neue Testament*), who says that Paul never abandoned his Judaism; or Gerd Lüdemann ("Paulus und das Judentum"), who says that "Paul did not change his religion at Damascus. At Damascus Paul recognized the Christ-event as the eschatological event promised in scripture together with his commission to bear the gospel to the Gentile world" (pp. 21-22; cf. p. 41).

132. Cf. William James, *The Varieties of Religious Experience: A Study in Human Nature* (New York: The Modern Library, 1929), pp. 231-232.

First of all, there are passages in Paul's Epistles that support the interpretation of his experience as a "conversion." In their reflection of his situation prior to faith, they omit any reference to inner preparation. A passage in Galatians reads:

> You have heard, no doubt, of my earlier life in Judaism. I was violently persecuting the church of God and was trying to destroy it. I advanced in Judaism beyond many among my people of the same age, for I was far more zealous for the traditions of my ancestors. (Gal. 1:13-14)

A second passage in Philippians reads:

> If anyone else has reason to be confident in the flesh, I have more; circumcised on the eighth day, a member of the people of Israel, of the tribe of Benjamin, a Hebrew born of Hebrews; as to the law, a Pharisee; as to zeal, a persecutor of the church; as to righteousness under the law, blameless. (Phil. 3:4-6)

Though some have appealed to Romans 7 in support of inner preparation (Rom. 7:23, for example, reads, "I see in my members another law at war with the law of my mind, making me captive to the law of sin"), it is possible to interpret that chapter as describing a kind of existence that Paul illustrates from his own experience but that is not applicable to him in every detail. So, for example, the statement in Romans 7:9, "I was once alive apart from the law," can scarcely be predicated of the man "circumcised on the eighth day, a member of the people of Israel, of the tribe of Benjamin, a Hebrew born of Hebrews." Thus, insofar as the identity of the "I" in Romans 7 is a matter of dispute, the chapter cannot be summoned in support of the idea of a psychological preparation. Regarding Paul's "conversion," Günther Bornkamm says:

> When he was encountered by the crucified and risen Christ and called by God, he was the very reverse of one haunted by qualms of conscience and gone to pieces because of his own inadequacy . . . no, he was a proud Pharisee, whose unremitting boast was his membership in the chosen people, God's Law, and his own righteousness.[133]

133. Günther Bornkamm, *Paul,* trans. D. M. G. Stalker (Minneapolis: Fortress, 1995), p. 23.

Much earlier, Albert Schweitzer had challenged the notion of Paul's "suffering inward distress from his experiences of the powerlessness of the law,"[134] a notion Werner Georg Kümmel arguably laid to rest in a monograph on Romans 7.[135]

But there are also passages in Paul's letters that support the interpretation of his experience as a "call." The three accounts of Paul's "defense" (recorded in Acts 9:1-19; 22:6-21; and 26:12-18) allow room for inner preparation. Whatever discrepancies may exist between the accounts, taken together they suggest an encounter that did not involve a conversion, since there was nothing in it to mark a break with Paul's religious past, nothing in it to alter Paul's posture toward the law. The differences between these narratives in Acts and Paul's account in Galatians are troublesome. In Acts, Luke has abbreviated but also expanded the Galatians account: he has omitted the period of Paul's three-year sojourn following the Damascus event and described him as proceeding immediately to Jerusalem (cf. Gal. 1:17-18). He has then expanded the account by interposing the separate event of a temple vision following Paul's return to Jerusalem, at which time he is commissioned to go to the gentiles (Acts 22:17-21). In Luke's account, it is Saul the Jew whom Jesus encounters and to whom Ananias announces that God has chosen him "to know his will, to see the Righteous One and to hear his own voice." It is Saul the Jew who enters the temple, receives the vision and the summons to leave the city, Saul the Jew who resists the gentile mission.

In favor of "call," and thus leaving room for the psychologically explicable, Otto Pfleiderer (1839-1908), pillar of the old History of Religions School, has written:

> Was not the conscientious Pharisee obliged to confess that he had never been able in his own case even to attain the ideal of righteousness to which he had aspired — that all his zeal for righteousness had failed to conquer, but had rather provoked and increased, the resistance of his sinful desires?

134. Albert Schweitzer, *Paul and His Interpreters,* trans. W. Montgomery (London: Adam and Charles Black, 1950), p. 105.

135. Werner Georg Kümmel, *Römer 7 und das Bild des Menschen im Neuen Testament* (Munich: Christian Kaiser Verlag, 1974), pp. 139-160.

Pfleiderer then appeals to Paul's exposition in Romans 7 as reflecting his own painful conflict before "the image of the crucified Jesus" presented itself to his "inward vision."[136] These comments could have had Friedrich Nietzsche (1844-1900) for their father. In the first book of his *Dawning of Day,* Nietzsche had this to say about Paul's experience:

> In his youth he had done his best to satisfy [the Law], thirsting as he did for that highest distinction which the Jews could imagine. . . . Now, however, he was aware in his own person of the fact that such a man as himself . . . *could* not fulfill the Law. . . . There were times when the thought struck him: "it is all in vain! The anguish of the unfilled Law cannot be overcome." . . . The Law was the Cross on which he felt himself crucified. How he hated it! What a grudge he owed it! How he began to look round on all sides to find a means for its total annihilation. . . . And at last a liberating thought, together with a vision . . . flashed into his mind. . . . There appeared on the lonely path that Christ, with the divine effulgence on His countenance, and Paul heard the words: "Why persecutest thou Me?" . . . His mind was suddenly enlightened, and he said to himself: "It is unreasonable to persecute this Jesus Christ! Here is my means of escape, here is my complete vengeance, here and nowhere else have I the destroyer of the Law in my hands!" The sufferer from anguished pride felt himself restored to health all at once, his moral despair disappeared in the air; for morality itself was blown away, annihilated — that is to say, *fulfilled,* there on the cross! . . . For from that time forward he would be the apostle of the *annihilation of the Law!*[137]

Without suggesting, as did Benjamin Bacon (1860-1932), that the accounts in Acts bring the apostle "so near the brink of perjury,"[138] the threefold repetition of Paul's "call" in Acts 9, 22, and 26 — together with his defense before "brothers and fathers" in Acts 22, a defense only obliquely related to the indictment — *could* be explained by Luke's larger purpose of conceiving Christian faith in unbroken continuity

136. Otto Pfleiderer, *The Influence of the Apostle Paul on the Development of Christianity,* trans. J. Frederick Smith (London: Williams and Norgate, 1885), pp. 31ff.

137. Friedrich Nietzsche, *The Dawn of Day,* trans. J. M. Kennedy (New York: Russell & Russell, 1964), pp. 67-70.

138. Benjamin Bacon, "Acts versus Galatians," *The American Journal of Theology* XI (1907), 456.

with Judaism, thus of the mission to the gentiles as part and parcel of true and genuine Judaism. At the same time, the interpretation of Paul's encounter as a "conversion" *could* hide an impatience with the kind of hermeneutic that emphasizes the pre-eminence of religious personality in history. In this view, the divine spirit and historically illuminable reality are thought to coincide in the self-consciousness of the individual. In other words, religious personality is conceived as the medium of transcendence determining the course of history. This opting for personality spells opting for what can be psychologically explained, thus opening the door to immanence, but closing it to transcendence, at least to transcendence conceived as prodigy, as miracle. Käsemann says of this view that it is incapable of understanding the power of grace.[139]

Nevertheless, as is clear from Krister Stendahl's argument in "The Apostle Paul and the Introspective Conscience of the West," the choice of "call" need not exist in tandem with the notion of psychic preparation.[140] In fact, it is precisely this view of "call," loosed from a psychological interpretation, that represents the "orthodox" position. In an essay entitled "The Concept of Tradition,"[141] Josef Pieper lists the concept's essential characteristics: first, it prohibits reciprocal action between transmitter and receiver; second, it conceives the receiver as the transmitter's pupil, or "disciple"; third, it connotes the place from which and to which what is transmitted is conducted, together with the site of the transmitter; finally, the concept involves transmitting something as true, holy, or sacred, since its source is in revelation and thus aloof from critical testing. It is clear from this description that the element of the personal is totally absent, whether in terms of observation, experimentation, verification, or dissent. Pieper says: "As soon as I accept a *traditum* as something verified by myself and rationally known it loses for me its character of tradition."[142] When one eliminates personality from the equation, the structure of existence remains the same after as well as before the reception of the tradition. Translated into the language of the Damascus event, it would mean that Paul's encounter

139. Ernst Käsemann, "A Pauline Version of the 'Amor Fati,'" in *New Testament Questions of Today,* trans. J. Montague (Philadelphia: Fortress, 1969), p. 229.

140. *Harvard Theological Review* 56, No. 3 (July 1963), 199-215.

141. Josef Pieper, "The Concept of Tradition," *The Review of Politics* 20 (1958), 465-491.

142. Pieper, "The Concept of Tradition," p. 473.

with Christ involved the assignment of an "office," not an alteration of existence. One of the ironies of theological history is that Bultmann's refusal to acknowledge the movement from unbelief to faith as involving change found him in the same pew with the orthodox who affirmed justification as an event occurring in the forum of heaven and thus leaving the structures of existence unaltered.[143]

Any interpretation of Paul's experience depends on understanding the degree of change it produced in his thought and way of life. If he held to the validity of the Torah's curse on "anyone hung on a tree" (Deut. 21:22-23) throughout his life, and if the central content of the Damascus encounter was that God had accepted the one cursed by the Torah, then he had to jettison an entire way of viewing God, the world, and himself — however incomparably grand or unique. Then Paul had to understand the change he had undergone as analogous, say, to the model applied by his older contemporary to the change in the patriarch, reared in the Chaldean confusion of Creator with creature, and in vision suddenly encountering the living God — "then opening the soul's eye as though after profound sleep . . . he followed the ray and discerned what he had not beheld before"[144] — or as analogous to the model applied to gentiles in the Jewish view.

More important, any interpretation of Paul's experience depends on understanding the character of the change that *he* believed it produced in his thought and life. In I Corinthians 9:1, Paul says: "Am I not free? Am I not an apostle? Have I not seen Jesus our Lord?" Later on, in I Corinthians 15:8, he declares: "Last of all, as to one untimely born, he appeared also to me." In II Corinthians 4:6, in which the plural is stand-in for the singular, his allusion to Damascus is clear:

> For it is the God who said, "Let light shine out of darkness," who *shone in our hearts* to give the light of the knowledge of the glory of God in the face of Jesus Christ. (Italics mine)

---

143. Cf. Roy A. Harrisville, "Bultmann's Concept of the Transition from Inauthentic to Authentic Existence," in *Kerygma and History, A Symposium on the Theology of Rudolf Bultmann*, ed. Carl E. Braaten and Roy A. Harrisville (Nashville: Abingdon Press, 1962), pp. 212-228; see also Harrisville, "Is the Coexistence of the Old and New Man Biblical?" *Lutheran Quarterly* VIII, 1 (Feb. 1956), 20-32.

144. *Abraham in Philo*, trans. F. H. Colson, Loeb Classical Library (Cambridge, MA: Harvard University Press, 1959), VI, 41.

Lastly, in Galatians 1:15-16, Paul declares:

> God, who had set me apart before I was born and called me through his grace, *was pleased to reveal his Son to me.*[145]

These references are twenty or more years subsequent to the event; but even allowing for embroidering, they register — together with the accounts in Acts — a Christophany, a sight of the one who had been crucified but whose appearance testified to his validation. This sight betokened the "fracture" of an entire theological world for the sake of another, in which the crucifixion of Jesus Christ as an act of divine mercy on humanity's behalf stood at midpoint. In Philippians 3, Paul sums up what he had come to abandon and what to apprehend.

There is more. In I Corinthians 9:14-18, Paul defends in dialectical fashion his right to claim support from his congregations but refuses to make use of it, adding, "I would rather die than that — no one will deprive me of my ground for boasting!" But in the next breath he proceeds to reject any boasting over his proclamation of the gospel — "for," as he says, "an obligation is laid on me." The term "obligation" translates another word used by the ancients to denote anonymous, blind destiny that seizes one from without, and to which even the gods are subject *(ananke)*. Paul uses the term to mark the sovereign power of God, which, fate-like, seizes a person. To resist it brings a curse ("Woe to me if I do not proclaim the gospel!"). For Paul, therefore, the gospel has assumed destiny's shape, and for this reason he can neither boast nor lay claim to a reward. And though remembrance of Damascus may obtrude here only as illustration and not as interpretation,[146] along with those references to an epiphany, it urges the conclusion that what Paul experienced was something in excess of a "call."[147] Whatever the purpose of Luke's accounts in Acts 9, 22, and 26, one factor tends to reinforce the

---

145. Italics mine.

146. Käsemann, "A Pauline Version of the 'Amor Fati,'" pp. 233-234.

147. Cf. Franz-Joseph Ortkemper, *Das Kreuz in der Verkündigung des Apostels Paulus*, p. 89; Peter Stuhlmacher, "Das Ende des Gesetzes," pp. 24-25; Christian Dietzfelbinger, *Die Berufung des Paulus als Ursprung seiner Theologie* (Neukirchen-Vluyn: Neukirchener Verlag, 1985), pp. 51-64; Helmut Merklein, "Die Bedeutung des Kreuzestod Christi," *Studien zu Jesus und Paulus* (Tübingen: J. C. B. Mohr, 1997), I, 7; Dieter Sänger, *Die Verkündigung des Gekreuzigten und Israel*, pp. 223, 292.

choice of the term "conversion" over "call." In the first account of the Damascus encounter, Luke uses the temporal adverb "immediately" *(exaiphnēs)* to indicate the suddenness of the event ("suddenly a light from heaven flashed around him" [9:3]), again *(eutheōs)* to report the removal of Paul's blindness following the event ("immediately something like scales fell from his eyes" [9:18]), and again *(eutheōs)* to document Paul's response to it ("for several days he was with the disciples in Damascus, and immediately he began to proclaim Jesus in the synagogues" [9:19b-20a]). In the second account, citing Paul's Jerusalem defense, Luke uses the adverb *(exaiphnēs)* to denote the suddenness of the event (Acts 22:6). And in the third account, which contains Paul's defense before Agrippa (Acts 26:12-13), the adverb is missing. In both the second and third accounts, however, just as in the first, the interval between event and response is collapsed into a tiny space: in the second account, directly following his report of Ananias's summons, Paul records his vision in the temple (Acts 22:17-21); in the third, directly following his recitation of Jesus' summons to go to the gentiles, he says that he "declared first to those in Damascus, then in Jerusalem and throughout the countryside of Judea, and also to the Gentiles, that they should repent and turn to God" (Acts 26:20). This collapsing of the interval between the epiphany and the attendant response hides a concession to the event as *anankē*. Willingly or not, Acts 9, 22, and 26 — like I Corinthians 9 — witness to Paul's encounter with an irresistible, ineluctable power that is intent on working its will whatever the opposition, and taking captive into its service whomever it seizes.

For all of this, neither "call," which implies a mere commission to a peculiar task or assignment to an office, nor "conversion," which implies a mere repudiation of the past, suffices to describe what Paul experienced at Damascus. Both terms and what they imply suffer "fracture" over the event of Paul's experience.

The Evangelists

The same collapse of interval between summons and response can be observed in the Gospel narratives of the calling of the disciples. Mark records that when Jesus passed by the Sea of Galilee, he saw Simon and Andrew casting their nets into the sea, and said to them, "Follow me. . . .

47

And immediately *(eutheōs)* they left their nets and followed him" (Mark 1:16-18).[148] In all three Synoptic Gospels, the call of Matthew or Levi evokes the same response:

> Jesus went out again beside the sea. . . . As he was walking along, he saw Levi son of Alphaeus sitting at the tax booth, and he said to him, "Follow me." And he got up and followed him. (Mark 2:13-14; Matt. 9:9; Luke 5:27-28)

No doubt, awareness of the illusions of source, author, and addressee attaching to the traditional historical-critical method[149] has made modern commentators cautious or silent about exploring the intent of the writer behind his account.[150] In the last century interpreters were intrigued by the collapse of interval between Jesus' summons and the disciples' response, and they rushed to broaden it. No less a conservative than Theodor Zahn (1838-1933), who avoided any psycho-historical interpretation of Paul's Damascus experience, followed in their train:

> Only people at home with Jesus' intentions and firmly persuaded of his calling to the task in which he wished to make them co-workers, could even take in his abrupt summons with the mind or follow it with a willing heart.[151]

To such interpreters it appeared psychologically impossible that Jesus should simply appear and summon persons who had no prior

148. Resistance in the NRSV to the use of "men" as synecdoche in translation has resulted in alteration of the noun to a verb in vs. 17: "I will make you fish for people."

149. See, e.g., the criticism of Paul Ricoeur in "Du Conflit à la Convergence des Méthodes en Exégèse Biblique," *Exégèse et hermeneutique* (Parole de Dieu), ed. X. Leon-Dufour (Paris: Seuil, 1970), pp. 36, 291-293.

150. Cf., e.g., Joel Marcus (in *Mark 1–8*, The Anchor Bible [New York: Doubleday, 2000], pp. 177-185), who draws no conclusions regarding the purpose of his narrative from his introductory statement that Mark is a "redemptive story re-enacted and re-experienced in the church's celebration of the compassionate, suffering, risen Lord who not only has gone before it . . . but is also present in its midst" (p. 69).

151. Theodor Zahn, *Das Evangelium des Matthäus* (Leipzig: A. Deichertsche Verlagsbuchhandlung, 1922), 4th ed., 172. Of Paul's response to Jesus' summons at Damascus, Zahn simply writes that "once he received this instruction from the very first he complied with it" (*Die Apostelgeschichte des Lucas,* 2d half, chs. 113-128, 3rd and 4th eds. [1927], 804).

knowledge of him but in one split second abandoned their livelihoods to follow him — a response given graphic representation in Franco Zeffirelli's movie *The Gospel according to St. Matthew.* But as one author notes, the real offense for the modern interpreter in these call-narratives lies in what was common to earliest Christianity: encounter with the Unconditioned, whose call made of the response to it a matter of course and at whatever cost:

> Our story . . . deals "only" with the miracle of the compelling word, in light of which it becomes senseless to ask whether it is man's free decision taking place here or the will of God reigning alone in majesty. What is peculiar to this experience is that both things occur simultaneously: the divine voice summons, and the person — precisely because he follows it — is totally free, that is, finally comes round to doing what he really wanted to do all along.[152]

If, in fact, unhesitating response to the Unconditioned marked earliest Christian faith, it would not be hazardous to assume that the call-narratives just cited anticipate a similar reaction from their readers. In the Fourth Gospel, the interval between the calling of Philip and Philip's invitation to Nathanael to "come and see" whether "anything good" comes from Nazareth leaves no time for deliberation:

> The next day Jesus decided to go to Galilee. He found Philip and said to him, "Follow me." Now Philip was from Bethsaida, the city of Andrew and Peter. Philip found Nathanael and said to him, "We have found him about whom Moses in the law and also the prophets wrote. . . ." (John 1:43-45)

The lack of interval between call and response in this account has elicited debate among modern interpreters. The one group attempts to widen it through the device of translation ("he found Philip *again*" — identifying him as one of the two in 1:35); through reference to Philip's shared citizenship with Andrew and Peter as a factor reinforcing Jesus' summons ("now Philip was from Bethsaida, the city of Andrew and Peter"); or through assimilation of the Marcan and Johannine accounts. The other group resists

---

152. Ernst Haenchen, *Der Weg Jesu: Eine Erklärung des Markus-Evangelium und der kanonischen Parallelen* (Berlin: Alfred Töpelmann, 1966), p. 80.

the argument from silence or geography, as well as the adjusting of the one account to the other, thus leaving Jesus' initiative unchallenged in the lack of interval between his call and the disciples' response.[153]

When one keeps in mind the entire context of the Fourth Gospel, those who resist widening the interval have the better of the argument. And again, despite the necessary caution regarding the "illusions" of the critical method, if we assume that the evangelist or "implied author" is pursuing some goal with his "implied reader," what is to prevent the suggestion that "Mark's Gospel exists to challenge those who read it to confront its Subject and to come to terms with him,"[154]specifically that the lack of interval allowed for response in this narrative is calculated to evoke a similar reaction in its reader/hearer? And would the demand for a like response on the part of his reader be appropriate if the evangelist or "implied author" himself had spent days or weeks weighing the pros and cons before throwing in with Jesus? And would resistance to such a suggestion merely reflect our inability to grasp what was characteristic of earliest Christianity?

The Fathers

Despite what William James called the mainstream Protestant aversion to "instantaneous conversion," three of its heroes attest to the absence of interval between call and response in their own experience. In his thirty-second year, Augustine, though mastered by his old sins, longed to devote himself entirely to God. During a severe struggle, he heard a voice from heaven, opened Scripture, and underwent sudden change:

153. Père Lagrange says that the fourth evangelist "deems it useless to state that Philip obeyed the call until he introduces him as a propagandist" (M.-J. Lagrange, *Evangile selon Saint Jean* [Paris: J. Gabalda et Cie, 1936], p. 49); Bultmann says that "verse 43 indicates that [Jesus'] brief word, 'Follow me!' makes Philip his disciple" (*The Gospel of John: A Commentary,* trans. G. R. Beasley-Murray [Philadelphia: Westminster, 1971], p. 103); Raymond Brown translates the verb *heuriskei* to mean simply "finds," not "finds again" (*The Gospel according to John [i–xii],* The Anchor Bible [New York: Doubleday, 1966], pp. 81-82) and C. K. Barrett remarks that using the Johannine to render the Marcan account more credible simply raises the level of irritation (*The Gospel According to St. John,* 2nd edition [Philadelphia: Westminster, 1978], p. 183).

154. Paul J. Achtemeier, *Mark, Proclamation Commentaries,* 2nd edition (Philadelphia: Fortress, 1986), p. 113.

Behold, I heard from a nearby house the voice of someone — whether boy or girl I know not — chanting, as it were, and repeating over and over: "Take it, read it! Take it, read it!" . . . Snatching it up, I opened it and read in silence the first passage on which my eyes fell: "Not in revelry and drunkenness, not in debauchery and wantonness, not in strife and jealousy; but put ye on the Lord Jesus Christ, and as for the flesh, take no thought for its lusts." No further did I desire to read, nor was there need. Indeed, immediately with the termination of this sentence, all the darknesses of doubt were dispersed, as if by a light of peace flooding into my heart.[155]

At some time after a quarrel with his father, whose bales of cloth he had stolen and sold to pay for the rebuilding of the local church, Francis of Assisi (ca. 1181-1226) disappeared underground. When he emerged, he vowed to restore what he had taken; he rent his garments, piled them in a heap, and, clad only in a hairshirt, left for the winter woods bursting into song. G. K. Chesterton (1874-1936) describes the change in these words:

> It was a profound spiritual revolution. The man who went into the cave was not the man who came out again; in that sense he was almost as different as if he were dead, as if he were a ghost or a blessed spirit. And the effects of this on his attitude towards the actual world were really as extravagant as any parallel can make them. He looked at the world as differently from other men as if he had come out of that dark hole walking on his hands.[156]

One year before his death, in the foreword to the first volume of his collected Latin works, Martin Luther wrote of his experience in the tower of the Black Cloister at Wittenberg, during the winter semester of 1512-1513 or the spring of 1513:

> Though I lived as a monk without reproach, I felt that I was a sinner before God with an extremely disturbed conscience. I could not believe that he was placated by my satisfaction. I did not love, yes, I hated the

155. *Saint Augustine's Confessions,* trans. Vernon J. Bourke, *The Fathers of the Church* (New York: Fathers of the Church, Inc., 1953), pp. 224-225.

156. G. K. Chesterton, *St. Francis of Assisi* (New York: Doubleday, Image Edition, 2001), p. 63.

righteous God who punishes sinners, and secretly, if not blasphe-
mously, certainly murmuring greatly, I was angry with God, and said,
"As if, indeed, it is not enough, that miserable sinners, eternally lost
through original sin, are crushed by every kind of calamity by the law
of the decalogue, without having God add pain to pain by the gospel
and also by the gospel threatening us with his righteousness and
wrath!" Thus I raged with a fierce and troubled conscience. Nevertheless, I beat importunately upon Paul at that place, most ardently, desiring to know what St. Paul wanted. At last, by the mercy of God, medi-
tating day and night, I gave heed to the context of the words, namely,
"In it the righteousness of God is revealed, as it is written, 'He who
through faith is righteous shall live.'" There I began to understand that
the righteousness of God is that by which the righteous lives by a gift
of God, namely by faith. . . . Here I felt that I was altogether born again
and had entered paradise itself through open gates.[157]

John Calvin wrote that while he was still a small boy his father decided that he should study theology; but after learning that the pursuit
of law led to greater wealth, the father changed his mind and dispatched
his son to the study of law. In obedience to his father, the son applied
himself to the study, but God, "by the secret guidance of his providence," gave a different direction to his life. Calvin continued:

And first, since I was too obstinately devoted to the superstitions of
Popery to be easily extricated from so profound an abyss of mire,
God by a sudden conversion subdued and brought my mind to a
teachable frame. . . . Having thus received some taste and knowledge
of true godliness, I was immediately inflamed with so intense a desire
to make progress therein, that although I did not altogether leave off
other studies, I yet pursued them with less ardour. I was quite sur-
prised to find that before a year had elapsed, all who had any desire after purer doctrine were continually coming to me to learn, although I
myself was as yet a mere novice and tyro.[158]

157. *Luther's Works,* Vol. 34, *Career of the Reformer,* IV, "Preface to the Complete
Edition of Luther's Latin Writings," trans. Lewis Spitz (Philadelphia: Muhlenberg Press,
1960), pp. 336-337.
158. *Commentaries on the Book of Psalms by John Calvin,* trans. James Anderson
(Grand Rapids: Baker Book House, 1979), I, xl. In his lectures on Calvin, Barth refused to

In Port-Royal-des-Champs, on November 23, 1654, the French physicist Blaise Pascal (1623-1662) retreated to his room, opened his Bible, and in it read the story of Christ's passion. He wept: Christ had forgiven him, and had shown him grace. He saw everything in a new light. Until that moment he had sought God through the reflection of the philosopher and scientist, but had reached only Descartes's (1596-1650) idea of God. Now he had discovered Christ and the living God who made himself known through love in the heart. He looked at his clock: it was half-past eleven. Shaken, feverish, he began to write. An hour later, he penned words from John's Gospel: "Righteous Father, the world has not known you"; then he added, "But I have known you." After he had written "according to the God of Abraham . . . not of the philosophers . . . ," he added, "certainty, certainty, feeling, joy, peace."[159]

Rosalyn Turek (1914-1999?), arguably the greatest Bach interpreter of the twentieth century, had a life-changing experience before her seventeenth birthday. After beginning work on the A minor Prelude and Fugue from Book I of the *Well-Tempered Clavier,* she suddenly lost consciousness. She wrote:

> I don't know for how long it was, but when I came to, I had a whole new insight into Bach's music. . . . I immediately dropped everything

interpret the Reformer's "conversion" in terms of a "temporal, historical datum" but rather as the "meaning, the whole of his biography." To the question of what Calvin might then have meant by the term, Barth replied: "I would put it more reservedly that he is becoming more and more awake, is coming to himself, discovering the theologian in himself." He added that Calvin's break with the church may have begun as early as at his parental home in Noyon (Karl Barth, *Die Theologie Calvins* [1922], ed. Hans Schnollk [Zürich: Theologischer Verlag, 1993], pp. 185, 190; cf. pp. 182, 184).

159. Cf. Emile Cailliet and John C. Blankenagel, *Great Shorter Works of Pascal* (Philadelphia: Westminster, 1948), p. 117. Such "conversions" are not limited to religious experiences. In *The God That Failed,* Arthur Koestler compared joining the Communist Party to a spiritual conversion: "To say that one had 'seen the light' is a poor description of the mental rapture which only the convert knows. . . . The new light seems to pour from all directions across the skull; the whole universe falls into a pattern like the stray pieces of a jigsaw puzzle assembled by magic at one stroke. There is now an answer to every question, doubts and conflicts are a matter of the tortured past. . . . Nothing henceforth can disturb the convert's inner peace and serenity — except the occasional fear of losing faith again, losing thereby what alone makes life worth living, and falling back into the outer darkness" (*The God That Failed* [New York: Harper, 1949], p. 23).

else I was studying in order to enter into this new way of thinking and to attempt to master this totally new technique. . . .[160]

A New World

The affirmation of a crucified Messiah effected a momentous change of "paradigm" with the New Testament authors. Paul Minear writes:

> Their perceptions of the world had been revolutionized: ideas about life and its hidden origins, about death and its equally hidden finalities, about society and its false certainties, about power and its deceptive efficacies. All had been changed.[161]

Paul's statement that by Christ's cross the world has been "crucified" to him and he to the world (Gal. 6:14) is but another way of saying that his world had been transformed. As Adolf Schlatter read it:

> Just as Paul sees the world gathered up into Jesus' cross, so . . . he appears to the world. . . . What God's grace gives us does not derive from what we have, as if it were already contained in that, were only a change of name for an old condition. A creation of God is beginning in us . . . to embrace our whole nature and transfigure our relation to each other. . . . For this reason, the apostle can let the whole world sink to the bottom with Jesus' cross. Something new and glorious is arising in its place: the new creation of God.[162]

Nowhere is the reference to Jesus' death as creating a new world clearer than in Paul's Second Letter to the Corinthians and its companion passage in Galatians. In II Corinthians 5:17, he says: "So if anyone is in Christ, there is a new creation: everything old has passed away; see, ev-

160. "Rosalyn Turek, A Portrait," *Johann Sebastian Bach: Goldberg Variations* (Hamburg: Deutsche Grammophon, 1999), pp. 10-11.

161. Paul Minear, *The Golgotha Earthquake* (Cleveland: Pilgrim Press, 1995), pp. xi-xii, 1; cf. Kurt Niederwimmer, "Erkennen und Lieben: Gedanken zum Verhältnis von Gnosis und Agape im Ersten Korintherbrief," *Kerygma und Dogma* 11 (1965), 85; Dieter Sänger, *Die Verkündigung des Gekreuzigten und Israel*, p. 234.

162. Adolf Schlatter, *Die Briefe an die Galater, Epheser, Kolosser und Philemon: Erläuterungen zum Neuen Testament* (Stuttgart: Calwer Verlag, 1963), p. 150.

erything has become new!" And in Galatians 6:15: "For neither circumcision nor uncircumcision is anything; but a new creation is everything!" The conjunction "so" *(hōste)* in II Corinthians 5:17, in addition to climaxing what precedes, relates the "new creation" to union with Christ in his death (vv. 14-15), a relationship reiterated in the phrase "in Christ" *(en Christō)* in verse 17. As in the Galatians passage, the term "creation" *(ktisis)* designates a new creative act. The "old" *(ta archaia)* refers first of all to knowledge "from a human point of view" *(kata sarka)* in verse 16.[163] Christ was formerly regarded as an object of knowledge together with all the other objects of human apprehension, a mere subject for inquiry whose true significance was not seen. The "old," however, goes deeper and demands the additional reference to origins: all that was in existence from the beginning till now passes away because Christ's death brings about a new creation. This knowledge evokes Paul's triumphant "see" *(idou)* in verse 17. This gives to the "new creation" a significance beyond the anthropological. The "new" epitomizes all that has occurred through Christ and points toward a final and ultimate realization.

In Galatians 6:15, Paul regards what has resulted from Christ's death (vs. 14: "the cross of our Lord Jesus Christ, by which the world has been crucified to me, and I to the world") from the viewpoint of the "Israel of God" (vs. 16). Circumcision and uncircumcision formerly denoted membership within one of the two divisions of humanity. These divisions have now lost their sociological significance, since what produced them has been made of no effect with Christ's death. For this reason, Paul's reply to those who maintain the necessity of circumcision in fulfillment of the Mosaic law is that what alone is of significance is the "new creation."

In the Fourth Gospel, the evangelist uses the narrative of a man born blind to indicate the emergence of the new on the heels of the old world, the old conceptual network. After he received his sight on the Sabbath, the blind man's interrogators bawl at him:

> "Give glory to God! We know that this man [Jesus] is a sinner." He answered, "I do not know whether he is a sinner. One thing I do know, that though I was blind, now I see." (John 9:24-25)

---

163. A verse from which Bultmann drew support for his opposition to the "Quest of the Historical Jesus," new and old; see Bultmann, *Exegetische Probleme des Zweiten Korintherbriefs* (Uppsala: Wretmans Boktryckeri, 1947), pp. 12ff.

A new world has come to displace the world in which life was lived according to judicial decree, according to a law that judged Jesus as Sabbath-breaker and sinner. This narrative in John comes as close as any in the Gospels to illustrating a fundamental conviction of Paul: if Jesus, under the curse of the law, had been declared to be "Son of God with power according to the spirit of holiness by resurrection from the dead" (Rom. 1:4), then the verdict of the law was clearly wrong, and righteousness had come to be revealed apart from the law.[164] "Here, in fact," writes Dieter Sänger, "we may speak of a hermeneutical paradigm change."[165]

The biblical authors use no uniform terminology to document their reaction to the total restructuring of their world that results from their encounter with a suffering, dying Christ. There is no "orthodox" view of the meaning of Jesus' death. For example, over against the characteristic narrative style of the Gospels and Acts, the Epistles and Apocalypse "metaphorize" the death of Jesus, offering representations in a profusion that defies attempts to arrive at a univocal meaning.[166]

Thus the biblical writers can agree in their identification of the model or matrix itself without agreeing on a full interpretation or rationalization of it.[167] They search for metaphors in hope of expressing something of their experience; and they use terms to visualize the event by alluding to ideas known to their hearers and readers. These terms and images are not always cleanly separated, but may be mingled and named in a single breath.[168] For this reason, utterances in the New Testament regarding the cross have links to all those theses that systematicians have later described and differentiated as "Abelardian," "Anselmian," and so forth. This does not involve disorder or self-contradiction; in fact, dis-

---

164. Cf. Morna D. Hooker, *A Preface to Paul* (New York: Oxford University Press, 1980), p. 40.

165. Dieter Sänger: "In view of his past as a strict Pharisee (Phil. 3:5; cf. Gal. 1:13; Acts 22:3; 23:6; 26:5) and zealot for the *patrikōn mou paradoseōn* (Gal. 1:14), i.e. for the Law, Paul was forced to relate the *nomos* to the content of his gospel, Jesus Christ, in a completely new way. Here, in fact, we may speak of a hermeneutical paradigm change" (*Die Verkündigung des Gekreuzigten und Israel*, p. 237).

166. Olivette Genest, "From Historical-Critical Exegesis to Greimassian Semiotics: A Christological Issue, The Meaning of Jesus' Death," *Semeia* 81 (1998), 105.

167. Cf. Kuhn, *The Structure of Scientific Revolutions*, p. 44.

168. Cf. Gerhard Friedrich, *Die Verkündigung des Todes Jesu im Neuen Testament*, pp. 45-46; Morna D. Hooker, *Not Ashamed of the Gospel* (Grand Rapids: Eerdmans, 1994), p. 139.

comfort arises only when a single idea to which even God is subject is involved.[169] Further, for the New Testament authors, and especially for Paul, the central recognition given the event of the cross did not eliminate the need for further reflection — for giving that recognition new shape and structure when the concrete situation required.[170]

Johann Georg Hamann (1730-1788), "Magus of the North," celebrated the advent of a new world through the crucified Messiah in these words:

> What a drama for the Creator and all the hosts of creation! World, angels and men share in this mystery. Spectators, players, subscribers. "It is finished" — this watchword, called by the Man of God on Golgotha deafened all nature, created a new heaven and a new earth, transfigured God, transfigured men; revealed to the world, angels, and men that God is righteous and that all would be righteous who believed in him.[171]

The Convert

Candidates for "conversion" have either been very young or very new to the area undergoing change. David Hume (1711-1776), the Scottish empiricist who inspired Europe's greatest thinker, Immanuel Kant (1724-1804), wrote his most important work, *Treatise Concerning Human Nature,* at the age of twenty-five but said that the idea for it came to him when he was fifteen. At the age of fourteen, Wolfgang Amadeus Mozart (1756-1791) had already composed a sonata, a symphony, an oratorio, and an opera, had been appointed concertmaster to the archbishop of Salzburg, and had been decorated by the pope. Both Isaac Newton (1642-1727) and Albert Einstein accomplished much of their work in their early twenties.[172] Werner Heisenberg (1901-1976) conceived of

169. Cf. Adolf Schlatter, *Jesu Gottheit und das Kreuz: Beiträge zur Forderung christlicher Theologie,* 2nd ed. (Gütersloh: C. Bertelsmann, 1913), p. 38.

170. Cf. Dieter Sänger, *Die Verkündigung des Gekreuzigten und Israel,* p. 294.

171. Johann Georg Hamann, *Entkleidung und Verklärung: Eine Auswahl aus Schriften und Briefen des "Magus im Norden,"* ed. Martin Seils (Eckart-Verlag, 1963), p. 16.

172. Cf. David Bodanis, $E = MC^2$: *A Biography of the World's Most Famous Equation* (New York: Berkley Books, 2000), p. 84.

quantum mechanics one night on a North Sea resort at the age of twenty-four.[173] Barth says that Calvin's reference to his obstinate devotion to the "superstitions of Popery," which God then "subdued by a sudden conversion," makes sense only if he was about seventeen or eighteen years old.[174]

Of Jesus himself, Luke writes that he "was about thirty years old when he began his work" (Luke 3:23). In the Fourth Gospel, Jesus' enemies scoff at his remark that "Abraham rejoiced that he would see my day," since he was "not yet fifty years old" (John 8:57). In Mark's Gospel, the events of his life frequently involve the young: the daughter of Jairus, synagogue ruler (5:21-24, 35-43); the daughter of the Syro-Phoenician woman (7:24-30); the boy with the dumb spirit (9:14-29); the children in his arms (10:13-16); the youth fleeing at the crucifixion (14:51-52) and the young man at the tomb (16:1-8).

Aside from questions of social and economic status, and aside from the age-old debate over the "Jesus movement" as composed of itinerant charismatics or of structured, settled groups, or both,[175] the summons to follow came to persons ripe for wandering, for pulling up stakes, leaving house and home, wife and child, mother and father (Mark 1:20; 10:29; Luke 18:29), who could let the "dead bury their dead" (Matt. 8:22) and take the lilies and birds as models (Matt. 6:26-30; Luke 12:24-28). The summons involved the basic and continually recurring themes of puberty and youth, in the call to detach ("If any want to become my followers, let them deny themselves and take up their cross and follow me" [Mark 8:34]); in the summons to decide for oneself ("Let anyone with ears to hear listen!" [Mark 4:9]); or in the call to sexual purity ("If your right eye causes you to sin, tear it out and throw it away; it is better for you to lose one of your members than for your whole body to be thrown into hell" [Matt. 5:29]).

173. Bodanis, p. 159.

174. Barth, *Die Theologie Calvins* (1922), p. 180.

175. Over ninety years ago, the jurist Rudolf Sohm insisted that primitive Christianity was initially an invisible, "purely religious" fellowship nourished by charismatics, whereas the historian Adolf von Harnack argued that earliest Christianity already had within it the seeds of an empirical, legal entity. See Harnack's analysis of Sohm's theory in *The Constitution & Law of the Church in the First Two Centuries,* trans. F. L. Pogson (New York: Williams & Norgate, 1910), pp. 176-258. See also current attitudes toward Sohm as noted in Ekkehard and Wolfgang Stegemann, *The Jesus Movement* (Minneapolis: Fortress, 1999), pp. 187-220.

Sociologically and psychologically, the Jesus movement was oriented to youth. Naturally, it also involved the mature, the elderly, and sedentary communities of believers. It is impossible to construe the movement as composed exclusively of persons prepared to abandon home, family, possessions, and protection. But these stable communities existed in a complementary relationship to the youth who were dependent on them. In Matthew's Gospel, Jesus says to the twelve:

> Whatever town or village you enter, find out who in it is worthy, and stay there until you leave. As you enter the house, greet it. If the house is worthy, let your peace come upon it; but if it is not worthy, let your peace return to you. If anyone will not welcome you or listen to your words, shake off the dust from your feet as you leave that house or town. (Matt. 10:11-14)

Whether or not the old, "whose hearts are dry as summer dust," tend to resist or suppress the new and novel, the evidence in terms of the requirement to attach oneself to the "Jesus movement" is on the side of youth. That later contemporary of Jesus who wrote what follows had been converted in his youth, in 31-34 C.E.:

> I am not ashamed of the gospel; it is the power of God for salvation to everyone who has faith, to the Jew first and also to the Greek. For in it the righteousness of God is revealed through faith for faith; as it is written, "The one who is righteous will live by faith." (Rom. 1:16-17)

Continuity and Contrast

If, for the New Testament authors, the new "paradigm" did not simply spring from the Old Testament, it is nonetheless true that they made use of the language and conceptuality of the Old Testament. The history of the Christian community's struggle to retain the Old Testament in its canon gives support to the contention regarding the condition that a new paradigm must fulfill. Fifty years ago, Rudolf Bultmann said that at the outset the Christian mission was supported by theological motifs and concepts stemming from the Old Testament-Jewish tradition.[176]

176. Bultmann, *Theology of the New Testament,* I, 84.

Motivation for a Christian theology derived not only from the need for interpreting the gospel message but also for understanding the Old Testament. If the God of Abraham, Isaac, and Jacob was also the God of Jesus Christ, then the Old Testament required reading and interpreting; its difficulties had to be overcome. But the Old Testament could also serve as a source of knowledge, with the proviso that it be read in accordance with its origin in a sovereign, divine deed:

> First of all, you must understand this, that no prophecy of Scripture is a matter of one's own interpretation, because no prophecy ever came by human will, but men and women moved by the Holy Spirit spoke from God. (II Pet. 1:20-21)

The New Testament, accordingly, is replete with reminiscences from the Old Testament. Many assume that the primitive community, faced with the "anomaly" of Jesus' death, gave that death positive meaning by means of Old Testament and late Jewish ideas of atonement, together with other ideas from the religious-historical context of the period.[177] The picture of Christ as the vicarious sacrifice by which the world is reconciled to God clearly points to an Old Testament idea, however we may trace its descent to older ethnic, even prehistorical roots, or trace its ascent from the cultic to the rational, ethical, or "pictorial."[178] That picture, or the picture of Christ, who through suffering and death pays the ransom by which the creature is redeemed from the lordship of sin and death, or the portrait of the one who takes upon himself the punishment the creature deserved — these portraits are anticipated in Old Testament figures.[179] In sum, the New Testament authors, whose world was revolutionized and altered by the cross, undertook to give to its reflection the moral and spiritual rigor of the Old Testament.

Nor is it inconceivable that the primitive Christian community used views or concepts that once were at home outside the old or new community of faith. The popular nineteenth-century view and its innumerable variations, according to which the Christology, soteriology, pneumatology, and sacramentology of the New Testament immediately derived from oriental or Hellenistic-Greek religion, has been challenged by a re-

177. Cf. Fritz Viering, *Der Kreuzestod Jesu,* p. 25.
178. Günter Bader, "Jesu Tod als Opfer," *ZThK* 80, No. 4 (1983), 413, 417.
179. Viering, p. 29.

appraisal of the sources. Some have been embarrassed by this,[180] and others have refused to be persuaded. Nonetheless, the language and conceptuality that the New Testament authors had to choose in order to convey their message thrust them into a context and world parallel to or at odds with their own. Striking similarities between sayings and narratives in the Gospels and in extrabiblical, non-Christian literature once forced an entire school to abandon the idea of novelty as a fundamental theological category in favor of the "religion of Jesus" or the "religion of Paul."[181] The result was a contest between those who affirmed Hellenistic-Jewish or Hellenistic-Greek religion and those who affirmed the religion of the Old Testament as the proper background for interpreting the New Testament — a contest that persists to the present hour.

Finally, it is just as conceivable that the Christian community drew from both the Old Testament tradition *and* from Hellenistic religion in order to declare convincingly within a given cultural context what God had done for humanity's salvation. In Judaism itself, the process of the intermingling of once mutually exclusive traditions had already begun with the appearance of the *Kethubim,* that final portion of the Old Testament "canon" of the Septuagint, and of the literature between the Testaments. This moves one commentator to say that in Paul's understanding of Jesus' death as sacrifice, for example, "the entire ancient world" appears; that the formula "Christ died for us" (Rom. 5:8) contains nothing other than the entire Greek experience, just as conversely the formula "God gave them up" (Rom. 1:24, 26, 28) embraces the entire Jewish experience.[182]

---

180. Note, e.g., Ernst Käsemann's reluctance concerning the English translation of his monograph on Hebrews, due to its dependence on the theory of the "redeemed Redeemer" in pre-Christian, Jewish-Hellenistic religion (*The Wandering People of God,* trans. Roy A. Harrisville and Irving L. Sandberg [Minneapolis: Augsburg, 1984], pp. 12-13). Note also his demurral over against Bultmann's theory of the fourth evangelist as editor of a pagan speech-source (in *Kirchliche Konflikte* [Göttingen: Vandenhoeck & Ruprecht, 1982], pp. 238-239).

181. Cf. *Die Religionsgeschichtliche Schule,* ed. Gerd Lüdemann (Frankfurt: Peter Lang, 1996), p. 13: "In the History of Religions School there was a curious gap between its discovery of community and cult as origin and situation-in-life of extensive portions of early Christian literature and its understanding of Jesus. For example, discovery of the community as the source of many early Christian sayings strangely conflicts with the high evaluation assigned to personalities, especially the personality and proclamation of Jesus."

182. Cf. Günter Bader, "Jesu Tod als Opfer," p. 424. See also Bultmann's discussion

Still, despite the New Testament writers' appropriation of concepts, metaphors, analogies, and comparisons from the world around them, the attempt to derive the New Testament in unilinear fashion from the Old Testament, together with intertestamental Jewish literature, whether enriched by Hellenistic elements or not — or to derive it from oriental, pagan tradition — contradicts the nature of the revolution effected by the "anomaly" of the death of the Messiah, Jesus. Whatever visual material the New Testament authors expropriated from other sources to describe its nature and significance ultimately did not suffice to explain the event. Bader says that the variety of New Testament utterances indicates that they have been shaped to the audience's capacity to understand. Nevertheless, the "ideational material of that time does not suffice but must be continually broken through if the significance of the Christ-event is to be explained."[183] Käsemann finds the New Testament witnesses "uncommonly open" to the world around them. And since it is tradition that "marks the message," because "tradition always determines communication," the authors draw from the most varied traditions without hesitation. Those traditions, however, are not allowed to stand unqualified or uncorrected. They do not give the proclamation its character — only its "handle."[184] Alteration of the tradition inevitably results, that is, provided the death of Christ was a true "anomaly" and not merely another stage on a continuum.

The debate among Christian interpreters over the real or alleged *diastasis* between the Old Testament as such and the Old Testament as employed by the New — thus over the legitimacy or illegitimacy of interpreting the one apart from the other — may never end. But this only means that some will always argue that the Old Testament is set within an entirely different horizon or emerges as an entirely new theological entity when viewed from the perspective of the New Testa-

---

of the "Good Shepherd" in John 10 as related to Old Testament as well as to Mandaean tradition (*The Gospel of John,* pp. 278, 280).

183. Cf. Gerhard Friedrich, *Die Verkündigung des Todes Jesu im Neuen Testament,* pp. 80, 143-145; cf. Bader, "Jesu Tod als Opfer," pp. 414-415; Manfred Oeming, *Gesamt Biblische Theologien der Gegenwart* (Stuttgart: W. Kohlhammer, 1987), pp. 125-126; and Stuhlmacher, "Achtzehn Thesen zur paulinischen Kreuzestheologie," p. 195.

184. Ernst Käsemann, "Erwägungen zum Stichwort 'Versöhnungslehre' im Neuen Testament," in *Zeit und Geschichte: Dankesgabe an Rudolf Bultmann zum 80. Geburtstag,* ed. Erich Dinkler (Tübingen: J. C. B. Mohr, 1964), pp. 55-57.

ment.[185] As earlier noted, in reacting to Bultmann's allegiance to the theory and practice of the History of Religions School, many neglected to pursue their reading of his *History of the Synoptic Tradition* to the final chapter, where he distinguishes the Gospels as *sui generis;* or they did not pursue their reading of his Fourth Gospel commentary to the point where he distances the author from his "pagan" sources, despite their kinship.[186]

At no other point in the Gospels is the incommensurability of the way Jesus came to bring with whatever preceded or paralleled it more clearly expressed than in his answer to the fasting question. In Mark's report, Jesus is asked why the Baptist's disciples and those of the Pharisees fast — but his disciples do not. Jesus first responds in a parable calculated to indicate that mourning, signaled in fasting, is inappropriate to celebration: "The wedding guests cannot fast while the bridegroom is with them, can they? As long as they have the bridegroom with them, they cannot fast" (Mark 2:19). For all its obliqueness, Jesus' reference to "the bridegroom" is as august a self-designation as may be found anywhere in the Gospel tradition. In a second parable, Jesus indicates the irreconcilable difference between the life he has come to bring and whatever may have come before:

> No one sews a piece of unshrunk cloth on an old cloak; otherwise, the patch pulls away from it, the new from the old, and a worse tear is made. And no one puts new wine into old wineskins; otherwise, the wine will burst the skins, and the wine is lost, and so are the skins; but one puts new wine into fresh wineskins. (Mark 2:21-22)

This aspect of contrast or irreconcilability between what has occurred with Christ and whatever may have preceded, paralleled, or followed it, is sounded again and again throughout the New Testament. To his contrary Galatians, Paul writes:

> Even if we or an angel from heaven should proclaim to you a gospel contrary to what we proclaimed to you, let that one be accursed! As we have said before, so now I repeat, if anyone proclaims to you a

185. Cf. Hans Hübner, *Biblische Theologie des Neuen Testaments,* pp. 66-67.
186. Cf. Bultmann, *The History of the Synoptic Tradition,* trans. John Marsh (New York: Harper and Row, 1968), pp. 368-374, and *The Gospel of John,* pp. 367, 382.

gospel contrary to what you received, let that one be accursed! (Gal. 1:8-9)

One tiny parable in Matthew's Gospel appears to contradict the argument regarding the incommensurability of the old with the new:

Therefore every scribe who has been trained for the kingdom of heaven is like the master of a household who brings out of his treasure what is new and what is old. (Matt. 13:52)

What is striking about this parable is that it is the only biblical passage in which the old is not disparaged: the scribe trained for the kingdom draws from his thesaurus both old and new. In the community represented and addressed by Matthew, it was inevitable that the question should arise concerning Jesus' relationship to what preceded him. Was he an innovator, or did he represent a transition from the legalism characteristic of reform movements to a less rigid piety? In response, the "Jesus of Matthew" defines his place in terms of its continuity with the old. The parable, however, does not merely intend to make room for the old within what is contemporary. If "old" and "new" in this context were not intimately connected with Jesus' teaching concerning the kingdom, which is the subject of the entire thirteenth chapter, the obvious conclusion would be that he enjoys a status on a par with other rabbis in Israel. But there is such a connection, and the fact that Jesus is compared to the scribe in verse 52 gives to the parable an ambiguity and force that extend beyond chronology. What the parable is calculated to conceal is that what Jesus teaches is not a mere novelty that enjoys equality with ancient and venerable interpretations, whose value and significance do not cease with age. Again, it is not that Jesus *also* brings the new, that perhaps by means of old, familiar forms and ideas he announces what "many prophets and righteous people longed to see" (Matt. 13:17). Taken in its context, this parable conceals the truth that the new that Jesus draws from his treasury possesses an intrinsic energy that guarantees to it a superiority that qualifies the old as valuable only because of its service to the new. The new is thus "eschatologically" new: that is to say, it possesses a dynamic that renders continuity with the old possible only on condition that the old retain its status as servant of the new.

CHAPTER TWO

The Death of Jesus in Paul

The Old Testament Cultic and Legal Tradition

Clues to the Pauline language and conceptuality as rooted in Judaism are everywhere. One need have no allegiance to a particular persuasion regarding the New Testament background to acknowledge that, to a great extent, Paul's theology developed from Old Testament Jewish thought, or to concede that the synagogue had already done a good piece of work before he arrived on the scene.

Use and Fracture of Wisdom, Sacrifice, and the Law

When, for example, Paul refers to Christ as "the wisdom of God" within the polemic of I Corinthians 1:18-31, he is using an idea that stretches from Hellenistic Judaism through Philo (ca. 20 B.C.E.–50 C.E.), Aristobulos (3rd to 2nd century B.C.E.), Josephus (37 B.C.E.-?), and apocalyptic to rabbinic Judaism. His argument in I Corinthians 2:7-8, for example, could well be a variation on an old wisdom myth that lies behind many Jewish texts.[1] For his interpretation of Jesus' death as sac-

---

1. The passage reads: "We speak God's wisdom, secret and hidden, which God decreed before the ages for our glory. None of the rulers of this age understood this; for if they had, they would not have crucified the Lord of glory." And the myth as cited in the apocalypse of Enoch reads: "Wisdom could not find a place in which she could dwell; but a place was found [for her] in the heavens. Then Wisdom went out to dwell with the children of the people, but she found no dwelling place. [So] Wisdom returned to her place

rifice, specific institutions of the Jerusalem cult will have furnished Paul a type. In Romans 3:25-26, he says that God put Christ "forward as a sacrifice of atonement by his blood."[2] The term relates to the highest point in the religion and theology of Israel, the great blood rite of Yom Kippur, the Day of Atonement. Against this Jewish, cultic background, Jesus, by means of his violent death, is conceived as having been installed as the locus of atonement. There is also legitimacy to the view that the apostle Paul interpreted his own "cruciform" existence in terms of the Old Testament Jewish tradition of the righteous sufferer.

Paul and Judaism are in formal agreement about righteousness as a divine activity rather than as an ethical quality in God. There is even material agreement between Paul and Judaism about righteousness as gift.[3] And despite portrayals of the pre-Christian Paul as anguished over the distance between what he was and what he should have been, as a Christian he developed his problems from out of the Jewish experience, which means that the question concerning the law concerned him incessantly.

Whether or not the apostle was dependent on specific, discrete strands of the Jewish Wisdom tradition may be moot; but the analogy of his writings to the literature of that tradition argues for a common heritage. At the same time, there is a striking difference between the two: it consists in the complexity of the one as opposed to the concentration of the other. In the Wisdom tradition, *Sophia,* or *Hokma,* is subject to variation or adaptation. In the Hellenistic Wisdom of Solomon, for exam-

---

and she settled permanently among the angels" (I Enoch 42:1-3, in *The Old Testament Pseudepigrapha,* I, 33). Erik Peterson locates the polemic of I Cor. 1:18-31 within Jewish liturgical tradition as reflected in a "homily" of Baruch 3:9–4:4 on Jer. 8:13–9:24, a text assigned for Yom Kippur. He finds the same liturgical thematic in a Jewish morning prayer and a prayer of the *Apostolic Constitutions.* Peterson concludes that the Baruch text may have suggested to Paul the possibility of transferring the *Sophia*-idea of Jewish liturgy to the *Sophia*-Christ and the word of the cross (Erik Peterson, "I Korinther 1, 18f. und die Thematik des Jüdischen Busstages," in *Frühkirche, Judentum und Gnosis* [Rome: Herder, 1959], pp. 43-50).

2. The phrase is the revisers' attempt to render the Greek *hilastērion,* in its turn a translation of the Hebrew *kapporeth,* which, to the despair of many, denotes, first of all, the site of a sacrificial transaction.

3. Qumran has decided the debate between Bultmann and Käsemann over Paul as its originator in Käsemann's favor; cf. Käsemann, "The 'Righteousness of God' in Paul," pp. 168-182, and Bultmann, "DIKAIOSYNE TOU THEOU," *JBL* 83 (1964), 12-16.

ple, Wisdom is a pre-existent being, a heavenly person who participates with the deity at creation; but for Josephus and rabbinic Judaism, the myth of pre-existence is tailored to serve the Torah. Furthermore, variants of the Wisdom tradition emphasize, while others wax polemical against, ranking knowledge over faith. In fact, if it does not represent a congeries of ideas, the Jewish Wisdom tradition at least represents a complex of ideas ultimately "alien to the faith of Israel" and "only with difficulty" adjusted to its structure.[4] For Paul, Wisdom is concentrated in a single subject, "Christ Jesus, who became for us wisdom from God" (I Cor. 1:30); beyond that personification, the concept resists all variation or adaptation. And since the benefit of this event is a given — not a performance — whatever the role of Wisdom in ancient tradition, whether adapted to Torah-theology (as in rabbinic thought) or united with it, is conditional on keeping the law (as in mysticism or apocalypticism): the sole and exclusive concentration of Wisdom in the crucified abandons all views of the divine activity conceivable within the context of the legal.[5] In other words, the event of the cross spells the death of a wisdom that attempts to get beyond creatureliness and thus forces one under the law.[6] As more than one researcher has noted, Paul's "striking semantics" in I Corinthians 1:18-25 has its explanation in the common and contemporaneous system of values that the cross event has compelled him to turn on its head.[7] Furthermore, whether or not the hymnic material in Philippians 2, Colossians 1, and Ephesians 2 contains "Pauline additions" and reflects a "cosmic-wisdom theology" in contrast to the "dialectic wisdom theology" of, say, I Corinthians 1 (the one theology denoting the exercise of divine power on a cosmic scale and the other emphasizing the cross as the evidence of power in weakness) — and however these seemingly antithetical views arrive at synthesis — the ultimate assertion of the crucified Christ as the "Lord of

---

4. Ulrich Wilckens, "Sophia," in *Theological Dictionary of the New Testament,* ed. Gerhard Friedrich (Grand Rapids: Eerdmans, 1971), VII, 509.

5. Cf. Klaus Haacker, "Die Fragestellung der biblischen Theologie als exegetischer Aufgabe," in *Biblisch-Theologische Studien* (Neukirchen-Vluyn: Neukirchener Verlag, 1977), p. 53; Thomas Söding, *Das Wort vom Kreuz* (Tübingen: J. C. B. Mohr, 1997), p. 82.

6. Cf. Hans Weder, *Das Kreuz Jesu bei Paulus* (Göttingen: Vandenhoeck & Ruprecht, 1981), p. 157.

7. Cf. Helmut Merklein, "Das paulinische Paradox des Kreuzes," *Studien zu Jesus und Paulus,* II, 288-289.

glory" (I Cor. 2:8), that is, the assertion of the power and universality attaching to his death, is never allowed to detract from the scandal of the cross.[8]

There is no mistaking Paul's use in Romans 3:25 of the priestly idea of atoning sacrifice to describe the soteriological significance of Jesus' death. Yet Paul cannot be interpreted as standing in smooth continuity with that idea.[9] First of all, and most important, his reference to Christ as the place of atonement *(hilastērion)* does not re-establish but supersedes the temple cultus, with its requirement of yearly sacrifice.[10] Second, Paul's statement that the "sacrifice of atonement by his blood" is "effective through faith" spells rejection of the priestly program for a cultically mediated holiness.[11] Third, that reference to faith breaches the boundaries of Jewish messianism, which awaited salvation always and only for Israel.[12] And while it may be too harsh to describe as "perverse" an interpretation that links the use of *hilastērion* in Romans 3 to Paul's concept of reconciliation *(katallagē;* cf. II Cor. 5:18-20), and then proceeds to explain the latter in terms of the former,[13] it is not too much to say that in light of that "linguistic" concentration on the sole event of Christ's death, its interpretation by way of cultic categories can only be typological.[14] In other words, the apostle's hermeneutic describes a move from the event of Christ to the Old Testament cultus. To this extent, Romans 3:25 spells the fracture of "P," the customary cipher for the cultic stratum of Old Testament tradition.

Incidentally, the ideational and speech-model of the "righteous sufferer" in Jewish thought undergoes a similar fate. Since it is the Messiah who steps into the role of sufferer, he cannot be merely one in a series,

8. For a discussion of these two "theologies" and their possible synthesis, cf. Barbour, "Wisdom and the Cross in I Corinthians 1 and 2," pp. 57-71.

9. Jürgen Becker rejects an "overleaping" of the centuries in the assumption that Paul is directly concerned here with the cultic idea; cf. "Die neutestamentliche Rede vom Sühnetod Jesu," *ZThK*, Supplement 8 (1990), 42.

10. Helmut Merklein, "Die Bedeutung des Kreuzestod Christi," *Studien zu Jesus und Paulus,* 33.

11. Merklein, "Die Bedeutung des Kreuzestod Christi," p. 73.

12. Franz-Joseph Ortkemper, *Das Kreuz in der Verkündigung des Apostels Paulus,* p. 18.

13. Gerhard Friedrich, *Die Verkündigung des Todes Jesu im Neuen Testament,* p. 99.

14. Merklein, "Die Bedeutung des Kreuzestod Christi," p. 31; "Der Tod Jesu als stellvertretender Sühnetod," *Studien zu Jesus und Paulus,* I, 86.

but is the one truly righteous one, which is why his death avails for many.[15] For this reason also — or as Paul says, by "becoming a curse for us" (Gal. 3:13)[16] — Jesus displaces Isaac in Galatians 3:16 as the descendant of Abraham through whom the gentiles are blessed.[17] As Levenson says, when Paul glosses the phrase "and to your offspring" in Genesis 12:7 and 22:17-18 with the words "who is Christ," he has so ruptured the association with Isaac that even Genesis testifies to the Christians' Messiah.[18] Nor can the event by which Christ became a curse ("Christ redeemed us from the curse of the law by becoming a curse for us") be clarified through an appeal to the sacral freeing of slaves in Jewish antiquity, since the slave could free himself or be released in the year of jubilee (see Lev. 25:47-55). For Paul, only one subject stands at the midpoint of the transaction, without any use being made of the figure of the one offering ransom or of the person to whom it is paid.[19] In that statement of Jesus' "becoming a curse for us," the hermeneutical move is from that event to the Old Testament cultic sphere, since Christ is identified on the basis of Deuteronomy 21:23, rather than on the basis of a concept of universal sin and the traditional-historical idea of atonement. In Paul this "fracture" of Jewish cultic and legal language and conceptuality at the point of the death of Jesus of Nazareth, the Messiah and God's Son, involves a radical qualification of the Sinai event. Rather than serving as a type of the saving activity of God, the Sinai covenant is set within the gradient of a continuum as an event inferior to the fulfillment in Christ.[20] Nowhere is this fact more forcefully emphasized than in the contrast between the two covenants in II Corinthians 3:6: "Our competence is from God, who has made us competent to be ministers of a new covenant, not of letter but of spirit; for the letter kills, but the Spirit gives life."

15. Kleinknecht, *Der leidende Gerechtfertigte,* pp. 375-376.

16. Paul is referring here to Deut. 21:23, which assumes a hanging following execution for a particular offense. In addition, he omits the phrase "[cursed] by God."

17. Several authors note that the reference to Deut. 21 in Gal. 3 occurs through debate with Jewish-Christian doers of the law, not through Jewish polemic against Jesus; cf. Gerhard Friedrich, *Die Verkündigung des Todes Jesu,* p. 130; Heinz-Wolfgang Kuhn, "Jesus als Gekreuzigter," pp. 32, 35. Friedrich goes so far as to say that initially Deut. 21:23 played no role in Jewish polemic against Jesus (p. 129).

18. Jon Levenson, *The Death and Resurrection of the Beloved Son,* pp. 211, 213.

19. Friedrich, *Die Verkündigung,* p. 83.

20. Cf. Helmut Merklein, "Die Bedeutung des Kreuzestod Christi," pp. 30-31, 33, 63.

The "letter" (*gramma*) refers to the codified law given at Sinai. It is not lifeless, as though the contrast between the two covenants were between deadness and life. Rather, "letter" characterizes the condition laid down for the ordering of the relationship between Yahweh and the Israelite community under the first covenant. It was the dominant characteristic of life under that covenant — and thus synonymous with "law" (*nomos*). To this characteristic Paul opposes the essence of the new covenant as "Spirit" (*pneuma*). Over against the "letter," an external quantity that makes demands from without and exacts an external compliance, the "Spirit" penetrates and dominates from within, thus effecting harmony between thought and action. Or again, whereas "the letter kills" — proof of its vitality and force — the Spirit "gives life." Whether or not Paul has the oracle of Jeremiah in mind here (Jer. 31:31-34), it is the presence of the Spirit that gives to the covenant its character as new. Hence, if God is directly manifested in the new, the way by which he was manifested in the old or through the written law cannot belong to the nature of the new. Judaism could never have spoken of a new covenant that should displace the old. Even in the community of Qumran, with its reference to a new covenant, nothing else was meant but a renewal of the covenant at Sinai. The law remained the sole way to salvation.[21]

In recent years, the discussion of Paul's posture toward the law has narrowed to an often bitter debate. The reading of Paul's critique of the Jew in Romans 2, for example, is divided among those who identify reliance on ethnic status *or* on the attempt to fulfill God's will through works as equally culpable, and those who object to such a reading as "sinister" or anti-Semitic and declare that Paul's critique does not extend to those who faithfully keep the law. The latter group contends that Paul and Judaism are, in fact, at one in condemning reliance on mere Jewishness for salvation rather than on obedience to Torah, and they deny that Judaism's perspective on the law can be seen in Paul's rejected version of it. For example, in a volume entitled *A Radical Jew: Paul and the Politics of Identity*,[22] Daniel Boyarin describes his reading of the apostle as closest in spirit to the work of Ferdinand Christian Baur,

21. Cf. Eduard Lohse, "Die alttestamentlichen Bezüge im neutestamentlichen Zeugnis vom Tode Jesu Christi," p. 103.
22. Berkeley: University of California Press, 1994.

whose position in turn is best represented by contemporary scholars such as James D. G. Dunn and Francis Watson. In the wake of the treatises of Krister Stendahl, W. D. Davies (1911-2001), and E. P. Sanders, this view judges the "Reformation," or "Lutheran," interpretation of Paul to be "unsupportable" from a scholarly point of view — as well as an "ethical scandal." In the section entitled "The 'Jew' as Symbol of Inferior Religion," Boyarin cites Bultmann and Käsemann as reviving a tradition according to which the term "Jew" symbolizes one who makes unsupportable demands of the deity. What is "truly sinister" about it, the author continues, is that not only the Jew who does *not* observe the law, but also the one who *does,* is described as accumulating the wrath of God to himself. The term *homo religiosus,* erroneously used of both types, in reality applies only to the observant Jew, whereas the apostle's attack applies exclusively to the *homo non religiosus,* the nonobservant Jew. Boyarin concludes that reference to the "Jew" or "the Jew within" (Ernst Käsemann) as a trope or allegory for what is morally reprehensible simply repeats a *topos* of anti-Semitic Nazism.[23] He adds that he learned from a study by William S. Campbell that Markus Barth was so offended by Käsemann's reference to the "devout Jew" as "Paul's adversary" — thus as mirror of his own past as well as symbol of the "religious man" — that he sought a retraction.[24] The fact is, however, that Markus Barth suggested to Käsemann that he may have had in mind a symbolic rather than literal or historical meaning of such terms as "essential adversary," "pious," and "Jew," a construction that Käsemann refused.[25]

Bultmann and Käsemann, whose record of opposition to Nazism is beyond challenge, may have (unwillingly) called up demons with their application of the term "Jew," "Jewishness," or "the Jew within" to anyone who raises a claim against God — observant of the law or not. Boyarin, however, does not mention the theologian who helped pave the way for such an identification, and who was neither an "existentialist" nor a "Lutheran." In the first edition of his *Römerbrief,* Karl Barth appended these words to his comment on Romans 2:17-24:

23. See Boyarin, *A Radical Jew,* pp. 11, 210-213.

24. William S. Campbell, *Paul's Gospel in an Intercultural Context* (Frankfurt: Peter Lang, 1992), p. 188, n. 9; p. 193, n. 65.

25. Markus Barth, "St. Paul — A Good Jew," *Horizons in Biblical Theology: An International Dialogue* I (1979), 38, n. 2.

The sacrament (of circumcision) *is* no longer fellowship with God. It only *signifies* it, and soon it no longer does that because it has totally lost its object. For a time one may still struggle to spiritualize and idealize the higher form, but these efforts already hide a leveling off which will turn the higher level of knowledge and the great possibility it embraces into just *one* more religion, *one* more point of view.[26]

And in the sixth edition, he says about Romans 2:8, 23:

Here again the Jew and the Greek, the men of God and the men of the world, are assembled together on one line under the threat of judgment. . . . The children of God present nothing peculiar, nothing new. . . . And so, after standing for a moment in amazement before the comedy of an unreal communion with God, the children of the world turn away supported and confirmed in their knowledge that, after all, the world is the world. With proper instinct for the truth, they do not permit themselves to be imposed upon, and they are thus protected against any turning towards the "God" of the pious man.[27]

Second, it is true that, beneath Paul's argument for righteousness by faith, there is the intention to encompass all humankind, Jew and gentile.[28] Addressing the gentile members of his audience concerning Israel, Paul says:

Just as you were once disobedient to God but have now received mercy because of their disobedience, so they have now been disobedient in order that, by the mercy shown to you, they too may now receive mercy. For God has imprisoned all in disobedience so that he may be merciful to all. (Rom. 11:30-32)

26. Karl Barth, *Der Römerbrief,* 1st ed. (1919), ed. Hermann Schmidt (Zürich: Theologischer Verlag, 1985), p. 63.

27. Karl Barth, *The Epistle to the Romans,* trans. Edwyn C. Hoskyns (London: Oxford University Press, 1933), pp. 63, 73. On page 8 of his "St. Paul — A Good Jew," Markus Barth fixes the origin of Käsemann's "apodictic" references in Bultmann's commentary on the Fourth Gospel, but also in his father's commentary on Romans, in which Jewish piety was identified with religion, and religion "with the most refined form of sin and rebellion against God."

28. This point is also made in an essay by Boyarin entitled "The Jews in Neo-Lutheran Interpretations of Paul," *Dialog* (Summer 1996), 193-197.

"That God may be merciful to all": Paul argues that the first covenant, with its law, was not intended to be the ultimate expression of his will. A promise was attached to it that, enjoying priority in time over the law (cf. Gal. 3:17), pointed to the end of an existence ordered according to judicial decree, and betokened the arrival of a new way by which to unite Israel's destiny with all believers. This *provisional* character of the law then sets the stage for the arrival of the Good News.[29] Scholars intent on construing Paul's thought on a continuum with the Jewish understanding overlook the apostle's emphasis on the law's provisional character and trivialize his statement that he counted his status in Judaism and righteousness under the law as "loss" (Phil. 3:6-7). The particular contribution of the writer to the Hebrews may have been to stress this aspect of the law's provisional character, an aspect that has left Paul's interpreters in a quandary.

The law, therefore, was not displaced because it had been broken. The covenant of the Old Testament community remained a *B'rith olam:* it had a "glory." It existed as an expression of the divine will, so that its supplanting could not be due to its temporality but to the appearance of a new and superior "glory," a new expression of that will (II Cor. 3:7-11).[30] True, the law *could* become an incentive to transgression, since it tied one's existence to the historical community of Israel, with which the desire to live for oneself could only collide. Of this situation Paul says:

> If it had not been for the law, I would not have known sin. I would not have known what it is to covet if the law had not said, "You shall not covet." But sin, seizing an opportunity in the commandment, produced in me all kinds of covetousness. Apart from the law sin lies dead. I was once alive apart from the law, but when the commandment came, sin revived and I died. . . . (Rom. 7:7-10)

The law, however, *was* capable of being kept. Of himself Paul says:

> If anyone has reason to be confident in the flesh, I have more: circumcised on the eighth day, a member of the people of Israel, of the tribe

---

29. Cf. Helmut Merklein, "Die Bedeutung des Kreuzestod Christi," p. 83; Sänger, *Die Verkündigung des Gekreuzigten und Israel,* p. 278.

30. Cf. Roy A. Harrisville, "The Concept of Newness in the New Testament" (Ph.D. diss., Princeton Theological Seminary, Princeton, NJ, 1953), pp. 284-290; cf. also Hans Hübner, *Biblische Theologie des Neuen Testaments,* p. 94.

of Benjamin, a Hebrew born of Hebrews; as to the law, a Pharisee; as to zeal, a persecutor of the church; *as to righteousness under the law, blameless.* (Phil. 3:4b-6; italics mine)

Paul's use of the adverb "more" in verse 4b suggests that the "blamelessness" was not a status the apostle reserved for himself. If his other autobiographical references (cf. Rom. 8:29; II Cor. 4:10; Gal. 6:14, 17) are not to be read as the exclusive experiences of one unusual individual or apostle,[31] neither can it be inferred from his statement here that he was sole owner of what he had abandoned. Whatever the difference between him and his coreligionists, it was one of degree. Fixing the displacement of the law in the impossibility of its keeping trivializes Paul's assertion that he was "blameless" as to righteousness under the law.[32]

In the final analysis, however, a discussion of the possibility or impossibility of fulfilling the law is an argument past Paul's true concern. E. P. Sanders' statement to the effect that what Paul regards as false in Judaism is that it is not Christianity[33] is correct if it allows the conclusion that Paul's evaluation of the law as weak, invalidated, death-dealing, or provisional in character is not an inference drawn from any empirically demonstrable deficit in the law.[34] It is rather the "Christological hermeneutics evident at the cross" that moves him to his evaluation.[35] It would hardly have occurred to Paul to assign the covenant at Sinai and its Torah merely provisional status if he had not been forced to "explain" the cross.[36] What was decisive for Paul was the "paradigm change" resulting from the acknowledgment of Messiah's death.[37] For if God determined to put humanity right in the cross of Jesus Christ, then the way of justification through works of the Torah was never a possibility.[38] It was thus the cross that elicited division in the

---

31. Cf. Charles B. Cousar, "Paul and the Death of Jesus," *Interpretation* 52, No. 1 (Jan. 1998), 47.

32. Cf. Merklein, "Die Bedeutung des Kreuzestod Christi," p. 39 and passim.

33. E. P. Sanders, *Paul and Palestinian Judaism*, pp. 17-18.

34. Cf. Sänger, *Die Verkündigung des Gekreuzigten und Israel*, pp. 270-271.

35. Merklein, "Die Bedeutung," p. 102; Sänger, *Die Verkündigung*, p. 268, n. 434.

36. Morna D. Hooker, *Not Ashamed of the Gospel*, pp. 31-33.

37. Sänger, *Die Verkündigung des Gekreuzigten und Israel*, pp. 270-271, n. 446.

38. Cf. Sänger, p. 287.

Corinthian and Galatian communities.[39] The Corinthians had interpreted the "riddle" of Christ's death in a way calculated to aestheticize it, and the Galatians believed they owed their ecclesial existence to observance of the law, not to the preaching of the Crucified. In response to E. P. Sanders' statement that Paul's thesis of justification merely answers the question about how one "gets in," Thomas Söding says that Paul's entire criticism of the law is disclosed from the Christological perspective, that is, the apostle intends to show from the "how" of God's self-communication, from his view into the innermost core of the event of Jesus' death and resurrection, that only faith in Christ, not works of the law, can justify.[40]

While Paul makes specific reference to the Crucified and his cross only in polemical contexts ("wisdom" in I Cor. 1–2; the law in Gal. 3–5; the new existence in Gal. 2:19 and Rom. 6:1-4), and while the doctrine of justification historically considered may be a late form of his theology, strongly conditioned by the situation, it is neither merely an anti-Jewish polemic nor an auxiliary crater of his thought.[41] In reality, the concept of justification, or the righteousness of faith, is nothing if not a Christological statement that takes its life from Jesus' death. The concept and the event are so indissolubly intertwined that affirmation or rejection of the one spells affirmation or rejection of the other.[42] The event itself witnesses to the divine initiative: here a death is fixed and foreordained by God himself; to its absolute saving sufficiency corresponds the *sola fide* ("by faith alone") of justification.[43] To construe it merely as a one-time occurrence giving order to the past is an error. God put Christ forward as sacrifice to show his righteousness by forgiving past sins (the phrase *dia tēn paresin* in Rom. 3:25 is poorly translated "passed over" in the NRSV) and "to prove *at the present time* that

39. Cf. Flemming Fleinert-Jensen, *Das Kreuz und die Einheit der Kirche: Skizzen zu einer Kreuzestheologie in ökumenischer Perspektive* (Leipzig: Evangelischer Verlagsanstalt, 1994), pp. 43-44.

40. Söding, *Das Wort vom Kreuz*, p. 169, note 53.

41. Cf. Udo Schnelle, *Wandlungen im paulinischen Denken,* Stuttgarter Bibelstudien (Stuttgart: Verlag Katholisches Bibelwerk, 1989), p. 91.

42. Cf. Hans Joachim Iwand, *Tod und Auferstehung, Christologie II, Vorlesung, Nachgelassene Werke,* n.s. (Gütersloh: Christian Kaiser Gütersloher Verlagshaus, 1999), II, 367.

43. Cf. Söding, pp. 156, 75-76.

he himself is righteous and that he justifies the one who has faith in Jesus." Justification of the sinner is established by virtue of being crucified with Christ (Gal. 2:19). A "new creation" is established in Christ's cross, which puts an end to existence by judicial decree (cf. Gal. 6:11-18);[44] and, since Christ took on himself the curse of the law, the gentiles now enjoy a share in the blessing of Abraham (cf. Gal. 3:13-14). For Paul, the death of Jesus confronts one with a decision like nothing else in the world.

Another variation on the theme of the law's displacement reads that it was part and parcel of Paul's conversion. Convinced that Jesus had been raised from the dead and thus had been vindicated by God (Rom. 1:4: "declared to be Son of God with power . . . by resurrection from the dead"), the verdict of the law, according to which anyone hanged on a tree was under a curse (Deut. 21:22-23), had been clearly wrong when applied to Jesus. For this reason, righteousness had to occur apart from the law.[45] The syllogism — anyone hanged upon a tree is under God's curse; Jesus was hanged on a tree; therefore, Jesus was under God's curse — appears inviolable until one returns to Paul's own variation in Galatians 3, which reads that God himself arranged such a fate for Jesus. The law, the very thing to deter the Jew — and initially Paul himself — from embracing Jesus as Messiah, was a means by which "the blessing of Abraham might come to the Gentiles" (Gal. 3:14). In face of its possible disparagement, bluntly expressed in "The Everlasting Gospel" by William Blake (1757-1827),[46] the law retained

---

44. Cf. Söding, p. 156.

45. Cf. Morna D. Hooker, *A Preface to Paul*, pp. 40-41. Peter Stuhlmacher takes a similar line when he says: "The Yes to the Crucified implies the No to the Torah which set the Crucified under a curse. . . . For Paul the epiphany of this very crucified man . . . had to be the infallible sign that God himself had thwarted and annulled the Torah's judgment of death . . . on the basis of Jesus' resurrection . . . the cross appears as the depotentiation of the Torah" ("Das Ende des Gesetzes," pp. 29, 30, 33). See also Jürgen Moltmann, who says that "the Law brought Jesus to his end on the cross, thus the risen and exalted Jesus is the end of the Law for every one who believes" (*Der Gekreuzigte Gott*, p. 127). Weder says: "The Crucified One lies within the sphere of law, but not the Risen One, thus also not God himself" (*Das Kreuz Jesu bei Paulus*, pp. 177, 191). Sänger says: "If the Torah had to demonstrate that the Crucified was accursed, God's acknowledgment of the Risen One effected the depotentiation of the Torah's cursing effect" (*Die Verkündigung des Gekreuzigten und Israel*, p. 278).

46. "If Moral Virtue was Christianity,/Christ's Pretensions were all Vanity,/And Cai[a]phas & Pilate, Men/Praise Worthy, & the Lion's Den/And not the Sheepfold, Alle-

integrity through its function as soteriological means, or as "witness to salvation."[47]

Finally, and briefly, in face of any possible disparagement of the law, Paul's view is that obedience to God, the keeping of commandments, is not an option for the believer. The apostle gives unheard-of weight to the ethical, to the point of puzzling the reader who is eager to purge it of matters of faith. He says: "It is not the hearers of the law who are righteous in God's sight, but the doers of the law who will be justified" (Rom. 2:13). In the twentieth century, to have insisted on faith as comprised of gift as well as of task *(Gabe und Aufgabe)* belonged to the contribution of Bultmann and Käsemann. There is no linear, continuous, and uninterrupted transition from Jewish cultic and legal tradition to the Pauline proclamation. However dependent he is on that tradition, Paul's warping of it to the singular event of the death of Jesus the Messiah marks its qualification, or fracture. If, as E. C. Hoskyns (1894-1937) and Francis Noel Davey (1904-1973) have said, Paul sees the Old Testament not as a body of legal precedent to which to appeal — and on which arguments may be based, and from which conclusions may be reached — but as the word of God whose concrete application is perceived only in the present,[48] what is that but the reflection of a gulf fixed between the Old Testament *as such* and the Old Testament *as used by Paul,* a *diastasis* of such proportions as to render the Old Testament a new theological entity, whatever the convergence of the two regarding their content? Let one of the most celebrated Jewish interpreters of Paul have the summing up:

> In spite of the fact that the *foundations* of all the teachings of Paul are Jewish, his *own* teaching is both the *contradiction of the Jewish religion* and the *rejection of the Jewish nation.*[49]

---

gories/Of God & Heaven & their Glories. . . . The Moral Virtues in Great fear/Formed the Cross & Nails & Spear,/And the Accuser standing by/Cried out, 'Crucify! Crucify!'" (The *Portable Blake,* ed. Alfred Kazin [New York: The Viking Press, 1946], p. 611).

47. Wolfgang Schrage, "Römer 3,21-26 und die Bedeutung des Todes Jesu Christi bei Paulus," in *Das Kreuz,* pp. 70-71; Stuhlmacher: "The law of Moses and the law of Christ . . . find their continuity only in the fact that the law of Moses must serve the grace of God also in its weakness" ("Das Ende des Gesetzes," p. 36, n. 46); Udo Schnelle, *Wandlungen im paulinischen Denken,* pp. 70-71.

48. Hoskyns-Davey, *Crucifixion-Resurrection: The Pattern of the Theology and Ethics of the New Testament* (London: S.P.C.K., 1981), p. 182.

49. Joseph Klausner, *From Jesus to Paul,* trans. William F. Stinespring (New York:

Use and Fracture of Apocalyptic

Stimulated by the researches of Albert Schweitzer, and before him, of Johannes Weiss (1863-1914),[50] most interpreters assign Jewish apocalyptic to the "paradigm" with which Paul came to encounter the "anomaly" of Messiah's death. In the decisive thrust of his thought, in his conceptuality and world of ideas, prior to — as well as after — his conversion, Paul was an apocalyptic theologian. He construed the ultimate promise encountering the world in Jesus not merely in qualitative but also in temporal fashion, thus refusing to speak of an end to history already transpired.[51]

Apocalyptic underlay Paul's Christology. It offered him the religious-historical background comparable to the "message about the cross" as a mystery replete with promise, pointing beyond itself to a future "radically discontinuous" with the present and effected by an act of God.[52] Despite his adoption of the terminology of his Corinthian opponents, with its reference to a "secret and hidden" wisdom that none of the "rulers of this age understood" but that is "revealed" to those who are "spiritual" (cf. I Cor. 2:6-16), Paul's embrace of the "cosmological and anthropological" aspects of apocalyptic thought distanced him from them.[53] By means of the "apocalyptic" theme of the worldwide rule of Christ, the idea of substitution that was derived from Old Testament cultic and legal tradition underwent "correction."[54]

The Macmillan Co., 1944), 591 [italics mine]; cf. Hübner, "Kreuz und Auferstehung im Neuen Testament, 2. Zur Kreuzesthematik," p. 188; Otto Kuss, "Die Rolle des Apostels Paulus in der theologischen Entwicklung der Kirche," *BLiTEc* 79 (1978), 52-53; Sänger, *Die Verkündigung,* p. 247.

50. Albert Schweitzer, *The Quest of the Historical Jesus;* Johannes Weiss, *Die Predigt Jesu vom Reiche Gottes,* ed. Ferdinand Hahn (Göttingen: Vandenhoeck & Ruprecht, 1964, originally published in 1892).

51. In 1947, Anton Fridrichsen said that, without attention to Paul's "fundamental eschatological conception, neither his apostolic self-consciousness nor his arguments and activity could be understood" (*The Apostle and His Message,* Uppsala Universitets Arsskrift [Uppsala: A. B. Lundesquistska Bokhandeln, 1947], p. 3).

52. Leander Keck, "Paul and Apocalyptic Theology," *Interpretation* 38 (1984), 234, 236, 241.

53. Stuhlmacher, "Glauben und Verstehen bei Paulus," *Evangelische Theologie* 26 (1966), 341-344.

54. Ernst Käsemann, "Erwägungen zum Stichwort 'Versöhnungslehre' im Neuen Testament," pp. 1, 53-55, 57.

The doctrine of the two eons as reflected in II Corinthians 10:3-4 (or in Rom. 6:3-5) has its home in Jewish apocalyptic. According to Paul, the ceremonial washings designed to reflect an inner purity by which one could minister in the tabernacle, or which designated the reinstatement of unclean persons and the initiation of proselytes into the community, were only relative in character. They could not convey the believer to the presence of the heavenly reality. But the "newness of life" (Rom. 6:4) that Christ accomplishes in the believer through their union in baptism denotes the presence of the heavenly reality within earthly existence. The argument in Romans 6 is as proximate to the hallmark of apocalyptic — that is, visibility — as any statement in the letters of Paul. Jewish apocalyptic is also validated in the apostle's addressing his communities as "saints," or as "elect," in his declaration that in Christ "there is neither Jew nor Greek" (Gal. 3:28) and in his communication of the "mystery" in Romans 11:25-27. Paul's anti-enthusiastic battle, so the argument reads, was fought out under the sign of apocalyptic, as was his battle with nomism.

One representative of the biblical wing of the "Pannenberg School" disagreed with this opinion. In the volume opening the fray with the so-called "kerygmatic theology," Ulrich Wilckens surveys the concept of revelation extending from Judaism to Jesus to the Fourth Gospel. Of the pre-Pauline Hellenistic and Jewish-Christian stage on this continuum, he has said that its unity lay in the acknowledgment of Jesus' resurrection as God's decisive deed interpreted within an apocalyptic context that held past, present, and future together. In Gnostic Corinth, however, this context had been abandoned. To the disparagement of the past (Jesus' resurrection) and future (the *eschaton*), the Corinthians regarded the presence of the Spirit as the one divine and eschatological deed. To confront this problem, Wilckens continued, Paul appropriated the conceptual weapon of his opponents, emphasized the presence of the Spirit, and as a result abandoned the apocalyptic context and left his theology in tension.[55] Years before Wilckens, Hans Lietzmann believed he had detected a collision of two theologies in Paul: one with its emphasis on the presence of the Spirit, or a theology *sub specie divina,* and

---

55. Ulrich Wilckens, "The Understanding of Revelation Within the History of Primitive Christianity," in *Revelation as History,* ed. Wolfhart Pannenberg, trans. David Granskou (New York: The Macmillan Co., 1968), pp. 57-121.

the other with its emphasis on the eschatological, or a theology *sub specie humana.*[56]

But what if the "tension" or "collision" lay elsewhere: not between the apocalyptic context or system of Paul's thought *and* his concession to the Corinthian error, but between that system along with whatever underlay the concession *and* the event he described as making foolish the wisdom of the world (I Cor. 1:20)? Whether or not the hallmark of Jewish apocalyptic is the visible appearance of God for judgment and salvation, whether or not primitive Christian preaching was nourished by that conceptuality, and whether or not the Christian revelation thus consists *solely* of the resurrection of Jesus Christ[57] — since it alone meets the test of "historical verification" demanded by that conceptuality — with the apostle Paul that conceptuality suffered fracture. It is not merely that the "utopian" aspect of the apocalyptic conceptuality (God's appearing for salvation) was retained, whereas the other, "catastrophic" aspect (God's appearing for judgment) was not "worked out."[58] And it is not enough to say that Paul subjected the outline of history in apocalyptic to criticism through giving its scheme of the two eons a "Christological sharpening."[59] Nor is it sufficient "historically" to concede Paul's application of apocalyptic thought *in concreto,* in light of the resurrection.[60] Whatever the view, apocalyptic still retains its independence, whereas the orientation of its conceptuality to the message about a man who died the death of a criminal, that is, the warping of the apocalyptic perspective to the finality and universality of a historical event, fractures the entire framework, demoting it to the status of means. This fact decides the issue, and not the differences from apocalyptic thought as commonly adduced (e.g., Paul's lack of interest in fixing the date of the final consummation, his disengage-

56. Hans Lietzmann, *Einführung in die Textgeschichte der Paulusbriefe an die Römer: Handbuch zum Neuen Testament* (Tübingen: J. C. B. Mohr, 1933), pp. 66-67.

57. "Einzig" in Wilckens: "Das Offenbarungsverständnis in der Geschichte des Urchristentums," p. 87.

58. Peter von der Osten-Sacken, "Die paulinische theologia crucis als Form apokalyptischer Theologie," *Evangelische Theologie* 39, No. 6 (Nov./Dec. 1979), 481.

59. Peter Stuhlmacher, *Gerechtigkeit Gottes bei Paulus,* 2nd ed. (Göttingen: Vandenhoeck & Ruprecht, 1966), pp. 204-207.

60. Von der Osten-Sacken, "Die paulinische theologia crucis als Form apokalyptischer Theologie," p. 488, n. 37.

ment of the future hope from any national basis, his understanding of the final events as already begun, thus transcending the apocalyptic scheme with its contrast between "now" and "then," and so forth). The difference between Paul and the Jewish hope lies in the collapse of apocalyptic as a whole, its fracture as a coherent scheme.

When the primitive Christian message announces the resurrection of Jesus Christ, the eschatological content of the gospel receives maximum emphasis by means of that concept. But since this utterance is linked to one who was crucified, who died a shameful death, the framework of apocalyptic expectation is broken, and the One who was crucified is proclaimed as present Lord.[61] The eschatological event of the crucified Christ has displaced the unknown eschatological salvation of apocalyptic thought — with its ambivalent messiahs.[62] For this reason the sharp line drawn by apocalyptic thought between this world and the next, which renders this world inhospitable to the divine presence, is perforated.[63] The rabbinic concepts of the "present age," subject to the evil one (Gal. 1:4), and the "age to come" (Eph. 1:21) are no longer merely concepts of time but also of quality.[64] The *eschaton* thus penetrates the present:[65] God's saving activity can be experienced here and now,[66] and life can be lived in this world, not merely in the next.[67] For this reason, suffering results from that irreducible tension between the "now already" and the "not yet,"[68] a plight no longer inevitable because the trials of this eon are a necessary entree to the new, but because Christ allows his own to participate in his suffering he "stigmatizes" them in their corporeality.[69]

In his volume on Jesus' preaching of the kingdom, Johannes Weiss

---

61. Eduard Lohse, "Apokalyptik und Christologie," in *Die Einheit des Neuen Testaments* (Göttingen: Vandenhoeck & Ruprecht, 1973), p. 135; cf. also pp. 137, 139, and 143.

62. Kleinknecht, *Der leidende Gerechtfertigte*, p. 218; Keck, "Paul and Apocalyptic Theology," p. 239.

63. Keck, p. 234; Kleinknecht, *Der leidende Gerechtfertigte*, p. 277.

64. Alois Stöger, "Die Christologie der Paulinischen and von Paulus abhängigen Briefe," in *Der historische Jesus und der Christus unseres Glaubens*, p. 174.

65. Stuhlmacher, "Glauben und Verstehen bei Paulus," *Evangelische Theologie* 26 (1966), 344.

66. Kleinknecht, *Der leidende Gerechtfertigte*, p. 275.

67. Weder, *Das Kreuz Jesu bei Paulus*, p. 180.

68. Keck, "Paul and Apocalyptic Theology," p. 240.

69. Cf. Gal. 6:17; Schrage, "Leid, Kreuz und Eschaton," p. 165.

declares that primitive Christianity firmly believed in the reality of salvation, but that this faith included an element of unresolved tension.
The Messiah had not yet acceded to his throne; the enemy of God still
raged. One lived in anticipation of the judgment, the devil's destruction,
the redemption of the elect, and the freedom of the glory of God's children. This mood, wrote Weiss, in which faith and hope combined but
where hope had the upper hand, was of great benefit to the individual.
In the long run, however, it could not persist without degenerating into
fanaticism. "What was needed," Weiss concluded, "was a religious genius of another type, able to experience the full content of faith in a new
form. Paul prepared for it."[70] For "religious genius" one can substitute
"recognition of the eschatological event of the crucified."

Wolfgang Schrage notes the "disconcerting" similarity between
Paul's worldview as reflected in I Corinthians 7:29-31 and the worldview
of the second-century Jewish apocalypse Fourth Ezra. Both pieces, for
example, negatively qualify the *kosmos,* and both refer to the final tribulation as signaling the end. The researcher finds in the I Corinthians
passage and Fourth Ezra 16 a particularly disturbing parallel, which
forces one to the conclusion that Paul was "captive" *(verhaftet)* to apocalyptic not only in form or motivation but also in substance. When
Schrage has concluded his study, however, he documents Paul's "profound" difference from the apocalypticist due to the warping of the
apocalyptic vision to his Christology. The apostle, unlike the apocalypticist, is not preoccupied with the world's passing away but rather
with the Lord in whom the future awaited by the apocalypticist has already broken in. The result is a correction of the two-eons scheme, a
construing of the "great tribulation" as present, and guidance for existence in the world versus the apocalyptic "prophylactic" against the
world. The essayist arrives at the conclusion that "with Paul . . . all these
elements of apocalyptic ideas are drastically reduced and all mythological speculations are leveled through criticism."[71]

For Paul, the cross in which God had appeared under the sign of his
opposite made totally unobservable and undemonstrable any qualitative or temporal change in history and human life. Accordingly, God's

70. Johannes Weiss, *Die Predigt Jesu vom Reiche Gottes,* p. 61.
71. Wolfgang Schrage, "Die Stellung zur Welt bei Paulus, Epiktet und in der
Apokalyptik," *ZThK* 61 (1964), 125-154; cf. 146.

victory in contradiction of the world was clear only to those willing to fly in the face of the empirical evidence. As he says in Romans 1:17, "The righteousness of God is revealed through faith for faith." If the hallmark of Jewish apocalyptic thought was the visibility, the observability of God's rule,[72] however secretly or modestly that rule was thought to begin, this is not apocalyptic. Paul's "revision" took the shape of what might be called his "doctrine of ambiguity," reflected in that dialectical style so characteristic of him:

> We are treated as impostors, and yet are true; as unknown, and yet well known; as dying, and behold we live; as punished, and yet not killed; as sorrowful, yet always rejoicing; as poor, yet making many rich; as having nothing, and yet possessing everything. (II Cor. 6:8-10)

"As impostors, and yet are true . . . as dying, and behold we live": the antithesis is absent in apocalyptic, or its second clause may appear in the future tense ("and yet will live").[73] Apocalyptic thought, of course, gave large place to suffering. If it had not done so, the idea would never have arisen that it originated in persecution. And for this reason the primitive Christian community may have found certain topics of the Jewish eschatology corroborated in its experience.[74] But such radical paradox as was expressed above or appears below is foreign to apocalyptic:

> He said to me, "My grace is sufficient for you, for my power is made perfect in weakness." So, I will boast all the more gladly of my weaknesses, so that the power of Christ may dwell in me. (II Cor. 12:9)

As Keck says, the problem of the relationship between Paul and apocalyptic is soluble only to those who think that Paul's entire thought is contained in the genuine Epistles. Since the apostle rethought everything in light of Christ's death and resurrection, whatever of apocalyptic theology he may reflect will have been transformed.[75]

---

72. Cf. Lohse, "Apokalyptik und Christologie," p. 132.

73. Cf. the antitheses in Enoch or the Testament of Judah: "Be hopeful, because formerly you have pined away through evil and toil. But now *you shall shine* like the lights of heaven" (Enoch 104:2). . . . "Those who died in sorrow *shall be raised in joy*" (Testament of Judah 215:4, *The Old Testament Pseudepigrapha*, I, 85, 802; italics mine).

74. Schrage, "Leid, Kreuz und Eschaton," p. 165.

75. Keck, pp. 230-231.

Use and Fracture of Stoicism

For some, the Stoics' influence on Paul, which came to him by way of the Hellenistic synagogue, counts for more than that of apocalyptic thought. Bultmann notes the extensive formal agreement between Paul and the Greek "preacher" in their use of dialogical and rhetorical devices, in their arrangement of ideas and their method of argumentation, and in their tone and mood. Bultmann's study led him to assert a "far-reaching formal agreement" between Paul and the Greek preacher, thus the apostle's dependence on Greek popular philosophy.[76] Troels Engberg-Pedersen applies to texts from the Stoics and Paul's letters to the Philippians, Galatians, and Romans a model that illustrates a shift from the perception of self as self-contained to the perception of self as belonging to something, and finally to the perception of self as one among others. This model, he believes, shows similarity between the anthropology and ethics of Paul and the Stoa, and he offers it as a tool for the interpretation of Pauline texts.[77]

A study of Paul and the Stoa legitimately involves a comparison in the matter of their thought content. Bultmann suggests that the far-reaching formal agreement between Paul and the Stoa involved agreement in the movement of ideas and thus reflected a "certain relation in spirit." The "relation in spirit" cannot be denied: for example, both Epictetus and Paul call for "nonengagement" toward this world's goods but without refusing to make use of them. Trouble begins when we forget that such things are given "for the present, not inseparably nor forever, but like a fig, or a cluster of grapes, at a fixed season of the year."[78] According to the Stoic, freedom derives from the application of this principle; and so it does for Paul. I Corinthians 7:29b-31 reads like a page torn from Epictetus's *Encheiridion*.[79] Johannes Weiss included one hundred and fifteen references to Epictetus in the footnotes of his exposi-

76. Rudolf Bultmann, *Der Stil der paulinischen Predigt und die kynisch-stoische Diatribe* (Göttingen: Vandenhoeck & Ruprecht, 1910), pp. 68, 71, 85.

77. Troels Engberg-Pedersen, *Paul and the Stoics* (Louisville: Westminster John Knox Press, 2000).

78. *Epictetus,* The Loeb Classical Library, trans. W. A. Oldfather (Cambridge, MA: Harvard University Press, 1966), Vol. II, Bk. 3, chap. 24, paras. 84-86, pp. 211-213; cf. Bk. 4, chap. 3, paras. 3-5, pp. 313-315; Bk. 4, chap. 7, para. 10, p. 363.

79. Cf. *Epictetus,* Vol. II, *The Encheiridion of Epictetus,* para. 19, p. 497.

tion of the first ten chapters of I Corinthians.[80] Perhaps the most interesting portion of his comparison of Paul and the Stoa deals with the concept of the body and its members in I Corinthians 12:12-17 and its analogies in Seneca (ca. 4 B.C.E.–65 C.E.), Marcus Aurelius (121-180 C.E.), and Epictetus.[81]

Paul was subject to the influence of Hellenism just as any modern person is subject to the formative forces of the technological age. The spiritual atmosphere in Tarsus, Antioch, Ephesus, Corinth, and Rome was, after all, vastly different from that of the "fortress of Pharisaic Judaism," which came to dominate in Jerusalem.[82] Nevertheless, in the conclusion of his study of Paul and the Cynic-Stoic diatribe, Bultmann remarks on the "profound difference" in the thought of Paul and the Greek preacher, stating that we should not conceal from ourselves the fact that "the impress of difference is greater than that of similarity." For example, with respect to Paul's use of parable, Bultmann notes both its similarity to but also its "very strong" difference from the diatribe, a difference rooted in the apostle's own nature:

He has too little of the artist, of the poet. Over all he is much too passionately engaged to take pleasure in words apart from their content. And he is too little an imitator, taking up rather what immediately serves his goal.[83]

Again, Bultmann says that Paul uses Greek forms of expression in a way peculiar to him, forms penetrated by devices that appear to have their origin elsewhere, and concludes:

80. Johannes Weiss, *Der Erste Korintherbrief: H. A. W. Meyer Kritisch-exegetischer Kommentar über das Neue Testament* (Göttingen: Vandenhoeck & Ruprecht, 1910).

81. Cf. Seneca, *Ad Lucilium Epistolae Morales,* The Loeb Classical Library, trans. Richard M. Gummere (Cambridge, MA: Harvard University Press, 1962), Vol. III, Epistle 95, para. 52, p. 91; *The Communings with Himself of Marcus Aurelius Antoninus, Emperor of Rome,* The Loeb Classical Library (Cambridge, MA: Harvard University Press, 1962), para. 27, p. 169; *Epictetus,* Vol. I, Bk. 2, chap. 10, paras. 3-4, p. 275.

82. Cf. Kuss, "Die Rolle des Apostels Paulus in der theologischen Entwicklung der Kirche," p. 56; cf., with qualification, Hans-Ruedi Weber, *Kreuz,* p. 110; cf. the Hellenistic doctrine of duty as underlying Rom. 5:7 in Kleinknecht's *Der leidende Gerechtfertigte,* p. 331.

83. Bultmann, *Der Stil der paulinischen Predigt und die kynisch-stoische Diatribe,* pp. 93-94.

So we can say that the mantle of the Greek rhetor does in fact hang on Paul's shoulders, but Paul has no taste for artistically correct drapery, and the lines of the alien shape show through everywhere.[84]

Differences in forms of expression reflect a difference in "spirit." For Epictetus, freedom can be achieved through an inner disposition (the distinguishing of mine from what is not mine). For Paul, nonengagement, distance, freedom from the world cannot be achieved on one's own but takes place via an external event, something outside the sphere of the Stoic's "moral purpose,"[85] toward which he could remain indifferent,[86] could call neither good nor evil, benefit or injury,[87] and over which he imagined he could be master.[88] And that event, totally removed from "mine" or "not mine," encompassing all of human existence and thus *extra nos,*[89] began a process whose end was in sight. The believer's "nonengagement" was necessitated by the fact that the future had already broken in with the cross and death of Jesus Christ. Epictetus could never have imagined the world as transitory or himself as leaning toward its end, since the world had neither beginning nor end; it was merely an eternal round of beginnings and endings. According to Paul, the believer was drawn into this event to the point where he could speak of himself or of his hearer/reader as "crucified" (Gal. 2:19), or as having "died with" Christ (Rom. 6:8; II Cor. 5:14; cf. Col. 3:3; II Tim. 2:11).

The distance between Paul and Stoic thought deserves demonstration by way of a comparison of their so-called *peristasen* catalogues, those tallies of "strokes of fate" undergone by the faithful or wise. In I Corinthians 4:12b-13a, Paul writes, "When reviled, we bless; when persecuted, we endure; when slandered, we speak kindly." And in II Corinthians 4:8, which has long furnished commentators occasion for citing Greek parallels, the apostle writes:

84. Bultmann, p. 108.
85. *Epictetus,* Vol. II, Book 4, chap. 7, para. 10, p. 363.
86. Cf. *Epictetus,* Vol. II, Book 4, chap. 7, para. 27, p. 371.
87. *Epictetus,* Vol. I, Book 2, chap. 5, paras. 4-5, p. 239.
88. *Epictetus,* Vol. II, Book 3, chap. 24, paras. 68-69, p. 207.
89. Schrage, "Die Stellung zur Welt bei Paulus, Epiktet und in der Apokalyptik," p. 153.

We are afflicted in every way, but not crushed; perplexed, but not driven to despair; persecuted but not forsaken; struck down, but not destroyed. . . .

And yet again in II Corinthians 6:8-10:

We are treated as impostors, and yet are true; unknown, and yet are well known; as dying, and see — we are alive; as punished, and yet not killed; as sorrowful, yet always rejoicing; as poor, yet making many rich; as having nothing, and yet possessing everything.

In his discourses, Epictetus says:

Show me a man who though sick is happy, though in danger is happy, though dying is happy, though condemned to exile is happy, though in disrepute is happy. Show him! By the gods I would fain see a Stoic![90]

Plutarch (46-120 C.E.), Greek biographer and essayist, writes of the sage:

He is not impeded when confined and under no compulsion when flung down a precipice and not in torture when on the rack and not injured when mutilated and is invincible when thrown in wrestling and is not blockaded by circumvallation and is uncaptured while his enemies are selling him into slavery; he is just like the boats that are tempest-tossed and shattered and capsized while they bear inscribed upon them the names *Bon Voyage* and *Providence* [and] *Protectress* and *Escort*.[91]

In his *Moral Essays*, Seneca celebrates the "spectacle" of Cato the Younger (95-46 B.C.E.), incorruptible opponent of Caesar and father-in-law of Brutus (ca. 85-42 B.C.E.), who, after shattering defeat, still stood erect:

Lo! Here is a spectacle worthy of the regard of God as he contemplates his works; lo! Here a contest worthy of God, — a brave man matched against ill-fortune.[92]

90. *Epictetus,* Vol. I, Book 2, chap. 19, para. 24, p. 367.
91. *Plutarch's Moral Essays,* 1057E, trans. Harold Chirniss, The Loeb Library of Classics (Cambridge, MA: Harvard University Press, 1976), Vol. XIII, Pt. II, 613.
92. Seneca, *Moral Essays,* trans. John W. Basore, The Loeb Library of Classics

Similarity in matters of style clearly exists between the utterances of Paul and the Stoics. No Gulliver's leap is required to assume that Paul made use of the rhetoric of the popular philosophy current in his day.[93] The dissimilarities, however, are equally patent. First of all, the Stoic "catalog" has in mind only the sufferer and the internal reaction to his suffering.[94] In Paul all spiritualizing or interiorizing of suffering is excluded.[95] The catalog in I Corinthians 4:12, for example, has to do with those who inflict suffering on their victims. Second, in the Stoa, the *peristasen* are merely an opportunity for the Stoic to demonstrate his indomitableness: the sufferer remains untouched by suffering. The *peristasen,* those "strokes of fate," are merely an occasion by which he demonstrates his *ataraxia,* or "nonengagement." Through an auto-suggestive feat of the will, evil is to be overcome, treated as nonexistent.[96] Third, in the Stoa suffering is a natural event. Seneca says:

> We do not suddenly fall on death, but advance towards it by slight degrees; we die every day. For every day a little of our life is taken from us.[97]

Paul's reference to his dying "every day," or putting himself and his companions in danger "every hour" (I Cor. 15:30-31), is leagues away from a reference to a natural event.[98] Finally, in the Stoa the ability to overcome evil lies within one's own power, as illustrated, for example, in Seneca's *Moral Essays:*

> What element of evil is there in torture and in the other things which we call hardships? It seems to me that there is this evil, — that the mind sags, and bends, and collapses. But none of these things can happen to the sage; he stands erect under any load. Nothing can subdue him;

(Cambridge, MA: Harvard University Press, 1963), Vol. I, *De Providentia,* chap. 2, para. 9, p. 11.

93. Schrage, "Leid, Kreuz und Eschaton," pp. 146-47; Kleinknecht, *Der leidende Gerechtfertigte,* pp. 258, 294; Niederwimmer, "Erkennen und Lieben," p. 81.

94. Kleinknecht, *Der leidende Gerechtfertigte,* p. 229.

95. Schrage, p. 150.

96. Schrage, p. 149.

97. Seneca, *Ad Lucilium Epistolae Morales,* trans. Richard M. Gummere (Cambridge, MA: Harvard University Press, 1967), Vol. I, Epistle 24, paras. 19-20, p. 177.

98. Kleinknecht, *Der leidende Gerechtfertigte,* pp. 238-239.

nothing that must be endured annoys him. For he does not complain that he has been struck by that which can strike any man. He knows his own strength; he knows that he was born to carry burdens.[99]

For Paul such "extraordinary power" belongs to God alone (II Cor. 4:7).

In all of this, the egocentric orientation of the Stoic ethic can scarcely be missed, but for Paul, dying "every day" has its issue in service to him who died and to those for whom he died: "We are convinced that one has died for all; therefore all have died. And he died for all, so that those who live might live no longer for themselves" (II Cor. 5:14-15). The essayist and commentator Richard Brookhiser assigns George Washington's (1732-1799) practice in "self-government" in part to Seneca's *Moral Essays,* available in print until well into the nineteenth century and always popular with Christians due to its "earnest moralizing." Brookhiser then adds that what meant much more to Washington were the "Rules of Civility," a set of precepts composed by sixteenth-century French Jesuits and copied out by Washington when he was sixteen years old. The "Rules" had to do with one's behavior toward the other, against which Seneca's preoccupation with the self and its peace of mind appears inert and torpid.[100]

It may be incorrect to say that the apostle has no interest in the existence of the individual,[101] but not incorrect to say that he is not *preoccupied* with the individual. Adolf Schlatter (1852-1938) says that Paul knows nothing of a lone, isolated man, an idea at which the Greeks arrived because their gods meant nothing to them. The Stoic lives for himself. He needs society, not to give content to the question about what he should do, but to win the applause that makes his moral performance worth desiring. Paul, whose very relationship to God sets him in community, needs "the other" to give content to the question concerning what he should do, but is free and independent of society when it comes to the enjoyable effects of his action.[102]

---

99. Seneca, Vol. II, Epistle 71, paras. 26-27, p. 89.

100. Richard Brookhiser, *Founding Father: Rediscovering George Washington* (New York: Simon & Schuster, 1996), pp. 123-128.

101. Cf. Käsemann, *Leib und Leib Christi: Eine Untersuchung zur paulinischen Begrifflichkeit, Beiträge zur historischen Theologie,* 9 (Tübingen: J. C. B. Mohr, 1933), p. 183; cf. pp. 111, 134.

102. Adolf Schlatter, "Paulus und das Griechentum," in *Das Paulusbild in der neueren*

Again, for Paul, unlike Epictetus, "nonengagement" has its limit —
in love:

> I know and am persuaded . . . that nothing is unclean in itself; but it is
> unclean for anyone who thinks it unclean. If your brother or sister is
> being injured by what you eat, you are no longer walking in love.
> (Rom. 14:14-15)

In place of "I know and am persuaded . . . that nothing is unclean in itself," one can substitute "in that which is another's never employ the
words 'good' or 'evil,' or 'benefit' or 'injury,' or anything of the sort."[103]
But nothing in Epictetus can substitute for "if your brother or sister is
being injured . . . you are no longer walking in love." There is only:

> If you kiss your child, your brother, your friend, never allow your
> fancy free rein, nor your exuberant spirits to go as far as they like, but
> hold them back, stop them, just like those who stand behind generals
> when they ride in triumph, and keep reminding them that they are
> mortal.[104]

As for Paul's and the Stoic's concept of the body and its members, with
all his celebration of their similarity, Weiss's contemporary notes the apostle's "alteration" of the Stoic doctrine. Rather than assuming a "body" or
society given with nature and inhering in "the organized body *(systema)* of
rational things," Paul has in mind a community newly arisen through an
"arbitrary determination" *(thesis),* that is, a body created when God sent
Christ to his cross and held together by the Spirit.[105] Judging Stoicism by
Marcus Aurelius, ruthless persecutor of Christians, may force us to the
conclusion that the movement remained an idea untranslatable into action.[106] But, though the Roman emperor may have been Stoicism's most
distinguished representative, he was certainly not its principal advocate,
any more than Torquemada (1420-1498) was of Christianity.

Deutschen Forschung, ed. K. H. Rengstorf (Darmstadt: Wissenschaftliche Buchgesellschaft, 1964), pp. 102-103.

103. *Epictetus,* Vol. I, Book 2, chap. 5, para. 5, p. 239.

104. *Epictetus,* Vol. II, Book 3, chap. 24, para. 85, pp. 211-213.

105. Cf. Lietzmann in Weiss, *Der Erste Korintherbrief,* p. 301, note 2.

106. P. T. Forsyth, *The Cruciality of the Cross* (Grand Rapids: Eerdmans, 1909; reprint, 1980).

It would be difficult to deny that Paul "unflinchingly"[107] uses concepts and forms of the popular thought of his day. Many more examples than those cited above indicate striking similarities. One can scarcely read I Thessalonians 2:1-12, for example, without being reminded of Stoic-Cynic criteria for distancing honesty from charlatanry, or I Corinthians 1:26-31 without recalling the contemporary substitution of the rhetoric of persuasion for the search for truth.[108] Finally, however, Paul appropriates neither the Stoics' understanding of self nor their understanding of the world. The cross stands in judgment on everything the world is and knows. The difference between Paul and the Stoa lies in the Stoa's fracture on the same event that created the distance between the apostle and the Jewish cultic-legal tradition or apocalyptic thought. Twenty-six years after the publication of his *Der Stil der paulinischen Predigt und die kynisch-stoische Diatribe,* Rudolf Bultmann could say that there was good reason for the current lack of interest in the influence of Stoic tradition on Paul, since "the Stoic perspective and conceptuality influenced Paul only in minor details."[109]

Use and Fracture of Gnosis

No doubt it corresponds to the universality of the gospel not merely to adopt a defensive stance against pagan culture and its religious traditions, but to give gentiles access to the gospel from the perspective of their own language and culture. This statement is as appropriate to Paul's use of the vocabulary and ideas of that curious phenomenon of late antiquity called Gnosis as to his use of Jewish or Hellenistic religiosity. Gnosis was not monolithic in structure, and for that reason, resistance to the message of the cross would not be representative of the whole. But even if it were, Paul would not be deterred from using whatever in it might serve as a vehicle for communication. From this perspective, the preoccupation of one wing of the History of Religions School with the apostle's "dependence"

---

107. Niederwimmer, "Erkennen und Lieben," p. 81.

108. Kleinknecht, *Der leidende Gerechtfertigte,* p. 202; Niederwimmer, "Erkennen und Lieben," p. 81.

109. Bultmann, "Die Neueste Paulusforschung" (*ThR,* n.s. 8, 1, 1936), in *Theologie als Kritik: Ausgewählte Rezensionen und Forschungsberichte,* ed. Matthias Dreher and Klaus W. Müller (Tübingen: Mohr Siebeck, 2002), p. 13.

on Gnostic thought was legitimate. From that school arose interest in a "pre-Christian Gnosis," with its dualistic-pessimistic attitude toward the world, its sacramentology and asceticism, its doctrine of the eons thought to have influenced Jewish eschatology, and its figure of the "redeemed redeemer" alleged to have "sat" for the New Testament portrait of the Christ. In a 1916 essay, Bultmann enumerates Gnostic ideas that presumably lay behind significant Pauline concepts such as the "unspiritual-spiritual" pair in I Corinthians 2:14-15; 14:14-15; the Adam-Christ contrast in Romans 5:14-15 and I Corinthians 15:21-22, 45; the descent of the heavenly Christ into the incognito of human form in I Corinthians 2:7-8 and II Corinthians 8:9; the "god of this world" in II Corinthians 4:4; and the giving of the law through angels in Galatians 3:19.[110]

There may be no clearer evidence of preoccupation with Gnosis as the presupposition for Pauline thought than Ernst Käsemann's 1933 study of the apostle's concept of the "Body of Christ." For example, Käsemann locates the Christ-Hymn of Philippians 2 within the context of the Lord's Supper liturgy, in which the community acknowledged Jesus as *Kyrios,* and in this manner concluded the drama that began with his death. In its worship the community called this drama to mind as the origin of its existence; but it also carried the drama to its conclusion by announcing that it was the foundation of the entire world and by proclaiming the Christ-Aion as the new order of divine salvation before which every knee in heaven, on earth, and under the earth should bow. The confession thus corroborated the status of Christ as the *anthrōpos,* or primal man, the image of the unknown God who embraces the world in its totality, obliging all to obey him.[111] Eric Voegelin says that a significant part of the blame for the crisis in modern statehood rests with the "Gnostic character" of Christianity, traces of which are to be found in Paul and John. Paul, Voegelin continues, did not maintain a balance over against the "shortcuts to immortality" of apocalyptic and Gnostic sectarians, but he engendered the "metastatic expectation of the Second Coming," an expectation that attempted to eliminate the tensions of existence, unlike Plato, who "did not permit enthusiastic expectations to distort the human condition."[112]

110. Bultmann, "Neueste Paulusforschung," p. 18.
111. Käsemann, *Leib und Leib Christi,* pp. 163, 179.
112. Eric Voegelin, *The New Science of Politics,* p. 126; *Order and History,* Vol. IV: *The*

Nevertheless, as was true of apocalypticism or Stoicism, the attempt to derive Paul's thought in linear fashion from Hellenistic religion or Gnosis ignores the fact that it had continually to be broken through in order to do service to his gospel. For example, in I Corinthians 1:18-25, Paul appropriates the Greek or Gnostic concept of "wisdom" with respect to its personification, but radically alters whatever of the transhistorical adheres to it through announcing that "Christ *crucified*" is the power and "wisdom of God" (I Cor. 1:23-24).[113] This emphasis on the historical arrival of a "foolishness wiser than human wisdom," particularly on the *manner* of that arrival in the event of the cross,[114] implies that the wisdom in vogue at Corinth was intent on absorbing the contingent in something greater, something larger, a wisdom loosed from history.[115] "The wisdom of God" and "the wisdom of the world" were thus incommensurables.

According to Ulrich Wilckens, Paul speaks, in I Corinthians 2:6-16, "like a perfect Gnostic."[116] He not only appropriates individual Gnostic terms and ideas, but he adopts the entire Gnostic train of thought in its language and conceptuality, atmosphere and pathos. On the other hand, Wilckens continues, the apostle nowhere speaks of "those who are spiritual" (vs. 14) as one in essence with the Spirit; and in 2:12, he interprets the content of the knowledge of revelation as "bestowed on us by God." The believer's union with Christ is thus not given in a "pneumatic materiality, but in the knowledge of the one crucified for him, given in the Spirit."[117] As for the idea of the "light fragments" of the primal man *(Urmensch),* or *anthrōpos,* imprisoned in the material, set free by a redeemer, and reunited with the primal man as furnishing the concept for Paul's description of the church as Christ's body — in the relationship between Christ and his own people — the personality differential is strictly maintained. There is no fusion or deification.

Ecumenic Age (Baton Rouge, LA: Louisiana State University Press, 1974), pp. 302-303, 306; cf. Michael Federici, *Eric Voegelin* (Wilmington, DE: ISI Books, 2002), p. xxxiii.

113. Cf. Wilckens, "Kreuz und Weisheit," a debate with Heinrich Schlier's *Die Zeit der Kirche* (Freiburg, 1956), in *Kerygma und Dogma* 3, No. 1 (1957), 84.

114. Cf. Weder, *Das Kreuz Jesu bei Paulus,* pp. 150, 156.

115. Cf. Weder, *Das Kreuz Jesus,* pp. 128-130, 134, 144, 154, 236.

116. Barbour agrees, at least to the extent that Paul uses "a quite different kind of language"; see "Wisdom and the Cross in I Corinthians 1 and 2," p. 61.

117. Quoted in Barbour, p. 185, n. 186.

Further on (in I Cor. 2:16), Paul warps the entire Gnostic train of thought to the preceding section (in 1:18-25) by describing the Spirit as the "mind of Christ," thus pressing the entire pathos of the Gnostic's self-consciousness into the service of the proclamation of the Crucified.[118] Later (in I Cor. 11:23-33), Paul interprets the Lord's Supper as a celebration between the event of the cross and the *parousia,* in opposition to the Gnostics' enthusiastic notion that the believer has already achieved perfection. Over against the scheme of epiphany and apotheosis in the Hellenistic myth, the Christ-hymn in Philippians 2 speaks of "a genuine Incarnation . . . and precisely for this reason of the exaltation of the humiliated One. . . ."[119] In its present condition, the myth of the pre-existent and exalted One has been carried to its conclusion, but under the condition of the radical alteration of its trans-historical character through the recitation of an actual death, "even death on a cross" (Phil. 2:8). It is possible that the Christ-hymn in Philippians 2 can only be understood against the background of mythical as well as biblical religiosity.[120] Nevertheless, the myth has undergone the same dialectic of expropriation and depotentiation as "wisdom" or "spirit" in the Corinthian correspondence. The origin of faith in the historical event of the death of Christ has made possible this use and usurpation of Hellenistic language and conceptuality. What Schlatter says of the earliest Christian community could have had even greater application to Paul:

> The primitive Christian poesy concerning Christ, begotten through fantasy and which gave clarity and plasticity to the description, did not lead to the fantastic or become a myth, because it did not loose itself from faith, but subjected itself to a powerful discipline.[121]

The fracture of Gnostic thought on the event of the crucified Christ later led Käsemann to express embarrassment over his use of the Gnostic *anthrōpos*-myth to interpret the place of Christ in his study of He-

---

118. Ulrich Wilckens, "Kreuz und Weisheit," p. 92. A bit further on, Wilckens refers to Paul's argument against his Corinthian opponents as harshly antithetical but also in "perilous accommodation" to Gnosis (p. 103).

119. Söding, *Das Wort vom Kreuz,* p. 123; cf. pp. 122-129.

120. See Söding, p. 121.

121. Adolf Schlatter, *Theologie des Neuen Testaments* (Calwer & Stuttgart: Verlag der Vereinsbuchhandlung, 1909), II, 532.

brews, and with it to repudiate the notion of the "redeemed redeemer" as portrayed by Richard Reitzenstein — to which his teacher, Rudolf Bultmann, had "seduced" him.[122]

Use and Fracture of the Pre-Pauline Christian Tradition

The apostle's use of the language and conceptuality of the community of faith that preceded him is extensive. Despite whatever differences existed between him and the Jerusalem "caliphate," he was not the inventor of a Christ cult but the inheritor of liturgical and creedal traditions birthed among those he had once sworn to eliminate. Clearly, he appropriated Christological and soteriological sayings about Jesus' death from the earlier community. The confession of Jesus' death as sacrifice or vicarious atoning death as it appears in Romans 3:25 belonged to the common store of faith of Jesus' Jerusalem adherents — and in this form came to Paul. The result of setting Jesus' death in this cultic context was the relativizing of temple and Torah, leading to conflict with those for whom they were a means of salvation, and ending in the banishment of the Hellenists, which in turn gave impetus to the "Antiochene" missionary tradition.[123] Paul developed from this atonement tradition his proclamation with its Christological concentration, its emphasis on righteousness by faith, and its critique of the law. The references in Romans 5:8; 8:32, and I Thessalonians 5:10 to Jesus' death as "for us," and "for us all," or in I Corinthians 15:3 and Galatians 1:4 to his death "for our sins," are part of the same pre-Pauline tradition. When Paul inquires in Romans 6 on behalf of his fictional opponent, "Should we continue in sin in order that grace may abound?" and replies that such is an impossibility since all who were baptized into Christ Jesus were baptized into his death, he is appropriating a link already forged in the primitive Christian tradition between Jesus' death and baptism, a link he assumes is already well known at Corinth (I Cor. 1:13).

Other passages in the Roman and Corinthian correspondence ar-

122. See Käsemann, *Kirchliche Konflikte,* p. 17.

123. Merklein, "Der Tod Jesu als stellvertretender Sühnetod," in *Studien zu Jesus und Paulus* (Tübingen: J. C. B. Mohr, 1987), I, 186; cf. Klaus Haacker, "Die Fragestellung der biblischen Theologie als exegetischer Aufgabe," in *Biblisch-Theologische Studien* (Neukirchen-Vluyn: Neukirchener Verlag, 1977), p. 42.

gue a dependence on earlier Christian tradition. Affirmations or confessions introduced by the masculine relative ("who"), such as the confession in Romans 1:4 or its variation in Romans 4:25, reflect a primitive Christian liturgical tradition. The use of the term "hand over" in the same passage, together with clauses beginning with the conjunction "that" in I Corinthians 15:3-5, recite pre-Pauline formulas. The argument concerning the two determinative acts of the "two corporate men" in Romans 5:12-21, the reference to the transfer of lordships in Romans 7:1-6, the paralleling of Christ's death and Passover in I Corinthians 5:7, the assigning of inclusive and eschatological significance to Christ's death in Romans 6:6 or I Corinthians 15:3 — all of these may derive from a complex of thought at home in the pre-Pauline community. The tables of duties in Romans, I and II Corinthians, and Galatians — reminiscent of lists in Hellenistic-Jewish, rabbinic literature and in Qumran, as well as in Greco-Roman and Hermetic writings — have all the earmarks of traditions containing instructions for catechumens about to receive baptism or instruction for those already belonging to the Christian community, all of it possibly harking back to such "primitive holiness codes" as appear in Leviticus 17-26.[124]

In a study entitled "The Atonement — An Adequate Reward for the *Akedah?*" Nils Dahl thought he detected, in Romans 3:25-26, 8:32a, and Galatians 3:13-14, fragments of a Jewish-Christian interpretation of Jesus' crucifixion in light of the *Akedah.* Appeal to the *Akedah,* Dahl concludes, helped the followers of Jesus overcome the scandal of the cross and understand what had occurred as an act of God's love and the manifestation of his righteousness.[125]

Paul's contrast between the old and new covenants, his reference to the promise of the revelation of faith in the old, thus to the temporal priority of the new covenant, his characterization of life under the old cov-

124. Cf. Philip Carrington, *The Primitive Christian Catechism: A Study in the Epistles* (Cambridge, UK: Cambridge University Press, 1940); "Essay II: On the Inter-relation of I Peter and Other N.T. Epistles," in E. G. Selwyn, *The First Epistle of St. Peter* (London: Macmillan, 1946), pp. 365-466; and Eduard Kamlah, *Die Form der katalogischen Paränese im Neuen Testament* (Tübingen: J. C. B. Mohr, 1964).

125. Nils Dahl, "The Atonement — An Adequate Reward for the *Akedah?*" in *The Crucified Messiah and Other Essays,* pp. 146-160; see also Max Wilcox, "Upon the Tree — Deut. 21:22-23 in the New Testament," *JBL* 96, No. 1 (1977), who, despite a minor detail, concurs with Dahl's study (p. 99).

enant and its law as bondage, and his description of the law's activity as provisional, preparatory to the revelation of faith (Gal. 3:14, 17, 23, 24; cf. vv. 19, 22), may all have been prepared for and stimulated by those "concealed behind the Lukan collective *Hellēnistai.*"[126] Those *Hellēnistai* may have originated the use of the term "spirit" to denote the eschatological content of the promise — in contrast to the sarkic, noneschatological character of the old covenant — and Paul's description of baptism as participation in Christ (Gal. 3:3, 5, 14, 26-29).

There is no question but that Paul appropriated from the community Christological and soteriological statements regarding Jesus' death. But Paul did not stop at appropriating traditional ideas and formulas. Due to the event that he believed was determinative of existence, he subjected what was traditional to reformulation, extension, and radicalization. Dahl, for example, does not neglect to point out the discontinuity between Jewish and Christian uses of the *Akedah*. He notes that Judaism stopped short at the crucial point of Abraham's sacrifice of his son.[127] Only an interpreter who believed the crucified Jesus to be the Messiah and Son of God could dare to follow the trend to its bitter end, stating that as Abraham offered up his son, so God offered up his own Son for Isaac's children.[128] Further, if that pre-Pauline passage in Romans 3:21-26 emphasizes an atonement-effecting forgiveness, Paul widens its scope to include the appearance of a new world broken in with Christ's death:

> [God did this] to prove at the present time that he himself is righteous and that he justifies the one who has faith in Jesus. . . . For we hold that a person is justified by faith apart from works prescribed by the law. Or is God the God of Jews only? Is he not the God of Gentiles also? Yes, of Gentiles also, since God is one. . . .[129]

In light of this "revision," Gerhard Friedrich (1908-1986) says that, since Paul does not appropriate the tradition in servile fashion, the in-

---

126. Cf. Sänger, *Die Verkündigung des Gekreuzigten und Israel*, p. 288.

127. Note Levenson's reference to the *Akedah* as "symbolic" in *The Death and Resurrrection of the Beloved Son*, p. 59.

128. Dahl, "The Atonement — An Adequate Reward for the *Akedah?*" p. 153; cf. Heb. 11:17-19 and Jas. 2:21-24.

129. Cf. Schrage, "Römer 3,21-26 und die Bedeutung des Todes Jesu Christi bei Paulus," in *Das Kreuz*, ed. Rieger (Göttingen: Vandenhoeck & Ruprecht, 1967), pp. 79, 85.

terpretation of *hilastērion* in Romans 3:25 as *kapporeth* ("covering," "mercy seat," "atonement," etc.) — hence as oriented to substitution — should finally be given up.[130] According to Käsemann, even in this instance to allow for the reformulation or radicalization of the traditional view is to say too much. For one thing, Paul's argument has nothing to do with the cultus; for another, he uses the tradition merely to give his own theology sharper focus. More important, salvation, according to Paul, is not first of all forgiveness of sins or the erasure of past guilt, but freedom from the power of sin and death, and the possibility of new life. The Cross is thus a theme that cannot be made to compete with the idea of Jesus' death as vicarious sacrifice.[131]

It is also significant that the concept of atonement has undergone revision in Paul's extension of the traditional *hyper*-formula to include the "ungodly" as beneficiaries of Christ's death: God proves his love for us in that, while we still were sinners, Christ died for us (Rom. 5:8; cf. II Cor. 5:21; Gal. 2:16-21; 3:10-14).[132] And in one stroke, "justification" as an event occurring through grace alone is all but exclusively tied to Christ's death.[133]

For Paul, then, the death of Jesus was not an event that only required interpreting in the light of traditional statements; rather, the traditional formulas required interpreting in the light of Jesus' death. As a result, the idea of sacrifice or expiation was wrenched from its sometimes tribal context and made to embrace an event reaching far beyond it.[134] And since, for Paul, reference to forgiveness or atonement did not clearly express the fact that Jesus' death not only put a period to the old but also effected the breaking in of the new, in Romans 5:9-10 he speaks of "justification" rather than of "sacrifice," that is, the gift of God's

---

130. Friedrich, *Die Verkündigung des Todes Jesu,* p. 64.

131. Käsemann, "Die Heilsbedeutung des Todes Jesu nach Paulus," in *Zur Bedeutung des Todes Jesu,* pp. 21-22; cf. Merklein, "Die Bedeutung des Kreuzestod Christi," p. 54.

132. Charles B. Cousar, "Paul and the Death of Jesus," p. 40; Jürgen Becker, "Die neutestamentliche Rede vom Sühnetod Jesu," p. 46.

133. Merklein, "Die Bedeutung des Kreuzestod Christi," pp. 23, 51; Söding, *Das Wort vom Kreuz,* pp. 156, 172.

134. P. T. Forsyth, *The Cruciality of the Cross,* p. 218; Schrage, "Römer 3,21-26 und die Bedeutung des Todes Jesu bei Paulus," pp. 79-80, 85, 101; cf. Cousar, "Paul and the Death of Jesus," p. 47.

peace given to those who once were enemies and now through the *pax Christi* are returned to obedience.[135]

Among the Christians at Corinth, the riddle of Christ's death may have been somewhere toward center, but it was interpreted in such a way as to be neutralized.[136] For Paul, on the other hand, the cross was the criterion, the principle of theological reflection.[137] Against what has often been correctly or incorrectly described as a Jewish-Gnostic-Sophia Christology, according to which the revelation of Christ was construed as a present knowledge by which to become wise, Paul declares that who God is and what God has done is revealed only in the cross, so that Christ is the power and wisdom of God (I Cor. 1:18-25). This personification of God's wisdom in the Crucified One resists all expectation of the divine activity as guaranteed through ecclesiastical acts:

> Each of you says, "I belong to Paul," or "I belong to Apollos," or "I belong to Cephas," or "I belong to Christ." Has Christ been divided? Was Paul crucified for you? Or were you baptized in the name of Paul? (I Cor. 1:12-13)

. . . or through pneumatic experience:

> You know that when you were pagans, you were enticed and led astray to idols that could not speak. Therefore I want you to understand that no one speaking by the Spirit of God ever says "Let Jesus be cursed!" and no one can say "Jesus is Lord" except by the Holy Spirit. (I Cor. 12:2-3)[138]

If Christ's death was an "eschatological atonement," that is, if it effected the breaking in of a new world, then no cult-ritual purification of believers is needed. This note requires expanding. If, on occasion, Paul can interpret the death of Jesus within a cultic setting (cf. Rom. 3:25-26; 5:8-9; 8:3), if he can transfer to Jesus all the specific institutions of the cult, then two conclusions may be drawn. The first is that Torah sacri-

---

135. Schrage, "Römer 3,21-26 und die Bedeutung des Todes Jesu Christi bei Paulus," p. 85; Käsemann, "Die Heilsbedeutung des Todes Jesu nach Paulus," p. 22.

136. Söding, *Das Wort vom Kreuz*, p. 75.

137. Weber, *Kreuz*, p. 145.

138. Fleinert-Jensen, *Das Kreuz und die Einheit der Kirche*, p. 16.

fice has not been invalidated or done away with, but rather fulfilled, absorbed in the death of Christ. In this case, obedience to Christ is not simply analogous to obedience to Torah, as, for example, the Pharisaic theory of obedience to Torah was analogous to the temple cult. Rather, obedience to Christ *is* obedience to Torah. Thus, following his cult-typological interpretation of Jesus' death in Romans 3:25-26, Paul asks, "Do we then overthrow the law by this faith?" and answers, "By no means! On the contrary, we uphold the law" (Rom. 3:31). The second conclusion is that obedience to Torah, when abstracted or loosed from the death of Christ as its fulfillment, is part and parcel of an institution from which Christians have been set free. The very cultic interpretation of Christ's death has made it impossible to participate in the Jerusalem cult.[139] Referring to Torah obedience loosed from the matrix of its fulfillment in Christ, Paul writes of his own people that

> they have a zeal for God, but it is not enlightened. For, being ignorant of the righteousness that comes from God, and seeking to establish their own, they have not submitted to God's righteousness. For Christ is the end of the law so that there may be righteousness for everyone who believes. (Rom. 10:2-4)

The apostle is not content to give to Christ's death a cult-typological interpretation, but, with that habit of pursuing an idea to its conclusion, he can use and warp it to his purpose of distinguishing life under the one covenant from life under the other.[140]

With the temple and its cult displaced, or rather fulfilled and absorbed, the Christians themselves can now be called "the church of God" (I Cor. 1:2), God's "temple," or the dwelling of the Spirit (I Cor. 3:16-17). If Christ became the prototype of a new humanity by means of

---

139. Cf. Merklein, "Der Sühnetod Jesu," p. 50.

140. Cf. Merklein, pp. 48, 50-51. When Merklein says (on p. 56) that, despite the difference between the Pharisaic theory of Torah obedience and the Christian interpretation of Jesus' death, "in either case the obligatory character of the *entire* Torah is basically preserved," he risks taking away with one hand what he gave with the other. He says (on p. 34) that the Old Testament cultic ideas serve as type so as to point to the antitype, the significance of which does not derive from the type but is merely made graphic by it. And on p. 59, he says that "the real difference" between Judaism and Christianity exists in their understanding of the grace of God — for the one, it is shown in the election and the covenant, for the other in the saving death of Jesus Christ.

his atonement, then those who are his have died with him.[141] In II Corinthians 5:14-15, Paul says:

> For the love of Christ urges us on, because we are convinced that one has died for all; therefore all have died. And he died for all, so that those who live might live no longer for themselves, but for him who died and was raised for them.

Whether or not this idea of representation was newly brought to Christology by Paul,[142] it is an advance over the traditional view of substitution reflected in the *hyper*-formula. That view may only have functioned "synchronically," that is, it may have conceived of Christ's death as atonement only for those at that moment in danger of punishment — without reference to those who should come after.[143]

In Galatians also, the traditional view of Christ's death lags behind what Paul wishes to say. At its center the apostle refers to Christ's "becoming a curse for us" — "that the blessing of Abraham might come to the Gentiles, so that we might receive the promise of the Spirit through faith" (3:13-14). Paul is not content to say that in dying Jesus took our place. He has replaced the idea of substitution or representation with that of identification. Nor is the idea of identification incidental or subordinate to what the apostle says elsewhere of Christ's death. Together with II Corinthians 5:21 ("for our sake [God] made him to be sin"), it marks the soteriological high point of his argument. In other words, Paul has moved the idea of Christ's death as vicarious and *punitive* toward that of its creating a new humanity, since by assuming our identity he has opened to us the possibility of assuming his identity.[144]

The traditional, early Christian view of Christ's death thus undergoes "fracture" in Paul's letters to the Romans, Corinthians, and

141. Merklein, "Die Bedeutung des Kreuzestod Christi," pp. 101-102; Jürgen Becker, "Die neutestamentliche Rede vom Sühnetod Jesu," p. 46.

142. Becker, "Die neutestamentliche Rede," p. 46.

143. Becker, p. 46. Commenting on Romans 6, Ortkemper suggests that, over against the traditional formula of living or rising with Christ on the one hand, and the formula of baptism into Jesus' death on the other, Paul created the expression of "being buried together with" or of "being crucified together with" Christ (*Das Kreuz in der Verkündigung des Apostels Paulus*, p. 86).

144. Cf. Merklein, "Das paulinische Paradox des Kreuzes," pp. 292-293, 297-298; see also Becker, "Die neutestamentliche Rede," pp. 46-47.

Galatians. Nowhere does Paul unequivocally describe Jesus' death as sacrifice. From here it is but a short step to conclude that his emphasis on the cross as that by which to interpret the community's Christological and soteriological statements and those statements themselves do not mutually assume or influence each other, but that the one gains mastery over the other to the point of excluding it.[145] And because of the degree of emphasis on the divine initiative in the death of Jesus, the events of offering and sacrifice can be described as "heightened beyond measure," even "to the point of the absurd."[146]

If the current interpretation of the Philippian correspondence has any merit, in pre-Pauline Christology the pre-existent, incarnate, and exalted one had taken such possession of the earthly one that there was reference only to the fact that he existed, not to *the way in which* he existed or was distinguished from other humans. Jesus' exaltation to the Father's right hand thus followed immediately from his crucifixion. The Easter appearances were mere manifestations of the one who was already exalted. And for Paul as well, the risen Christ accedes to lordship, but not by way of the cross as a means to an end: the risen Christ would have no identity other than that of the crucified. For this reason Paul warps to the cross a traditional hymn for which Jesus' death may have spelled only the last stage of his humiliation. The hymn opens with the relative pronoun signaling its origin in earliest Christian worship: "*Who, though he was in the form of God, did not regard equality with God as something to be exploited*" — then proceeds to affirm Christ's "emptying." Then, at the point of describing his obedience to death as the move toward exaltation, the hymn is interrupted to read that his obedience involved "death on a cross" (Phil. 2:5-11). If the cross, prior to Paul, was the question to be answered by the resurrection, with Paul the observation was reversed: the risen Christ was identifiable with Jesus of Nazareth only as the crucified.[147] Becker says that if the mere allusion to the idea of substitution in I Thessalonians is worth noting (I Thess. 5:9-10), the pointed reference to a theology of the cross in Philippians without the slightest mention of substitution is all the more remarkable.[148]

145. Käsemann, "Die Heilsbedeutung," pp. 21-22.

146. Ebeling, "Der Sühnetod Christi als Glaubensaussage," p. 19.

147. Käsemann, "Die Heilsbedeutung des Todes Jesu nach Paulus," pp. 31-32; cf. Schrage, "Römer 3,21-26 und die Bedeutung des Todes Jesu Christi bei Paulus," pp. 85-86.

148. Becker, "Die neutestamentliche Rede," p. 45.

If in Paul the theme of Christ crucified is not the reappearance in altered form of traditional ideas, whether Jewish or Greek, Stoic or Gnostic, neither is it a supplement to "traditional" Christian interpretations. That long list of observers who labeled Paul "the second founder of Christianity" had half the truth on their side. There is nothing of "correlation" about his work, that feature of response that allows a question to remain as it is, unchallenged and in control of the dialogue. With Paul, discontinuity has the upper hand; nothing is left unaltered. What the old philologist said of the style of Paul's letters — "this is Paul, none but Paul; it is neither private letter nor yet literature, something between that cannot be imitated though imitated again and again"[149] — can be said of their content. When the apostle has completed the process of "editing" the tradition, every page has been blue-penciled to the point where the original is scarcely recognizable.

Still, the question about what gave rise to this massive reworking of inherited or received tradition in Paul is of far greater weight than the question of the dependence or independence of his thought. Contemporary relish for setting the apostle on a continuum with Jewish or Greek thought, or at least with pre-Pauline Christian tradition, as well as anxiety over his possible loss of integrity in the face of the parallels to his ideas, are both propelled by the notion of uniqueness as a fundamental category — the one advocating it, the other reacting to it. But "newness" in the New Testament is never an exclusively chronological designation, a name for something having recently arrived on the scene. Its truest definition concerns what is *qualitatively* new, a characteristic adhering to it by virtue of an inherent dynamic. Translated in terms of the Pauline language and conceptuality, the event of the cross is the theme throbbing throughout the apostle's work, and the character of his work needs to be discerned in that light. With Paul, that event has a life of its own. It exists outside him, an object toward which his feeling, thinking, and willing are directed. At least that is his confession.

In his "Epistemology at the Turn of the Ages," J. Louis Martyn writes of the epistemological issue in I and II Corinthians. The Gnostics, addressees of the first Epistle, no doubt consented to Paul's stric-

---

149. U. v. Wilamowitz-Moellendorf, quoted in Feine-Behm, *Einleitung in das Neue Testament* (Heidelberg: Quelle & Meyer, 1950), p. 123. (The quotation is absent in subsequent editions.)

tures regarding a "knowledge according to the flesh" *(ginōskein kata sarka)* but failed to hear the apostle's criticism of their position since they assumed that, as *pneumatikoi,* they existed altogether in the new age. The "super-apostles" of II Corinthians no doubt agreed with the Gnostics regarding the true way of knowing but construed it as a knowing "face to face" *(kata prosōpon),* claiming to have seen God and to have mirrored the event in their own faces. For Paul, however, it was not nature but an event that constituted the epistemological watershed. For this reason, the opposite of knowing "according to the flesh" was not a knowing "according to the spirit" *(kata pneuma)* but a knowing "according to the cross" *(kata stauron).* The essential failure of the Gnostics lay in their determination to live *after* the cross, and the failure of the super-apostles was in their determination to live *before* the cross — neither of them *in* the cross.[150]

The conclusion to be drawn is that the dialectic of appropriation and depotentiation inherent in Paul's use of terms and concepts from the world around him is "the linguistic reflex of the activity of God in the cross of Jesus."[151] For this reason, the incorporation of his proclamation into any given religious-historical context cannot represent it as a mere modification. For the apostle, the historical event of the cross of Christ involved a qualification — more, a fracture of whatever setting he may have lent it.

Put positively, in Merklein's words, the "'word of the cross' forms the basis for its own semantic, and creates its own [linguistic] world. It constitutes a semantic change of paradigm and requires its execution."[152]

The Pauline Experiential Theology

It is impossible to determine whether the encounter with his tradition and the religious thought within the culture of his day furnished Paul the occasion for reflection on the death of Jesus, or whether that reflec-

150. J. Louis Martyn, "Epistemology at the Turn of the Ages: 2 Cornthians 5:16," *Christian History and Interpretation: Studies Presented to John Knox* (Cambridge, UK: Cambridge University Press, 1967), pp. 279, 283-286.

151. Weder, *Das Kreuz Christi bei Paulus,* p. 166.

152. Merklein, "Das paulinische Paradox des Kreuzes," p. 285.

tion had already occurred and made it possible for him to take a stance toward that tradition and culture. In any case, if not beyond dispute, it is an assumption as legitimate as any other that the dialectic of expropriation and depotentiation that the tradition and culture underwent at Paul's hands was directly linked to his own experience.[153] Pauline theology, with its criticism of human wisdom and righteousness, whether nursed in a Judaizing nomism, Stoic moralism, or Gnostic enthusiasm — and with its emphasis on the sovereignty of God in effecting humanity's redemption in the crucified Christ — corresponds with what Paul himself experienced at his conversion.

When his biographer records the third and final narrative of his conversion, this time on the occasion of his defense before Agrippa, Paul refers to his membership in the "strictest sect of our religion," his persecution of Christians, the appearance of Christ and his charge, concluding with the statement that God had helped him to that hour, that his witness was a recitation of Mosaic and prophetic tradition affirming that the Messiah must suffer, and by rising from the dead would proclaim light to "our people" and to the gentiles (Acts 26:1-23). The narrative refers to the basic ingredients of Pauline theology: first to the ingredient of contrast, that is, the abandonment of hostility to a faith originating in allegiance to another, itself abandoned; the second, to the ingredient of continuity, that is, the affirmation that the new allegiance had its anticipation in the allegiance he earlier possessed; and finally, to the announcement of the event that created this continuity and contrast — "that the Messiah must suffer." In this theology, the lion's share went to contrast, not by eliminating continuity, but because continuity did service to it. Martin Kähler (1835-1912) says:

> For this man of deep feeling and acuity the tangled knots of his own life, of his people's history, and of the great sweep of humanity were loosed beneath the cross. . . . Such a shattering is not borne without firm support or something gained to balance it. The God of the Fathers, the God of history gave him support. . . . He found gain in that, and with the Crucified living in him he mastered his world-embracing task.[154]

153. Ulrich Luz, "Theologia crucis als Mitte der Theologie im Neuen Testament," p. 128; cf. Söding, *Das Wort vom Kreuz*, p. 176.

154. Martin Kähler, *Das Kreuz: Grund und Mass der Christologie*, p. 314.

If it is true that Paul's encounter with the crucified Messiah evoked the dialectic of continuity and contrast that inheres in his thought, and for which reason whatever vehicle he used to convey it underwent both expropriation and depotentiation, then the orientation of his thought to that event cannot be set down as one-sided, restricted to the moment or situation, or in need of supplementing. Over against approaches to Paul's letters that he believes honor neither their specificity nor their relationship to the heart of his gospel, J. Christiaan Beker (1924-1999) distinguishes the "coherent core and contingent contextualism" in Paul's thought. He says that the way the core of Paul's theology achieves depth and relevance in every contingency of the human situation constitutes his particular contribution to theology, "a feat — with perhaps the exception of Luther — no other apostle or theologian has achieved."[155] The interest of this present study is parallel to Beker's to the extent that it emphasizes a "core" in Paul's thought that cannot be reduced to statements that are relativized or conditioned only by the situation. Nor is that "core" a timeless, abstract thing randomly inserted by the apostle into any given situation. On the other hand, this study is not so much concerned with the service that the contingent renders to the core of Paul's thought than with the effect of the core on the contingent — on the given situation. Furthermore, I construe the contingent less in terms of the sociological, economic, and psychological, as is true with Beker, than in terms of language and conceptuality. For this reason, the "apocalyptic setting" of Paul's gospel of "Christ crucified and risen" to which Beker gives emphasis is noted less for its enhancement of the gospel than for its fracture by the gospel.

There is nothing new about the debate over the existence or absence of a theme persisting throughout Paul's Letters, despite the situations to which it is applied. It is as old as the "debate" between William Wrede (1859-1906) and Albert Schweitzer on the one hand, and Heinrich Julius Holtzmann (1832-1910) and Rudolf Bultmann on the other, regarding the core of Paul's theology. What may be new is the refusal to assign priority to the "coherent" or to the "contingent."[156] Newer yet may be the relegating of Paul's thought to illogic. For example, Heikki Räisänen

155. J. Christiaan Beker, *Paul the Apostle,* pp. 23-36.
156. Cf. the tendency toward this view in Udo Schnelle, *Wandlungen im paulinischen Denken,* p. 97.

urges the pursuit of whatever insights Paul might have arrived at by "intuition," without attempting to locate coherence in his thought, particularly where his view of the law is concerned.[157] A 1991 novel entitled *Das riskierte Ich* (roughly translatable as "the wagered self") consists of a fictional account of Paul's theology as occasioned by his infatuation with a woman.[158]

After saying that large portions of experience gained by the old paradigm or disciplinary matrix are transformed into "different bundles" linked "piecemeal" to the new paradigm, Thomas Kuhn says that coming to grips with a new paradigm, or as he puts it, the "resolution of revolutions," may occur without benefit of a set goal.[159] Paul did, in fact, have a set goal; there is a discrete and definite point of orientation to his thought, but this is not to say that he developed it in a final or exhaustive way. Despite Paul's allegiance to the "new paradigm," one can detect a certain tension in its application. For example, aside from the ambiguity attaching to his view of the law's provisional character, in one instance he regards its total fulfillment as a possibility (Phil. 3:6) and in another views that possibility as hypothetical (Gal. 3:12; Rom. 10:5). Or again, his argument against the Corinthian enthusiasts and his defense of his apostleship appear to represent conflicting applications of his "paradigm." In opposition to the enthusiasts, who imagine that the new eon has already totally displaced the old, he hammers away at the "not yet":

> Already you have all you want! Already you have become rich! Quite apart from us you have become kings! Indeed, I wish that you had become kings, so that we might be kings with you! For I think that God has exhibited us apostles as last of all, as though sentenced to death, because we have become a spectacle to the world, to angels and to mortals. (I Cor. 4:8-9)[160]

But where his apostleship is under suspicion, he hammers away at the "now already":

157. Cf. Heikki Räisänen, *Paul and the Law*, (Philadelphia: Fortress Press, 1986), pp. 264-269.

158. Susanne Krahe, *Das riskierte Ich* (Munich: Christian Kaiser Verlag, 1991).

159. Kuhn, *The Structure of Scientific Revolutions*, pp. 123, 149, 172-173.

160. Note the irony in the repeated "already" of v. 8, denoting the present possession of salvation; cf. Heinz-Wolfgang Kuhn, "Jesus als Gekreuzigter," p. 30.

Thanks be to God, who in Christ always leads us in triumphal procession, and through us spreads in every place the fragrance that comes from knowing him. For we are the aroma of Christ to God among those who are being saved and among those who are perishing; to the one a fragrance from death to death, to the other a fragrance from life to life. (II Cor. 2:14-16)[161]

Other examples of tension or "onesidedness" in Paul's application of his "paradigm" could be cited, together with their manifold explanations. Ortkemper says that Paul himself recognized imperfection in his utterances when he sought to thrust toward the one event of cross and resurrection, but "had continually to lag behind the fullness and richness of Christian truth."[162] Kuss says that when Paul takes up a tradition by thinking it through anew and altering it to the extent of incorporating it into a "system," the system is "not at all unified or thought through in all its consequences." He refers to the "embarrassment" over a "certain conceptual immaturity" in Paul, a "vagueness about thinking through consequences or the relationships between various statements and perceptions."[163]

Embarrassment arises from experiencing unfulfilled expectation in oneself or in another. If one expects Paul's theology to exhibit not simply a "coherent core" but a fully integrated system, an architectonic structure with all pieces in place and interrelated, a system to rival any other, its absence will obviously defeat expectation. Leaving to debate whatever Paul may have intended, since every vehicle he used to convey his gospel suffered fracture, it was inevitable that whatever emerged as his own had to suffer the same fate. The "minus sign" he drew over what others had said or thought required drawing the same over what he himself had said or thought. The apostle could not master his theology in any ultimate way because it never existed as a system; in fact, it could not, since the event at its core spelled the death of system. If it corresponds to the theology of the cross that "it cannot be contained in a final theological system, but continually puts all systems into question,"[164]

161. Kleinknecht, *Der leidende Gerechtfertigte*, p. 281.

162. Ortkemper, *Das Kreuz in der Verkündigung des Apostels Paulus*, p. 102.

163. Otto Kuss, "Die Rolle des Apostels Paulus," p. 43.

164. Ulrich Luz, "Theologia crucis als Mitte der Theologie im Neuen Testament," p. 130.

no other option was left to Paul's own conceptuality. He may well have been the first to affirm this, for it was he, after all, who said, "For now we see in a mirror, dimly . . ." (I Cor. 13:12a).

Thus the "excuses" raised for Paul's occasional violation of the canons of logic, such as that he was "first and foremost a missionary, a man of practical religion" who developed one line of thought when struggling with one problem but contradicted it when struggling with another;[165] or that whatever was opposed to his exposition of faith had little substance except to serve as an antithesis;[166] or the older, "classical" explanation that whatever he wrote was conditioned by a specific, discrete occasion obtaining among his readers[167] — all these tend to give short shrift to the undeniably historical event at the core of the Pauline literature. From out of this core radiates reflection on whatever object requires it, and because of this core — the event of the death of Jesus of Nazareth, confessed as Savior and Lord — no reflection, whatever its object, can enjoy ultimacy.

Paul and the Cross in the Believer's Life

In the interpretation of Paul it is customary to distinguish the doctrinal from the ethical sections of his letters to the point of separation. The apostle has often been read as setting down first what God has done, then declaring what is expected of the believer. It may be that centuries of reading the Epistle to the Romans as separating believing from doing has furnished this reading its stimulus. The alleged structure of Romans — the "doctrinal" section in chapters 1–8, the "ethical" section

---

165. Cf. Räisänen, *Paul and the Law,* pp. 266-268; E. P. Sanders, *Paul, the Law, and the Jewish People,* p. 199.

166. Cf. D. A. Campbell, "The Meaning of ΠΙΣΤΙΣ and ΝΟΜΟΣ in Paul," *JBL* III, No. 1 (1992), 91-103. Räisänen refers to Paul's "all-pervasive concern for the Gentiles," which led him to misrepresent Jewish Christianity and Judaism ("Legalism and Salvation by the Law," in *Die Paulinische Literatur und Theologie* (Göttingen: Vandenhoeck & Ruprecht, 1980), pp. 63-83.

167. Cf. William Wrede, *Paul,* pp. 113-114; Albert Schweitzer, *The Mysticism of Paul the Apostle,* trans. William Montgomery (New York: The Johns Hopkins University Press, 1998), p. 225; Georg Strecker, "Befreiung und Rechtfertigung," in *Rechtfertigung,* Festschrift für Ernst Käsemann (Göttingen: Vandenhoeck & Ruprecht, 1976), p. 487; Schnelle, *Wandlungen im paulinischen Denken,* pp. 85-87, 97.

in chapters 12–15, and the two separated by "at best a digression, and at worst a completely alien interpolation,"[168] an "intermezzo," an apologia for God's activity in history — appears to have been superimposed on the Pauline correspondence as a whole. The implications of this separation are legion. I refer to three of them below.

First, it may be argued that when Paul describes what is to be believed, he speaks of an event occurring apart from human activity, but also apart from existence. Justification takes place in the heavenly forum (in foro coeli): God credits the sinner's account with the merits won by Christ's substitutionary satisfaction, and thus looks upon the sinner as though the sinner had not sinned. Then the argument continues: when Paul turns to ethical matters, he speaks of what must be done in response to God's gracious act in Christ. God justifies, and humans respond to the divine initiative with a holy life. Or again, the argument reads that the saving event establishes one's existence, but it is also a way on which one must travel. Or what God has given is not a possession that cannot be lost but a gift that must be seized ever anew. Or life must be reached by the standard already reached; those who grasp Christ first as "their righteousness" must strive to make him actual in their lives. In language that has achieved popularity among the interpreters of the New Testament, the "imperative follows or grows out from the indicative."

One assumption behind this view is that the imperatives are capable of being carried out. The writer of IV Maccabees takes this position with respect to the law: "Verily, when the Law orders us not to covet, it should, I think, confirm strongly the argument that the Reason is capable of controlling covetous desires" (IV Macc. 2:6). Since the incorporeal, incorruptible Word of God entered our world, becoming flesh so as to make death disappear from us as utterly as straw from fire (Athanasius), a similar action, though in miniature and empowered by grace, is expected in return. What remains is a question of tactic. Whether or not this scheme derives from a tradition that emphasizes merit to the disadvantage of the sovereignty of divine grace,[169] it has become a commonplace among scholars.

168. The quotation is in J. C. O'Neill, *Paul's Letter to the Romans* (Harmondsworth: Penguin, 1975), p. 145.
169. Cf. Klaus Schwarzwäller, "Kreuzestheologie — Politische Theologie," *Theologische Rundschau* 52, No. 1 (Feb. 1987), 91.

Second, the "imperatives" may be read as calculated to indicate the impossibility of their fulfillment. God regards the sinner in Christ as though the sinner had not sinned. But when Paul turns to matters of doing, he does not speak of what can or must be done in response to God's gracious act, but rather of what cannot be done. In other words, the admonition, the "imperative," constitutes a deliberately impossible demand whose purpose is to call to a new confession of sin and a flight to God for forgiveness. Thus the summons to a holy life, far from assuming its achievement, assumes quite the opposite: that God has acted and nothing can be done in response. The structures of existence are incapable of change or alteration, whether empowered by grace or not.

Third, an attempt at an alternative may be made by appealing to Christian existence as a "way." Accordingly, justification involves what one scholar describes as a "basis for an ethical reformation of life."[170] However imperceptible at first may be the alteration in the structures of existence, the life of the Christian consists in a gradual — though not necessarily progressive — approximation to the will of God.[171] The "imperative," addressed to believers at any point on their journey toward holiness, is thus a summons to become in actuality what they are potentially. Though for the moment they may be unable to render their life conformable to the life of Christ, that is their goal. This view appears to avoid the optimism of the first, which assumes that conformity to Christ can be immediately achieved, and avoids the pessimism of the second, which assumes that it can never be a reality.

The apostle himself could be cited in favor of each of these interpretations. Regarding the first, the interval in the book of Acts between Saul's conversion and Paul's proclamation of Jesus as Son of God (Acts 9:17-20) is brief enough to suggest that his obedience to Christ was not a delayed reaction to his conversion. Regarding the second, one could refer to Paul's description of the conflict between "the law of the mind" and "the law of sin" in Romans 7:23-24 (a conflict that moves the apostle to cry, "Who will rescue me . . . ?") — or at least to Augustine's, Luther's, and Calvin's interpretation of it. Respecting the third interpreta-

---

170. Hans Lietzmann, *Einführung in die Textgeschichte der Paulusbriefe an die Römer*, p. 66.

171. Cf. Erich Seeberg's view of Luther's understanding of justification as a process, *Luthers Theologie in ihren Grundzügen* (Stuttgart: W. Kohlhammer Verlag, 1950), pp. 121-123.

tion, Paul's word at the conclusion of Philippians 3, "I press on toward the goal for the prize of the heavenly call of God in Christ Jesus" (Phil. 3:14), appears to suit the notion of progression.

These three views do not yet arrive at the heart of Paul's thought, not merely because separating believing from doing relegates doing to the status of an ethic,[172] or denies obedience to Christ where it cannot be proved. The reason, chiefly, is that the separation ignores the similarity — even the identical nature of the content — in the indicatives and imperatives in Paul's letters.

For example, in one breath Paul will say to the Romans, "Consider yourselves dead to sin" (Rom. 6:11), and in the next he will issue a summons to disallow it: "Do not let sin exercise dominion" (Rom. 6:12). Or he will encourage the Philippians to "join in imitating me" (Phil. 3:17; cf. I Cor. 4:16; 11:1), and yet write to the Thessalonians that "you *became* imitators of us and of the Lord" (I Thess. 1:6; cf. 2:14). That is, Paul can supply the indicative and the imperative with the same content, which is a characteristic feature of the Pauline admonitions.[173] The significance of this identification is that, for Paul, Christ is the subject of believing *and* doing inasmuch as he has made the believer one with himself. Neglect of this thought in Paul marks the three views I referred to above, and it explains why they emphasize immediate response, no response, or gradual response to the divine saving act. Furthermore, beneath these emphases lies the assumption that the self of the believer retains its independence, has an identity all its own, and is given definition apart from some other thing, some other one. It is Paul's contention, however, that what gives definition to Christian existence is "no longer I . . . but Christ" (Gal. 2:20). Paul's use of local constructions such as "in Christ" or "in the Lord" (cf. Rom. 6:11; 8:1, 39) denotes a change of existence, so that the noetic aspect of the divine activity is made to serve the ontical.[174] Be-

---

172. Cf. Käsemann, *Commentary on Romans,* trans. G. W. Bromiley (Grand Rapids: Eerdmans, 1980), pp. 182, 234. Cf. the statement of Joachim Jeremias to the effect that everything in the New Testament that does not reflect Jesus' own situation-in-life belongs to the category of echo and is subordinate (*Das Problem des historischen Jesus* [Stuttgart: Calwer Verlag, 1960], pp. 23-24).

173. Cf. also Romans 6:11-12: "So you also must consider yourselves dead to sin and alive to God in Christ Jesus. Therefore, do not let sin exercise dominion in your mortal bodies, to make you obey their passions."

174. Cf. Hübner, *Biblische Theologie des Neuen Testaments,* I, 231-232.

lievers are not merely set free from the compulsion of posing as the acting subjects of their lives by agreeing to their identity as constituted by the past event of the cross.[175] Such "agreement" allows the "I" its independence over against whatever is agreed to. Whatever the historical antecedents of his conviction, it is Paul's conviction that the new life is new to the extent that its subject is not "I" but the risen Crucified.[176]

If Christ is Paul's "I," then it is possible to say not only that the believer *can* or *ought* or *must* respond to the divine gracious activity — or *must* regard the Incarnation as a model for life. It is not a matter of the believer's deciding to allow such to occur, or of "concretizing in all his activity what once occurred on the cross toward his being a Christian."[177] Nor, contrary to Bultmann's existential interpretation, is it Paul's idea that the fellowship with Christ in suffering occurs by way of the resolution of faith and is thus a goal ever to be won or a process continually occurring in the believer's life.[178] Finally, whether or not intended to rescue the apostle from "transcendental irrelevance," the suggestion that Paul must "balance" his indicatives with imperatives due to his "realism about the continuing human situation" ignores the Pauline conviction that, by his divine power, the risen and exalted Lord makes his "epiphany" in the believer.[179] The believer *is* Christ's own appearance in the world.

From these observations we may draw three obvious conclusions. The first is that, according to Paul, the Christian's life is shaped by and conformed to the life of the Incarnate One. To the charge that his teaching concerning justification through faith and not by deeds of the law inevitably leads to moral laxity, Paul responds that that is an impossibility since the Christian shares the life of Jesus Christ:

> How can we who died to sin go on living in it? Do you not know that all of us who have been baptized into Christ Jesus were baptized into his death? Therefore we have been buried with him by baptism into

175. Cf. Weder, *Das Kreuz Jesu bei Paulus,* p. 179.

176. Cf. Söding, *Das Wort vom Kreuz,* p. 172.

177. Gerhard Delling, *Der Kreuzestod Jesu in der urchristlichen Verkündigung,* p. 39.

178. Rudolf Bultmann, *Theology of the New Testament,* trans. Kendrick Grobel (New York: Charles Scribner's Sons, 1955), II, 182.

179. Stephen J. Patterson, *Beyond the Passion* (Minneapolis: Fortress, 2004), pp. 55, 139 n. 19.

death, so that, just as Christ was raised from the dead by the glory of the Father, so we too might walk in newness of life. (Rom. 6:2-4)

The second conclusion is that, according to Paul, Christian existence is conformed to the sufferings and death of Christ. "In a unique train of thought" in Romans 6,[180] Paul maintains that, since Christ has died, the believers have died: they have been "crucified together with him" in the baptism that gives contemporaneity to the once-for-all event of Christ's death (Rom. 6:2, 6, 10). In other words, it is not Christ's dead body on the cross in which baptism gives a share. Nowhere does Paul speak of the believers' conformity in such a way, not even in I Corinthians 10:16. In that passage, the rhetorical question "The cup of blessing which we bless, is it not a sharing in the blood of Christ?" has its clarification in the parallel to follow: "The bread that we break, is it not a sharing in the body of Christ?" That is, since the "body of Christ" is always the body of the risen Lord, who nonetheless never ceases to be the Crucified, he is able to give his people a share in his blood, that is, draw them into the event of his death. He is thus not a cultic deity who makes himself known, nor is his death an event followed by a vacuum. Rather, it has become the sphere of the believers' life.[181]

In the *peristasen* catalogs, the lists in which Paul enumerates the sufferings and deprivations, distresses and dangers that mark Christian existence, he makes especially clear the inclusive significance of the suffering and dying of Christ.[182] In II Corinthians 4, which was presumably directed against an enthusiastic, false *pneuma*-theology, most of the characteristics of the catalogs appear:

> But we have this treasure in clay jars, so that it may be made clear that this extraordinary power belongs to God and does not come from us. We are afflicted in every way, but not crushed; perplexed, but not driven to despair; persecuted, but not forsaken; struck down, but not destroyed; always carrying in the body the death of Jesus, so that the

180. Egon Brandenburger, "*Stauros,* Kreuzigung Jesu und Kreuzestheologie," p. 40.

181. Cf. Brandenburger, p. 40; E. C. Hoskyns and Francis Noel Davey, *Crucifixion-Resurrection,* p. 189; Hübner, *Biblische Theologie des Neuen Testaments,* p. 184; Robert C. Tannehill, *Dying and Rising with Christ: A Study in Pauline Theology* (Berlin: Töpelmann, 1967), pp. 1, 80.

182. Schrage, "Leid, Kreuz und Eschaton," p. 158.

life of Jesus may also be made visible in our bodies. For while we live, we are always being given up to death for Jesus' sake, so that the life of Jesus may be made visible in our mortal flesh. (II Cor. 4:7-11)[183]

In Schrage's words, "the *peristasen* are the preferred site of the *theologia crucis,* in which the theology of the cross is extended and articulated in world- and historical-experience."[184]

On the other hand, Christology and "autobiography" are nowhere as intimately connected as in Paul's letter to the Philippians. Chapter 2 contains the Christ-hymn:

Christ Jesus, who, though he was in the form of God, did not regard equality with God as something to be exploited, but emptied himself, taking the form of a slave, being born in human likeness. And being found in human form, he humbled himself and became obedient to the point of death — even death on a cross. Therefore God also highly exalted him and gave him the name that is above every name. (Phil. 2:5-9)

Close on the heels of the hymn follows Paul's autobiography:

Circumcised on the eighth day, a member of the people of Israel, of the tribe of Benjamin, a Hebrew born of Hebrews; as to the law, a Pharisee; as to zeal, a persecutor of the church; as to righteousness under the law, blameless. Yet whatever gains I had, these I have come to regard as loss because of Christ. More than that, I regard everything as loss because of the surpassing value of knowing Christ Jesus my Lord. For his sake I have suffered the loss of all things. . . . I want to know Christ and the *power of his resurrection and the sharing of his sufferings* by becoming like him in his death. (Phil. 3:5-10; italics mine)

The hymn and the autobiography have the same parabola shape. At the zenith appears "in the form of God," or "under the law, blameless." At the nadir appears "obedient to the point of death," or "suffered the loss of all things." And, once more at the zenith, "highly exalted," or "I want to know Christ and the power of his resurrection." Clearly, the acting subject of the hymn and of the autobiography is the same: Jesus Christ.

183. Cf. also the catalogs in Romans 8 and II Corinthians 4, 6, 11, and 12.

184. Schrage, "Leid, Kreuz und Eschaton," p. 164; cf. also Kleinknecht, *Der leidende Gerechtfertigte,* p. 10.

And the mode of existence in both is the same: servanthood and suffering. It is the same because the earth remains the sphere of Christ's activity, whether in his humiliation or exaltation. Thus, while Paul lives, his existence is cruciform, for in this mode the crucified and risen Christ makes his appearance.

The idea of the believer's existence as conformed to the sufferings and death of Christ is echoed in the remainder of the New Testament. In the Synoptic Gospels, the first passion prediction makes explicit that not only must the Son of Man suffer, but the disciple must also be prepared to bear his cross (cf. Mark 8:34; Matt. 10:38; Luke 9:23, and the doublet in Matt. 16:24 and Luke 14:27). In Hebrews 13:12-13, the pattern of the Messiah and the pattern of discipleship are linked. Each must pass through a suffering intrinsic to obedience.

The third conclusion to be drawn from our observations is that what is said of Paul as the epiphany of Christ may be said of any believer. Only in II Corinthians 10–13 does he appear to assign his sufferings a special position, no doubt due to the situation that that portion of his correspondence reflects.[185] In every other instance, Paul does not single out the sufferings of Christ as the peculiar mark of his existence. In Romans 6:5, he says that through baptism (the *homoiōma,* or "likeness") believers have grown together into the shape of his death; and in Romans 8:16-17, he says that "we are children of God, and if children, then heirs . . . if, in fact, we suffer with him. . . ." When, in II Corinthians 1:3-7, he refers to "our affliction," to "the sufferings of Christ . . . abundant for us," to our "being afflicted," or to patiently enduring "the same sufferings that we are also suffering," it is clear that participation in Christ's death is a continuing aspect of the existence of the ordinary believer.[186] Even in II Corinthians 2:14–7:3, which has the apostolic office as its theme, "what characterizes the apostolic existence at bottom also gives to Christian existence as such its character."[187] No more can Galatians 2:19-20, with its "not I, but Christ," be limited to Paul's personal experience.[188] Even such an intensely personal reflection as appears in Galatians 6:17 ("I carry the marks of Jesus branded on my

185. Cf. Kleinknecht, *Der leidende Gerechtfertigte,* pp. 372-373.

186. Tannehill, *Dying and Rising with Christ,* pp. 86, 96, 98; Kleinknecht, *Der leidende Gerechtfertigte,* p. 246.

187. Schrage, "Leid, Kreuz und Eschaton," pp. 158-159.

188. Tannehill, p. 57.

body") is not the exclusive experience of one unusual individual but an example of how the preaching of the Good News works itself out in the life and service of the believer.[189] In Philippians 1:29-30, the apostle says that the "struggle" that his readers observed in him at their first meeting, and in which he is still engaged, is theirs as well since they have been granted "the privilege not only of believing in Christ but of suffering for him as well."[190] And of the Thessalonians he writes that they became "imitators of us and of the Lord" (I Thess. 1:6; cf. 2:14).[191]

To return to the Christ-hymn and the "autobiography" in Philippians 2 and 3, the exhortation that immediately precedes the hymn ("let the same mind be in you that was in Christ Jesus" [Phil. 2:5]) and that immediately follows the autobiography ("brothers and sisters, join in imitating me" [Phil. 3:17]) forms an *inclusio,* or frame, which suggests that Paul is not eager to reserve the epiphany of Christ for himself as the specific mark of his life or office. "What happens to the Redeemer, or happened while he tarried in human form on earth, happens to his whole *sōma.*"[192] In fact, the contrasts perforating the *peristasen* of I Corinthians 4:6-13 ("Already you have all you want! Already you have become rich! Quite apart from us you have become kings!") serve as an irony calculated to stun the readers into the consciousness that exactly the opposite is true. They, too, like Paul, are a

> spectacle to the world, to angels and to mortals . . . fools for the sake of Christ . . . weak . . . held in disrepute . . . hungry and thirsty . . . poorly clothed and beaten and homeless . . . weary from the work of [their] own hands . . . reviled . . . persecuted . . . slandered . . . become like the rubbish of the world, the dregs of all things.

Now the question arises as to how Paul conceives of the relationship between the crucified Christ and the believer. First of all, if his concept of conformity may be read against the background of the Stoic notion of the universe and everything in it as organism, or against the Gnostic notion,[193] we might just as legitimately appeal to the idea of "corporate per-

---

189. Cf. Cousar, "Paul and the Death of Jesus," p. 47.
190. Cf. Kleinknecht, *Der leidende Gerechtfertigte,* p. 310.
191. Cf. Luz, "Theologia crucis als Mitte der Theologie im Neuen Testament," p. 122.
192. Bultmann, *Theology of the New Testament,* I, 299.
193. In the preface to his *Dying and Rising with Christ,* Tannehill refers to the rele-

sonality" as illustrated in Hebrew prophetism, according to which a group is seen as incorporated in a single person. Thus, for example, Ezekiel addresses Israel as "the harlot" in chapter 16, and Second Isaiah speaks to "Zion" and "Jerusalem" (40), or to "Israel, my servant, Jacob whom I have chosen" (41), and so forth.[194] The idea of corporate personality is perhaps assumed whenever Scripture refers to the "people of God" or to Adam, "the primal ancestor," as extended to the body of humanity. Yet, as Käsemann insists, the New Testament offers no incontestable support for the idea, and the question about the extent to which it was still alive in primitive Christianity is unanswered.[195] More important is the ninety-year-old reminder of Traugott Schmidt that, for Paul, existence "in" is not automatic but occurs through faith. The synonymy of existing "in faith" and "in Christ" is amply illustrated in II Corinthians 13 and Galatians 2:

> Examine yourselves to see whether you are living *in the faith.* Test yourselves. Do you not realize that *Jesus Christ is in you?* (II Cor. 13:5; italics mine)

> It is *Christ who lives in me.* And *the life I now live* in the flesh *I live by faith in the Son of God.* (Gal. 2:20; italics mine)

Equally important is Schmidt's conclusion that what can be referenced of "corporate personality" in the Old Testament and Judaism does not extend beyond isolated poetic comparison.[196]

Second, to read Paul's understanding of the believer's conformity

---

vance of Gnostic material for understanding certain aspects of Paul's use of the idea of Christ as inclusive *anthrōpos,* and Bultmann says of Paul's concept of union with Christ that it is conceived "in the cosmological terminology of Gnosticism, but factually accomplished by the decision of faith" (*Theology of the New Testament,* I, 351). On the other hand, E. Kamlah regards Paul's idea of the sufferings of Christ now at work in him as prefigured in the suffering righteous ones of the Old Testament ("Wie beurteilt Paulus sein Leiden? Ein Beitrag zur Untersuchung seiner Denkstruktur," *Zeitschrift für neutestamentliche Wissenschaft* 54 [1963], 228).

194. Cf. Tannehill, p. 29.

195. Käsemann, *Commentary on Romans,* p. 337.

196. Traugott Schmidt, *Der Leib Christi: Eine Untersuchung zum urchristlichen Gemeindegedanken* (Leipzig: A. Deichert'sche Verlagsbuchhandlung, 1919), pp. 114, 128. In George Steiner's novel *The Portage to San Cristobal of A. H.,* the protagonist exclaims: "It is not poetry, Rolf, that has produced the most vivid fictions or complex metaphors!" (New York: Simon and Schuster, 1981), p. 127.

to the Crucified in terms of "imitation" has sanction elsewhere in the New Testament, as well as in a long history of Christian interpretation. To his readers, the author of I Peter says:

> For to this you have been called, because Christ also suffered for you, leaving you an example, that you should follow in his steps. (I Pet. 2:21)

In the earliest account of Christian martyrdom outside the New Testament, that of Polycarp of Smyrna (ca. 156 C.E.), his biographer says that the martyr "waited to be betrayed as also the Lord had done, that we too might become his imitators."[197] Ignatius, Tertullian, Origen, and Ludolph the Saxon (ca. 1377),[198] down to the perennial bestseller by Charles M. Sheldon (1857-1946),[199] all counsel the necessity of imitating Christ.

To return to the "autobiography," the use of the passive voice throughout makes clear that the apostle is not describing himself as the actor but as the one acted upon: "For his sake I have suffered the loss of all things" (3:8); "and be found in him" (3:9); and "becoming like him in his death" (3:10) — the clumsy translation of a phrase completely at odds with the notion of adopting a likeness at will *(symmorphizomenos tǭ thanatǭ autou)*. And however the "sharing of his sufferings" in verse 10 may be construed, its place in the context indicates that the sharing is not self-chosen and thus does not remain within the limits of the moral.[200] The same is true of the final verse in the autobiography: "If somehow I may attain the resurrection from the dead." For if Christ is the acting subject of the hymn *and* autobiography, then that "if somehow" cannot refer to anything that Paul must

---

197. *The Apostolic Fathers,* The Loeb Library of Classics, trans. Kirsopp Lake (New York: G. P. Putnam's Sons, 1930), Vol. II, *The Martyrdom of St. Polycarp, Bishop of Smyrna,* Book I, paras. 1-2, p. 313.

198. Cf. the relevant references in Sloyan, *The Crucifixion of Jesus,* pp. 123, 128, 140.

199. Since its first printing, Sheldon's *In His Steps* (New York: Wilbur B. Ketcham, 1896), has sold more than 300 million copies.

200. Though Bultmann interprets the *koinōnia tōn pathēmatōn autou* as "factually accomplished by the decision of faith," he is adamant in opposition to its being "artificially induced by an *imitatio*" (see *Theology of the New Testament,* I, 351); cf. also Walter von Loewenich, *Luther's Theology of the Cross,* trans. Herbert J. A. Bouman (Minneapolis: Augsburg, 1976), pp. 109-110.

achieve, or a mandate he must fulfill, but refers to the ever-present possibility of *losing* what he had gained, that is, the "surpassing value of knowing Christ Jesus my Lord," a righteousness "through faith in Christ" (3:8-9). Furthermore, Paul's summons to his readers to "join in imitating me" is not an appeal to follow Jesus as a model,[201] nor even consciously to imitate the apostle, but rather to show the power of the gospel at work in their lives so that a clear pattern results.[202] In his variation on *Communion of the Christian with God* by Wilhelm Herrmann (1846-1922), Kähler says that what is at issue is Christ's constant activity by which he mediates his life to those who are his. "There is no doubt," he adds, "this presence in our hearts is the presence of the Risen and Living One."[203]

Third, in II Corinthians 3:18, one verse beyond the favorite of G. F. W. Hegel (1770-1831),[204] Paul speaks in a way that may be interpreted as eliminating the difference between Christ and the believer,[205] as conceiving them in terms of their "natural consubstantiality." The idea has had a long history, reaching as far back as the mystics, with

---

201. Cf. Fleinert-Jensen, *Das Kreuz und die Einheit der Kirche,* p. 48.

202. Note Tannehill's references to Philo's use of the term *mimeomai* so as to exclude conscious imitation in any literal sense (*Dying and Rising with Christ,* p. 103; cf. also pp. 100, 104, 111). Referring to Jesus' word about discipleship in Matthew 16:24, Gerhard Koch says that it does not read "whoever does not take up *my* cross," but "whoever does not take up *his* cross and follow me cannot be my disciple." Discipleship of Jesus, therefore, cannot simply be an "imitatio." Cf. Koch, "Kreuzestod und Kreuzestheologie," *Herder Korrespondenz* 29 (1973), 151.

203. Martin Kähler, *Der Verkehr des Christen mit Christus* (Korntaler), ed. Hans Brandenburg und Fritz Grünzweig (Stuttgart-Hohenheim: Hänssler Verlag, n.d.), p. 125.

204. II Corinthians 3:17: "Now the Lord is the Spirit, and where the Spirit of the Lord is, there is freedom."

205. "All of us, with unveiled faces . . . are being transformed into the same image from one degree of glory to another." In this connection, Hübner attempts to free Bultmann of the age-old charge of altering theology into anthropology by saying that, although *beginning* with anthropology, theology is clearly Bultmann's goal, that at the preliminary stage of his inquiry Bultmann's question is whether or not the human is capable of receiving the divine revelation or whether the idea of revelation is such a mythological notion that demythologizing requires its surrender. If the latter, then bid farewell to the dialectical theology of Barth, to its existential variant in the theology of Bultmann, and even to Wolfhart Pannenberg's attempt to replace a theology of direct revelation with a theology of indirect revelation through history (see Hübner, *Biblische Theologie des Neuen Testaments,* I, 203-205).

their concept of salvation as a union of "generic likes." Johannes Tauler (1300?-1361) and Jean de Gerson (1363-1429), for example, could speak of a "spark of soul" *(synteresis rationis et voluntatis)* that is eternally one with God, which not even the Fall could erase. And it may even be that Bernard of Clairvaux (1090-1153) could conceive only of a corporate Christ, the head and the members, never of a redeemer with a past amenable to investigation.[206] Hundreds of years later, all of a sudden, in a discussion of the parable of the two sons in Luke 15, Johann Peter Lange, David Friedrich Strauss's replacement at Zürich, writes of the apparent contrast between the two, then adds that, on closer inspection, there emerges from the elder brother's "hidden *Seelengrund*" features of the same prodigality for which the younger is reproached.[207]

Such a view, however, would not only ignore the use of the phrase to denote the community *together* with its head, but would also ignore the "personal-differential" reflected in what the Pauline "autobiography" omits from the hymn. Paul could say of himself:

> . . . circumcised on the eighth day, a member of the people of Israel, of the tribe of Benjamin, a Hebrew born of Hebrews; as to the law, a Pharisee; as to zeal, a persecutor of the church; as to righteousness under the law, blameless . . . (3:5-6)

but obviously not:

> . . . who was in the form of God (2:6). . . . God also highly exalted him, [etc.] (2:9-11)

206. Cf. Sloyan, *The Crucifixion of Jesus*, p. 135. Joachim Jeremias's designation of Christ in Ephesians 2:15; 4:24, and Colossians 3:10, as "the new man absolutely" tends in the same direction; cf. his article on "Ἄνθρωπος," *Theological Dictionary of the New Testament*, I, 365. The NRSV likewise translates the simple, generic term *anthrōpos* in the phrase *kainos anthrōpos* as "the new humanity" or "new self." But cf. the following sentences from Bernard: ". . . this is the principal reason why the invisible God willed to be seen in the flesh and to converse with men as a man. He wanted to recapture the affections of carnal men who were unable to love in any other way, by first drawing them to the salutary love of his own humanity . . ." (cited in Dennis E. Tamburello, *Union with Christ: John Calvin and the Mysticism of St. Bernard* [Louisville: Westminster John Knox Press, 1994], p. 74).

207. Johann Peter Lange, *Das Leben Jesu nach den Evangelien*, vol. 2, *Die einheitliche Darstellung der Geschichte des Lebens Jesu*, part 3 (Heidelberg: Universitätsbuchhandlung von Karl Winter, 1844), p. 381.

and he could only await as hope what had already occurred to Christ:

> . . . if somehow I may attain the resurrection from the dead. (3:11)

In a history written from the perspective of "co-inherence," that is, of the natural world's reconciliation with the world of God's kingdom, Charles Williams gives this setting to Ignatius' last word, "My Eros is crucified":

> He who is *Theos* is *Anthropos,* and all the images of *anthropos* are in him. The Eros that is crucified lives again, and the Eros lives after a new style: this was the discovery of the operation of faith.

"Not," Williams adds, in the word of the Athanasian Creed, "by conversion of the Godhead into flesh but by taking of the manhood into God."[208]

The question as to how Paul conceives the believer's conformity with Christ requires another framework. Aside from the "poetic" or the metaphorical, existence "in" does not come about through imitation of Christ as model or prototype, nor through an absorption in Christ's passion, cultically experienced and resulting in something physically induced — an imitation and mystical absorption that leaves the conditions of this world unchanged and erases the difference in time and person between Christ and the believer. Rather, it is by his divine power that the risen and exalted one makes his epiphany in those who are his, and in cruciform shape.[209] This means that the framework within which Paul sets his references to union with Christ is eschatological. The Jewish ceremonial washings that betokened an inner purity by which the priest could minister in the temple, or that involved the reinstatement of unclean persons or the initiation of proselytes into the community, did not convey the believer into the presence of a heavenly reality, nor did

---

208. Charles Williams, *Descent of the Dove* (New York: Living Age Books, 1956), pp. 46, 59, 235. Also, by contrast, Luther recognized that the believer's union with God is simultaneously the full recognition of one's unlikeness and opposition to God, and in a footnote on one of Tauler's sermons he substituted the word "faith" for *Seelengrund;* cf. Stephen Pfürtner, "Die Paradigmen von Thomas von Aquin und Martin Luther," in *Theologie-wohin? Auf dem Weg zu einem neuen Paradigma,* ed. H. Küng, D. Tracy (Mainz: Matthias Grünewald, 1988), pp. 168-192.

209. Cf. Käsemann, *Commentary on Romans,* pp. 225, 231-232.

they bring that reality to earth. According to Paul, the "newness of life" that Christ accomplished in the believer on the basis of his union with him in baptism denoted the presence of the heavenly reality within the believer's present existence. Similarly, there is no congruence of Paul's idea with events in the mysteries.[210] In the latter, the myth is timeless, the alternation of dying and rising is continually repeated; but according to Paul, Jesus' death and the baptism "in" Christ has to do with an unrepeatable fact. It is because the cross is an eschatological and inclusive event that the temporal-historical distance between his death and the believers' union with him does not separate but collapses.[211] Furthermore, the various terms joined with the prefix *(syn)* in Romans 6 and 8 do not affirm the initiate's deification, as in the mysteries.[212] Contrary to knowledge gained through mystical experience or vision, or to a union taking place via the external act of baptism, it is the death of Jesus that "in its once-for-allness . . . extends into the present."[213] It is the effect of the cross that the old self and old world are destroyed, and this is the reason why Paul can say that the believer has died with Christ. And it is the effect of the cross that induces Paul to use "corporate patterns of thought" to express its significance for Christian existence.[214]

Later, the author of Ephesians will highlight the connection between Christ's death and the new, believing existence. In Ephesians 2:14-15 he describes the old condition of life prevailing among Jews and Greeks as a reciprocal "hostility" produced by the "dividing wall" of Israel's exclusivity. In Christ's "flesh," that is, in his death, what formerly separated the two was abolished, and "one new humanity" created "in himself" — not merely a union of two formerly hostile parties, but a new "man" different from any other — totally reconciled to God. In retrospection on this event, the author can speak of Christ as "our peace."

---

210. Cf. Friedrich, *Die Verkündigung des Todes Jesu im Neuen Testament,* p. 90.

211. Cf. Friedrich, p. 89.

212. Romans 6:4: *syntaphō;* 6:5: *symphytoi;* 6:6: *systauromai;* 8:17: *synklēronomos, sympaschō, syndoxazō;* 8:26: *synantilambanō;* 8:29: *symmorphos.*

213. Cf. Friedrich, p. 89. Alois Stöger's definition of baptism as occurring "under the veil of cult-symbolic appearance which makes it possible for the believer himself to cooperate in the divine deed" comes perilously close to the Hellenistic view (see "Die Christologie der Paulinischen und von Paulus abhängigen Briefe," p. 179).

214. Tannehill, *Dying and Rising with Christ,* p. 126.

Finally, this life with Christ is hidden. However the new, eschatological existence may be defined, its hallmark is that of hiddenness.[215] And the event that establishes such hiddenness is the cross by which God made his appearance under the sign of its opposite. Here lies the contrast with Jewish apocalyptic, for which visibility is the hallmark, or with systems such as Stoicism, according to which the ideal is visibly achieved in a moral progression (which is why the Stoic needs an audience). It is this hiddenness that renders the "imperative" both command and promise: command because the Christian still lives in this world, and promise because Christ, who is the believer's life, will someday be Lord of all. The promise, however, is the beating heart of the imperative. As the epiphany of the Incarnate Christ, what believers are will someday be known to them and to all: "For the creation waits with eager longing for the revealing of the children of God" (Rom. 8:19). Hence, for Paul, the answer to the question of the relationship between believing and doing is that the subject of life, of existence, is the incarnate, crucified Lord, whose death establishes the mode of the cruciform as the mark of conformity with him. Thus Paul "presses on," not by ordering his life to a standard or extrinsic decree but "because Christ Jesus has made me his own" (Phil. 3:12), or, as he promises the Philippians at the close of his letter, because "God will fully satisfy every need of yours according to his riches in glory in Christ Jesus" (Phil. 4:19). The distance between believing and doing is thus not bridged by an imperative to which one responds as to an external command. The distance lies first of all in the nature of what God has given: himself, pressing toward a consummation yet to come. This is precisely what the Pauline imperatives intend to make clear — as offering the possibilities of the new life. God's will shall be done, because another is the subject of life. And it is precisely the nature of what God has given that the acceptance of suffering cannot imply a sanctioning of the status quo. As Karl Theodor Kleinknecht says, the Pauline texts neither give flat theological justification to sufferings nor speak of "God's reconciliation with misery." Rather, because they reflect on suffering from the perspective of the relationship to Christ — and link its sense to that relationship — what results is a battle against suffering and death.[216]

---

215. Tannehill, p. 74.

216. Kleinknecht, *Der leidende Gerechtfertigte,* p. 386; cf. Schrage, "Leid, Kreuz und Eschaton," p. 156.

CHAPTER THREE

The Death of Jesus in Mark

The Scheme

There have been variations without number on the theme of Mark's purpose with his Gospel. Was the purpose apologetic? Did he, for example, superimpose the "messianic secret" on the Jesus tradition in order to convince his readers that none recognized Jesus' identity during his lifetime because he traveled incognito?[1] Or does his Gospel perhaps combine an unmessianic tradition of the "life" of Jesus with the church's Christological confession in order to win a pre-Easter Jesus community for the churchly kerygma?[2] Preoccupation with such questions may reflect captivity to one or all of the illusions Paul Ricoeur describes as attaching to the historical-critical method — the illusions of source, author, and addressee.[3] In any event, for the majority of interpreters, the orientation of Mark's Gospel to the death of Jesus of Nazareth is a fact too difficult — or impossible — to deny.

The formal structure of the Gospel itself yields evidence of its orientation. When one reads the Gospel from end to beginning, that is, from Jesus' cry of dereliction on the cross in 15:34 to the report of John the Baptist's arrest in 1:14, the death motif is easily recognizable as a

1. Cf. William Wrede, *The Messianic Secret,* trans. J. C. G. Greig (Cambridge, UK: J. Clarke, 1971 [first published in German in 1901]).

2. Cf., e.g., Walter Schmithals, "Kein Streit um des Kaisers Bart," *Evangelische Kommentare* 2 (1970), 80-82.

3. Paul Ricoeur, "Du Conflit à la Convergence des Méthodes en Exégèse Biblique," *Exégèse et Herméneutique,* ed. Leon-Dufour (Paris: Seuil, 1971), pp. 36, 291-293.

constant. The motif is clearly present in chapter 14, opening with the hierarchs' plot and Judas' intent to betray, which frame the Bethany anointing, continuing with the resolve of the chief priests to put Jesus to death as the prelude to the Sanhedrin hearing, and ending with Peter's denial. In the Last Supper scene in 14:22-25, Jesus interprets his death as salvific for the first time. As for chapter 13, or the "Little Apocalypse," more than fifty years ago, R. H. Lightfoot (1883-1953) successfully demonstrated its close ties with chapters 14 and 15 in terms of proximity, motifs, and usage.[4] The insertion of the eschatological discourse in chapter 13 within the context of the passion makes clear that the time of Jesus up to the *parousia* is determined by his death.[5] Immediately before the prophecy of the appearing of the Son of Man in power (13:26-37), chapter 12, with its parable of the vineyard, concludes with the intention of Jesus' hearers to arrest him (12:1-12). On the occasion of the temple-cleansing in chapter 11, the chief priests and scribes look for a way to kill him (11:18). Chapter 10 contains the third passion prediction (10:32-34): there Jesus, for the second time, interprets his death as saving (10:45). Chapter 9 contains the second prediction following the event of the Transfiguration (9:30-32). In contrast to the other two predictions,[6] its simple reference to the Son of Man's betrayal "into human hands" may reflect authentic Jesus material. Chapter 8 contains the first prediction, following Peter's confession at Caesarea Philippi, together with Peter's attempt to remove Jesus from suffering, which Jesus fends off as if it were a satanic temptation (8:31-33). The death motif is less clearly sounded in chapter 7, but may still be heard in the reference to the "spies" from Jerusalem, who embroil Jesus in a debate over the tradition (7:1-15). Chapter 6 records Jesus' rejection at Nazareth, as well as the Baptist's death — an event that Mark reports as an omen of what will later happen to Jesus. Chapter 5, with its report of drownings (5:13), of a

4. R. H. Lightfoot, "The Connexion of Chapter Thirteen with the Passion Narrative," in *The Gospel Message of St. Mark* (Oxford: Clarendon Press, 1950), pp. 48-59.

5. Hans Conzelmann, "Historie und Theologie in den synoptischen Passionsberichten," in *Zur Bedeutung des Todes Jesu*, p. 45.

6. Cf. Mark 8:31: "Then he began to teach them that the Son of Man must undergo great suffering, and be rejected by the elders, the chief priests, and the scribes, and be killed, and after three days rise again"; see also Mark 10:33: "See, we are going up to Jerusalem, and the Son of Man will be handed over to the chief priests and the scribes, and they will condemn him to death; then they will hand him over to the Gentiles."

child at the point of death (5:23), of a woman suffering from hemorrhage (5:25), and of the child's raising (5:41-42), simply enhances the motif.

Of all the chapters in the Gospel, chapter 4 least clearly reflects the death motif, though the word of Isaiah, echoed in Jesus' explanation of the parables, ends with the prediction of cities laid waste and a land utterly desolate (Isa. 6:9-13).[7] In chapter 3, following two Sabbath conflicts, the Pharisees and Herodians resolve to put Jesus to death; the same chapter contains the first reference to Judas, with its ominous relative clause, "who betrayed him" (3:19). In chapter 2, Jesus first responds to the question about fasting in the bridegroom logion with the words "the wedding guests cannot fast while the bridegroom is with them, can they?" and ending with the prediction that "the days will come when the bridegroom is taken away from them, and then they will fast on that day" (2:20). If Jesus' disciples may be identified with the "wedding guests" (the meaning of the Greek is "sons of the bridechamber" [v. 19]), the identity of "the bridegroom" cannot be in doubt, however oblique. Finally, in chapter 1, the verb "I hand over" or "betray" *(paradidōmi)* is used for the arrest of John the Baptist; with only two exceptions (4:19 and 7:13), this verb will be used only of Judas' betrayal, Jesus' passion, or the passion of his disciples predicted in 13:9, 11, and 12.

Whether or not the earliest Gospel is an apology for the scandal of the cross, written for those who were perplexed by the death of Jesus or possibly even offended by it[8] (pace Gottfried Schille[9]), suiting the Jesus tradition to Jesus' suffering and dying is "the authentic theological performance of Mark."[10]

---

7. "Go and say to this people: 'Keep listening, but do not comprehend; keep looking, but do not understand.' Make the mind of this people dull, and stop their ears, and shut their eyes, so that they may not look with their eyes, and listen with their ears, and comprehend with their minds, and turn and be healed . . . until cities lie waste without inhabitant, and houses without people, and the land is utterly desolate . . ." (Isa. 6:9-13).

8. Hooker, *Not Ashamed of the Gospel,* p. 48.

9. "Two things I cannot at all recognize: that Mark has laid the foundation for his theology in his adaptation of the passion story, and that he wanted to set forth a passion narrative extended rearwards. . . . Mark has recognized and evaluated the theological ideas decisive for the passion narrative only by-the-by" (*Offen für alle Menschen,* p. 77).

10. Luz, "Theologia crucis als Mitte der Theologie im Neuen Testament," p. 132.

Old Testament Theology

Use and Fracture of the Servant Motif

Many have seen in Mark's Gospel the reflection of early Jewish theology[11] as contained in Deutero-Isaiah's description of the Servant of God. There is no doubt that Mark's passion narrative "bulges"[12] with features reminiscent of the Fourth Servant Song (Isa. 52:13–53:12), and that it is penetrated by the idea of the Servant to a greater degree than the Gospels of his coevangelists.[13] The description of the Servant's "pouring out himself to death," or the Lord's laying on him "the iniquity of us all" in Isaiah 53:6, 12, *could be* echoed in the statement about Jesus' going "as it is written of him," or in his word at the Last Supper about his blood as "poured out for many" (Mark 14:21, 24), perhaps even in the exchange of Jesus with Barabbas (15:6-15). Zechariah's and Second Isaiah's references to the striking of the shepherd and the scattering of the sheep (Zech. 13:7; Isa. 53:6) *could* be repeated in Jesus' prediction that all would become deserters: "For it is written, 'I will strike the shepherd,

11. Cf. Gottfried Schille, *Offen für alle Menschen: Redaktionsgeschichtliche Beobachtungen zur Theologie des Markus-Evangeliums* (Stuttgart: Calwer, 1974), p. 77; Christian Maurer, "Knecht Gottes und Sohn Gottes im Passionsbericht des Markusevangeliums," in *Redaktion und Theologie,* p. 132.

12. Dennis Macdonald, *The Homeric Epics and the Gospel of Mark* (New Haven: Yale University Press, 2000), p. 16.

13. Cf. Christian Maurer, "Knecht Gottes und Sohn Gottes im Passionsbericht nach den Synoptikern," p. 117; August Strobel, "Die Deutung des Todes Jesu im ältesten Evangelium," in *Das Kreuz Jesu,* pp. 46, 50; Maurer, arguing that the Marcan tradition, with its Suffering Servant, belongs to an older layer than the tradition underlying Matthew and Luke, sees the Servant idea reflected in the report of Jesus' temptation, in his transfiguration, in the cry of the demon-possessed at Capernaum, in the absence of the term "Son" (= "Servant") in Peter's skewed confession, and in Jesus' confession before the high council ("Knecht Gottes und Sohn Gottes," pp. 133, 142, 144, 146-148). Despite Hooker's "demolition of the argument" (with "virtual silence resulting") that Mark or his coevangelists were in any way influenced by the figure of the Servant, her suggestion that the idea of the Servant may lie behind Mark 10:45 is sufficient concession to inhibit demolition. If the intention is to challenge the tradition of the Servant as a unilinear phenomenon moving into the New Testament with *heilsgeschichtlich* necessity from the Old, other factors serve that end. See Morna Hooker, *Jesus and the Servant,* pp. 89, 94, 159; William L. Schutter, *Hermeneutic and Composition in I Peter,* Wissenschaftliche Untersuchungen zum Neuen Testament, 2nd series (Tübingen: J. C. B. Mohr, 1989), pp. 138-139.

and the sheep will be scattered'" (Mark 14:27). Jesus' silence before the high priest and Pilate (14:61; 15:4-5) *could* echo the Servant, who, like a sheep before its shearers, "did not open his mouth" (Isa. 53:7); the recital of the indignities Jesus endured at the hands of his captors in Mark 14:65 *could* be reminiscent of the Servant's report in the Third Servant Song.[14] Jesus' crucifixion between two thieves (Mark 15:27) urges comparison with the Servant's being "numbered with the transgressors" in Isaiah 53:12. Finally, the confession of the centurion beneath the cross (Mark 15:39) *could* reflect Isaiah's statement of the Servant as startling "many nations," of kings shutting their mouths "because of him" (Isa. 52:15); and the burial in the rock-hewn tomb narrated in Mark 15:42-47 *could* be reminiscent of the Servant's making his grave with the rich (Isa. 53:9).

What would have moved the evangelist to cast Jesus in this role is the Servant's intimate relationship with God: his suffering understood as obedience toward God, firmly grounded in God's will and plan to atone, thus rendering God transparent.[15] In other words, Mark *could* foot on a tradition determined by the proof from the prophecy in Isaiah 53.[16] The Servant idea may thus have been present at the beginning of the Jesus tradition. This leads Christian Maurer to suggest that the idea, if not in all details, goes back to Jesus himself.[17]

I have already noted the distance between the New Testament and late Jewish interpretation of the Isaian Servant. Whether that interpretation construed the *Eved* as a collective, as Joachim Jeremias argued,[18] or as an individual, or was not limited to one or the other, Judaism's politicization of the figure, its silencing or restricting of his suffering to the despising of his royal mien or to his impatience in paradise, and finally its splitting him

14. Isa. 50:6: "I gave my back to those who struck me, and my cheeks to those who pulled out the beard; I did not hide my face from insult and spitting."

15. Maurer ("Knecht Gottes und Sohn Gottes," pp. 114-115) argues that Mark 15:28, with its reference to the fulfillment of Scripture in Jesus' crucifixion between two thieves, does not belong to the original text, but, together with Jesus' words to his captors (14:48-49), clearly alludes to Isa. 53:12 in a form suggestive of an older tradition that is traceable to the Hebrew text and birthed in the attempt to move from a *de facto* to a *de verbo* Scripture proof (pp. 119, 128).

16. Cf. Strobel, "Die Deutung des Todes Jesu im ältesten Evangelium," p. 58.

17. Maurer, pp. 120, 129, 145-146.

18. Cf. Joachim Jeremias, "παῖς θεοῦ," in *Theological Dictionary of the New Testament*, V, 683-684.

in two — the first come to wage war for a second to appear in kingly glory — have little to do with Mark's suffering and dying Christ.

Research on the Old Testament and Jewish background of the passion narrative often links the Isaian Servant and the concept of the righteous one, who atones by his suffering, thus assigning Judaism an idea reflected in the Gospel accounts. Hans-Ruedi Weber says that, when the early church searched the Old Testament for key texts to interpret the crucifixion, it soon discovered the significance of Isaiah 53. He adds that the discovery was facilitated by a link already forged in the intertestamental period between the Isaian passage and Psalm texts dealing with the suffering righteous one.[19] Ten years later, Kleinknecht said that, in the earliest Christian formation of the tradition, Jesus' suffering and death were interpreted and articulated by way of the concept of the suffering righteous one along with that of the servant of God.[20] Twenty years later, Wolfgang Reinbold said that the central Old Testament interpretive category of the earliest passion narrative underlying the Gospel accounts, and particularly Mark's, is the category of the "suffering Righteous One."[21]

If, however, that late Jewish idea of the righteous sufferer has its deposit in the evangelical tradition and thus in Mark,[22] one aspect of Mark's narrative severs the link, setting the idea of the righteous sufferer's atonement adrift from a connection with the Servant. The Fourth Book of Maccabees contains two passages about the righteous sufferer that have been identified as closest to the theology of Mark. The first records the prayer of the priest Eleazar, who was put to the rack and thrown in the fire for his refusal to eat unclean food:

> "You know, O God, that though I could have saved myself I am dying in these fiery torments for the sake of the Law. Be merciful to your people and let our punishment be a satisfaction on their behalf. Make my blood their purification and take my life as a ransom for theirs." (IV Macc. 6:27-29)

The second describes the martyrdom of the seven sons and their mother under the tyrant Antiochus Epiphanes (175-164 B.C.E.):

19. Weber, *Kreuz*, p. 95.
20. Kleinknecht, *Der leidende Gerechtfertigte,* pp. 178, 195.
21. Wolfgang Reinbold, *Der älteste Bericht über den Tod Jesu,* pp. 200-201.
22. Cf. Weber, *Kreuz*, p. 174.

These then, having consecrated themselves for the sake of God, are now honored not only with this distinction but also by the fact that through them our enemies did not prevail against our nation, and the tyrant was punished and our land purified, since they became, as it were, a ransom for the sin of our nation. Through the blood of these righteous ones and through the propitiation of their death the divine providence rescued Israel, which had been shamefully treated. (IV Macc. 17:20-22)[23]

Aside from the fact that these martyrs' deaths were due to their faithfulness to the law, and thus atoned for their own sins, the atonement achieved for others is restricted to the nation and people of Israel. For Mark, however, the death of Jesus is his surrender to the nations, as the second passion prediction ("the Son of Man is to be betrayed into human hands") and the phrase "for many" *(hyper pollōn)* in the words of the Supper make clear (Mark 9:31; 14:24). As if to emphasize this universal effect, Mark's Gospel does not separate but rather couples the roles of the Jewish and Roman authorities, thus overstepping the limits of Jewish trial legislation and of the Jewish nation, despite the fact that everything occurs in the city of God.[24]

Use and Fracture of Apocalyptic

Many have noted the presence of apocalyptic thought in Mark's Gospel; in it Jesus at once emerges as the "stronger one" in the struggle with evil. Following John the Baptist's announcement in 1:7 ("the one who is more powerful than I is coming after me") and the laconic reference to the wilderness struggle in 1:12-13, the first deed Mark reports is Jesus' exorcism of the unclean spirit in the Capernaum synagogue. From that point onward, Mark's Gospel abounds in narratives of Jesus' conflicts with

---

23. *The Old Testament Pseudepigrapha,* II, 552, 563.

24. Cf. George Strecker, "Die Leidens- und Auferstehungsvoraussagen im Markusevangelium," *ZThK* 64, No. 1 (1967), p. 34; Schille, *Offen für alle Menschen,* pp. 79-80; Maurer, "Knecht Gottes und Sohn Gottes," pp. 117, 129-131. Maurer argues that, since the idea of the Servant's suffering is not — as in Maccabees — an addition to the supererogatory suffering for others, Mark's Gospel has less affinity with these late Jewish parallels than with Isa. 53 (cf. p. 131).

dark and evil forces, from which he always emerges the victor. James M. Robinson refers to what he calls the "cosmic language" of Mark, which exceeds the immanence of human interaction, and he refers to the "transcendent cosmic and spirit-world forces at work in history." When it occurs within the body of the Gospel, Robinson says, this language does not detract from the bulk of the narrative but actually advances the historical action.[25]

Whatever its conclusions, the Marcan portrait of Jesus involved in cosmic struggle has its antecedents in Jewish apocalyptic thought. In this kind of thought, reflection on the messianic age or the end-time becomes "the universal horizon of theology as a whole,"[26] and it is marked by the use of a peculiar, discrete treasury of symbols from which one generation after another might draw.

Mark's use of the impersonal *dei* in the first passion prediction ("the Son of Man *must* undergo great suffering" [Mark 8:31]) and in the "little apocalypse" ("this *must* take place" [Mark 13:7]), a use that becomes thematic in Luke, is a circumlocution for "God has willed it." The usage has its stimulus in an apocalyptic eschatology for which a fixing of times was essential. Accordingly, the time for the appearance of God's kingdom — of the Messiah or the end of the world — was seen as determined beforehand.[27]

25. James M. Robinson, *The Problem of History in Mark* (London: SCM Press, 1957), cf. pp. 35-42, 49-53; cf. also his earlier "Mark's Understanding of History," *The Scottish Journal of Theology* (1956), 8.

26. Jürgen Moltmann, *Theology of Hope,* trans. James W. Leitch (New York: Harper & Row, 1965), pp. 325-329.

27. The verb appears in an apocalyptic context in the *Testament of Naphtali* 7:1, in Testaments of the Twelve Patriarchs, I, 813; and in *Apocalypsis Henochi Graece* 9:11, in *Fragmenta Pseudepigraphorum Quae Supersunt Graeca,* ed. M. Black (Leiden: E. J. Brill, 1970), III, 24. This view of happenings as determined is reflected throughout the literature of Qumran. According to the War Rule, the day when the "Sons of darkness" fall is "appointed from ancient times" (1:9b, 10; cf. 13:14b, 15). The Commentary on Habakkuk refers to all the ages of God as reaching their "appointed end" (7:13f.), and the Community Rule (3:15) refers to the Master who instructs the sons of light regarding their "visitation for chastisement, and the time of their reward." This peculiarly apocalyptic view is especially clear in the Thanksgiving Hymn: "In their ages Thou hast allotted to (the earth's inhabitants) tasks during all their generations, and judgement in their appointed seasons according to the rule [of the two spirits. For Thou hast established their ways] for ever and ever, [and hast ordained from eternity] their visitation for reward and chastisements; Thou hast allotted it to all their seed for eternal genera-

Next, since 1864 scholars have given varying degrees of assent to the hypothesis that a Jewish apocalyptic leaflet underlies the "Little Apocalypse" of Mark 13:3-37. Aside from the question of the leaflet's original occasion and its possible revision at Mark's (or another's) hand, the widest ripple in the pond is the chapter's reflection on the return of Christ and its use of imagery at home in Jewish apocalyptic theology. The disciples' question and Jesus' response in verses 3-8 echo Jewish expectation of the tribulation, or "Woes of the Messiah," preceding the end. The false messiahs are introduced by a phrase calculated to recall the Old Testament oracles of Yahweh (v. 6: "I am he"). The theme of martyrdom in verses 9-13 reflects Jewish expectation of persecution as belonging to the "Footsteps of the Messiah."

At the head of Mark 13:14-23 appears the prophecy of the "desolating sacrilege" *(to bdelygma tēs erēmōseōs)*. The phrase translates a code name *(Shiqquts Shomem)* that appears in Daniel's prophecy of the destruction of Jerusalem and its sanctuary prior to the end:

> From the time that the regular burnt offering is taken away and the abomination that desolates is set up, there shall be one thousand two hundred ninety days. (Dan. 12:11; cf. 9:27, and 11:31)

Verses 24-27, with their picture of the Son of Man gathering his elect (vs. 27), echo another word from Daniel (Dan. 7:13). The section contains nothing that could not appear in Jewish apocalyptic thought. Finally, set within a cluster of sayings in verses 28-37, Jesus' disclaimer regarding knowledge of the coming of the Son of Man answers precisely to Jewish apocalyptic thought, which is characterized by a curious contradiction between the exact fixing of a date for the end (cf. Mark 9:1) and ignorance of its arrival. However truncated or dissociated these themes, they have their origin in apocalyptic expectation.

Usually the link between the passion narrative and chapter 13 is seen as forged from the passion narrative toward chapter 13, and not the other way around — in concert with the understanding of the cross as the point of orientation of Mark's Gospel. The result is that the "ambiguous" character of the apocalyptic perspective is removed through the

---

tions and everlasting years. . . . In the wisdom of Thy knowledge Thou didst establish their destiny before ever they were" (IQH I, 13-20, in Geza Vermes, *The Dead Sea Scrolls in English*, p. 191).

reference to the historical event of the cross. But if Mark is in any way dependent on the apocalyptic perspective, the relationship between chapter 13 and the passion narrative may be that of a two-way street, though the one is less wide than the other. The passion narrative takes on, through that link, the apocalyptic flavor.

Käsemann insists that the earliest Christian community regarded apocalyptic thought as the most appropriate expression of the fact that in Jesus the ultimate promise of the world appears.[28] In that case, Mark's portrait of Jesus as "the Stronger One," victor in the cosmic struggle with evil, is an offspring of "the mother of Christian theology." But there is sufficient evidence to indicate the Gospel's correction — or even fracture — of the apocalyptic perspective. For example, if Jesus' self-designation as "Son of Man" is reminiscent of the figure of the end-time in Daniel 7:13 and Enoch, the passion predictions alter it through orientation to the passion:

> Then he began to teach them that the Son of Man must undergo great suffering, and be rejected by the elders, the chief priests, and the scribes, and be killed. . . . He was teaching his disciples, saying to them, "The Son of Man is to be betrayed into human hands, and they will kill him. . . ." He took the twelve aside and began to tell them what was to happen to him, saying, "See, we are going up to Jerusalem, and the Son of Man will be handed over to the chief priests and the scribes, and they will condemn him to death. . . ." (Mark 8:31; 9:31; 10:32-33)

The contrast with the figure in Daniel and Enoch is obvious. There the Son of Man bears no features of suffering, only of glory.[29] This link between the Son of Man title and the passion predictions underscores the tension between the Son of Man in Daniel and Enoch and the one in Mark. According to Mark, it belongs to his office — his commission — that the Son of Man should suffer.[30]

If it is true that Mark's chapter on the end of time and the coming of the Son of Man provides the organizing principle behind the remainder

---

28. Käsemann, "On the Subject of Primitive Christian Apocalyptic," in *New Testament of Today* (Philadelphia: Fortress Press, 1969), p. 124.

29. Cf. Strecker, "Die Leidens- und Auferstehungsvoraussagen," pp. 28-29; Maurer, "Knecht Gottes und Sohn Gottes," p. 132.

30. Cf. Delling, *Der Kreuzestod Jesu in der urchristlichen Verkündigung*, p. 59.

of his Gospel,[31] it is also true that the "Little Apocalypse" is oriented part and parcel to the passion. For example, with the passion begins the distress referred to in chapter 13, which sets the disciples in the succession of the Lord on his way to suffering and death. Mark 8:31-38, which links the first passion prediction with the summons to radical self-denial and cross-bearing, has its parallel in 13:9-13:

> If any want to become my followers, let them deny themselves and take up their cross and follow me (8:34). They will hand you over to councils; and you will be beaten in synagogues. . . . Brother will betray brother to death . . . and you will be hated by all because of my name. (13:9-13)

The "hour" of the coming of the Son of Man in 13:32 is altered to the "hour" of his passion in Mark 14:35, 41. Mark 13:33-37, which contains Jesus' injunction to "keep alert," functions as a transition to the Gethsemane scene (14:33-42), with its sleeping disciples. Or again, the statement in 13:24-25 ("in those days . . . the sun will be darkened, and the moon will not give its light") has its referent in 15:33: "When it was noon, darkness came over the whole land. . . ."[32]

Something more than "correction"[33] is happening with this reorientation. If, as Adolf Schlatter once said, "Israel's hope was always directed to theophany,"[34] that is, if the hallmark of the apocalyptic perspective was the expectation of a direct, visible demonstration of the power of God, Mark's narrative severs, for one last time, the link between Jesus and such "historical verifiability."[35] The chief priests and scribes taunt: "Let the Messiah, the King of Israel, come down from the cross now, so that we may see and believe. . . . Let us see whether Elijah will come to take him down" (15:32, 36). And Jesus dies with a loud cry (15:37). In the decisive moment, the one portrayed as thaumaturge in excess of any other Gospel does no miracle, and God does not save him

---

31. A. Edward Gardner, "The End of the Age: The Coming of Christ, Jesus' Death, Resurrection and Wisdom Thinking," *Encounter* 60, No. 1 (1999), 75.

32. Cf., e.g., T. A. Burkill, "St. Mark's Philosophy of the Passion," p. 266.

33. Joachim Gnilka, "Die Verhandlungen vor dem Synhedrion und vor Pilatus nach Markus 14:53–15:5," in *Redaktion und Theologie*, p. 303.

34. Adolf Schlatter, *Jesu Gottheit und das Kreuz*, p. 25.

35. Luz, "Theologia crucis als Mitte der Theologie im Neuen Testament," p. 134.

through a miraculous intervention. Why Elijah might be expected to come and rescue Jesus is left unexplained. In fact, however, he cannot come, for he is already dead: "I tell you that Elijah has come, and they did to him whatever they pleased . . ." (9:13).[36]

Contrary to taunt or expectation, this crucified, slain Jesus would not mount the pinnacle of Jerusalem's temple and announce the time of deliverance to Israel, liberate her from foreign rule, wreak vengeance on her enemies, compel her allies to pay her tribute, and establish a golden age of peace — reigning in a city come down in infinite glory from heaven to earth. He was not the one to return the scattered remnants from Mesopotamia and Egypt to their homeland, purge the *yetzer hara,* the "evil impulse" from Israel's heart, make all humans prophets, and transform the theaters and circuses of the Romans into Bible yeshivas. With Mark, the crucifixion occurred in Jerusalem, the city of God, but it had exceeded the bounds of Jewish trial legislation and nationhood.[37] If, by this "historicizing" or warping of the apocalyptic material to Jesus' passion, Mark was alerting his audience to the dangers of being caught up in an enthusiasm that anticipated a near end to the world, it was all a by-product of his linking the imminent expectation to the event of the cross:

> When in Mark it is said of Jesus, crying for his God in the abandonment of death and thus dying, "truly, this man was God's Son" . . . this means that in the event of this death the deity of the Son of God became event.[38]

Use and Fracture of the Divine Man

The comparison of Luke's Gospel with the ancient genre of reverential biography, or "aretalogy," made by Moses Hadas (1900-1966) and Morton Smith (1915-1991) has been echoed in recent studies of Mark.[39] If the first evangelist did not actually introduce the Hellenistic tradition of the Divine Man *(theios anēr* or *theios anthrōpos)* into the store of church thought, he

36. Hooker, *Not Ashamed of the Gospel,* pp. 49-51.
37. Cf. Schille, *Offen für alle Menschen,* p. 79.
38. Eberhard Jüngel, "Vom Tod des lebendigen Gottes," p. 107.
39. Moses Hadas and Morton Smith, *Heroes and Gods: Spiritual Biographies in Antiquity* (New York: Harper and Row, 1965).

clearly seems to have moved in its traces. His constant use of the temporal adverb "suddenly" or "immediately" *(euthus, eutheōs)* yields one clue.[40]

Other aspects of the Gospel reflect an epiphanic character. The dissonance in the resolve of the high priests and the actual course of events in Mark 14:1-2; Peter's denial and the double crowing of the cock foretold in 14:30; the dependence of Jesus' enemies on his silence, and his speech that gives him into their hands in 14:61-62 — all these suggest that the actors in this drama were able only to carry out alien decisions, a "determinism" calculated to enhance the figure of the Divine Man.[41] Further, Mark's use of the title "Son of God" is calculated to enhance the portrait of Jesus as a colossus reminiscent of Jewish or pagan deity. However the evangelist may have conceived it, the title's appearance at the beginning and end of his Gospel allows the inference that he prefers it. Or again, despite the similarity between the Qumran Teacher and Jesus in their consciousness of mission and relationship to their communities, Jesus' claim to majesty is singular. He speaks on his own authority, an authority that is set above the Torah.

Nowhere, however, are the intimations of deity more striking than in the so-called bridegroom logion, the first half of Jesus' reply to the fasting question. First, by referring to himself in his customary oblique fashion as bridegroom and to the disciples as wedding guests (Greek: "sons of the bridechamber"), Jesus indicates that his relationship to them is determined by a future consummation that conditions all of their activity in the present. Second, the imagery of the bridegroom and wedding guests indicates that it is a more august claim than the claim to messiahship that the Jesus of Mark is raising here. The imagery conjures up a welter of associations with deity. The *olam haba',* the coming age, has arrived: Yahweh, God, the Lord, the bridegroom of Hosea 2 and Isaiah 54,[42] is in

---

40. Cf. 1:10, 12, 18, 20, 21, 23, 29-30, 42; 2:8; 3:6; 4:15-16, 29; 5:2, 29, 30, 42; 6:25, 27, 54; 7:25; 9:15, 20; 10:52; 11:2; 14:43, 45, 72; 15:1; cf. also the contested reading in 5:42 and 9:15.

41. Cf. Maurer, "Knecht Gottes und Sohn Gottes," p. 122.

42. Hos. 2:19-20: "I will take you [Israel] for my wife forever; I will take you for my wife in righteousness and in justice, in steadfast love, and in mercy. I will take you for my wife in faithfulness; and you shall know the Lord." Isa. 54:5-6: "For your Maker [of Jerusalem and Judah] is your husband, the Lord of hosts is his name; the Holy One of Israel is your Redeemer, the God of the whole earth he is called. For the Lord has called you like a wife forsaken and grieved in spirit, like the wife of a man's youth when she is cast off, says your God."

the midst, gathering his elect. It is his presence that exceeds the normal expediencies of life.

Even the report of Jesus' death is suggestive of aspects attaching to the Divine Man. Mark says that, after Jesus "gave a loud cry and breathed his last,"

> the curtain of the temple was torn in two from top to bottom. Now when the centurion who stood facing him saw that in this way he breathed his last, he said, "Truly this man was God's Son!" (15:38-39)

Reflections on similarities often lead to assumptions regarding origins. Lawrence Wills says that Mark's Gospel belongs to a genre of reverential biography called "aretalogy," which has parallels in the eastern Mediterranean and relates the "charter myth" of a specific community in order to justify the object of its worship, its "hero cult," such as is reflected in the Greek *Life of Aesop* (ca. 6th century B.C.E.). Short of fixing Mark's origin in *The Life,* the author says that the myth animating it provides the basis "for very suggestive parallels with the Jesus tradition."[43] In addition to similarities in content, the author notes similarities between Mark and *The Life* in literary technique, such as the sandwiching of one episode within another.[44] Thus, the argument reads, because of its aretalogical character, Mark's Gospel does not represent a break with tradition but participates in an already existent genre.

More recently, it has been urged that the key to Mark's composition has less to do with genre than with his imitation of specific texts. Dennis Macdonald describes Mark's Gospel as a prose epic modeled after the *Odyssey* of Homer (ca. 9th century B.C.E.) and the ending of the *Iliad.*[45] Coupled with such literary activity as that of Homer in Mark's cultural milieu, the similarities and differences between his Gospel and the Homeric epics yield the criteria for concluding that Mark emulated Homer.[46]

---

43. Lawrence M. Wills, *The Quest of the Historical Gospel: Mark, John, and the Origins of the Gospel Genre* (New York: Routledge, 1997), pp. 29, 33-34, 46, 156.

44. In Mark 5, Jesus, on his way to raise the synagogue leader's daughter, has an encounter with a woman suffering from hemorrhages; in chapter 65 of *The Life,* Aesop is sent on an errand for his master, and on his way has an encounter with the governor, and when the episode is concluded, resumes his errand.

45. Macdonald, *The Homeric Epics and the Gospel of Mark,* p. 3.

46. Macdonald, pp. 8-9, 176. In face of the "density" and frequent agreement in or-

Once the evangelist tumbled to the similarity between Jesus' sufferings and those of Odysseus, he found in the Homeric epics a reservoir of plot devices for crafting his own narrative. For his narrative of Jesus' death, Mark "transvalued" the *Iliad,* just as he had the *Odyssey.* In harmony with Macdonald's criterion of dissimilarity, Mark, unlike Homer, leaves the burden of the happy ending to the reader.

Similarities do in fact exist between Mark's portrait of Jesus and the contemporaneous Hellenistic idea of the Divine Man. According to Macdonald, Mark was no slave to Homer's *Odyssey,* but he "emulated" it, with the result that Jesus "trumps" Odysseus. For example, Homer's hero awakes in the middle of a storm and holds on for dear life waiting for calm; Mark's hero awakes and stills the storm. Odysseus leaves Polyphemus blind or leaves Tiresias in Hades sightless; Jesus leaves the Gerasene demoniac cured. Odysseus tells his son Telemachus he is no god, merely his father; a voice from heaven declares Jesus to be the Son of God. Odysseus predicts quiet return to his estate; Jesus predicts his return to the whole world in a cosmic display of splendor. Odysseus visits Hades and returns, never having died; Jesus actually dies and is raised to life.

Mark's use of the story of Hector in the *Iliad* answers to the same "criterion of interpretability." The Trojans wrongly consider Hector a god; Jesus is the Son of God. The epic ends with Hector's tragic and permanent death; the Gospel ends with Jesus' triumph over death. Unlike the three Trojan women, the three women in Mark discover an empty tomb. The conclusion, writes Macdonald, is inescapable: Mark imitated Homeric epic. Furthermore, uninhibited in his creation of theological fiction, he created a hero who could outdo "the cultural monuments" of Greece. The result is that nearly every episode with parallels in Homer displays this "theological rivalry." Macdonald concedes Mark's indebtedness to tradition, to written sources and Jewish scriptures, while underscoring their diminished influence.[47]

To conclude that similarity between authors argues dependence of the one upon the other need not be false, though it flies in the face of re-

---

der between Homer and Mark, Macdonald, in what the Germans would call a "Kannegiesserkritik," expresses surprise that the evangelist's "conscious and extensive imitation" of Homer has evaded readers for two thousand years (pp. 145, 187).

47. Macdonald, pp. 188-190.

cent studies, according to which the literatures of disparate and unrelated cultures reveal common structures. But if, in the midst of their similarities, one of the narratives could be shown to exhibit a striking dissimilarity to the other, then the hypothesis of dependence would at least be challenged. Such dissimilarity does in fact exist, as was already noted in those instances in which Jesus "trumps" Odysseus or Hector. Gottfried Schille concedes that at various points Mark moves in the traces of Hellenistic-epiphany thought, though he denies that the miracle tradition had no intra-Christian history, or that it was possible to trace an earlier *Theos-Anēr*-Christology beneath Mark's Son-of-God perspective. He also observes that Mark's Gospel has far exceeded its sphere of ideas, stating that the "key word" *euthus* not merely denotes the execution of a command (as in a healing) but signals everything connected with the appearance of Jesus, in whom God's affair occurred "immediately."[48]

On the other hand, when, as with Macdonald, this dissimilarity is seized on as "evidence of emulation," informal logic is strained, and the move from the observation of similarity in genre to insistence on actual mimesis is perilous. In that old essay on the passion narrative, Dibelius signals the dissimilarity. After noting its Old Testament allusions, he says:

> We must put aside the modern error — that the earliest narrator evaluated things much as our present-day consciousness does, and meant to describe stirring and heroic events, or to illumine a historical happening. The earliest Passion story was neither stirring nor heroic. It contained no word speaking of the human greatness of Jesus in suffering, none intended to appeal to the human feelings of the reader. We can express this view with complete confidence because Mark's Passion story itself shows the same character. If we read, say, the story of the arrest or the trial before Pilate without reading any construction into the text, we shall be astonished at the bareness of the description and the absence of any traits that show the feelings of those who took part and that work upon the feelings of the readers.[49]

Referring to Mark's use of *euthus* in the report of Jesus' baptism, Schille says that the evangelist "breaks off the epiphany in the moment of the

48. Schille, *Offen für alle Menschen*, pp. 49, 52, 70.

49. Martin Dibelius, "The Passion Story," in *From Tradition to Gospel*, trans. Bertram Lee Woolf (New York: Charles Scribner's Sons, n.d.), pp. 185-186.

epiphany." Rising out of the water Jesus "immediately" sees the Spirit, who "immediately" drives him into the wilderness (1:10, 12). The result of Mark's work with his "key word," Schille concludes, is that the unequivocal epiphany of God is lit up only to be extinguished again.[50]

If, at the beginning of Mark's Gospel, Jesus' activity and the events surrounding it could tempt his readers to assign to him the lineaments of the Divine Man, any possible misunderstanding was soon cleared up in that ominous note of 3:6: "The Pharisees went out and immediately conspired with the Herodians against him, how to destroy him."[51] And if, at the end of his Gospel, Mark reversed the procedure and drew back the veil at the moment Jesus seemed least divine (15:39), more than one generation of readers would attempt to exempt the divine from the human, would postulate a "temporary suspension for the Incarnation,"[52] and thus put asunder what the evangelist did not think to divide. Conzelmann puts the matter simply: Mark found ready to hand a passion narrative together with a portrait of Jesus as thaumaturge and Divine Man that he then interpreted in terms of the passion theology.[53]

Use and Fracture of the Pre-Marcan Tradition

Despite the suspicion toward form- and redactions-critical research, the examples cited above are evidence of contemporary preoccupation with Mark's sources, and they give legitimacy to consulting such source-pioneers as Martin Dibelius (1883-1947). In two essays on the passion, Dibelius says that Mark was not the first to provide a narrative of Jesus' suffering.[54] The narrative was more or less complete before Mark put pen to paper, though it may have contained pieces that first circulated in

50. Schille, *Offen für alle Menschen*, p. 70.

51. Charles B. Cousar, "Eschatology and Mark's Theologia Crucis," *Interpretation* 24 (1970), 335.

52. Cf. Alan E. Lewis, "The Burial of God: Rupture and Resumption as the Story of Salvation," *Scottish Journal of Theology* 40, No. 1 (1987), for references to Irenaeus and Calvin.

53. Conzelmann, "Historie und Theologie in den synoptischen Passionsberichten," pp. 41-42.

54. Martin Dibelius, "Das historische Problem der Leidensgeschichte," *Botschaft und Geschichte*, I, 248-257; "The Passion Story," in *From Tradition to Gospel*, pp. 180-189.

isolated form.[55] This narrative was furnished with such Old Testament details as alluded to the events leading up to and including the crucifixion. Dibelius believed he detected another source beneath Mark's narrative in actual eyewitness accounts. For example, the anonymity of the fleeing disciple in Mark 14:51-52, or the reference to the sons of Simon of Cyrene, who carried Jesus' cross, features omitted by Mark's coevangelists, suggest that the readers of the earliest report were eyewitnesses to Jesus' arrest and knew what persons were meant.[56] Alongside eyewitness reports Dibelius sets whatever appeared to contradict Mark's data, such as the introduction to the passion narrative in 14:1-2, in which Jesus comes into his opponents' power *before* the feast of Passover.[57] In addition, he assigns to the pre-Marcan report the narrative of the Last Supper and the sayings of Jesus, such as his declaration against the temple in 14:58. In Dibelius's opinion, the scene of Peter's denial may also have belonged to that oldest report.[58]

Like Dibelius, contemporary scholars are hesitant to speculate regarding the age and genre of the earliest narrative, though they agree it may have emerged decades before Mark composed his Gospel and been stamped by community theology.[59] To the extent that contemporary research locates the decisive utterances regarding Jesus' passion in Mark's community, despite its demurrer it is involved in a search for sources.

It has been argued more than once that Mark was dissatisfied with the

55. "Das historische Problem der Leidensgeschichte," pp. 248-249; "The Passion Story," pp. 179-180.

56. "Das historische Problem der Leidensgeschichte," pp. 252, 255; "The Passion Story," p. 183.

57. "Das historische Problem der Leidensgeschichte," pp. 250, 255; "The Passion Story," p. 181.

58. "Das historische Problem der Leidensgeschichte," p. 255; "The Passion Story," pp. 183, 215.

59. Rudolf Pesch, "Die Überlieferung der Passion Jesu," in *Redaktion und Theologie des Passionsberichtes nach den Synoptikern,* pp. 358-359; Joachim Gnilka, "Die Verhandlungen vor dem Synhedrion," p. 302; George Strecker, "Die Leidens- und Auferstehungsvoraussagen im Markusevangelium," pp. 27, 31, 32, 35-36; Heinz-Wolfgang Kuhn, "Jesus als Gekreuzigter," p. 34; Gottfried Schille, *Offen für alle Menschen,* p. 78. Regarding the Gospels as "aetiological narratives," written to justify existing practices and beliefs of a given community, see Benjamin W. Bacon, "The Purpose of Mark's Gospel," *JBL* 29 (1910), 43, or "Jesus Christ," in *The New Schaff-Herzog Encyclopedia of Religious Knowledge* (New York: Funk and Wagnalls, 1910), VI, 160.

tradition he had received. One variation of that argument reads that he believed "the orthodox confession" of the Christ was in danger of calcifying, and thus proceeded to unlock its significance by emphasizing the necessity of the passion of the Son of Man.[60] Another says that the pre-Marcan tradition reflected a *heilsgeschichtlich* thematic with its emphasis on Davidic rule and the temple, thus with the identification of Israel and the church. With Mark this thematic undergoes radical delimitation: he appropriates the Davidic title but no longer interprets it with recourse to Israel. He simply tells of the healing of the blind man (Mark 10:46-52), the entry into Jerusalem (Mark 11:1-11), the debates (Mark 11:27-33; 12:28-37), and the passion. "This One," Mark declares, "is David's Lord."[61]

According to yet another variation, the result of Mark's "Christological deepening" is that Jesus' injunctions to silence do not hinder understanding but make clear that the recognition of his identity does not come about as a direct consequence of his deeds. Jesus' "real" secret, therefore, is not that he is the veiled messiah but that previous church teaching did not correctly understand him. In this way Mark forces his church to submit its credo to the test.[62] According to the same variation, Mark consciously stands beyond a threshold Paul had not yet reached. While Paul might take up various fragments of alien theologies, largely in order to reject them, Mark, writing in a period that needed a radical rethinking of the tradition, allows the diverging traditions to flow into the wide stream of his work.[63]

The argument, with its variations and counter-arguments, may have speculation for its father, but superimposed or not, a dialectic of hiddenness and revelation threads throughout Mark's Gospel. At the Gospel's high watermark, the dialectic appears in the move from Peter's confession of Jesus as the Messiah to Jesus' reference to the Son of Man (8:29, 31):

> He asked them, "But who do you say that I am?" Peter answered him, "You are the Messiah." . . . Then he began to teach them that the Son of Man must undergo great suffering. (Mark 8:29-31a)

60. Gnilka, "Die Verhandlungen vor dem Synhedrion," p. 306.
61. Cf. Hans Conzelmann, "Historie und Theologie in den synoptischen Passionsberichten," p. 44.
62. Schille, *Offen für alle Menschen,* p. 47.
63. Schille, p. 38.

In contrast to the messiah title that belonged to the community's Christological confession, the "Son of Man" title had its home in nonmessianic, apocalyptic tradition, and thus lacked any reference to suffering.[64] Aside from whether or not Jesus used the title and was misunderstood, or he intended to be misunderstood so as not to end his work before its time — and aside from whether or not the title was transmitted by a "nonmessianic Jesus-tradition" — Mark wedded it to the messiah of the community's confession and made it serve his motif of the "secret," a mystery hidden from Jesus' contemporaries but revealed to his readers. In other words, Mark was the first to speak of the suffering Son of Man.[65] Further, whether or not we are to see here a correction of the earliest community's Christ-predicate in the limiting of Peter's confession to a single noun *(ho Christos)*, or the correction of a "deficient" nonmessianic Jesus-tradition in its linkage to the other tradition of the messiah,[66] it is clear that the linkage is made to serve a unified portrait. Further still, whether or not this treatment constitutes Mark's "central contribution to forming a Christological confession within the whole church,"[67] the result is in fact epochal, which we can see in the dependence of his coevangelists. The secrecy motif is further augmented by Jesus' injunction to silence in 8:30 ("and he sternly ordered them not to tell anyone about him"). In chapter 9, the dialectic of revelation and hiddenness appears in Jesus' prediction of his passion and resurrection, and in the disciples' fear and ignorance (9:30-32). In Mark 10:32-38, alongside the revelation theme in the passion prediction appears Jesus' intention to remain hidden, coupled with the theme of ignorance reflected in the Zebedees' petition.[68]

Contrary to the thesis of William Wrede, according to which Mark inherited the "Messianic secret" and superimposed it on the traditional

---

64. Cf. Erik Sjöberg's response to Joachim Jeremias' contention that I Enoch and IV Ezra yield evidence of the suffering of the Son of Man ("Känna 1 Henok och 4 Estra tanken pa den lidande Människosonen?" *Svensk Exegetisk Arsbok* V [1940], 178, 183).

65. Cf. Walther Schmithals, "Die Worte vom leidenen Menschsohn, Ein Schlüssel zur Lösung des Menschensohn-Problems," in *Theologia Crucis — Signum Crucis,* pp. 424, 436 n. 62.

66. Cf. the discussion in Schmithals, pp. 433, 435-436, 438, 441-442.

67. Schille, *Offen für alle Menschen,* pp. 48, 50, 53.

68. Strecker, "Die Leidens- und Auferstehungsvoraussagen im Markusevangelium," pp. 37-39.

material for the sake of convincing suggestive audiences that the reason why no one recognized Jesus' true identity during his lifetime was that he traveled incommunicado,[69] it was the event of the cross as throwing the entire "Jesus-movement" into doubt that furnished the riddle yielding the second of the two great contradictories in Mark's revelation-and-hiddenness dialectic. This dialectic of hiddenness and revelation echoes a refrain already repeated by Paul: principally in the Christ-hymn of Philippians 2, but all throughout the Paulines, there is that continual movement between the picture of Christ's cross and the fullness of God in him. Let Romans 8:31-39 serve for them all:

> He who did not withhold his own Son, but gave him up for all of us, will he not with him also give us everything else? . . . It is Christ Jesus, who died, yes, who was raised, who is at the right hand of God, who indeed intercedes for us.

Not for nothing did Albrecht Dürer (1471-1528) set Paul in front of Mark in his portrait of the evangelists.

---

69. Wrede, *The Messianic Secret*, p. 145.

CHAPTER FOUR

The Death of Jesus in Matthew

The Scheme

The definition of Matthew's passion narrative as "the way of the humiliated Christ"[1] need not be restricted to the three chapters toward the end of his Gospel. In all the sections that Matthew shares with Mark or Luke, the death motif is clearly present. Taken together with the sections that Matthew does not share with his coevangelists, his passion narrative clearly is not merely an epilogue, unconnected with the main work.[2] Over a century ago, Johann Peter Lange said that "the feature of Messianic suffering moves through the Gospel as a prevailing idea."[3]

According to the leanest and most workable hypothesis, Mark's Gospel — and thus its passion narrative — was known to Matthew, as well as to the community within and for which he wrote. In fact, the greatest portion of Matthew's passion narrative suggests a reworking of Mark.[4] It is also clear, however, that Matthew does not simply revise the Marcan report. Aside from his dependence on a particular churchly community in which various traditions were alive and in which study of the Old Testament may have been undertaken,[5] the

1. Cf. Nils Dahl, "Die Passionsgeschichte bei Matthäus," in *Redaktion und Theologie des Passionberichtes nach den Synoptikern*, p. 213.

2. Weber, *Kreuz*, p. 179.

3. Johann Peter Lange, *Das Leben Jesu nach den Evangelien*, book 1, part 7, p. 241.

4. Cf. Dahl, "Die Passionsgeschichte bei Matthäus," pp. 206, 208-209, 212.

5. Cf. Dahl, p. 205, where he expresses his doubt that Matthew used written sources other than Mark for his passion narrative.

evangelist's portrayal of Jesus' sojourn through opposition toward suffering and death contains features that set him apart from his fellow Gospel authors.[6]

In Matthew 1:21, the angel announces to Joseph that he shall name the newborn child Jesus, "for he will save his people from their sins," an announcement replacing the message of Israel's deliverance known to Old Testament readers. Matthew 2 describes the family's flight into Egypt, the massacre of the innocents, the family's return, and Herod's intent to destroy the child. Herod thus functions as a counterpart to the Egyptian pharaoh, making use of state power to exterminate the God-sent child (2:13). Similarly, the massacre of the innocents at Bethlehem (2:16-18) answers to the Egyptian massacre of the children in Exodus 1. The chapter continues with references to the death of those "seeking the child's life" (2:20) and to Joseph's avoidance of Judea, now under the rule of Herod's son (2:22). Chapter 3 describes Jesus' submission to John's baptism as "fulfilling all righteousness" (3:15), that is, as assuming the divine demand that he adopt the status of sinner — a feature given special emphasis in the crucifixion narrative, where Jesus is abandoned by God. From the outset of his activity, Jesus appears as one fated for suffering; for that reason the divine glory illumines him at his baptism: "And a voice from heaven said, 'This is my Son, the Beloved, with whom I am well pleased'" (3:17). In chapter 4, Jesus is "led up by the Spirit into the wilderness to be tempted by the devil," first of all to change stones to bread, second, to throw himself from the temple's highest point (4:5-7) — a plunge he will risk, writes Adolf Schlatter, when God's will "leads" him to the cross.[7]

At the outset of the Sermon on the Mount (Matt. 5–7), Jesus addresses beatitudes to the poor, to those who mourn and are powerless, to the merciful and the peace-makers, and finally to the persecuted, who in this way share the destiny of the Crucified.[8] Suffering for Jesus' sake, they make known the divine election in the train of the prophets:

> Blessed are you when people revile you and persecute you and utter all kinds of evil against you falsely on my account. Rejoice and be

6. In tracing the death motif, I am in large part indebted to Ernst Käsemann's 1957 Göttingen lectures.

7. Adolf Schlatter, *Der Evangelist Matthäus* (Stuttgart: Calwer Verlag, 1948), p. 107.

8. Fleinert-Jensen, *Das Kreuz und die Einheit der Kirche*, p. 15.

glad, for your reward is great in heaven, for in the same way they persecuted the prophets who were before you. (5:11-12)

All throughout his Gospel, Matthew, like Mark, will describe discipleship as following the suffering Messiah, but then deepen it in terms of persecution from outsiders (cf., e.g., 5:11-12; 10:16-23; 24:9-14; 25:31-46).[9] If at the outset of the Sermon the community of believers becomes visible as persecuted, in what follows it is summoned to act in midst of its persecution:

> You are the salt of the earth. . . . You are the light of the world . . . let your light shine before others, so that they may see your good works and give glory to your Father in heaven. (5:13-16)

Again, reading Matthew's portrayal of Jesus in chapter 5 as setting Moses' authority aside and replacing it with his own (5:21, 27, 31, 33, 38, 43), the evangelist's audience will have little difficulty arriving at the reasons for his execution. Or again, it will require no great feat to construe Jesus' death as the actualization of his summons in the Sermon to overcome evil with suffering and love (5:38-42). In Matthew 8, Jesus' exorcisms and healings are viewed in terms of the Servant of Yahweh's role: "He took our infirmities and bore our diseases" (8:16-17; cf. Isa. 53:4). Aside from Jesus' word at the Last Supper, this is the only instance where the concept of vicarious suffering suggests itself to Matthew.[10] He obviously did not feel obliged to enter more closely into the redeeming consequences of Jesus' death.[11] Chapter 9, in a slight variation of the Marcan parallel, includes Jesus' reply to the fasting question in the double parable and the bridegroom logion, with its ominous ending: "The days will come when the bridegroom is taken from them . . ." (9:15).

9. Cf. Luke Timothy Johnson, *The Real Jesus*, p. 154.

10. Of Matthew's use of Isaiah 53 here, Morna Hooker says that "the early Christian communities did not always use scripture in the ways that seem to us to be obvious and appropriate" (*Not Ashamed of the Gospel*, p. 86). Earlier she had written that this application to other spheres of quotations that would make evident the identification of Jesus with the Servant proves that such an application was never made, either by Jesus or his followers (cf. *Jesus and the Servant*, p. 83).

11. Birger Gerhardsson, "Jesus, Ausgeliefert und Verlassen — nach dem Passionsbericht des Matthäusevangeliums," p. 265.

In the commissioning of the Twelve in chapter 10, the prospect of the disciples' arraignment before local Jewish courts, their betrayal and death, spells the continuation of a trial and execution yet to come (10:17-25). In the same chapter, in an "eschatological openness" ("What I say to you in the dark, tell in the light; and what you hear whispered, proclaim from the housetops" [10:27]), Jesus promises that the world will not get free of its victims. Even in death his voice will be heard through his witnesses:

> ... have no fear of them; for nothing is covered up that will not be uncovered, and nothing secret that will not become known. . . . Do not fear those who kill the body but cannot kill the soul; rather fear him who can destroy both soul and body in hell. (10:26-28)

At the conclusion of this chapter, the motif of the disciples' suffering resumes, this time with specific reference to the cross as the way of their salvation: "Whoever does not take up the cross and follow me is not worthy of me" (10:38). Since this variant does not yet point to Jesus' crucifixion, it may hark back to Jesus himself.[12]

In Matthew 11 — and in a statement reflecting oldest tradition but evoking sufficient debate to suggest that the Christian community has been unable to master it — Jesus refers to the "kingdom of heaven" as having "suffered violence . . . from the days of John the Baptist until now" (11:12). According to the likeliest interpretation, in this passage Jesus does not understand the kingdom as elsewhere in Matthew, that is, as a rule or reign enforced with the majesty of a Judge to come, but rather as something to which one may do harm. Violent men seize hold of the kingdom to prevent others from entering it. Thus, however intimately John the Baptist and Jesus may be united ("for all the prophets and the law prophesied until John came" [Matt. 11:13]), according to the one the kingdom is in the offing, while for the other it is already present, and for that reason it is vulnerable, prey to attack. As Ernst Käsemann says in the essay that initiated the so-called Second Quest of the Historical Jesus:

> Who but Jesus himself can look back in this way over the completed Old Testament epoch of salvation, not degrading the Baptist to the

12. Cf. Kleinknecht, *Der leidende Gerechtfertigte*, p. 175.

position of a mere forerunner as the whole Christian community and the whole New Testament were to do, but drawing him to his side and — an enormity to later Christian ears — presenting him as the initiator of the new aeon? But who then is this, who thus does justice to the Baptist and yet claims for himself a mission higher than that entrusted to John? Evidently, he who brings with his Gospel the kingdom itself; a kingdom which can yet be obstructed and snatched away, for the very reason that it appears in the defenceless form of the gospel.[13]

According to Matthew, Jesus' invitation in chapter 11 ("Come to me, all you that are weary and are carrying heavy burdens" [11:28-29]) receives its authority from his forsakenness on Golgotha. In becoming last of all and servant of all, he is able to give rest from the burdens that exhaust those who are struggling to become first.[14]

Matthew 12 opens with a reference to Jesus' awareness of the Pharisees' conspiracy. Whatever may have moved the evangelist to restrict the summary of the Isaian Servant's activity to Jesus' deeds of healing, the identification of Jesus as the suffering Servant of Yahweh is deeper and more intense than that in the Gospels of Mark or Luke. In chapter 12, following a reference to Jesus' injunction to silence, Matthew applies to his activity a passage from Isaiah that the Targum had already interpreted of the Messiah:

> This was to fulfill what had been spoken through the prophet Isaiah: "Here is my servant, whom I have chosen, my beloved with whom my soul is well-pleased. I will put my Spirit upon him, and he will proclaim justice to the Gentiles. He will not wrangle or cry aloud, nor will anyone hear his voice in the streets. He will not break a bruised reed or quench a smoldering wick until he brings justice to victory; and in his name the Gentiles will hope." (12:17-21)[15]

This quotation reflects Matthew's penchant for painting in black and white. Jesus makes no stir ("he will not wrangle or cry aloud"), and

13. Käsemann, "The Problem of the Historical Jesus," in *Essays on New Testament Themes,* trans. W. J. Montague (London: SCM Press, 1964), p. 43.

14. Minear, *The Golgotha Earthquake,* p. 114.

15. Cf. H. L. Strack and Paul Billerbeck, *Das Evangelium Matthäus, erläutert aus Talmud und Midrasch* (Munich: C. H. Beck'sche Verlagsbuchhandlung), p. 630.

his enemies force him out into the open. Or, as recorded earlier (v. 15), he heals and helps ("many crowds followed him, and he cured all of them"), and his enemies plan murder. Later on in the chapter, Jesus at once denies and affirms his opponents' desire for a sign: "No sign will be given [an evil and adulterous generation] except the sign of the prophet Jonah" (12:39). The evangelist has in mind Jesus' death and resurrection (12:40), and he takes his chronology approximating the time between Good Friday and Easter from Jonah 1:17. The sign for Jesus' petitioners, however, is merely Jonah's burial in the belly of the fish, and it is of no use to them.

If the parables in the Synoptic Gospels, and thus in Matthew, do not merely aim at a point where picture and meaning come together to yield a general religious maxim *(tertium comparationis),* but rather have at their center one in whom God's kingdom is present,[16] then a relationship exists between the sayings and doings of Jesus in Matthew's Gospel, specifically between his recitation of the parables and the narrative culminating in his passion. If that is true, the results of the seed sown in the opening verses of chapter 13 may not simply reflect the fate of the earliest community's proclamation, but also — or even principally — that of Jesus himself:

> Some seeds fell on the path, and the birds came and ate them up. Other seeds fell on rocky ground, where they did not have much soil . . . when the sun rose, they were scorched; and since they had no root, they withered away. Other seeds fell among thorns, and the thorns grew up and choked them. (13:4-7)

The idea that the kingdom was manifest in what Jesus did, that God's almighty grace was at work in him, struck some of his hearers as inconceivable, unreal. For such the parable assumed the shape of an enigma lacking explanation.[17] But that was only a minor consequence of its telling.

In Matthew 14, in a lengthy narrative punctuated with dialogue, Matthew records the arrest, imprisonment, and death of John the Baptist (14:1-12). Whatever the judgment regarding the narrative's historical details, and whatever the view of its source, Herod's confusion of

16. Adolf Schlatter, *Der Evangelist Matthäus*, p. 428.
17. Schlatter, p. 428.

Jesus' identity with John's ("This is John the Baptist; he has been raised from the dead" [14:2]); Herod's fear of the crowds initially deterring him from his intent (". . . though Herod wanted to put him to death, he feared the crowd, because they regarded him as a prophet" [14:5]); and his final succumbing to pressure and allowing John to be beheaded ("out of regard for his oaths and for the guests . . . he sent and had John beheaded in the prison" [14:9-10]) — all these call up associations with the later passion narrative. There Pilate raises the question concerning Jesus' identity ("Are you the King of the Jews?" [27:11]). He is reluctant to turn Jesus over to his executioners ("he realized that it was out of jealousy that they had handed him over" [27:18]), an attitude reinforced by a word from his wife, reversing the woman's role in the account of the Baptist's death ("Have nothing to do with that innocent man, for today I have suffered a great deal because of a dream about him" [27:19]). Finally, the governor succumbs to the crowd's demand that Jesus be crucified.

In Matthew 15, Jesus once more strides beyond the Jewish rabbi or prophet by striking at the rules for ritual purification, instead locating the source of evil in the human heart: "It is not what goes into the mouth that defiles a person, but it is what comes out of the mouth that defiles" (15:11). In other words, the sanctioning of behavior — thus implicating a legal command or requirement — is not a matter of external decree. Corresponding to the Hellenistic Enlightenment, with its urging of the heart, or *ratio,* as the locus of ethical judgment,[18] this statement spells an attack on the Mosaic Torah and its requirement of unquestioning formal obedience. Whoever strikes at Moses in this way has ceased to be a Jew. For this reason, the chief priests and Pharisees, who later level at Jesus the epithet *planos* ("one who leads astray" [NRSV: "imposter"]) in their demand that Pilate secure his tomb (27:63), may have more in mind than his "sign of Jonah" — three days and nights in the belly of the whale (12:40).[19]

In chapter 16, Jesus once more dialectically rejects and accepts the demand for evidence by referring to the sign of Jonah, of which his

18. Käsemann, "Matthäusevangelium" (unpublished lectures given at Tübingen, n.d., II, 44 [Part I was delivered in the summer semester of 1957]).

19. Cf. Ulrich Luz, *Das Evangelium nach Matthäus: Evangelisch-Katholischer Kommentar zum Neuen Testament* (Neukirchen-Vluyn: Neukirchener Verlag, 2002), 4, section 392.

death and resurrection will be the repetition (16:4). Later, following the confession of Peter at Caesarea Philippi as its antithesis, Jesus predicts his suffering and death in Matthew's parallel to Mark's first passion prediction.[20] As with Mark and Luke (Mark 8:31; Luke 9:22; 24:44), Matthew's use of the verb *dei* in the note that "Jesus began to show his disciples that he *must* go to Jerusalem and undergo great suffering" (16:21) does not express the inexorable power of fate but rather the necessity of fulfilling the divine saving will.

More than once suspicion has been aroused about the portrayal of Jesus as predicting his suffering. The passion predictions have often been regarded as the later community's attempt to render intelligible the enigmatic event of his passion. They have been labeled *vaticinia ex eventu,* prophecies, or kerygmatic summaries trajected back into the mouth of the historical Jesus; but the consequence of this is to render the disciples' flight at his death inexplicable.[21] Whatever side we take in the debate concerning their historicity, for Matthew and his coevangelists the passion predictions make clear that Jesus voluntarily and resolutely enters upon his suffering. For this reason he cannot be identified with Schweitzer's apocalypticist, who by his death resolves to force God's kingdom to come once he has met defeat at the hands of his own people.[22]

20. Cf. Mark 8:31.

21. Rather than agree with Bultmann that, in referring to the Son of Man as about to suffer, Jesus was pointing away from himself to another, Käsemann regards the passion predictions as prophecies after the fact (see Käsemann, "Matthäusevangelium," II, 111). There may be yet another alternative to Bultmann's "fantastic" thesis.

22. According to Schweitzer's reading of Matthew 10, Jesus had awaited the inbreaking of the kingdom at harvest time, for which reason he sent out the Twelve. His expectation was not fulfilled. The disciples returned, but Jesus' exaltation as Son of Man, thought to happen simultaneously with the kingdom's coming, did not occur. As Schweitzer says, "The actual history disavowed the dogmatic history on which the action of Jews had been based." The nonevent set Jesus at a crossroads. From now on he no longer spoke of the tribulation awaiting those who belonged to him prior to the kingdom's coming, but only of his own: his death would compel the kingdom to come. In its essential details, Schweitzer's scheme is so strikingly similar to that of Johannes Weiss's *Die Predigt Jesu vom Reiche Gottes* (published fourteen years before the first edition of Schweitzer's study [1906]), that, lacking evidence of a common "ancestor," Schweitzer's dependence on Weiss is the only conclusion to be drawn. Cf., e.g., Weiss's discussion of Jesus' expectation of a sudden victory of God's affair as reflected in his sending the disciples on their mission throughout Jewish territory. The expectation, Weiss continued,

The chapter concludes with Jesus' word that discipleship without suffering does not deserve the name. To be a disciple and to bear the cross are synonymous:

> If any want to become my followers, let them deny themselves and take up their cross and follow me. For those who want to save their life will lose it, and those who lose their life for my sake will find it. For what will it profit them if they gain the whole world but forfeit their life? Or what will they give in return for their life? (16:24-26)

The context of Matthew 17, with its narrative of the Transfiguration, reflects the author's concern to depict the Son as marked for suffering, the one bathed in glory about to be *Crucifixus:*

> From the cloud a voice said, "This is my Son, the Beloved; with him I am well pleased; listen to him!" Jesus ordered them, "Tell no one about the vision until after the Son of Man has been raised from the dead. . . . Elijah has already come, and they . . . did to him whatever they pleased. So also the Son of Man is about to suffer at their hands." (17:5-12)

Not merely intent on revealing Jesus as the Son of God, despite the fact that he undergoes suffering, the narrative appears bent on emphasizing his suffering as *proof* of his Sonship. Toward the conclusion of the chapter, clearly adhering to a fixed scheme followed by his coevangelists, Matthew records Jesus' second prediction of his passion (17:22-23), this time not merely "at the hands of the elders and chief priests and scribes" but "into human hands" — so as to allow for Roman as well as Jewish complicity.

In Matthew 18, Peter's question about the limit of forgiveness ("How often should I forgive — as many as seven times?"), and Jesus' response in the parable of the unforgiving servant, furnish a variation on the theme of discipleship (18:21-35). As Schlatter says, the parable makes clear the incompatibility of two actions: the king's acquittal of his slave

---

was not fulfilled. Since he was rejected by his people, his death would be their redemption, the means for bringing in the kingdom. On this account, Jesus' teaching lacked any systematic ethic, since the imminent appearing of the end ruled out any protracted existence (cf. Weiss, *Die Predigt Jesu vom Reiche Gottes,* pp. 100, 103, 139, 143, and Schweitzer, *The Quest of the Historical Jesus,* pp. 327, 347-348).

and the slave's treatment of his debtor. The one act does not allow the other: the slave's acquittal is canceled if he does not acquit his debtor. What the disciple has received from God through Jesus thus functions as a model for his own activity. Further, there is a causal connection between the two actions: since the grace of God has become the disciple's own and remains so only when he acts toward another in accordance with it, he is obliged fully to forgive.[23]

Following another variation on the theme of discipleship as synonymous with suffering in chapter 19 ("everyone who has left houses or brothers or sisters or father or mother or children or fields," etc. [19:29]), Matthew 20 records Jesus' third and last prediction of his death and resurrection (20:17-19). Jesus is thus one who has divine foreknowledge at his disposal and goes voluntarily to his death. But this time, just as with Mark, in the "school speech" dealing with the disciples' dispute over rank, Jesus describes his death as substitutionary:

> Whoever wishes to be first among you must be your slave; just as the Son of Man came not to be served but to serve, and to give his life a ransom for many. (20:28; cf. Mark 10:45)

By now it is obvious that the death motif is as evident in Matthew as it is in Mark. At this point in his Göttingen lectures, Käsemann says that the question of the historicity of Jesus' word in 20:28 is of no concern — that this word encompasses the entire Gospel.[24]

In Matthew 21, Jesus makes an appeal to the Baptist, whose end throws its shadow over his own destiny:

> Did the baptism of John come from heaven, or was it of human origin? And they argued with one another, "If we say, 'From heaven,' he will say to us, 'Why then did you not believe him?'" (21:25)

At the close of chapter 21, following the parable of the wicked tenants, Matthew not only charges the chief priests and Pharisees with ignorance but with conscious thoughts of murder. The evangelist says that the authorities, realizing that they were in fact the subject of Jesus' parables, "wanted to arrest him." More than fifty years ago, C. W. F. Smith

---

23. Adolf Schlatter, *Der Evangelist Matthäus*, p. 561.
24. Käsemann, "Matthäusevangelium," II, 108.

(1905-1993) said that "Jesus used parables and Jesus was put to death. The two facts are related and it is necessary to understand the connection."[25] Matthew could scarcely have made the connection any clearer.

In chapter 22, Jesus' question regarding the messiah represents the high watermark of his encounter with his opponents. Over against his Marcan parallel (Mark 12:35-37), Matthew has set the scene in the context of a dialogue, and he ends it with the Pharisees' retreat. First, the Pharisees appear en masse: "Now while the Pharisees were gathered together. . . ." Next, Jesus takes the initiative: "[He] asked them the question: 'What do you think of the Messiah? Whose son is he?'" Then the Pharisees thrust at him: "They said to him, 'The son of David.'" Jesus parries the thrust: "How is it then that David by the Spirit calls him Lord . . . ?" And Jesus holds the field: "No one was able to give him an answer, nor from that day did anyone dare to ask him any more questions." In this scene, rabbinic identification of the messiah with David's son, gleaned from the Old Testament and reflected in the acclamation of the crowds upon Jesus' entry into Jerusalem (21:9), appears to be critiqued from the perspective of Psalm 110: "The Lord says to my lord, 'Sit at my right hand . . .'" (Ps. 110:1). Apart from the question of whether or not this scene (as in Mark) reflects a certain ambivalence toward the Son-of-David title as applied to the messiah and thus a preference for the alleged Hellenistic title *Kyrios,* the dialogue as such — and particularly the identification of Jesus' interlocutors, who at this point are intent on his arrest or his death — marks a further stage in the journey toward the passion: Jesus, in full consciousness of his messiahship, is striding toward his fate.

In Matthew 23, Jesus accuses his opponents of filling the measure of their fathers to the brim through killing and crucifying him (obviously) and those who belong to him (23:32-34), with the result that they have brought judgment down upon themselves:

> So that upon you may come all the righteous blood shed on earth, from the blood of righteous Abel to the blood of Zechariah son of Barachiah, whom you murdered between the sanctuary and the altar. (23:35)

---

25. Charles W. F. Smith, *The Jesus of the Parables* (Philadelphia: Westminster, 1948), p. 17.

The chapter closes with Jesus' lament over Jerusalem, which in turn concludes with an apocalyptic vision. The one whom Israel has rejected as its Messiah has now abandoned it and will appear as Israel's Judge at the *parousia:*

> See, your house is left to you, desolate. For I tell you, you will not see me again until you say, "Blessed is the one who comes in the name of the Lord." (23:38-39)

For this reason, the phrase "you will not see me again until . . ." is yet one more passion prediction.

I have referred above to the intimate relationship between the passion narrative and the predictions and parables in Matthew's Gospel. In those earlier portions, Matthew was preparing his readers to detect meanings inherent in the passion, while the passion itself enacted truths earlier hidden in the predictions and parables. For example, Jesus' submission to his Father at Gethsemane (26:39, 42) yields a clue to his earlier declaration (in chapter 20): "The Son of Man came not to be served but to serve and to give his life a ransom for many "(20:28). Or again, the darkness over the earth at the time of Jesus' crucifixion completes the revision of the apocalyptic forecast in Matthew 24 (v. 29). Or again, Matthew's twofold reference to Jesus' cry as "with a loud voice" (27:46, 50) yields the clue to those signs of the apocalyptic judgment in chapter 24 (vv. 21, 24, 31; 7:27). Finally, the parabolic images of the Son of Man in Matthew 25 are precisely those assigned to the leaders of a persecuted community.[26] In the statement about the great division in chapter 25, the figure of the Son of Man merges with that of the king and "the members of [his] family," to the effect that the clause "I was in prison and you visited me" may be applied to any of those three (25:31-46).

In the passion narrative itself, Matthew has enlarged the story through insertions from the Old Testament, such as the thirty pieces of silver, the gall mixed with the drink offered to Jesus on the cross, and the content of the mockery of passers-by (26:15; 27:34, 43). He has also added the details of Judas's death, the dream of Pilate's wife, the hand-washing scene, and the watch set at the grave (27:3-10, 19, 24-25, 62-66; 28:11-15). If Matthew's sole reference to vicarious suffering occurs in re-

26. Cf. Minear, *The Golgotha Earthquake,* pp. 82-96.

lation to Jesus' healing activity, only his account of the Last Supper contains the reference to forgiveness, "one of the rare statements in the Gospels that attempts to explain what the death of Jesus achieved."[27] The statement about the "blood of the covenant" (26:28) will have its explanation in subsequent events, in Judas's confession ("I have sinned by betraying innocent blood" [27:4]), in Pilate's avowal of innocence ("I am innocent of this man's blood" [27:24]), and in the people's accepting responsibility for Jesus' death ("his blood be on us and on our children!" [27:25]). All these will be the "many" for whose forgiveness the blood of the covenant will be poured out. Chapter 27 concludes with the miracles that occur at Jesus' death, including the appearance of the risen saints following his death on the cross (27:51-54) and his resurrection despite the guard at the tomb (27:62-66).

One by one the interpreters follow Dibelius's argument that, in Matthew's Gospel, Jesus completely dominates the situation from the beginning of his passion, that in midst of his sufferings he remains the Son of God equipped with power.[28] From his birth onward, Jesus is in peril. Evildoers seek his life, but their attempts are doomed to fail. In fact, whenever the situation darkens, Jesus is removed or "withdraws" — an action signaled in Matthew's repeated use of the word *anachōrein*. Jesus is "taken" to Egypt, or to Galilee, to avoid danger to his life (2:14, 22). When he hears that John has been arrested, he "withdraws" to Galilee (4:12), just as he does when he learns of the Pharisees' plot (12:14-15). In the latter instance, Matthew uses the term *gnous* of Jesus as a discerner of hearts ("when Jesus became aware . . ."), thus removing the motive of anxiety from his withdrawal. Following the news of John the Baptist's death, Jesus "withdraws" to a deserted place (14:13). The only instance in which Jesus' "withdrawal" is not to avoid danger is his journey to the district of Tyre and Sidon before his encounter with the Canaanite woman.[29]

This perspective allows Matthew to record the predictions of Jesus'

27. In *Not Ashamed of the Gospel* (p. 71), Hooker notes that the phrase "for the forgiveness of sins" is used of John's baptism by Mark and Luke, but not by Matthew, and she inquires whether Matthew deliberately transferred it from John's baptism to Jesus' death.

28. Cf. Dibelius, "The Passion Story," pp. 197-198; Dahl, "Die Passionsgeschichte bei Matthäus," p. 213; Gerhardsson, "Jesus, Ausgeliefert und Verlassen — nach den Passionsbericht des Matthäusevangeliums," pp. 265, 268; Albert Vanhoye, "Struktur und Theologie der Passionsberichte in den Synoptischen Evangelien," pp. 232-233.

29. Cf. Matt. 15:21-28.

passion in greater detail. In Matthew 12, Jesus refuses to give empirical evidence of his authority; then he adds that, just as Jonah was in the belly of the whale for three days, so the Son of Man will be in the heart of the earth for three days and nights (12:40). In chapter 16, in his parallel to Mark's first passion prediction (see Mark 8:31), Jesus says that it is to *Jerusalem* that he must go and undergo great suffering (16:21). In Matthew's second prediction, Jesus makes explicit the parallel between his fate and that of John the Baptist:

> I tell you that Elijah has already come, and they did not recognize him, but they did to him whatever they pleased. So also the Son of Man is about to suffer at their hands. (17:12)

Jesus' third prediction (17:22-23) is followed by a fourth (20:18-19, 28), and even a fifth (26:2, 24, 45).

The perspective is reinforced by the observation that, throughout his narrative, Matthew — more strongly than Mark — emphasizes the fulfillment of Jesus' own word. In the "colophon" at the head of the narrative, Matthew writes:

> When Jesus had finished saying all these things, he said to his disciples, "You know that after two days the Passover is coming, and the Son of Man will be handed over to be crucified." (26:1-2)

That same theme is struck in the chief priests' and Pharisees' demand that Pilate secure the tomb: "Sir, we remember what that impostor said while he was still alive, 'After three days I will rise again'" (27: 63). And it appears again in the angel's word to the women: "Do not be afraid; I know that you are looking for Jesus, who was crucified. He is not here; for he has been raised, as he said" (28:5-6). As Dahl suggests, one motive for Matthew's including the story of Judas (27:3-10) was to describe the fulfillment of Jesus' woes on the betrayer:

> The Son of Man goes as it is written of him, but woe to that one by whom the Son of Man is betrayed! It would have been better for that one not to have been born. (26:24)

There is a limit to this being equipped with power and its attendant features. When Jesus' "time [*kairos*] is near," or his "hour [*hōra*] is at hand" (26:18, 45), he is powerless. Cunning, force, and weapons are let loose, and his enemies do with him whatever they wish (26:50; cf. 17:12). And then he is "handed over" by a disciple, by the "people of God," and by the worldly power — all links in the same chain. In each instance, as the passive construction indicates,[30] the one acting behind these events is God: it is God who hands Jesus over, allows his enemies to overpower him without hindrance. Nowhere, perhaps, is this feature given greater emphasis than in the context of the crucifixion itself. There, despite everything, Jesus dies without being put to death:

> And about three o'clock Jesus cried with a loud voice, 'Eli, Eli, lema sabachthani?' That is, 'My God, my God, why have you forsaken me?' When some of the bystanders heard it, they said, 'This man is calling for Elijah.' At once one of them ran and got a sponge, filled it with sour wine, put it on a stick, and gave it to him to drink. But the others said, 'Wait, let us see whether Elijah will come to save him.' *Then Jesus cried again with a loud voice and breathed his last.* (27:46-50; italics mine)

Jesus dies — but not by human hands.[31]

But beyond this, Jesus hands himself over. Ultimately, the Son of God, with all his power and authority, refuses to make use of it. More than one scholar has suggested that the crucifixion narrative contains strong reminiscences of the temptation. For example, Jesus' refusal to exercise the power at his disposal in the garden "so that the Scriptures of the prophets may be fulfilled" (26:51-54) recalls his resistance to the devil's urging with the threefold reference to what "is written" in Matthew 4 (vv. 4, 7, 10). Even his refusal to drink the wine mixed with gall (27:34) may be intended to recall the story of the temptation.[32] When the passers-by at the crucifixion shake their heads and say, "Save yourself! If you are the Son of God, come down from the cross" (27:40), they are echoing the devil's summons for Jesus to plunge from the pinnacle of the temple: "If you are the Son of God, throw yourself down" (4:6).

---

30. "The Son of Man is *going to be betrayed* into human hands" (17:22); "the Son of Man *will be handed over* to the chief priests and scribes" (20:18); "the Son of Man *will be handed over* to be crucified" (26:2); "woe to that one by whom the Son of Man *is betrayed*" (26:24); "the Son of Man *is betrayed* into the hands of sinners" (26:45); italics mine.

31. Cf. Gerhardsson, "Jesus, Ausgeliefert und Verlassen," pp. 271-273, 275.

32. Cf. Weber, *Kreuz*, p. 181.

This abuse heaped on Jesus at his execution, as well as the earlier temptations, has at its base the expectation that God will deliver his righteous one from peril ("if you are the Son of God"), a theme that is not limited to the literature between the Testaments. For example, in his introduction to the Psalms, Hermann Gunkel (1862-1932) says that, in Psalms 56:9 and 140:12, the reference to "knowing" ("that God is for me . . . that the Lord maintains the cause of the needy") is best explained on the assumption of its being prefaced by an oracle guaranteeing deliverance, and that Jeremiah's certainty that his complaint and prayer will be heard assumes a similar oracle (Jer. 11:18-20).[33] In any case, by calling up associations with the temptation narrative in chapter 4, Matthew appears to want to describe the crucifixion as Jesus' last and hardest "test," a repetition of the more "theoretical" temptations following his baptism. It would never have occurred to Matthew, however, that in the moment when Jesus experienced total abandonment by God, he would have "lost" his faith. His submission to the "curse" of crucifixion was thus not merely his last and hardest test, but it was the highest point of his resistance to temptation and of his obedience to God.[34] Minear writes of the significance of Matthew's "timing" of Jesus' cry: "It comes not at the onset of darkness but about three o'clock, when light overcomes the darkness. The cry is synchronized with the return of light."[35]

Use and Fracture of Old Testament Theology and Apocalyptic

In a work for which Jesus' death is at the midpoint of a triangle formed by Old Testament, synagogue, and church,[36] Matthew's passion narrative will obviously be described in an Old Testament context. I have referred above to the "frame" of Matthew's passion narrative as reflecting formulations in Deuteronomy. For example, at the outset of the narrative, the phrase "when Jesus had finished saying all these things" (26:1) echoes the phrase in Deuteronomy, "when Moses had finished speak-

33. Cf. Hermann Gunkel, *Einleitung in die Psalmen: Die Gattungen der religiösen Lyrik Israels* (Göttingen: Vandenhoeck & Ruprecht, 1933), pp. 243-247.

34. Cf. Gerhardsson, "Jesus, Ausgeliefert und Verlassen," pp. 277-279, 283.

35. Minear, *The Golgotha Earthquake,* p. 103.

36. Dahl, "Die Passionsgeschichte bei Matthäus," p. 217.

ing" or "reciting all these words" (Deut. 31:1; 32:45).[37] Similarly, at the close of Matthew's Gospel, Jesus' commissioning of the disciples (28:20) echoes Moses' command that Israel "obey the Lord, observing all his commandments" (Deut. 30:8).[38] The opening and closing of Matthew's passion narrative thus reflect its Old Testament framework.

Within the narrative itself, the Last Supper scene opens with Jesus' statement that the Son of Man goes "as it is written of him" (26:24). The saying is a general reference, reflecting earliest Christian conviction that the Old Testament attested to Jesus' death, and is without connection to any specific text. It appears in Mark (Mark 14:21) and is of the same type as the opening sentence of the *paradosis* in I Corinthians 15:3. After the Supper, Jesus and the disciples go to the Mount of Olives, where Jesus predicts their desertion in his nuancing of what the Lord of hosts says to his sword in Zechariah 13 (Matt. 26:31).[39] In the next moment, encountering the crowd that has arrived, he asks, "Have you come out with swords and clubs to arrest me as though I were a bandit?" He then adds, "But all this has taken place so that the scriptures of the prophets may be fulfilled" (26:56). In chapter 27, Matthew appends to his account of the death of Judas a quotation from Jeremiah 32:9; and he records Jesus' cry from the cross in the words of Psalm 22:1.

In addition to reflecting Old Testament Scripture generally, Matthew's passion narrative clearly reflects features of apocalyptic Judaism. Without subscribing to Schweitzer's portrait of Jesus as driven and ultimately shattered by the imminent expectation of the kingdom, one can acknowledge that his uncovering of passages in Matthew suggestive of apocalyptic thought does have merit.[40] With regard to Jesus' word in

---

37. Cf. also Deuteronomy 31:24; 32:45.

38. Cf. also Deuteronomy 29:9; 30:10, 16; 31:12; 32:46.

39. Zechariah 13:7: "'Awake, O sword, against my shepherd, against the man who is my associate,' says the Lord of hosts. 'Strike the shepherd, that the sheep may be scattered.'"

40. For example, Schweitzer notes that the entire commissioning discourse in Matt. 10:16-23, with its promise of the arrival of the Son of Man preceded by turmoil, belongs to a prediction of events of the end-time, and locates its most striking parallel in the Syrian Baruch Apocalypse (2nd century C.E.): "Behold, the days are coming and it will happen when the time of the world has ripened and the harvest of the seed of the evil ones and the good ones has come that the mighty One will cause to come over the earth and its inhabitants and its rulers confusion of the spirit and amazement of the heart. And they will hate one another and provoke one another to fight. And the despised will rule over

Matthew 11:12 concerning the kingdom as suffering violence, Schweitzer says that Johannes Weiss mistakenly assigned all initiative or "activity" to the kingdom. In reality, he argues, the verse restores activity to Jesus' preaching — but as conditioned by a "thorough-going eschatology":

> The secret of the Kingdom of God . . . amounts to this, that in the movement to which the Baptist gave the first impulse, and which still continued, there was an initial fact which drew after it the coming of the kingdom, in a fashion which was miraculous, unintelligible, but unfailingly certain, since the sufficient cause for it lay in the power and purpose of God.[41]

In his interpretation of the parable of the banquet and the man without a wedding garment in Matthew 22:1-14, Schweitzer sees a characteristic feature of "thorough-going eschatology" that cannot be explained dogmatically but nonetheless obtrudes in Jesus' teaching and public activity: the idea of predestination.[42]

Weiss notes that, in those passages of the Gospels that reflect Jesus' idea of the kingdom, the future tense has the lion's share. He says that, in Matthew, striving for righteousness is given a "sharply eschatological" point because it is harnessed to keeping in view the otherworldly kingdom still to come; he concludes that the command to love one's enemies perfectly suits Jesus' eschatological preaching: it gives instruction for the final period of struggle in which the divine judge will put an end to all human strife, and "all too soon." The promise in Matthew 8:11-12 that the elect will sit at table with Abraham, Isaac, and Jacob thus envisions an "altogether otherworldly blessedness, without analogies to this world."[43]

Käsemann locates traditional Jewish material in Matthew 24, perhaps an apocalyptic "leaflet" or its fragment from the time of the Jewish War. Thus, the "flight" predicted in verses 15-22 amounts to a sketch of

---

the honorable, and the unworthy will raise themselves over the illustrious. And many will be delivered to the few. . . . And it will happen that everyone who will save himself and escape from all things which have been said before . . . will be delivered into the hands of my Servant, the Anointed One" (70:2-4, 9-10 [*The Old Testament Pseudepigrapha*, I, 644-645]).

41. Schweitzer, *The Quest of the Historical Jesus*, p. 326.
42. Schweitzer, p. 335.
43. Weiss, *Die Predigt Jesu vom Reiche Gottes*, pp. 71-73, 112-113, 147-150.

the apocalyptic message of disaster drawn from earlier motifs. Similarly, verses 29-31, with the prediction of the heavenly signs accompanying the coming of the Son of Man, recall the oracles of Isaiah, Ezekiel, and Joel,[44] to say nothing of the predictions with which the apocalyptic writings of later Judaism are aswarm. Interpreting the chapter as an event that brings back the chaos existing before the creation, Käsemann regards the whole of it as determined by Old Testament Jewish tradition. Only the identification of the Son of Man with Jesus and the tendency to emphasize hope more strongly mark its specifically Christian element.[45]

In his relentless contrast between the Jewish ecclesiastical authorities and Jesus, Matthew replicates the division of humanity into the good and the wicked that is characteristic of the dualism of apocalyptic thought. He draws other, lesser contrasts,[46] which function for the most part only to heighten the contrast between Jesus and the religious authorities. In the chapters immediately preceding his passion account, Matthew — again in concert with apocalyptic thought — deals with the ultimate fate of the wicked.

From a purely formal aspect, Matthew's repeated reference to an event's taking place "to fulfill what had been spoken by the Lord through the prophet" reflects apocalyptic perspective.[47] This use of the prophecy-fulfillment feature is reminiscent of the historical review that is part of the apocalyptic genre, calculated to engender confidence in present occurrence as part of a predetermined divine plan, thus related to what Schweitzer termed the "eschatological-predestination" idea inherent in the apocalyptic scheme.

Yet another aspect of the apocalyptic perspective is reflected in

---

44. Isa. 13:10: "For the stars of the heavens and their constellations will not give their light; the sun will be dark at its rising, and the moon will not shed its light"; Isa. 34:4: "All the host of heaven shall rot away, and the skies roll up like a scroll"; Ezek. 32:7: "When I blot you out, I will cover the heavens, and make their stars dark: I will cover the sun with a cloud, and the moon shall not give its light"; Joel 2:31: "The sun shall be turned to darkness, and the moon to blood, before the great and terrible day of the Lord comes."

45. Käsemann, "Matthäusevangelium," II, 143, 149, 151, 152-154.

46. Between Judas and Jesus (26:21-25, 48-50), the disciples and Jesus (26:31), Peter and Jesus (26:33-35, 69-75), the crowds and Jesus (26:47; 27:20-23, 25, 39, 49), Pilate's guard and Jesus (27:27-31), the bandits and Jesus (27:44).

47. Cf. Matthew 1:22; 2:5, 15, 17, 23; 3:3; 4:14-16; 8:17; 12:17-21; 13:35; 21:4-5; 26:56; 27:9.

Matthew's language. In the midst of the barbarity of the crucifixion, Matthew says that the curtain of the temple was torn in two, the earth shook, rocks were split, tombs were opened, and bodies were raised and crawled out of their tombs (27:45-54). In announcing judgment to Israel, Jeremiah speaks of the sun going down during the day (Jer. 15:9). In Isaiah, Judah's hymn of victory sings that the "dwellers in the dust" awake (Isa. 26:19). In Ezekiel's vision of the dry bones, God says, "I am going to open your graves, and bring you up from your graves, O my people" (Ezek. 37:12).[48] In the vision of Daniel, Michael, protector of Israel, will arise, and "many of those who sleep in the dust of the earth shall awake, some to everlasting life, and some to shame and everlasting contempt" (Dan. 12:2). Albert Vanhoye refers to Matthew's staging the effects of Jesus' death by emphasizing its eschatological compass, by adding "cosmic shock" to the rending of the veil "in order better to indicate the end of the old age."[49] Add to this Matthew's description of the shaking of the disciples' expectations, the priests' prestige, the scribes' righteousness, and the soldiers' power at the resurrection — a "revolution" to which "only language that is inherently apocalyptic can do justice."[50]

In a monograph entitled *Apocalyptic Eschatology in the Gospel of Matthew*,[51] David Sim argues that Matthew's particular "apocalyptic-eschatological scheme" originated with a "sectarian Jewish" group undergoing a crisis following the Jewish war. It had departed from the parent Jewish body and was now in conflict with it; it was also threatened by a law-free Christianity in ascendance since the destruction of the Jerusalem church, and was imperiled by the gentile world. These factors led to the withdrawal of Matthew's community, and to its need to seek support from within its own borders. It thus became an apocalyptic community. To satisfy his readers' need for consolation, but also for vengeance, as well as to maintain the group's solidarity, Matthew designs his apocalyptic-eschatological scheme, trajecting it back into the

48. In his "Die Passionsgeschichte bei Matthäus," p. 225, n. 34, Dahl notes Harald Riesenfeld's demonstration of the agreement between Matt. 27:51-53 and Ezek. 37 in the synagogue paintings at Dura-Europos.

49. Vanhoye, "Struktur und Theologie der Passionsberichte in den Synoptischen Evangelien," p. 255.

50. Minear, *The Golgotha Earthquake*, p. 107.

51. Society for New Testament Studies, Monograph Series 88 (Cambridge, UK: Cambridge University Press, 1996).

mouth of Jesus, the Son of Man who would return at the *eschaton* and preside over the judgment.[52]

It is not merely that the concern of Matthew, "the catechist or rabbi," is not rapture but discipleship of the crucified, hence *paraenesis.*[53] There is no mistaking the eschatological-apocalyptic nature of his thought: it is the language of the end-time as it appears in the Old Testament and the literature between the Testaments, language used to mark an epiphany,[54] the *visible* appearance of God for judgment and deliverance. Visibility, the epiphanic, is in fact the hallmark of the apocalyptic perspective. But it is precisely at this point that it suffers fracture in Matthew's Gospel. For Matthew, Jesus' death is the apocalyptic event par excellence, the beginning of the end of the world, as the events that he uses to surround it and that he subordinates to it make clear. As Paul Minear puts it, whereas Caesarea Philippi marks the verbal disclosure of God's identification of Jesus as the Son, Golgotha and the earthquake disclose his actual identification.[55] But by warping the eschatological-apocalyptic scheme to the event of the crucifixion, Matthew voids it of its hallmark. Where is the epiphany, the visibility, the God manifest to every eye in that man hanging on the tree and cursed according to the law? Earlier in the Gospel, visibility has been challenged. In chapter 10, the Son of Man has linked his return to the completion of the disciples' assignment, not to an epiphany (10:23). In chapter 18, Jesus' response to the disciples' question about rank is that greatness does not go through glory but humility (18:1-4). And the "Doom Chapter" warns against a misunderstanding of Jesus' messiahship inherent in apocalyptic speculation (24:4-5).[56] Not even the event that gave Matthew the reason for composing his Gospel escapes the challenge to visibility. He says that, upon seeing the resurrected Jesus, his disciples "worshiped him; but some doubted" (28:17). According to Matthew, the appearance of the risen Lord was as ambiguous as his life and death.

This wedding of apocalyptic perspective to Jesus' crucifixion spells

52. Sim, *Apocalyptic Eschatology in the Gospel of Matthew*, pp. 242-243, 248.
53. Cf. Käsemann, "Matthäusevangelium," II, 92, on Matt. 8:23-27.
54. Weber, *Kreuz*, p. 182.
55. Minear, *The Golgotha Earthquake*, p. 13.
56. Minear, pp. 86, 90; Fleinert-Jensen, *Das Kreuz und die Einheit der Kirche,* p. 38; Daniel Patte, *The Gospel according to Matthew* (Philadelphia: Fortress, 1987), p. 336.

a serious qualification, if not total abandonment, of the old paradigm. The universal notion of the visible day of God has been supplanted by what cannot be seen — by ambiguity or hiddenness. In light of that qualification, everything said by prophets and seers requires adjustment, alteration, qualification, even cancellation. For the sake of this event, attention to the Old Testament becomes a matter of "reverse English," since this event gives integrity to what has been done and said in the past, however much interpreters such as Matthew appear to move from prophecy to fulfillment, from the Old Testament to the New.

Aside from construing Matthew's scheme as a means to the end of group solidarity, and thus assigning penultimate status to the words and deeds of Jesus — a procedure scarcely restricted to Sim but sufficient to recall a word of Screwtape to his nephew[57] — the study of Matthew's "apocalyptic-eschatological scheme" aimed at protecting his community against formative Judaism and law-free Christianity hides a confidence in scholarly method that recalls the heyday of form- and redaction-criticism.

Käsemann, whose description of Matthew's community Sim's study resembles, is sanguine about the results to which the form-critical method can take him. He admits that its preoccupation with the original situation-in-life of a given speech or narrative reduces its concern for historical individuality. Nevertheless, he believes that the method is sufficiently accurate to determine the life of a speech or narrative and thus the situation of the community it reflected before being included in a Gospel. From his reading of Matthew, Käsemann believes he sees in it vestiges of the apocalyptic dream of a once robust but now defunct Palestinian Christianity. Here, for the first time in church history, he says, the theological conception — and a church struggling to give it shape — went under. The limiting of mission to Palestine, the expectation of an imminent in-breaking that obviates further preparation, messianic restitution of the twelve-tribe people — it all broke apart on the fact of the gentile church. This tradition Matthew proceeds to combine with a gentile Christianity in order to combat a Judaism that kept the Torah but

---

57. "We do want, and want very much, to make men treat Christianity as a means; preferably, of course, as a means to their own advancement, but, failing that, as a means to anything" (C. S. Lewis, *The Screwtape Letters: Screwtape Proposes a Toast* [New York: Macmillan, 1967], pp. 119-120).

denied Jesus' messiahship, and to combat a fanaticism that appealed to inspiration and the Spirit's authority for recognition of its position. Against these opponents, Käsemann continues, Matthew makes a unified charge: hypocrisy. Thus, whereas Sims interprets Matthew's purpose as primarily defensive, that is, to ensure the solidarity of a group that has withdrawn from the wider world and sought support within its own borders, Käsemann understands the evangelist's purpose to be in essence offensive, that is, as an attack on the two fronts of Pharisaism and enthusiasm.[58]

The differences between Sim and Käsemann are as clear as their similarities, and from them one may infer that whatever criteria are used to determine the situation of a given community, they are more heuristic in nature, have more the nature of incitement to discovery than of certainty. If, as I have noted earlier, the event of Jesus' death is given such place in a Gospel seldom associated with a *theologia crucis,* then Matthew's use, say, of the Jewish apocalyptic tradition may have less to do with maintaining group solidarity or with opposing legalism and fanaticism than with pointing up this event as the beginning of the end of the world. Then it is not so much the use — or, as with Käsemann, the resuscitation of a tradition and to whatever it is linked — that deserves attention, but the point toward which everything is warped and bent, and for that reason suffers fracture. For Matthew, the event of Jesus' death requires a sea change in perspective involving a radical alteration of whatever "mental furniture" he has used to view the world, himself, and God. With him this event also refuses to take second seat to the need for group solidarity or control, or to a struggle against legalism and enthusiasm, which are coincident to the main purpose.

Use and Fracture of Nomism

In his study of the Christian Church in the first three centuries, Ferdinand Christian Baur says that the principal content of the utterances and speeches in Matthew's Gospel is not the person of Jesus and his divine nature but rather "the human and familiar," which makes direct appeal to the "moral and religious consciousness." This, Baur says,

---

58. Käsemann, "Matthäusevangelium," I, 81, 107-108; cf. II, 68, 98, 140.

is the simple answer to the question of what one's attitude must be and what one must do in order to enter the kingdom of God. In the teaching of Jesus, Baur adds, the Old Testament concept of theocracy had been so spiritualized that everything connected with one's relationship to the kingdom rested exclusively on moral conditions.[59]

The number of those following in Baur's train is past counting. Johannes Weiss says that in the soul of Jesus, "this powerful, joyfully active man," the predestinarian-eschatological and ethical-imperatival aspects juxtapose without colliding.[60] Bacon argues that Matthew's Gospel demonstrates the use to which the Jesus tradition could be put by a Jewish-Christian, neolegalistic community. Accordingly, its portrait of Jesus is that of teacher of the law or a second Moses, corresponding to the Gospel's construction according to five books of Christian Torah.[61] Käsemann says that the thematic division of the Sermon on the Mount indicates that Matthew understood it as Torah and portrays Jesus as a (Christian) rabbi.[62] Nils Dahl points out that the evangelist understood his work as a kind of counterpart to the Pentateuch, that in his Gospel two ideas cohere: Jesus as the Christ and Jesus as *Didaskalos,* as crucified Son of God and a new Moses.[63] Birger Gerhardsson says that two questions were uppermost for Matthew: what is righteousness? and how did Jesus, the righteous one, live? Matthew was thus the "ethicist" among the evangelists.[64]

One by one, interpreters who describe the Jesus of Matthew as the bringer of a new Torah must concede a dialectic in his relationship to the law. Baur says that the affirmative relationship Jesus adopts toward the law also contains opposition to it, since the inner is opposed to the outer, the disposition giving the deed its true worth as opposed to the mere doing of it. This is a "new principle," Baur says, essentially different from Mosaism insofar as what the law contains "but only implicitly *(an sich)* is

59. Baur, *The Church History of the First Three Centuries,* trans. Allan Menzies (London: Williams and Norgate, 1878), I, 26, 35, 37, 77.

60. Weiss, *Die Predigt Jesu vom Reiche Gottes,* pp. 7-8.

61. See a review of Bacon's argument in Roy A. Harrisville, *Benjamin Wisner Bacon, Pioneer in American Biblical Criticism* (Missoula, MT: Scholars Press, 1976), pp. 41-45.

62. Käsemann, "Matthäusevangelium," II (synopsis of part I), 1; II, 77, on Matt. 7:1-5 and 7:28-29.

63. Dahl, "Die Passionsgeschichte bei Matthäus," pp. 217-218.

64. Gerhardsson, "Jesus, Ausgeliefert und Verlassen," pp. 266, 280.

now made the chief thing and principle of the moral." This "expansion," he concludes, automatically turns into a "qualitative difference."[65]

Weiss argues that it is understandable that, since the period of rationalism, when the eschatological-messianic had become foreign to it, Christian theology should hold more and more to what Jesus had to say about this life. But, he adds, the historian will readily recognize that this is only one side of the picture, for Jesus does not always appear in the "pure clarity of a fully harmonious nature." For example, his encounter with his opponents strikes sparks from his spirit that ignite the entire structure of Pharisaic nomism. His statement to the effect that no one is made unclean through outward defilement but only through sin is not merely something new; it attacks the very basis of a system built totally on the notion of levitical purity. Weiss remarks that a great number of Jesus' ethical ideas arise in debate with the law and with Pharisaism, and for this reason they lie outside his eschatological preaching. He assigns the same subordinate status to passages such as Matthew 12:28,[66] which reflect moments of prophetic inspiration in which Jesus' consciousness of victory overwhelms him. Jesus does not speak in this way every day, Weiss adds; that is, such a statement does not mark his basic mood but represents his experience at its height. But for all that, it is a declaration that topples "modern ethicizing expositions with one blow." Again, anticipating Schweitzer's description of Jesus' ethical sayings as tailored to a discipleship within the interim before the end *(Interimsethik)*,[67] Weiss denies to Jesus any systematic ethical legislation calculated to regulate the life of a community over the years.[68]

Similarly, Benjamin Bacon notes an exception to the Gospel's "neo-legalism" in how Matthew describes Jesus' attitude toward the law. As evidence, he refers to the Sermon on the Mount, in which the legalist's expectation is "met to the ear" but "broken to the hope." That is, the requirement is rendered so exorbitant that all mercenary righteousness collapses before it.[69] Dahl says that, though Matthew and many mem-

---

65. Baur, *Church History,* I, 30.

66. "If it is by the Spirit of God that I cast out demons, then the kingdom of God has come to you." See what may be the more original reading in Luke 11:20: "If it is by the finger of God that I cast out the demons, then the kingdom of God has come to you."

67. Schweitzer, *The Quest of the Historical Jesus,* pp. 454-455.

68. Weiss, *Die Predigt Jesu vom Reiche Gottes,* pp. 88, 90, 95, 136-137, 139.

69. Harrisville, *Benjamin Wisner Bacon,* pp. 44-45.

bers of his community are of Jewish origin, the Gospel itself is not Jewish-Christian but "universal," evidence that not all Jewish-Christians remained aloof in particularistic fashion.[70] Finally, Käsemann refers to Jesus' dialectical relationship to the law in the Synoptic Gospels: in one instance he affirms it, in another he exceeds it, and in still another he shoves it aside. Hence, though Matthew may describe Jesus as the first Christian rabbi and his teaching as *didachē*, or Torah, he nonetheless distinguishes him from the rabbis. The Jewish rabbi, authorized through ordination, teaches only in dependence on the tradition; Jesus, on the other hand, speaks of the will of God directly and without constant reference to Scripture.[71] Where he does refer to the tradition, he radicalizes Moses or distances himself from him — as he does in the Sermon. He accords decisive significance to his eschatological mission and holds himself to be inspired. Whether or not he reflects on his person, he is conscious of himself as the bringer of the messianic Torah, which annuls the Torah of Moses.[72] If this "Torah" that Jesus brings is a summons to radical love and voluntary obedience, it has its anticipation in the deed that should "save his people from their sins" (1:21), that is, in the death of Jesus obedient to the will of his Father (26:53-54). In this way the rabbinic, nomistic, and legalistic have also suffered fracture.

In one of his last published pieces, Käsemann gave his own answer to the question of how Matthew had avoided the formulas of sacrifice and atonement other Christian interpreters had applied to Jesus' death. For Matthew, Käsemann wrote, God had come to the poor in Jesus, to the mourning and the hungering (Matt. 5:3-6), to sinners and the heavy laden (Matt. 9:13; 11:28-30), to the little ones (Matt. 18:10), to the thirsty, the strangers, the naked, and the sick (Matt. 25:34-36). This is precisely why he died. And his death took place where profanity showed itself on all sides, in order not to abandon the weary and the rejected, and in order to block the path of all those who are captive to the illusion that God is absent where he does not reveal himself in visible power. At the cross, at the place where Christ did not forsake the Father and died for us, God

---

70. Dahl, "Die Passionsgeschichte bei Matthäus," p. 216.

71. In fact, Käsemann assigns the bulk of scriptural quotations in the New Testament to community theology (see "Matthäusevangelium," I, 82).

72. Cf. Käsemann, "Matthäusevangelium," I, 82-83; II, 94.

and the ungodly come together — "'Look, the virgin shall conceive and bear a son, and they shall name him Emmanuel, which means, 'God is with us'" (Matt. 1:23) — and the distinction between the holy and the profane, the attractions of power, the illusion that the existence of God can be believed only where it can be proved, or that piety can be established on the evidence of one's own eye — all of that pales.[73]

73. Ernst Käsemann, "Die Gegenwart des Gekreuzigten," in *Kirchliche Konflikte,* pp. 76-83.

CHAPTER FIVE

The Death of Jesus in Luke

Luke and the *heilsgeschichtlich* Scheme

For years scholars have declared outright or implied that in Luke's Gospel and the Acts of the Apostles there is nothing of "anomaly" attaching to Jesus' death, nothing to precipitate a crisis or transition from one paradigm to another. In 1930, J. M. Creed (1889-1940) wrote that Luke contains no *theologia crucis* beyond the affirmation that the Christ must suffer, since prophetic Scripture had thus foretold.[1] In his studies on the theology of Luke, Hans Conzelmann (1915-1989) says that the Gospel has worked out no direct interpretation of Jesus' suffering or death, and that in Acts the concept of the cross plays no role for preaching.[2] In an essay on the history and theology of the Synoptic passion narratives, he acknowledges that for Luke the passion is in fact the condition for salvation, that this view is strongly set forth in the widening of Jesus' journey toward the passion and in the detailed description of his teaching in the temple; and yet he inquires whether the passion is, for Luke, only a passage that is over with the exaltation of Jesus.[3]

Charles Kingsley Barrett says that Luke stood far enough from the historical Jesus to have digested the raw, perplexing traditions that appear in Mark in all their crudity — and to have made of them something

---

1. J. M. Creed, *The Gospel according to St. Luke* (London: Macmillan, 1930), p. lxxii.

2. Conzelmann, *The Theology of St. Luke,* trans. Geoffrey Buswell (New York: Harper and Brothers, 1960), p. 201.

3. Conzelmann, "Historie und Theologie in den synoptischen Passionsberichten," p. 52.

less scandalous and more easily assimilable.[4] According to James D. G. Dunn, "an important corollary" to the concentration on Jesus' resurrection in Acts is the absence of any theology of Jesus' death, mentioned "only as a bare fact."[5] In one of his last novels, among the best works of prose fiction in the last century, Albert Camus (1913-1960) records the "confession" of a down-at-the-heel, one-time Parisian lawyer whose musings on his life include this reflection on Jesus' death:

> . . . he was not upheld, he complained, and as a last straw, he was censored. Yes, it was the third evangelist, I believe, who first suppressed his complaint. "Why hast thou forsaken me?" — it was a seditious cry, wasn't it? Well, then, the scissors![6]

Absence of the "anomaly" in Luke's Gospel has been assigned to his *heilsgeschichtlich* scheme, according to which the divine plan of salvation consists of a continuum with successive stages marked by repeated attempts at thwarting the divine purpose but ultimately made to serve it; it is also characterized by ever-new revelatory events, all culminating in Christ's return.[7] Within this scheme, the death of Jesus is an interlude in the history of salvation, a passage toward his exaltation, reflected in his words to the two Emmaus travelers: "Was it not necessary that the Messiah should suffer these things *and then enter into his glory?*" (Luke 24:26 [italics mine]). For Luke, the argument reads, the death of Jesus is a tragic crime, unjustly committed by malicious Jewish leaders against the will of the Roman authorities and the better part of the Jerusalem citizenry,[8] a crime that God fortunately corrects after three days through his glorious intervention, but which lives on in the indictments contained in the sermons of Acts.[9]

On this view, the soteriological understanding of Jesus' death in

4. Barrett, *Luke the Historian in Recent Study* (London: Epworth Press, 1961), p. 23.

5. Dunn, *Unity and Diversity in the New Testament* (Philadelphia: Westminster, 1977), p. 17.

6. Albert Camus, *The Fall,* trans. Justin O'Brien (New York: Alfred A. Knopf, 1957), p. 113.

7. Cf., e.g., Oscar Cullmann, *Salvation in History,* trans. Sidney G. Sowers and the editorial staff of SCM Press (New York: Harper and Row, 1967), pp. 125-126.

8. Cf. Luke 23:48: "And when all the crowds who had gathered there for this spectacle saw what had taken place, they returned home, beating their breasts."

9. Luz, "Theologia crucis als Mitte der Theologie im Neuen Testament," p. 120.

Luke's Gospel retreats. Troeger says that, in all the Lukan literature, the idea of the substitution and atoning suffering of Jesus plays no role.[10] Another says that it is difficult to assume that Luke assigned saving significance to the cross of Jesus, that awareness of the church's tradition is indicated only once in the Gospel — in the so-called Words of Institution at the Last Supper (Luke 22:19-20).[11] In his exposition of the passion narrative, Dibelius contrasts the reports of the centurion's confession in Luke and Mark. Luke allows the centurion to reach knowledge accessible to human comprehension; thus his statement "this man was innocent" (Luke 23:47) reflects merely a "psychological miracle," the executioner convinced by the martyr. Mark is dealing with a "greater miracle, the conversion of an unbeliever by the dying Savior."[12] Friedrich says that, while no other New Testament author speaks so much of the forgiveness of sins, nowhere does Luke connect it with the death of Jesus; and he refers to two passages in Acts that deal with Jesus' death without specifically mentioning his resurrection. The first is in the narrative of Philip and the Ethiopian eunuch in 8:26-40, which recites verses from the Fourth Servant Song in Isaiah 53. Friedrich notes that the recitation breaks off immediately before the words that the sufferer was "stricken for the transgression of my people" (Isa. 53:8). The second passage is in Acts 20:28, which records Paul's address to the Ephesian elders, whom he admonishes to "shepherd the church of God that he obtained with the blood of his own Son." According to Friedrich, Luke makes it clear here that, though of minor importance to his theology, the community's statements of faith regarding Jesus' death are known to him, the implication being that he could scarcely have suppressed them.[13]

The consensus appears to read that Luke's theological reflection assigns only secondary significance to the death of Jesus. Luke depicts Jesus' passion, a mere passage toward exaltation, as the martyrdom of the Righteous One for whose death the Jews bear responsibility.[14] And

---

10. Troeger, *Die Passion Jesu Christi in der Gnosis nach den Schriften von Nag Hammadi*, p. 138; Delling, in *Das Kreuzestod Jesu in der urchristlichen Verkündigung* (p. 88), flatly declares that Luke does not apply the idea of substitution to the death of Jesus.

11. Delling, *Das Kreuzestod Jesu in der urchristlichen Verkündigung*, pp. 82, 92, 93-94.

12. Dibelius, "The Passion Story," p. 195.

13. Friedrich, *Die Verkündigung*, p. 20; cf. Hooker, *Not Ashamed of the Gospel*, p. 93, and Delling, *Der Kreuzestod Jesu in der urchristlichen Verkündigung*, p. 94.

14. Delling, *Der Kreuzestod Jesu in der urchristlichen Verkündigung*, pp. 82, 84; Weber,

since he portrays Jesus' death in this way, he emphasizes the ethical aspect of that death. Thus it is not the saving significance of his death but rather its paradigmatic character that Luke emphasizes. Jürgen Becker does not restrict this characterization to Luke but regards "the oldest form of the synoptic passion report" as a variation on the idea of the righteous sufferer, for which reason the death of Jesus is not assigned saving significance.[15] According to Schmithals, the question of Luke's intention behind his subtraction of saving significance from the passion has not yet found a satisfactory answer.[16] If the scholarly consensus regarding Luke's nonsoteriological interpretation is correct, then Camus's lawyer was in error:

> He left us alone, though people naturally tried to get some help from his death: After all, it was a stroke of genius to tell us: "You're not a very pretty sight, that's certain! Well, we won't go into the details! We'll just liquidate it all at once, on the cross!"[17]

A Second Reading

There is another way of reading Luke. After the decades-old control of Lukan studies that sharply distinguished the period of Jesus' passion from the remainder of his life and career conceived as a "Galilean springtime," studies began to appear challenging the separation, contending that it had ignored certain aspects in Luke's view of Jesus' death. According to Frieder Schütz, once we recognize the relationship between the theme of Jesus' rejection and his passion in Luke-Acts, we may infer that Luke's community was in crisis: it awaited the kingdom's coming, and yet it suffered persecution. To meet this crisis, the evangelist drew a portrait of Jesus calculated to assist his readers in coming to grips with their fate. The portrait was that of the rejected and crucified Jesus whose fate

---

Kreuz, p. 191. Wilckens says that in Luke the death of Jesus is naturally foreseen in the divine plan but receives no soteriological significance (*Die Missionsreden der Apostelgeschichte*, p. 126).

15. Becker, "Die neutestamentliche Rede vom Sühnetod Jesu," p. 37.

16. Walter Schmithals, "Die Worte vom leidenden Menschensohn: Ein Schlüssel zur Lösung des Menschensohn-Problems," in *Theologia Crucis–Signum Crucis*, p. 421.

17. Camus, *The Fall*, p. 113.

took its origin from his status as the Christ. That is, Jesus was not the Christ because he suffered; he suffered because he was the Christ. Accordingly, his community had to regard its persecution as marking its fellowship with the one destined to judge the living and the dead. Thus, Schütz concludes, there is no time free of rejection in the life and career of Jesus, which is then followed by the passion, a peripheral happening more or less distinguishable from the other events of his life.[18]

A rereading of the Gospel makes clear that, though Luke may not reflect on the death of Jesus in the same way his coevangelists do, he does not construe it as "a bare fact."[19] Whatever terms and concepts served his old paradigm, among them a view of salvation history as a vast panorama or cavalcade moving inexorably toward its goal, they may still dot the Gospel's landscape but cannot absorb the event of the cross, thus rendering it a mere "corollary" to the resurrection. For Luke, the cross of Jesus is a sign standing over his earthly path from the very beginning.[20]

The first hint of the passion occurs as early as Luke 2:34-35, in the prophecy of Simeon at the time of Jesus' circumcision:

> This child is destined for the falling and the rising of many in Israel, and to be a sign that will be opposed so that the inner thoughts of many will be revealed.

Chapter 4 contains the passion in miniature, but with what has been termed "an interesting reversal": instead of Jesus' death and resurrection leading to the gentile mission, the suggestion that he brings salvation to the gentiles enrages his countrymen (4:28-30): "They got up, drove him out of the town, and led him to the brow of the hill on which their town was built, so that they might hurl him off the cliff."

In Luke 9, Jesus stands with Moses and Elijah on the Mount of Transfiguration, where all three speak of the "departure" he is about to "accomplish" at Jerusalem (9:31). "Departure" — or more exactly "exodus" — is a term Luke obviously uses to link Jesus' death with the history of Israel's deliverance, its journeying and settling in Canaan; for

---

18. Frieder Schütz, *Der leidende Christus: Die angefochtene Gemeinde und das Christuskerygma der lukanischen Schriften. Beiträge zur Wissenschaft vom Alten und Neuen Testament* (Stuttgart: W. Kohlhammer Verlag, 1969).

19. Sänger, *Die Verkündigung des Gekreuzigten und Israel*, p. 221.

20. Sänger, p. 80.

this reason it embraces the whole of Jesus' activity culminating in his suffering and his ultimate vindication by God. Of all the evangelists, Luke alone conceives of Jesus' journey to Jerusalem and its outcome as his *exodos*. The Transfiguration scene is framed by two of the three great Passion predictions in Luke:

> The Son of Man must undergo great suffering, and be rejected by the elders, chief priests, and scribes, and be killed, and on the third day be raised. (9:21-22)

> Let these words sink into your ears: The Son of Man is going to be betrayed into human hands. (9:44)

The second prediction contains no hint of resurrection, and like the third (18:31-34), it draws attention to the word's concealment from the disciples.

From the outset, Luke's so-called "journey report" (9:51–19:44) is characterized as one of Jesus' suffering stubborn rejection. Following the metamorphosis on the mountain, Luke reports that when "the days drew near for him to be taken up, he set his face to go to Jerusalem" (9:51). If the first half of the verse, with its reference to the ascension (Acts 1:2), hides a victory motif, what follows in the second half warns against telescoping or assigning a subordinate role to the events leading toward it. The result of Jesus' decision is a resounding rejection by the Samaritans, calling to mind their repudiation of Elijah in II Kings 1:2-16. But unlike the Elijah narrative, in which the prophet's rejection ends in the death of the Samaritans and their king, an event that James and John suggest might be repeated ("Lord, do you want us to command fire to come down from heaven and consume them?" [9:54]), the rejection of Jesus is unrelieved. "Within this dynamic framework," says David Moessner, "in the chilling cadences of the Deuteronomic prophetic fate Luke sets the reception accorded Jesus the prophet like Moses."[21]

Jesus' journey to the temple seals the fate of the prophet like Moses and that of the nation. In Luke 11, following his attack on the Pharisees as approving the deeds of their fathers by building the tombs of the prophets they killed, the scribes and Pharisees grow more hostile and wait to catch him in his speech (11:47-51). Chapter 12 contains a double-speech in which

---

21. David Moessner, "'The Christ Must Suffer': New Light on the Jesus-Peter, Stephen, Paul Parallels in Luke-Acts," *Novum Testamentum* 28, No. 3 (1986), 238.

Jesus appears not only as actor ("I came to bring fire to the earth, and how I wish it were already kindled!") but also as acted upon ("I have a baptism with which to be baptized, and what stress I am under until it is completed!" [12:49-50]). In Luke 13:33, as in the report of the Transfiguration (9:31), the evangelist describes Jerusalem as the city of Jesus' death.[22] In reply to the Pharisees' warning of Herod's intention to kill him, Jesus says:

> Yet today, tomorrow, and the next day I must be on my way, because it is impossible for a prophet to be killed outside of Jerusalem. (13:33; cf. 9:31)

Once more, in chapter 17, Jesus' prophetic sending to Jerusalem spells a recapitulation of the tragic fate of Israel's prophets (17:25-30). "This generation" will inflict suffering on the Son of Man.

Equal in importance to early allusions are the scenes that enjoy a reciprocal relationship with the passion. For example, from the perspective of the passion, the portrait of Herod undergoes gradual "disfigurement." In Luke 3 he imprisons John the Baptist (3:19-20); in chapter 9 he is "perplexed" about Jesus, his allegedly resuscitated victim (9:7-9); in chapter 13 he is an active threat (13:31); and in chapter 23 he is directly involved in Jesus' trial (23:6-12). Likewise in chapter 3, a heavenly voice confirms Jesus' baptismal experience of *sonship* (3:21-22), a theme that Luke isolates as the immediate cause of handing Jesus over to Pilate by the Sanhedrin (22:70–23:1). Chapter 4 describes Jesus' temptation and Satan's challenge ("if you are the Son of God . . ." [4:9]), to which the exorcism of the demon in 9:37-43 and the voice at the Transfiguration ("my Son, my Chosen" [9:35]) give the response.[23]

The implication of the passion prediction immediately following the Transfiguration is that the disciples are unable to perform the exorcism because they do not understand Jesus' statement about suffering (9:43b-45). The temptation is repeated at the crucifixion ("If you are the King of the Jews, save yourself!" [23:37]) and at its outcome in the "exorcism" — in Jesus' "crying with a loud voice" and "breathing his last" (23:46). Finally, in his reply to the warning against Herod, Jesus links his "exodus" to his healings and exorcisms, another connection ignored by those who sepa-

---

22. Gerhard Delling suggests that 13:31-33 is taken from an oral or written source (see *Der Kreuzestod Jesu in der urchristlichen Verkündigung*, p. 79).

23. Hooker, *Not Ashamed of the Gospel*, p. 81.

rate a "Galilean springtime" from the passion: "Listen, I am casting out demons and performing cures today and tomorrow, and on the third day I finish my work" (13:32). The result is a three-way connection between the Transfiguration, the exorcism, and the passion prediction.[24] As Hooker says, by eliminating Mark 9:9-13, 21-24, 26-29 from his narrative of the exorcism, and by adding the reference to Jesus' "departure" in 9:31 and to his "taking up" in 9:51, Luke has made the links between glory and suffering even more stark, reminding us that what is occurring in Jesus' ministry, death, and resurrection is Satan's defeat. Chapter 18 contains Luke's third great passion prediction: it opens with the words "See, we are going up to Jerusalem," suggestive of the "exodus" or "departure" in 9:31 and of the time drawing near for his "taking up" in 9:51 (18:31-34). In the statement that "everything that is written about the Son of Man by the prophets will be accomplished," Luke uses a verb *(teleō)* that he took up at 12:50 in the curious little saying about Jesus' "baptism," and that he repeats in 22:37[25] and in Acts 13:29. And again, as with the second prediction (9:43b-45), the meaning of Jesus' statement is hidden from the disciples (18:34).

Nowhere in Luke's Gospel is the division between belief and unbelief, between the voluntary and involuntary, between human culpability and the divine decree, between the earthly or mundane and the cosmic or transcendent — and finally nowhere the interweaving of an individual's fate with that of his people — more marked than in the Good Friday scene of Luke 23. *They* bring Jesus to the place called "the Skull," *they* crucify him, and *they* cast lots to divide his clothing (23:33-34) — while "the people" stand by watching (23:35). To the right and left of the victim hang two criminals, the one adding to the leaders' and soldiers' mockery ("let him save himself"), the other witnessing to Jesus' innocence and pleading to be remembered (23:39-42). On the one hand, a willful deed of execution; on the other, acknowledgment of the perpetrators' ignorance: "They do not know what they are doing" (23:34). On the one hand, leaders and soldiers as subject of the action; on the other, a death construed as submission to divine decree: "Father, into your hands . . ." (23:46). On the one hand, an altogether earthly, natural-

---

24. Cf. Delling, *Der Kreuzestod Jesu in der urchristlichen Verkündigung,* p. 77.

25. This is the only instance in which Isaiah 53 is used in Luke's Gospel, not as a dogma, but as proof text that these things happened to the Messiah. Acts 8:32-33 reflects the same use; cf. Hooker, *Jesus and the Servant,* p. 151; cf. p. 113.

historical event — one more crucifixion, with all the politicizing that serves as its preface — and on the other, a cosmic, transcendent event:

> It was now about noon, and darkness came over the whole land until three in the afternoon, while the sun's light failed; and the curtain of the temple was torn in two. (23:44-45)

On the one hand, scoffing and mocking; on the other, an inscription that spoke better than it knew: "This is the King of the Jews" (23:35-38). On the one hand, God's exaltation of the crucified Jesus as prophet and servant like Moses contains reproof of Israel and a demand for repentance; on the other, an offer of forgiveness and life for both Jew and gentile: "Father, forgive them. . . . Truly I tell you, today you will be with me in paradise . . ." (23:34, 43). On the one hand, an exodus; on the other, a standing at God's right hand in the presence of those who destroyed him. This subtle interweaving in Luke's narrative sets him on a par with the ancient dramaturgists, but it is precisely *what* he weaves that sets him apart from the literature of tragedy he has come to know.[26]

In the final chapter of his Gospel, Luke gives the word of the risen Jesus to his disciples:

> Look at my hands and my feet; see that it is I myself. Touch me and see; for a ghost does not have flesh and bones as you see that I have. (24:39)

This statement appears in the section of Luke 24:36-42 in which the risen Lord is identified with the crucified Jesus. In contrast to the traditional *heilsgeschichtlich* conception that reduces the passion to subordinate status, the resurrection and exaltation are in fact the passion's continuation; more exactly, the passion has Jesus' resurrection as its goal. And, according to Luke, it is the risen one himself who furnishes the impetus for this interpretation of his death:

> Was it not necessary that the Messiah should suffer these things and then enter into his glory? Then beginning with Moses and all the prophets, he interpreted to them the things about himself in all the scriptures. (24:26-27; cf. 44-46)[27]

26. Roy A. Harrisville, *Holy Week, Proclamation 2*, Aids for Interpreting the Lessons of the Church Year (Philadelphia: Fortress Press, 1981), p. 58.

27. Weber, *Kreuz*, p. 187. Regarding the death-motif in Luke, cf. Delling, *Der*

The link Luke forges between Jesus' death and the last times constitutes a further challenge to the *heilsgeschichtlich* perspective. For example, in Luke 12:49-56, following his response to Peter's question concerning the "parable" of the thief, and the summons to alertness in view of the coming of the Son of Man (12:39-40), Jesus speaks the parable of the slave "whom his master will find at work when he arrives" (12:42-48). He then continues the discourse, prefacing it with this declaration: "I came to bring fire to the earth, and how I wish it were already kindled!" What follows in the references to bringing ("casting" in the original) fire, to division and to war among members of the same household, belongs to the stock of apocalyptic perspective. For example, there is a striking similarity between this text in Luke and Micah's prediction of Jerusalem's fall:

> The faithful have disappeared from the land . . . the powerful dictate what they desire; thus they pervert justice. . . . The day of their sentinels, of their punishment, has come; now their confusion is at hand. Put no trust in a friend, have no confidence in a loved one . . . for the son treats the father with contempt, the daughter rises up against her mother, the daughter-in-law against her mother-in-law; your enemies are members of your own household. (Mic. 7:2-6)

More important, by means of that curious reference to "baptism" in verse 50 ("I have a baptism with which to be baptized"), Luke clearly and deliberately sets Jesus' death within the context of the events of the end-time. It is precisely because the "last things" *and* his death have not yet taken place that Jesus experiences straitening: "How I wish it were already kindled! . . . what stress I am under until it is completed!" Then, turning from the disciples to the crowds (12:54a), Jesus gives reverse application to a traditional maxim:

> When you see a cloud rising in the west, you immediately say, "It is going to rain." You hypocrites! You know how to interpret the appearance of earth and sky, but why do you not know how to interpret the present time?

Kreuzstod Jesu in der urchristlichen Verkündigung, p. 79; Hooker, *Not Ashamed of the Gospel,* pp. 78, 80-82; Moessner, "'The Christ Must Suffer,'" pp. 238-241; Peter Doble, *The Paradox of Salvation: Luke's Theology of the Cross* (Cambridge, UK: Cambridge University Press, SNTS Monograph Series, 1966), pp. 7, 22, 68, 211-213.

Jesus aims this epithet at an incapacity resulting in a contradiction between weather-prediction and interpreting the "present time." By setting this within the context of Jesus' discourse to the disciples, but also to the crowds concerning the approaching *eschaton,* the evangelist clearly intends to set "the present time" — that is, Jesus' activity culminating in his death — at the heart of the apocalyptic vision. For all its vaunted (verbal) similarity to this text, the Gnostic Gospel of Thomas omits a feature absolutely essential to Luke: the link between Jesus' ultimate fate and the events to occur at the end of time.

Finally, it is astonishing to note the extent to which Luke has described the life of Jesus as the way of the suffering Christ. Even the titles he applies to Jesus throughout his two-volume work resist the notion of Jesus' death as a mere passage toward exaltation. In the Gospel, the "Christ" predicate, whether used as appellative or personal name, is never reserved for the exalted one. Of the three exceptions to this use in Acts, only one passage refers solely to the Messiah's resurrection (Acts 2:31), while the others refer to the necessity of his death (Acts 17:3: *hoti ton Christon edei pathein;* Acts 26:23: *ei pathētos ho Christos).* Of the more than twenty-five uses of the Son-of-Man title in the Gospel and in Acts, half refer to the shame, rejection, or suffering of this figure.[28]

Use: Martyrs and Wisdom

Fidelity to the *heilsgeschichtlich* interpretation did not silence other attempts at uncovering the language and conceptuality of the third evangelist. In his form-critical study, Dibelius suggests that Luke's Gospel is the story of the man of God who, embattled by evil forces, in patience and forgiveness becomes a model of innocent suffering. The literary consequence of this view was the description of Jesus' passion as a martyrdom. According to Dibelius, since pieces such as the martyrdom of Isaiah or II and IV Maccabees in edited form were known among Christians, Luke could expect understanding and appreciation from his readers.[29]

---

28. Cf. Luke 6:22; 7:34; 9:22, 26, 44, 58; 12:10; 18:31-33; 22:22, 48; 24:7. Cf. Moessner, "'The Christ Must Suffer,'" p. 234; Sänger, *Die Verkündigung des Gekreuzigten und Israel,* p. 220.

29. Dibelius, "The Passion Story," p. 201.

A newer, more elaborate but yet related theory relates to Wisdom literature as the context out of which Luke wrote his Gospel, his passion narrative in particular. According to this theory, Wisdom, with its story of salvation mediated through God's loyal and saintly people,[30] furnished Luke with a coherent matrix around which to rework the passion story as a defense of Jesus' death. Whether or not the tradition of the crucifixion that Luke received directed him to Wisdom's model, or whether he had already begun to think of Jesus in such terms, his substitution of Psalm 31:5 ("Father, into your hands I commend my spirit") for the cry of dereliction in Mark as Jesus' last word, together with his report of the centurion's declaration that "this man was innocent" *(dikaios),* coincides with what Wisdom affirmed would be the lot of the "righteous man," God's *dikaios.* Wisdom, together with the Psalms, thus furnished Luke two distinct but convergent sources leading to his model. These two strains precluded any cry of desolation. "My God, my God, why have you forsaken me?" (Ps. 21:1) could not have been Jesus' last word on the cross in Luke's Gospel. Luke's model and the Psalms agree that God had not abandoned his *dikaios.* The model demanded a final word that reflected a mood of quiet confidence in God. The Marcan crucifixion narrative was thus subsumed under a larger model. In that model the *dikaios* was resented because

> . . . he said he was God's Son: we are considered by him as something base, and he avoids our ways as unclean; he calls the last end of the righteous happy, and boasts that God is his father. (Wisdom 2:16)

In his reply to the council's question, "Are you, then, the Son of God?" Jesus answers, "You say that I am," to which they respond, "What further testimony do we need? We have heard it ourselves from his own lips!" (Luke 22:70-71).

In that model the death of the *dikaios* was also a testing:

> Let us test what will happen at the end of his life; for if the righteous man is God's child, he will help him, and will deliver him from the hand of his adversaries. (Wisdom 2:17b-18)

---

30. In "Struktur und Theologie der Passionsberichte in den Synoptischen Evangelien," pp. 249-250, Vanhoye says that the humiliation of Jesus represents the realization of a prophetic tradition attesting to the need for personal sacrifice — and which rests on the history of the men of God.

At the cross the leaders scoff and say, "He saved others; let him save himself if he is the Messiah of God, his chosen one!" The soldiers mock and say, "If you are the King of the Jews, save yourself!" And one of the criminals derides him and says, "Are you not the Messiah? Save yourself and us!" (Luke 23:35-39).

In this model the sufferer displays gentleness and forbearance in the face of his tormentors: "Let us test him with insult and torture, so that we may find out how gentle he is, and make trial of his forbearance" (Wisdom 2:19). Luke reports that, when they crucified Jesus at the place called "the Skull," he said, "Father, forgive them, for they do not know what they are doing" (Luke 23:34). At this point the Wisdom-theory points to the ignorance theme that threads throughout the Gospel and Acts and parallels Luke's assigning Jesus' death to specific groups. He strikes this theme initially in the report of the people's "beating their breasts and wailing" on their way to the cross and again on their return home (23:27, 48). The theme runs on into Acts, where Peter clearly assigns the "men of Judea and all who live in Jerusalem" responsibility for Jesus' death (Acts 2:14, 22-23); but in his address to the people at Solomon's portico he says, "And now, friends, I know that you acted in ignorance, as did also your rulers" (Acts 3:17). According to the theory, this theme likewise originates in Luke's molding of his passion narrative around the Wisdom-matrix. In the Wisdom of Solomon the enemies of the "righteous man . . . were led astray, for their wickedness blinded them, and they did not know the secret purposes of God" (Wisdom 2:21-22).

The theory of the Wisdom-matrix is not limited to Luke's passion narrative; it notes Luke's use of the "language of entrapment" throughout his Gospel. Again and again Luke describes Jesus' opponents as watching him "so that they might find an accusation against him" (6:7); as "testing" him (10:25; 11:16); as "lying in wait for him, to catch him in something he might say" (11:53-54); and as "watching him closely" (14:1). This theme, begun as early as Luke 5 — with the scribes' and Pharisees' "questionings" following the healing of the paralytic[31] — is thought to be redolent of the oppressors of the *dikaios* in Wisdom's model:

31. Cf. Luke 5:17-26.

Let us lie in wait for the righteous man, because he is inconvenient to us and opposes our actions; he reproaches us for sins against the law, and accuses us of sins against our training. (Wisdom 2:12)

Thus, according to this theory, beneath Luke's story of Jesus' being spied upon, humiliated, crucified, and raised — all of it construed as his *exodus* — there lay the model of the humiliated, killed, and vindicated *dikaios* or "righteous man" of the Wisdom of Solomon.[32]

Fracture: The Divine Necessity

However suggestive the theory of Wisdom's "righteous one" *(dikaios)* as furnishing Luke the matrix for his composition might be, it encounters one significant challenge. Threading throughout his "history" — or better, obtruding on it at its beginning, midpoint, and conclusion — is the repeated reference to the *necessity* of Christ's death. Like Mark and Matthew, Luke transmits early church tradition concerning the divine "must" of Jesus' suffering; in addition, he makes this tradition the central theme of his narrative. Further, while one or the other coevangelist may refer to Scripture as requiring its fulfillment in the suffering of the Son of Man,[33] and may also speak of its divine necessity,[34] Luke combines the two ways of speaking into a unity.[35]

This emphasis on necessity has precedent neither in the Old Testament nor in the later rabbinic literature. When the prophets speak of what is to come, they do not refer to something that "must" occur. Among the Writings, only Daniel refers to a divine necessity determining the course of the world as destiny, a usage suggestive of Greek or

32. For this exposition of Luke's Gospel against the background of the Wisdom-motif, cf. Doble's *The Paradox of Salvation.*

33. Cf. Mark 9:12: "How then is it written about the Son of Man, that he is to go through many sufferings and be treated with contempt?" See also Mark 14:21: "For the Son of Man goes as it is written of him. . . ."

34. Cf. Mark 8:31: "Then he began to teach them that the Son of Man must undergo great suffering"; or Matt. 16:21: "From that time on, Jesus began to show his disciples that he must go to Jerusalem and undergo great suffering"; or Matt. 17:22: "As they were gathering in Galilee, Jesus said to them, 'The Son of Man is going to be betrayed into human hands.'"

35. Weber, *Kreuz,* p. 193; see also Friedrich, *Die Verkündigung,* p. 34.

Hellenistic influence.[36] Apparently, the language of ineluctable fate is not at home in Jewish thought. For this reason, when Doble writes of Jesus' testing at his crucifixion as modeled in the fate of Wisdom's *dikaios,* he can at best only speak of it as "implied."[37]

There is a relentlessness in Luke's use of the term for necessity in his portrait of Jesus. In 4:43, Jesus says: "I must proclaim [*euangelisasthai me dei*] the good news of the kingdom of God to the other cities also...." In the first great passion prediction of 9:22, he says: "The Son of Man must undergo great suffering [*dei ton huion tou anthrōpou polla pathein*]...." In 13:33, Jesus announces: "Yet today, tomorrow, and the next day I must [*dei me...poreuesthai*] be on my way...." In this last passage, Jesus' reference to his death in Jerusalem as by divine necessity sets aside the earlier warning against Herod (13:31), as does verse 32, with its use of the verb *teleioō* in the passive (inaccurately translated "I finish my work"). God will set the end to Jesus' activity. In Luke 17:25, Jesus refers to the "initial or supreme" necessity of the suffering of the Son of Man *(prōton de dei auton polla pathein).* In 19:5, Jesus says to the tax collector Zacchaeus, "I must stay at your house today" *(dei me meinai).* In chapter 23, not one in the cast of characters — not Pilate, Herod, the chief priests, the elders, or the people — is the cause of the action. The crucifixion as a Jewish crime or a travesty of Roman justice is only the human, historical side of an event whose ultimate cause is signaled in verse 34: *"Father,* forgive them, for they know not what they do" — the reverse side of the divine necessity. It is not sufficient merely to say that the Jews led Jesus to his cross.[38] Three times in the last chapter of his Gospel, Luke emphasizes the necessity of Jesus' death. In 24:7, the men standing at the tomb remind the women of Jesus' statement that "the Son of Man *must* be handed over to sinners" *(dei paradothēnai);* in 24:26, Jesus reproaches the two on the way to Emmaus for their slowness of heart to believe "that the Messiah *should* suffer these things" *(tauta edei pathein);* and in 24:44, in a final meal with his disciples, Jesus

36. Cf. Dan. 2:28-29, 45. In his interpretation of Nebuchadnezzar's dream, Daniel tells the king that God has revealed to him "what will happen at the end of days," "what is to be," or "what shall be hereafter" (LXX: *dei genesthai*).

37. Cf. Wisdom 3:1, 5: "But the souls of the righteous are in the hand of God.... Having been disciplined a little, they will receive great good, because God tested them and found them worthy of himself." Cf. Doble, *The Paradox of Salvation,* p. 171.

38. Cf. Reinbold, *Der älteste Bericht über den Tod Jesu,* p. 66.

reminds them that everything written of him in the law, the prophets, and the psalms *"must* be fulfilled" *(dei plērōthēnai).*[39] Whether or not Luke and his coevangelists guessed that some day Jesus' path toward death would be seen as an accident or due to human arbitrariness and for this reason prefixed the "must,"[40] the theme of necessity is part and parcel of the passion narrative.

The theme of Jesus' death by divine necessity runs on into Luke's second volume. Acts 1:3 speaks of Jesus' "suffering" as a fixed station of his career. In Luke's report of Peter's address to the Israelites at Pentecost, Peter speaks of the crucified Jesus as "handed over to you according to the definite plan and foreknowledge of God" (Acts 2:23). And once more, as in his Gospel, Luke strikes here in Acts the motif of human ignorance alongside that of the divine necessity. To his audience in Solomon's portico Peter says, "I know that you acted in ignorance," but it was precisely in this way that "God fulfilled what he had foretold through all the prophets, that his Messiah would suffer" (3:17-18). And the same link between Jewish ignorance and divine destiny is forged in Acts 13:27:

> Because the residents of Jerusalem and their leaders did not recognize him or understand the words of the prophets that are read every Sabbath, they fulfilled those words by condemning him. (13:27)

Therefore, to the Jews' "subjective" guilt over Jesus' death corresponds the deed as "objectively" predestined in the plan of God: the Christ *had to suffer.*[41] In Acts 4:27-28, after the Jerusalem council releases Peter and John, their friends join in praise to God, who through Herod, Pilate, "the Gentiles and the peoples of Israel" did "whatever [his] hand and [his] plan had predestined to take place." Acts 6–7 contains the narrative of Stephen's martyrdom, clearly patterned after Jesus' passion. The *dramatis personae* are the same: the synagogue, the people, the elders

---

39. Delling, *Der Kreuzestod Jesu,* p. 79.

40. Hans Joachim Iwand, *Tod und Auferstehung,* ed. Hans-Iwand Stiftung (vol. II, *Christologie*), p. 397.

41. Ulrich Wilckens, *Die Missionsreden der Apostelgeschichte,* pp. 133-134. Wilckens says that neither in 3:17 nor in 13:27 is the Jews' *agnoia* intended in the moral sense. According to Luke, the Jews are absolutely guilty; their ignorance relates to their ignorance of the divine plan of salvation proclaimed beforehand by the prophets.

and scribes, the council, the high priest. "They" could not withstand the wisdom and Spirit with which Stephen spoke; "they" secretly instigated men; "they" stirred up the people and the elders and scribes (6:10-12); "they" came upon him and seized him (6:12); "they" were enraged; "they" ground their teeth against him; "they" cast him out of the city and stoned him (7:54, 58). Only Pilate and Herod are missing, replaced by "Saul," who consented to Stephen's death (8:1). Again, all of this is merely the human, historical side of an event whose ultimate cause is signaled in Acts 7:60: "And [Stephen] knelt down and cried with a loud voice, 'Lord, do not hold this sin against them.'" In the synagogue at Antioch in Pisidia, Paul stood up to recite the events of salvation history culminating in the death of Jesus, whom "the residents of Jerusalem and their leaders" killed and thus "fulfilled" the words of the prophets, and after carrying out everything "written about him," took him down from the tree and laid him in a tomb (13:27, 29). In Acts 17:3, Paul contends with the Jews of Thessalonica, "explaining and proving that it was necessary for the Messiah to suffer and to rise from the dead." Finally, in chapter 26, characterizing his preaching before King Agrippa, Paul says:

> I stand here, testifying to both small and great, saying nothing but what the prophets and Moses said would take place: that the Messiah must suffer [*ei pathētos ho christos.* (26:22-23)]

This constant harking back to Old Testament scriptures as fulfilled in Jesus' death is not — at least not principally — an apologetic aimed at the Jewish community. That would have rendered Luke's work anachronistic, since the problem of Jewishness largely belonged to an earlier period of Christian history. The emphasis on Scripture's fulfillment in Jesus' death is the obverse side of the insistence on its necessity. For this reason, the Old Testament could not be left behind; it belonged to the setting that enabled Luke to speak of the death and resurrection of Jesus.[42]

In Acts, suffering marks the authentic discipleship of the Messiah. Peter, Stephen, and Paul, like Jesus, are called to a journey involving suffering and rejection. The nation's leaders reject Peter before the people once more reject salvation from "the prophet like Moses" (Acts 4:5-31;

---

42. Cf. Hoskyns-Davey, *Crucifixion-Resurrection*, p. 178.

5:17-41; 12:1-17). Stephen suffers rejection and violent death as a transition figure between the leaders' opposition and the people's rejection (Acts 7:54–8:4). Paul suffers rejection from the people as a whole, so that the "glory of Israel" is extended to Ephesus, Macedonia, and Greece (Acts 19:21–28:31).

Therefore, the apostles and the communities "must" suffer rejection as their Messiah did because suffering is the way that messianic history is fulfilled according to the plan and purpose of God. In his exposition of the passion summaries in Luke, Wilckens says that the conclusion is irrefutable that Luke adapted and interpreted whatever he found in the tradition available to him so as to serve his description of the apostolic proclamation with its leading motif: that Christ must suffer.[43] We can thus detect two tendencies in Luke: in his Gospel he proclaims the Christ as the one destined to suffer; in Acts he depicts the suffering Christ as the one appointed for the world's salvation. In the Gospel the Christ is the suffering Jesus; in Acts the suffering Jesus is the Christ.

43. Wilckens, *Die Missionsreden der Apostelgeschichte,* pp. 116-117.

CHAPTER SIX

Synoptic Confession of the Crucified

In the face of the occasional contention that denying Jesus' anticipation of his death or reflection on its significance in relation to his mission robs his teaching of its Jewish particularity,[1] the majority of New Testament scholars have argued that the passion predictions in the Gospels correspond so completely in language, style, and sequence to the narratives of the passion, that the evangelists trajected back into the mouth of Jesus the later account of his trial and death. These passages are thus taken to be *vaticinia ex eventu*, prophecies after the fact. It is true, for example, that the passion narrative is so central for Mark that its language, style, and sequence appear to have influenced the remainder of his Gospel — in form as well as in content. It is difficult to compare the passion predictions in Mark with his narrative of the passion in chapters 14 and 15 without arriving at this conclusion. Schmithals says that Mark himself gave shape to the passion predictions, that their form thus emerged *ad hoc* on the basis of the passion narrative and in conjunction with doctrinal and confessional formulae derived from the early communities. He adds that, even if a different form-critical judgment were arrived at, the question regarding the redactional intention of the predictions would remain.[2] But it is not merely the striking formal and material correspondence between the

---

1. See, e.g., Peter Stuhlmacher, *Was geschah auf Golgotha?*, p. 281. But note the vacillation in Hooker: "Is it not more likely that Jesus spoke of the *probability* of rejection and of his willingness to drink the cup *if it were necessary?*" (*Not Ashamed of the Gospel*, p. 62).

2. Schmithals, "Die Worte vom leidenden Menschensohn," pp. 417, 420, 422.

predictions and the passion narrative that has led a majority to this conclusion. The use of that puzzling and much-debated "Son of Man" title in all three predictions in Mark, repeated in the parallels of Matthew and Luke with but one exception (and that due to the context; cf. Matt. 16:21), has tended to reinforce the notion that the predictions are redactional.

Approaching these predictions on the assumption that they are somehow liturgical or creedal in character may help to explain their origin, though it may not rescue them from the historian's critical eye. First, the argument from language that von Rad once adduced with regard to Old Testament creedal statements[3] may be of little help. The language of the predictions is in fact *agendarisch* (memorandum-like), reflective of a moment of great intensity, a characteristic that could simply be due to the actual historical context, at least as viewed by the Synoptists, rather than to any solemn, liturgical moment. Second, the fact that the general substance of these predictions repeatedly occurs throughout the entire New Testament may reflect merely the Christian community's insistence on the necessity of Christ's death, and not dependence on a creedal or liturgical formula. In fact, as I have noted above, the theme of necessity is clearly struck in that little word *dei,* which heads the first prediction in each of the Synoptics. In the face of the defeat that the death of Jesus spelled — and the consequent disbelief of Jew and Greek — the primitive community was eager to demonstrate the necessity of that death. Third, in every Matthaean and Lukan parallel but one,[4] the prediction concludes with the statement that the Son of Man will rise "on the third day," whereas Mark always reads "after three days" (Mark 8:31; 9:31; 10:34; cf. Matt. 16:21; 17:23; 20:19; Luke 9:22; 18:33).

Despite these embarrassments to the hypothesis, what is striking is that in each instance the passion predictions appear within a confessional context.[5] The frame for the first prediction is Peter's confession.

3. Gerhard von Rad, *Das formgeschichtliche Problem des Hexateuchs* (Stuttgart: W. Kohlhammer, 1938), pp. 12, 18-20, 29-31, 38, 40, 44-46, 51-55, 61-63.

4. Luke contains no reference to the rising in his second prediction (9:44).

5. Schmithals says that in all three predictions the words concerning the "suffering Son of Man" are linked to a central Christological confession. This feature indicates that the predictions are redactional, and more, that they are intended progressively to instruct the reader: first, in giving the fundamental data of the kerygma; second, in supplying an

In all three Synoptic Gospels, the prophecy of the passion immediately follows Peter's acknowledgment of Jesus as the Christ. That this linking of confession with prediction is not due to allegiance to Mark's outline is indicated by the fact that the setting for Peter's confession is not identifiable in Luke. Just prior to his narrative of the confession and first prediction occurs Luke's "Great Omission," an elimination of almost three chapters of Mark (Mark 6:45–8:26). The context of the second prediction is equally confessional in character. In all three Synoptists, the prophecy of the passion follows hard on the Transfiguration and the witness to Jesus as "my beloved Son" (Mark 9:7; Matt. 17:5), or as "my Son, my Chosen" (Luke 9:35). Again, the factor of Luke's independence, his telescoping of events surrounding the first and second predictions so as to include them within the space of twenty-six verses — whereas Mark and Matthew require twice that amount — indicates that the link between confession and prediction is not due to slavish pursuit of Mark's outline.

The same is true of the third prediction. In all three evangelists it occurs as a prelude to Jesus' entry into Jerusalem and the crowd's hosannas. And again, Luke's shuffling of his material between the prediction and the entry, requiring twice the space allowed in Mark and Matthew, indicates his independence over against Mark's outline. In each of his predictions, Luke appears to follow the general pattern of Mark. It is only prior to his prophecies of the passion that he omits or interpolates material. Before the first prediction he omits Mark 6:45–8:26, and before the third he interpolates the so-called Journey Report (9:51–18:14); but with 18:15 he returns to the path of Mark's Gospel. This independence with respect to Mark, where he is assumed to be following him, suggests that historical sequence and chronology are not always Luke's primary concern. In an overview of the predictions from the angle of Luke's or Matthew's agreement with Mark rather than their independence from him, Luke Timothy Johnson says:

> Each retains the Markan passion account and develops it even further. Each maintains the threefold prediction of the passion. By this means, they place Jesus' ministry of teaching and wonder-working

---

interpretation of the data; and third, in use of the concept *paradidonai* (cf. "Die Worte vom leidenden Menschensohn," pp. 429, 432).

within the framework of rejection and suffering. Something more than respect for a source is at work here. Matthew and Luke feel free to alter virtually every other aspect of Mark, but this image of the suffering One they do not alter in the least.[6]

In fact, the primary function of the passion predictions is not to yield any kind of historical context but rather to "interpret" the events that precede or follow them. Thus the Christ confessed by Peter, the Son witnessed to by the Transfiguration voice, and the crowd's hailing of "the One [the "King" in Luke 19:38] who comes in the name of the Lord" is then interpreted in all three passion predictions as marked for suffering and death.[7] Such an "interpretation," whether originally or only subsequently affixed to the event interpreted, could well have had its situation-in-life in a creedal formulation of the primitive Christian community, a formulation that reflected that community's first and bitterest contest with Jew and gentile.

In the Synoptic accounts of the resurrection appearances, there is little similarity: in fact, what Mark, Matthew, and Luke share can be reduced to under three verses. It is surprising, then, that in Luke 24, the portion of his narrative most peculiar to him, there are instances in which Luke's language, style, and the content of his narrative are similar to the passion predictions. First of all, Luke 24:6-7 repeats the third prediction that the Son of Man will be handed over to "sinners" ("to the Gentiles" [Luke 18:32]). Second, among Jesus' captors, verse 20 refers to the "chief priests" *(archiereis),* listed in the first prediction, and uses the verb *paradidōmi* ("I deliver up"), which appears in the second prediction. Third, verses 26 and 44 refer to the necessity of Jesus' passion by way of the verb *dei,* which occurs in the first prediction. Finally, verses 26 and 44 repeat the substance of the third prediction in 18:31: "Everything that is written about the Son of Man by the prophets will be accomplished."

Why this similarity with the passion predictions, and why at this

---

6. Johnson, *The Real Jesus,* p. 154.

7. In Mark, just as the statement regarding Jesus' "majesty" is always followed by the prediction of his suffering, so the prediction is always followed by *paraenesis* in the form of a summons to the disciples to suffer or to serve (Mark 8:34-35; 9:35; 10:43-44). In *Das Kreuz und die Einheit der Kirche,* Fleinert-Jensen says that it is scarcely accidental that, following the three passion predictions, Mark introduces examples denoting a denial of power (p. 74).

juncture? Matthew, normally so loyal to Mark, has gone his own way; so it is not inconceivable that Luke 24 simply reflects a particular theological posture rather than dependence on Mark or on a tradition known to all three evangelists. But it is also possible that all of Luke 24, with its obviously liturgical overtones — reflected, for example, in the episodes of Jesus' prayer at the breaking of bread (Luke 24:30) and his request for food (Luke 24:41-43) — is nothing but a theological supplement to the *dei* in the credo of the first prediction. From Luke's third prediction ("everything that is written . . . will be accomplished"), as well as from his statement in 9:51 to the effect that Jesus "set his face to go to Jerusalem," it could be inferred that such a supplement as the Emmaus incident and Jesus' rebuke of those "slow of heart to believe all that the prophets have declared" (Luke 24:25) would inevitably follow. On this view, Luke would emerge as von Rad's Yahwist, that is, as collector and gatherer of the tradition, but responsible for its historicizing or theological "penetration."[8] If the predictions are either a creedal statement of the primitive community or its historicized deposit, then its expansion might be due precisely to that tendency toward the "theological maximum" that von Rad believed was characteristic of the final editor of the Hexateuch.

In the third passion prediction — and in all three Synoptic Gospels — Jesus says: "See, we are going up to Jerusalem" (Mark 10:33; Matt. 20:18; Luke 18:31). Up from where? The evangelists allow us to infer "up from Jericho": the journey from there to Jerusalem involves a considerable climb. But if the geographical settings of Mark, and hence of Matthew and Luke, are furnished by the evangelist and not by the tradition, that command to go up could reflect a time in the ancient church when the holy sites still stood, when pilgrims began their tour of the sacred precincts from the Golden Gate west of the Kidron valley, and with some such shout as, "See, we are going up!" In his biography of Constantine, Eusebius (ca. 260-340 C.E.) reports the construction of the Church of the Sepulcher and assumes that the Christians in Jerusalem were still aware of the location of Jesus' grave.[9] Furthermore, the

---

8. According to von Rad, it was left to the Yahwist, that first great theologian of the *Heilsgeschichte*, to wed the two traditions of the giving of the land and the law, which resulted in the emphasis on the two basic elements of all biblical proclamation, the law and the gospel.

so-called *Peregrinatio Silviae ad loca sancta* describes fourth-century observance of the stations of the cross on the eight days of Easter in the
church of Constantine:

> On the first Lord's day (Easter Sunday), there is a procession toward
> the larger church, i.e. the Martyrium (the basilica), also on the second
> and third day, but in such fashion that when mass is over there is al-
> ways a procession from the Martyrium to the Anastasis (smaller
> church of the resurrection) with hymns. Then on the fourth day there
> is a procession to Eleona (the Mount of Olives chapel), on the fifth to
> the Anastasis, on the sixth to Zion, on the Sabbath in front of the
> Cross (westward, at the foot of Golgotha, just outside the basilica),
> but on the Lord's day, that is on the eighth, again toward the larger
> church, i.e. the Martyrium.[10]

The letters of Paula and Eustochium to Marcellus, preserved in the library of St. Jerome (ca. 342-420 C.E.), assume such pilgrimages had
continued — not unbroken, obviously — from the time of Christ's ascension to their own. Bishops and martyrs, they wrote, men eloquent
in church doctrine, had visited Jerusalem, supposing themselves to be
less religious, less knowledgeable, even less manly, until they had
adored the Christ at those spots from which the gospel first shone
forth.[11]

For years, a series of exegetes have not been content with deriving the
Synoptists' dating of Jesus' passion purely from human experience, but
they have regarded it as reflecting rituals observed by the Christian community. In 1918, Karl Ludwig Schmidt (1891-1956) explained the difference between the passion report and the remainder of gospel narrative in
terms of the report's special, formal position. That is, it will have been
read in a *lectio continua* during worship. For this reason, before it could be

9. Eusebius, *Life of Constantine,* trans. Averil Cameron and Stuart G. Hall (Oxford:
Clarendon Press, 1999), III, 25-40, 132-134.

10. *Silviae vel potius Aetheriae peregrinatio ad loca sancta: Sammlung vulgärlat-
einischer Texte,* ed. W. Heraeus und H. Morf (Heidelberg: Carl Winter's Universitätsbuchhandlung, 1929), XXXIX, 2, 44-45. Cf. references to Silvia-Aetheria in Joachim
Jeremias' *Golgotha* (Leipzig: Verlag von Eduard Pfeiffer, 1926), pp. 14-15, 49-50, 61.

11. Eusebius Hieronymus (Jerome), *Paulae et Eustochii ad Marcellam, Epistola* XLVI,
206: 9, *Opera Omnia,* Vol. I, J.-P. Migne, *Patrologia Latina* (Turnholt [Belgium]: Typo-
graph Brepols Editores Pontificii, n.d.), vol. XXII, 489.

honed or polished as the material outside the passion narrative, it had already been fixed and could not be altered.[12] In a virtual extension of Schmidt's hypothesis, Philip Carrington (1892-1975) argued that Mark's Gospel, throughout, consists of a series of lections for use in Christian worship, the passion narrative or longer continuous lection reserved for annual commemoration of the Christian Pascha.[13] In 1955, Schille said that Bultmann offered no help with respect to the origin of the unity of the passion tradition, and further that Dibelius's discussion assigned more weight to missionary apologetic as point of origin than it could really hold. As to the situation or need of the community that might have evoked its forms of the passion tradition, Schille referred to baptism and the Lord's Supper, to those events within the cultic community in which it was accustomed to remember Jesus' suffering in detail. The form of Jesus' confession in the passion narrative was adjusted to that of the general baptismal confession, and the reflection on Jesus' suffering was adjusted to the celebration of the Lord's Supper, with its *anamnesis*. The Gospel passion tradition thus stemmed from celebration.[14] Twenty years later, Hans-Ruedi Weber referred to the "more probable supposition" that the passion narrative was collected for a "worship function" and in the early church transmitted "chiefly in worship."[15] A year later, Hans Klein said that the situation-in-life of the earliest passion tradition reflected in Mark and John was "presumably" the passion and Easter *anamnesis*.[16] In 1981, Gnilka pointed to the repetitive nature of Mark's passion narrative, a fea-

12. Karl Ludwig Schmidt, "Die Literarische Eigenart der Leidensgeschichte Jesu," in *Redaktion und Theologie*, pp. 17-19; cf. also Vanhoye, "Struktur und Theologie der Passionsberichte in den Synoptischen Evangelien," p. 228.

13. Philip Carrington, *The Primitive Christian Calendar: A Study in the Making of the Markan Gospel* (Cambridge, UK: Cambridge University Press, 1952); *According to Mark: A Running Commentary on the Oldest Gospel* (Cambridge, UK: Cambridge University Press, 1960).

14. Gottfried Schille, "Das Leiden des Herrn," in *Redaktion und Theologie des Passionsberichtes nach den Synoptikern*, pp. 154-164, 167-169, 172, 174, 181-182, 188, 190-193, 195, 197.

15. In an argument highly reminiscent of Carrington's thesis, Weber says that the passion narrative, with its division into three parts by the hours of the day, could derive from the retelling of the crucifixion during the three daily hours of prayer in the Jewish-Christian order; see *Kreuz*, pp. 78-80.

16. Hans Klein, "Die Lukanisch-Johanneische Passionstradition," in *Redaktion und Theologie des Passionsberichtes nach den Synoptikern*, p. 395.

ture intended to serve remembrance, perhaps at the earliest community's worship. By way of illustration, Gnilka referred to the "intentional" parallelism between the high priest's question and Jesus' answer in Mark 14:61-62 and the hearing before Pilate in 15:2 as giving precision to Jesus' response in terms of the community's confession.[17] In 1992, Hans Hübner said that the "total, integrated life" of the Christian community was focused on the *anamnesis* of Christ's death at the Supper, and that the community's practice of the Supper furnished both the setting and the impetus for the development of the passion narrative.[18] In 1998, Helmut Koester spoke of the earliest community's setting the narrative of Jesus' passion within the context of a cultic action rooted in a ritual practice instituted by Jesus himself. The cult, anchored in the traditional language of Israel, together with the story of Jesus' suffering and death, furnished the constitutive elements in the community's self-definition.[19]

Earlier than any of the above-named, Bacon had argued that the earliest Christian community recognized only two types of Gospel composition — the "sayings and the doings" of Jesus — and that these two types furnish the clue to the two foci about which the anecdotes in the Synoptic Gospels were agglutinated: baptism and the Lord's Supper.[20] Bacon also attributed the dissimilarity in the evangelists' references to the rising of the Son of Man to a difference in liturgical practice.[21]

The uncovering of creedal formulations does not solve the relationship between the event and its interpretation. Conzelmann, noting that Mark's summary of the passion-kerygma in the three predictions re-

17. Gnilka, "Die Verhandlungen vor dem Synhedrion," pp. 295-296, 300.

18. Hübner, "Kreuz und Auferstehung im Neuen Testament, 2. Zur Kreuzesthematik," p. 71.

19. Koester, "The Memory of Jesus' Death and the Worship of the Risen Lord," *HTR* 91, No. 4 (1998), 348-349.

20. Benjamin Wisner Bacon, "Gospel Types in Primitive Tradition," *The Hibbert Journal* IV (1906), 878; *Jesus the Son of God or Primitive Christology: Three Essays and a Discussion* (New Haven: Yale University Press, 1911), p. 27; *The Apostolic Message: A Historical Inquiry* (New York: The Century Co., 1925), pp. 120, 124.

21. Bacon, "The Resurrection in Primitive Tradition and Observance," *American Journal of Theology* XV (July, 1911), 3; cf. "Raised the Third Day," *The Expositor* XXVI (December 1923). In his monograph on the topological data in John's Gospel, Karl Kundsin suggests that its passion narrative appears to reflect the liturgical or festival calendar of Holy Week; cf. Kundsin, *Topologische Überlieferungsstoffe im Johannes-Evangelium* (Göttingen: Vandenhoeck & Ruprecht, 1925), p. 10, n. 1.

veals the connection between *credo* and gospel, nevertheless cautions against citing the liturgy as condition for the emergence of the passion narrative. He says that the passion does not become contemporaneous in the worship through cultic repetition, but by the fact that it is narrated. He then adds that one cannot alter a hermeneutical theory regarding the manner of narration into an explanation of historical causes.[22] But while transferring allegiance from the passion predictions as *vaticinia* to the passion predictions as creedal does not rescue them from the historian's critical eye, it nevertheless helps to make clear the point where the contingent event in which the community believed it saw the hand of God and its understanding or conception of that activity converge. The *credo* thus gave faith and fact their connection and made impossible extracting naked facts from their interpretation or extracting interpretation as some alien thing added to the fact.

The larger question about what may have induced the Christian community to wed the contingent event and the "web" of its interpretation in precisely this way, in the *credo,* is answered in part by the community's belief that it encountered God as immediately present in the proclamation. This was certainly the case with Paul, whose silence at the point where he is most heavily engaged, that is, regarding the actual circumstances of Jesus' death — a feature Käsemann describes as "shocking"[23] — makes clear that for him the saving deeds could not be loosed from or played out against their interpretation in the preaching. In fact, Paul had already committed one act of "suppression." He had allowed the life and career of Christ to pale in light of the cross rather than allowed the cross and its atonement to disappear behind his historical life.[24] At any rate, due to the community's encounter with God as present, it was both bound to and free from the naked fact and the mythical. It was bound to the fact insofar as it acknowledged that God had been "there" before it believed, and it was free from the fact insofar as it selected and "theologized," or "historicized," the events for the sake of their actualization. It was bound to the "mythical," or "myth-like," when human existence furnished it no analogy to the activity of God, when,

---

22. Conzelmann, "Historie und Theologie in den synoptischen Passionsberichten," pp. 38-39.

23. Käsemann, "Die Heilsbedeutung des Todes Jesu nach Paulus," p. 26.

24. Forsyth, *The Cruciality of the Cross,* p. 141.

for example, it wanted to say something of God's activity at the beginning or end of time; but it was free of the mythical insofar as it announced that God had indeed been met in the contingent events of history. In the recognition of Yahweh as a God who roams, nomad-like, through time, always "before" his people, and in the recognition of the crucified Christ as risen, exalted, and reigning, the creeds of Israel and of primitive Christianity — and hence their literatures — not only have their justification but quite possibly their source as well.

CHAPTER SEVEN

The Death of Jesus in John

The Debate

Opinion is sharply divided over the significance of Jesus' death in John's Gospel. The division is most clearly reflected in Günther Bornkamm's (1905-1990) debate with Ernst Käsemann following the latter's interpretation of John 17.[1] In that piece, which reprises his earlier Göttingen inaugural lecture,[2] Käsemann says that the glory of Jesus so dominates the Christology of the Fourth Gospel that the passion narrative poses a problem. Apart from a few early hints, it appears only at the conclusion of the Gospel. The temptation is to regard it as a mere postscript, says Käsemann, because the author could not overlook it and yet could not organically insert it into his work. He happened on the expedient of stamping it with the features of Christ's victory.[3] For this reason, Käsemann continues, John uses Jesus' earthly life "merely as a backdrop for the Son of God proceeding through the world of man and as the scene of the inbreaking of the heavenly glory."[4] Thus John knows nothing of a real humanity of Jesus, tempted and exposed to suffering and death. Passing un-

---

1. Ernst Käsemann, *The Testament of Jesus,* trans. Gerhard Krodel (Philadelphia: Fortress, 1968); Günther Bornkamm, "Zur Interpretation des Johannes-Evangeliums: Eine Auseindersetzung mit Ernst Käsemanns Schrift 'Jesu letzter Wille nach Johannes 17,'" in *Geschichte und Glaube* (Munich: Christian Kaiser Verlag, 1968).

2. Ernst Käsemann, "Ketzer und Zeuge: Zum johanneischen Verfasserproblem," Inaugural Lecture in Göttingen, June 30, 1951, *ZThK* 48 (1951), 292-311.

3. Käsemann, *The Testament of Jesus,* p. 7.

4. Käsemann, p. 13.

troubled through death, which ends his earthly limitation, the one sent from heaven victoriously and joyfully ascends whither he descended as the one who has fulfilled his mission and has now been called back to the kingdom of freedom.[5] Such a description, says Käsemann, eliminates any contrast between present and future, since the earthly Jesus already personifies resurrection and life. This Christology so determines the Incarnation and the passion that it renders the former a projection of preexistence and the latter a return to it. In such a gospel, a *theologia crucis* no longer has any room. From all this we may infer the Gospel's origin in a "conventicle with Gnosticizing tendencies."[6]

Aside from questions of the evangelist's conceptuality, this interpretation has had its defenders. Bultmann gave it support when he said that, since Jesus' exaltation on the cross is his "enthronement," not only is his exaltation situated in the crucifixion, but the cross is in a certain sense projected into the glory. He further supported it when he said that John describes the entire earthly activity of Jesus in such a way as it can and hence should be understood in light of the end — thus as eschatological event.[7] Stöger describes the Jesus of John as acting, not suffering; as seizing the initiative and disposing of his enemies; as the knower whom no occurrence surprises; as the one whose word is fulfilled like the word of Scripture. Jesus, he says, *seems* to be the object of the process, but he is actually in charge. He gives up his spirit from free decision, just as he voluntarily assumes his death.[8] Kuhn refers to the fourth evangelist as "repressing" the aspect of Jesus' suffering, adding that the offense of the cross cannot easily be built into John's theology; and he cites with approval Käsemann's reference to John's passion as "lagging behind" (*nachklappt*).[9] Friedrich says of the prologue that "it lacks any reference to the death or even to the saving significance of Jesus' death."[10] Roland Bergmeier notes the two *eidōs*-clauses in John 18:4 and 19:28, which read

5. Käsemann, pp. 19-20.

6. Käsemann, *The Testament of Jesus,* pp. 20, 51, 73.

7. Rudolf Bultmann, "Zur Interpretation des Johannesevangeliums," *Theologie als Kritik* (*ThLZ* 87, 1962), 498.

8. Stöger, "Das Christusbild im Johanneischen Schrifttum," in *Der historische Jesus und der Christus unseres Glaubens,* pp. 154-155.

9. Heinz-Wolfgang Kuhn, "Jesus als Gekreuzigter in der frühchristlichen Verkündigung bis zur Mitte des 2. Jahrhunderts," p. 25; Weber, *Kreuz,* p. 208.

10. Friedrich, *Die Verkündigung des Todes Jesu im Neuen Testament,* p. 19.

that Jesus knew "all that was to happen to him," and "that all was now finished," and which thus form the *inclusio* framing John's passion narrative.[11] Hooker says that, while the ideas of suffering and glory are held together in the Synoptic tradition, in John they have coalesced to the point where one verb *(doxazō)* does duty for the two in Mark *(stauroō* and *doxazō).* Hooker then refers to the "blunting" of the horror of Mark's passion narrative, and views as "startling" Jesus' reference to his death as his glorification.[12] More recently, John Ashton refers to "Käsemann's case" as a strong one, adding that "the extent to which John suppresses the painful — and especially the shameful — elements of the passion story is truly remarkable"; he concludes that, with regard to the Fourth Gospel, the use of the term "passion" is a "misnomer."[13]

After his review of Käsemann's interpretation, Bornkamm proceeds to an independent analysis of the Gospel, beginning with Jesus' "farewell discourse." Here, Bornkamm says, Jesus' death is not only a "passing through" but a "breaking through" — to glory. The one who speaks in the farewell discourse is the one who dies, insofar as he discloses the benefit of his death for believers. What follows in the passion narrative takes place under this aspect. For this reason, Bornkamm says that he does not understand Käsemann's assertion that the passion narrative proved an embarrassment for John. Further, he says that the prediction of Jesus' death courses through the entire Gospel: he calls to mind John the Baptist's confession in 1:26 and 29, as well as the numerous passages scattered from the Cana story onward that speak of Jesus' "hour" (2:4; 7:30; 8:20) until they reach fulfillment in John 12:23-27; 13:1, 31; and 17:1. He refers to the temple-cleansing, with its mysterious reference to Jesus' death (2:13-22), and to the speech concerning the descent, ascent, and paradoxical exaltation of the Son of Man in Jesus' conversation with Nicodemus (3:12-15). These predictions are woven more tightly together in the shepherd-discourse in John 10, in the raising of Lazarus in chapter 11, and in Jesus' anointing and the speech about the seed in chapter 12. Equally important, Bornkamm adds, are the future revelation of the Son of Man at the end of the call of Nathanael (1:51) and

11. Roland Bergmeier, "Τετέλεσται in John 19:30," *Miszellen, Zeitschrift für Neutestamentliche Wissenschaft,* 79 (1988), vol. 3/4, 286.

12. Hooker, *Not Ashamed of the Gospel,* p. 95.

13. John Ashton, *Understanding the Fourth Gospel* (Oxford: Clarendon Press, 1991), p. 487.

the miracle of the feeding and the discourse at its conclusion (6:61-65). One should also note the transition to the first-person plural in the community's later testimony (1:14; 3:11-12). Bornkamm concludes this section by saying that the Gospel intends to be understood in "reverse direction" *(von rückwarts aus),* that is, from the witness of the Paraclete, whose message attests to the one glorified in death who will judge the world.[14] Bornkamm adds that, if we interpret the story of Jesus in John in linear and undialectical fashion as the story of God striding over the earth, stamped by Docetism and robbed of the reality of the cross event, then we have encountered the pre-Johannine tradition but not John.[15]

This interpretation has also had its defenders. In a monograph entitled *Jesu Gottheit und das Kreuz,* Adolf Schlatter insists that "the Johannine Gospel contains little else than passion history." In its fifth chapter, he says, we are already in the midst of the passion, and from there we get nothing more than the report of Jesus' journey toward death. In the first word of his exaltation, Jesus becomes what the serpent in the desert was for Israel (3:14-15). In the shepherd-discourse it is clear that, since humans are his possession and he is bound to them by an indissoluble bond, he goes unto death for them (10:11). Or again, in chapter 13, inasmuch as the one who has gone out from God is himself *of* God, he dies. And since he goes to the Father no earlier and not otherwise than through his death, this creates as its necessary result a dual — though in itself totally unified — love.[16] In the same vein, Hoskyns-Davey say that the reality of Jesus' death and its immediacy in the context of his mission to the Jews are more constantly insisted on by John than by any other New Testament writer. In evidence they refer to John's use of the same term to signify the crucifixion and exaltation of Jesus; the insistent looking for "the hour" that comes only with his death; the "glory" that can be apprehended only with his "glorification"; and the prediction of the Spirit that is withheld until he dies. All this and more, they add, point in only one direction.[17]

In the last three decades, Käsemann's thesis has evoked a chorus of objections. Alan E. Lewis says that John by no means suggests that the

14. Bornkamm, "Zur Interpretation des Johannes-Evangeliums," pp. 112-114.
15. Bornkamm, p. 117.
16. Schlatter, *Jesu Gottheit und das Kreuz,* pp. 29-31.
17. Hoskyns-Davey, *Crucifixion-Resurrection,* p. 153.

perfecting of Christ's glory on the cross was accomplished without or despite its physical misery and terminal mortality. Jesus himself, "in effect bringing Easter Saturday forward into the Upper Room," makes clear the necessity of termination, farewell and absence, sorrow and bereavement in order for the Spirit to come. The resurrection is thus not permitted to "verge back upon the cross . . . death is given space and time to be itself."[18] Writing of John's conception of Jesus' passion as saving event, predicted in Scripture as the will of God and sealed through Jesus' last word ("It is finished" [19:30]), Bergmeier says that the integration of the passion narrative into his Christology had already been prefigured, that the evangelist was not concerned to eliminate the saving significance of Jesus' death but to anchor it firmly in the Christology.[19] In an extended argument against assigning a "naïve docetism" to the Fourth Gospel, Martin Hengel says that, while John's Gospel may lack the Marcan theme of the Christ assailed by the distance and silence of God, it nevertheless has its own *theologia crucis,* as shown, for example, by the reference to Jesus as "troubled in spirit" in 13:21; to his carrying his own cross in 19:17; and especially to the record of events in 19:28-30 and 19:1-6, narratives composed with "extreme subtlety" and totally lacking in naivete, much less the "naïve docetism" attributed to the Fourth Gospel by Hengel's friend and neighbor Ernst Käsemann. "No author in the New Testament," Hengel concludes, "ventures to speak of the suffering and death of God in the man Jesus in this way, provocative as it would have sounded to the ears of people of antiquity."[20]

Fleinert-Jensen refers to the dominant role of the cross in the structure of all the Gospels and says that the cross supplies the perspective from which the signs in John's Gospel can be understood.[21] According to Luke Timothy Johnson, in the Fourth Gospel the supreme "work of God" that Jesus accomplishes is his passion and death. Together with his resurrection, it is the supreme revelation of God's glory, the effective presence of God in the world. The passion, writes Johnson, is no more an afterthought for John than it was for the Synoptists. It is the climax

18. Alan E. Lewis, "The Burial of God: Rupture and Resumption as the Story of Salvation," *ScotJT* 40 (1987), 344.

19. Bergmeier, "Τετέλεσται," p. 289.

20. Martin Hengel, *The Johannine Question,* trans. John Bowden (London: SCM Press, 1989), pp. 68-72.

21. Fleinert-Jensen, *Das Kreuz und die Einheit der Kirche,* pp. 34-35, 37.

shaping everything that precedes it.[22] Questioning the worth of engaging in the perennially debated alternative of a Christology of the cross versus one of glory in John, Ulrich Müller appears to side with the critics of Käsemann: he says that the passion is the "narrative orientation-point of the entire presentation, the high point or denouement of the narrative drama." On the other hand, he opposes the collapsing of the concepts of death and exaltation into a paradox, saying that the death can be an integral part of the event of exaltation only because everything depends on the Son's return to the Father. By showing that Jesus' death does not lead to a dead end, but opens the way on which he will prove to be the "heavenly steward" by preparing a dwelling for his own with the Father, John intends to overcome Jewish objections to the cross as a challenge to the legitimacy of his being sent from God. The real interest of the evangelist, therefore, is not in Jesus' crucifixion but in its interpretation as exaltation. In view of this pragmatic dimension, according to Müller, the death of Jesus gains no special theological significance.[23]

Finally, Helge Kjaer Nielsen, noting that Bultmann does not regard Jesus' death as having real or independent significance in John, and adverting to Bornkamm's criticism of Käsemann's reading, says that in the emphasis on Paul's preaching about the cross there is a clear tendency to overlook his statements about Jesus' glory and power. He says that, whatever conclusion can be drawn regarding John's understanding of Jesus' death, the thought of death in his concept of exaltation cannot be dismissed, because the script of Jesus' drama is written by God, and in that drama his death is the central event. In opposition to positions such as those assumed by Müller, Nielsen contends that it cannot justifiably be claimed that the evangelist's particular perspective precludes a recognition of the significance of Jesus' death on the cross; and he suggests that, instead of speaking of a *theologia gloriae* and a *theologia crucis* as alternatives, we would do better to link them together in John's Gospel.[24] Interestingly, Käsemann adds a qualification to his estimate of the place of Je-

22. Johnson, *The Real Jesus,* p. 156.

23. Ulrich B. Müller, "Zur Eigentümlichkeit des Johannesevangeliums: Das Problem des Todes Jesu," *Zeitschrift für neutestamentliche Wissenschaft* 88, No. 2 (1997), 26, 38-41, 43, 46.

24. Helge Kjaer Nielsen, "John's Understanding of the Death of Jesus," in *New Readings in John,* ed. Johannes Nissen and Sigfred Pedersen (Sheffield, UK: Sheffield Academic Press, 1999), pp. 232-233, 237-238, 254.

sus' death in John: he says that the hour of the passion and death of Jesus is "in the most marked sense also the hour of his glorification," and in the footnote attached says, "insofar Jesus' death, pace Bultmann, *Theologie*, 405, is crucial in character."

The Scheme

A review of the passages in John that explicitly refer to Jesus' death should decide whether or not the passion is integral to the Gospel. The last sentence of the prologue in chapter 1 reads:

> And the Word became flesh and lived among us, and we have seen his glory, the glory as of a father's only son, full of grace and truth. (1:14)

If the same synonymy of "glory" with "cross" that threads elsewhere throughout the Gospel underlies this statement as well, then it is a confession in retrospect of Christ's glory as anchored in the event of the cross.[25] The first unambiguous signal of Jesus' death, however, lies in John the Baptist's identification of him as the "Lamb of God" (1:36).

Next, in John 2, the first of the two "hidden passion predictions"[26] appears, and like its twin in 7:6, it is linked to a misunderstanding:

> The mother of Jesus said to him, "They have no wine." And Jesus said to her, "Woman, what concern is that to you and to me? My hour [*hōra*] has not yet come." (2:3-4)

> His brothers said to him, "Leave here and go to Judea so that your disciples also may see the works you are doing. . . ." Then Jesus said to them, "My time [*kairos*] has not yet come. . . ." (7: 3, 6, 8)

What happens at Cana points forward to Jesus' death. Later, in John 2:19, to the demand for a sign to justify the temple-cleansing, Jesus responds: "Destroy this temple, and in three days I will raise it up." The next chapter

---

25. Cf. Bornkamm, "Zur Interpretation des Johannesevangeliums," p. 18; Hoskyns-Davey, *Crucifixion-Resurrection*, p. 149. Friedrich, *Die Verkündigung*, p. 19, holds the contrary view, saying that the Prologue lacks any reference to Jesus' death or to its saving significance.

26. Fleinert-Jensen, *Das Kreuz und die Einheit der Kirche*, p. 39, n. 8.

(3:14) emphasizes the necessity *(dei)* of the Son of Man's being "lifted up" *(hypsōthēnai),* an event clearly identified in 12:32-34 as his crucifixion:

> "I, when I am lifted up from the earth, will draw all people to myself." He said this to indicate the kind of death he was to die.

If the theme of laying down one's life for one's friends (cf. 15:13) is not an accidental marginal phenomenon but the central motif and structural principle of the Johannine passion narrative and Christology, then John 3:16 cannot be merely a piece of appended tradition unessential to John's Gospel, but it has been correctly cited as the quintessence of Johannine theology.[27] Two chapters ahead, in 5:16-18, following the healing of the lame man, "the Jews started persecuting Jesus." Because he called God his Father, they "were seeking all the more to kill him." In chapter 6, the "bread of God" that gives "life to the world" (v. 33) is Jesus' "flesh" (v. 51) — hence the summons to his disciples to "eat the flesh of the Son of Man and drink his blood" (vv. 53-56). The same chapter contains the initial references to Jesus' betrayal (6:64, 70-71). Chapter 7 opens with Jesus' avoidance of Judea "because the Jews were looking for an opportunity to kill him." In 7:19, Jesus attacks his opponents' failure to keep the law and their search for an opportunity to kill him, an intention registered by the crowds (7:25) but frustrated because his "hour" *(hora)* has not yet come (7:30). Again, in 8:20, Jesus avoids arrest "because his hour had not yet come." At the outset and all throughout, these repeated references to Jesus' "hour," his "time" (or, as in 8:21-22, his "going away" [*hypagō*]), can only be calculated to depict his entire ministry as a progress toward death. John 8:28 cites the Son of Man's "lifting up" as proof of his being sent from the Father:

> When you have lifted up the Son of Man, then you will realize that I am he, and that I do nothing on my own, but I speak these things as the Father instructed me.

In 8:37 and 40, responding to his enemies' boast concerning their paternity, Jesus says: "I know that you are descendants of Abraham; yet you

---

27. Hartwig Thyen, "Niemand hat grössere Liebe als die, dass er sein Leben für seine Freunde hingibt" [15: 13] ("Das johanneische Verständnis des Kreuzestodes Jesu," *Theologia Crucis — Signum Crucis,* p. 476).

look for an opportunity to kill me." The shepherd-discourse of chapter 10 is replete with references to Jesus' death:

> The good shepherd lays down his life for the sheep. . . . I know my own and my own know me. . . . And I lay down my life for the sheep. . . . For this reason the Father loves me, because I lay down my life. . . . No one takes it from me, but I lay it down of my own accord. I have power to lay it down, and I have power to take it up again. (10:11, 14, 15, 17, 18)[28]

The intent of this discourse is to set forth the precondition for the reciprocal relationship between Christ and his followers: the surrender of Christ's own life.[29]

In chapter 11, Jesus raises another man from the dead, and his fate is immediately sealed. At a final consultation of the council, called by the chief priests and Pharisees to decide his fate, the high priest says: ". . . it is better for you to have one man die for the people than to have the whole nation destroyed" (11:50). "This," the evangelist explains, "he did not say on his own, but being high priest that year he prophesied that Jesus was about to die for the nation" (11:51). Then he adds: ". . . and not for the nation only, but to gather into one the dispersed children of God" (11:52). From the outside, Jesus appears to be the victim of a plot on the part of his Jewish opponents; but to "the insider," to the evangelist and his community, his death is a willing sacrifice for others. As the high priest — the "outsider" — unwittingly prophesies, his death will ultimately mean the gathering of the scattered people of God. In chapter 12, introduced by the account of the Greeks' request to see him, Jesus' words "the hour *[hōra]* has come for the Son of Man to be glorified" and "unless a grain of wheat falls into the earth and dies"[30] are the

---

28. In the good shepherd's statement that he "lays down his life" for the sheep *(tithenai tēn psychēn)*, Joachim Jeremias sees a reminiscence of the Servant's life having made "an offering for sin" in the Hebrew of Isa. 53:10, and his pouring "out himself to death" in the Aramaic of 53:12. He concludes that a comparison of these passages with the expression *didonai tēn psychēn* in Mark 10:45, together with the *hyper*-formula elsewhere, reflects early Christian meditation on the Servant-idea (see Jeremias, "Παῖς Θεοῦ," in *Theological Dictionary of the New Testament*, V, 708, 710-711).

29. Nielsen, "John's Understanding of the Death of Jesus," p. 245.

30. Of this saying, Hoskyns-Davey declare that "it contains, as no other single saying does, the heart of the Gospel" (see *Crucifixion-Resurrection*, p. 171).

signal that the high priest's prophecy of his death for "the dispersed children of God" has already begun to be fulfilled (12:23-24). Here, in what Morna Hooker has called a replacement for the Synoptic passion predictions,[31] as well as later in chapters 13 and 17, whatever veil lay over that "hour" till now is about to be thrown off. That hour is not only the hour of his glorification, however, but also of his agitation: "Now my soul is troubled. And what should I say — 'Father, save me from this hour'? No, it is for this reason that I have come to this hour" (12:27-28).

If this report echoes the Gethsemane scene in Mark 14:33-34,[32] Jesus' prayer that the Father's name be glorified and the answer ("I have glorified it, and I will glorify it again" [12:28-29]), the only voice "from heaven" in the Gospel, furnish the evangelist's interpretation of the Synoptic voice at the baptism and transfiguration: "You are my Son, the Beloved; with you I am well pleased" (Mark 1:11; Matt. 3:17; Luke 3:22). After brushing aside his own suggestion that he should be saved from "this hour," Jesus once more refers to his "lifting up" (in John 12:32) as the "judgment of this world," as the "driving out" of the "ruler of this world." The event of the cross has displaced spectacular apocalyptic. If readers wish to see divine power miraculously revealed at the crucifixion, says Craig Koester, they must leave John and go to the Synoptics. Noting the link between Jesus' statement concerning the arrival of his "hour" and his reference to the dying seed (12:23-24), as well as between the statement about the Son of Man's glorification and Judas' departure for betrayal, Koester remarks that, in either instance, death or betrayal and glory are inseparably joined.[33]

Commenting on the first half of the Gospel (extending from 2:1 to 12:50), and including what he calls "The Book of Signs," C. H. Dodd (1884-1973) speaks of Jesus' journey from Galilee to Jerusalem in all the Gospels as a *via dolorosa,* and of the "symbolic value" of this journey as "deeply embedded in the scheme of the Fourth Gospel." He adds that the "central core of the *kerygma*" in John is not represented in successive chronological stages as in the Synoptic Gospels and Acts, but as "as-

---

31. Hooker, *Not Ashamed of the Gospel,* p. 96.

32. Cf. Bergmeier, "Τετέλεσται in John 19:30," p. 282.

33. Craig Koester, "The Death of Jesus in the Gospel of John," *Tidsskrift for Teologi og Kirke* 75 (2004), 272.

pects of each single saving act of Christ," confident that a backward glance over the seven "signs" or episodes would make this clear.[34]

With John 13:1 — its reference to Jesus' "hour" *(hōra)* as having come and its final "having loved his own who were in the world, he loved them to the end" — John's passion narrative begins in earnest and, as Thyen writes, spans an arc that ends in the cry "it is finished" in 19:30.[35] Agreeing that the story of the footwashing in chapter 13 is one of the most important texts for an understanding of Jesus' death in John's Gospel, Nielsen says that in that act Jesus gathers into a single symbol his entire mission now nearing its culmination. For this reason the story, with its "elaborate introduction," enjoys such a central position in the Gospel.[36] Then, in 13:10-11, 18-19, just as in 6:70-71, Jesus again makes veiled reference to his betrayer, and, following a final prediction of his betrayal, singles Judas out and virtually sends him off to do his work (13:21-30). The conclusion to the farewell discourse in 14:27-31 summarizes the vision by which Jesus' followers are to gain a new understanding of his death. It will be a salvation-bringing return to the Father — thus an occasion for joy, not anxiety (14:27-28). It will be an act of Jesus' sovereignty, since the "ruler of this world" has no power over him (14:30), and it will manifest Jesus' obedience to the Father (14:31).[37] Thyen says that John 15:9-16 structurally assumes the place taken by the passion predictions in the Synoptic Gospels; he con-

34. C. H. Dodd, *The Interpretation of the Fourth Gospel* (Cambridge, UK: Cambridge University Press, 1958), p. 384.

35. Thyen refers to the odd grammatical construction of John 13:1-4, which has led scholars such as Bultmann to discard it, and says that, whatever its genesis, its structure is materially linked to that of the narrative following it. Its double-sidedness corresponds precisely to the twofold explanation of the footwashing, and, like the latter event, points beyond itself to its fulfillment in Jesus' death (Thyen, "Niemand hat grössere Liebe als die, dass er sein Leben für seine Freunde hingibt," pp. 472-473). The text reads: "Now before the festival of the Passover, Jesus knew that his hour had come to depart from this world and go to the Father. Having loved his own who were in the world, he loved them to the end. The devil had already put it into the heart of Judas, son of Simon Iscariot, to betray him. And during supper Jesus, knowing that the Father had given all things into his hands, and that he had come from God and was going to God, got up from the table, took off his outer robe, and tied a towel around himself."

36. Nielsen, "John's Understanding of the Death of Jesus," p. 241.

37. Cf. Müller, "Zur Eigentümlichkeit des Johannesevangeliums: Das Problem des Todes Jesu," p. 29.

tinues that the theme of love fulfilled in giving one's life for one's friends is a central motif and structural principle of the Johannine passion, not a merely accidental phenomenon, as Käsemann supposed. In contrast to Dibelius, who regarded 15:13-15 as an alien body, a "midrash-like deviation," Thyen says that the passage actually mediates what Dibelius and entire generations of theologians believed was absolutely incapable of mediation, that is, human and Christian love — *erōs* and *agapē*. He provides an extensive quotation, the ending of which reads:

> Humiliation and exaltation are prefigured by love's self-negating condition. Whoever loves, does not merely go calmly to meet his impending death. He anticipates suffering and death as the highest possibility of a lasting life-fellowship with his friend, a certainty distinct from everything accidentally given or taken. . . .[38]

In John 18:1 a change occurs. The reader is taken across the winter brook Kidron to view the "stations" of Jesus' suffering. The arrest scene in 18:1-12 and the threefold confession in 18:5, 6, and 8 ("I am he . . . let these men go!") further interpret the love of Jesus as fulfilled in dying for his friends. Finally, in chapter 19, with the mother and the beloved disciple under the cross (19:25-27), the event reaches its climax in the statement "it is finished" (19:30). Now the free deed of love will set the promise of the Paraclete in motion. The Gospel's emphasis on Jesus' initiative at his arrest, his lordly dignity at the hearing, and his victory in going to the Father may all represent the evangelist's individual production. Nevertheless, it can be seen from the Synoptic Gospels that the presuppositions for this understanding were already present in the community.

Hoskyns-Davey sum up the argument for the centrality of Jesus' death in John's Gospel:

> The reality of the death, and its urgent immediacy in the whole context of his mission to the Jews, are far more constantly insisted upon by the fourth evangelist than by any other New Testament writer. . . . The use of the same word to signify the crucifixion and exaltation of

---

38. Thyen, "Niemand hat grössere Liebe als die, dass er sein Leben für seine Freunde hingibt," pp. 467, 470, 476-477; cf. Johnson, *The Real Jesus*, p. 156.

Jesus; the insistent looking for the "hour" which comes only with his death, for the "glory" which can be apprehended only with his "glorification," the prediction of the Spirit which, until he dies, is withheld by that grim "not yet" because the Spirit can be given only if he goes away — all these point in one direction.[39]

Use and Fracture of Judaism

Adolf Schlatter, in a 1902 essay, says that the language of John's Gospel reflects a reality no one interested in historical truth could ignore, namely, that its author was a Palestinian who thought in Aramaic, read his Hebrew Bible, and in the first half of his career taught chiefly in Palestine. Schlatter concludes that the link between the Aramaic and the Greek in John's consciousness has to do not merely with the forms of words but with the content of his thought and speech. On this strict unity of language and thought-forms, all attempts at parceling the Gospel out into sources shattered.[40] In 1922, C. F. Burney (1868-1925) advanced the hypothesis that the Fourth Gospel is the translation of a single Aramaic document,[41] a theory cited later by T. W. Manson (1893-1958), who expressed "the growing conviction" that the Gospel of John and the First Epistle of John are "fundamentally Hebraic" in character.[42] Burney was followed by Ernst Haenchen (1894-1975), who said that the Gospel was not a "historical documentary film" but the community's witness of faith, the colors of which derive from the Old Testament, just as in Mark.[43]

In John's Gospel, reminiscences of Old Testament themes and utterances are abundant and striking. Chapter 1 identifies the beloved son,

---

39. Hoskyns-Davey, *Crucifixion-Resurrection*, p. 153.

40. Adolf Schlatter, "Die Sprache und Heimat des vierten Evangelisten," *Beiträge zur Förderung christlicher Theologie*, 6 (1902) (Gütersloh: C. Bertelsmann), 7-8, 12, 171-172.

41. C. F. Burney, *The Aramaic Origin of the Fourth Gospel* (Oxford: Clarendon Press, 1922).

42. T. W. Manson, *Studies in the Gospels and Epistles*, ed. Matthew Black (Manchester University Press, 1962), p. 118.

43. Ernst Haenchen, "Historie und Geschichte in den johanneischen Passionsberichten," in *Zur Bedeutung des Todes Jesu*, p. 60; cf. also pp. 58, 61, 63.

the paschal lamb, and Jesus in the account of his baptism, echoing the rite by which a sheep is substituted for the first-born son destined for sacrifice, described in Exodus 34:20. John 1:29 correlates with 19:36, in which the one who takes away the sin of the world dies according to the laws governing the offering of the paschal sacrifice.[44] The report in 19:34-36 that the soldiers did not break Jesus' bones reflects the commandment of Exodus 12:46 and Numbers 9:12 regarding the slaughter of the paschal lamb. In John 3:14 and 8:28 — and in 12:33-34, where the event is supplied with a theological interpretation — the evangelist refers the type of Jesus' execution to the Old Testament.[45]

Of greater importance is the Gospel's dating of Jesus' death on Nisan 14, the day of preparation for the Passover, with the result that Jesus' death coincides with the slaughter, and not — as per the Synoptists — with the eating of the Passover lamb. In this way the evangelist has set Jesus' story within the framework of the Passover narrative.[46]

The "I-am" speeches, used without modifier in 8:24 and 13:19, or used with metaphors in 6:35 ("I am the bread of life"), in 8:12 ("I am the light of the world"), in 10:9 ("I am the door"), in 10:11 ("I am the good shepherd"), in 11:25 ("I am the resurrection and the life"), in 14:6 ("I am the way, the truth and the life"), and in 15:1, 5 ("I am the true vine") — all hark back to the Old Testament theophanic formula "I am Yahweh." In fact, the entire life of Jesus is described as a theophany. Thus his revelation fulfills or exceeds whatever was prior: the creation (1:1), the revelation to Moses (1:17), to Jacob (1:51), to Daniel (5:26), to Abraham (8:56), to Isaiah (12:41), and to Zechariah (19:37).

Some have detected links between John and Jewish Wisdom literature. Siegfried Schulz contends that the author of the Fourth Gospel knew of the Jewish-Hellenistic Wisdom speculation as reflected in the Odes of Solomon and Sirach, or The Wisdom of Solomon — and that the influence of this speculation is reflected in the "pre-Johannine Logos-hymn."[47] According to the myth in its Old Testament and early Christian form, Wisdom is a person or hypostasis who was in the begin-

---

44. Cf. Levenson, *The Death and Resurrection of the Beloved Son*, p. 208.

45. Cf. Num. 21:8-9.

46. Cf. John 19:14, 31 with Mark 14:1-2, 12, 17; 15:1; Matt. 26:1-2, 17, 20; 27:1; Luke 22:1-2, 7, 66.

47. Siegfried Schulz, *Das Evangelium nach Johannes: Das Neue Testament Deutsch* (Göttingen: Vandenhoeck & Ruprecht, 1987), p. 11.

ning with God, and by whom God created the cosmos.[48] Stöger points
to the "Johannine logion" in Matthew and Luke (Matt. 11:25-30; Luke
10:22) as the bridge between John and the Wisdom literature, as well as
between John and the Synoptists.[49]

Scholars have likewise been eager to note the Gospel's connection
with Hellenistic Judaism. For example, Joachim Jeremias says that the
idea of the *logos* as instrument of revelation is much older than Philo of
Alexandria; he concludes that the title predicated of Christ derives from
the Septuagint.[50] Others who share Jeremias's theory of the Gospel's
reflecting Hellenistic-Jewish influence nonetheless assume that the
evangelist's education took such form as Philo represents: they refer in
particular to the Alexandrian's doctrine of the *logos*.[51]

Several have referred to the similarity between John's Gospel, the
Epistles, and the apocalyptic literature of Judaism. The similarity is further enhanced by the Gospel's use of the "Son of Man" title, reminiscent
of the Book of Daniel and the Similitudes of Enoch.[52] Particularly regarding its dualistic view, there are striking similarities between the
Fourth Gospel and the literature of Qumran. According to Qumran
teaching, a prince of light engages in battle with an angel of darkness,
unrighteousness, and ruin (1QS III, 18, 20, 24 and 19, 21; IV, 12). Both figures are conceived as personal beings who help or oppress humankind
(1QS III, 24-25; 1 QM XIII, 10); they also wage war in the human heart
(1QS IV, 23-24). This struggle of the prince of light and his company
against the prince of darkness and his cohorts continues until the end-
time (1QS IV, 16-17, 25).

If an author is more than a one-dimensional creature, assigning his
conceptuality to one kind of thought does not necessarily rule out assigning it to another. The fact that Bultmann and his students, for exam-

48. Cf. The Wisdom of Solomon 9:9.

49. Stöger, "Das Christusbild im Johanneischen Schrifttum," p. 158. Cf. Sirach
6:26-28; cf. also 24:19-22; 51:23-27.

50. Joachim Jeremias, *Der Prolog des Johannesevangeliums* (Stuttgart: Calwer Verlag,
1967), pp. 26-29.

51. Emil Schürer, "Über den gegenwärtigen Stand der johanneischen Frage,"
Johannes und sein Evangelium, ed. Karl Heinrich Rengstorf (Darmstadt: Wissenschaftliche Buchgesellschaft, 1973), pp. 20-21.

52. Stöger, "Das Christusbild im johanneischen Schrifttum," pp. 134-135; cf. Dan.
7:13-14, and 1 Enoch 46:1-6; 48:2-7; 62:5-9, 14; 63:11; 69:26-29; 70:1; 71:17.

ple, interpret the Johannine conceptuality against the background of Gnosis, and thus minimize the influence of the Old Testament, does not spell the absence of any such influence. The parallels between John and Wisdom, between the Johannine *logos*-idea and Hellenistic Judaism, and between the Fourth Gospel and the apocalyptic literature of Judaism are too numerous to be denied.

Nevertheless, a divide does exist between the Johannine conceptuality and Old Testament Jewish and Hellenistic thought. For all its link with Wisdom, a great gulf is fixed between John and Wisdom at one signal and decisive point: the statement in John 1:14 according to which the heavenly *logos* has become man in Jesus represents something unique and completely new over against Wisdom speculation — however much of it may once have underlain the hymn. Traditionally, the shape of "Wisdom" or of the *logos* was conceived as incorporated in a species of the wise or the devout, *not* in a particular man. This does not automatically give the nod to Gnosis in our attempt to uncover John's "mental furniture"; but it does furnish an occasion for it. Further, the suggestion that the prehistory of the *logos*-idea is to be found in Hellenistic Judaism such as Philo represents,[53] or that John's idea of Jesus' sonship is shaped according to the Old Testament idea of the prophet's relationship to God, assumes an idea of "consubstantiality" that Jewish and Hellenistic thought did not manage.[54] In the Judaism of the apocrypha, the pseudepigrapha, the rabbinic writings, and Qumran, God came more and more to be conceived of as transcendent, so that mediating creatures were needed to convey the divine activity. Angels, demons, spirits, sons of God came to inhabit the entire world. Though initially these "little Yahwehs" represented only a hypostasizing of the divine attributes, they came more and more to be personified, with the result that Judaism was liable to ditheism, to atomizing its concept of God, and was thus unable to throw off the threat of polytheism.[55] The dogmatic reflection of the ancient church, however, united Christ more and more with God, and the Gnostic danger was countered with Trinitarian doctrine according to which the Three led back to the One.

53. Cf. Joachim Jeremias, *Der Prolog des Johannesevangeliums,* pp. 26-27.

54. Cf. Bultmann's criticism of this view as presented in Dodd's *The Interpretation of the Fourth Gospel,* in *Theologie als Kritik,* p. 465.

55. Cf. the role of Metatron, "Prince of the Divine Presence," in "The Appendix to 3 Enoch," *The Old Testament Pseudepigrapha,* I, 303-315.

The differences between John's Gospel and the literature of apocalyptic Judaism are likewise apparent. According to the Apocalypse of Baruch, for example, the messiah returns in his glory as soon as he has established his kingdom;[56] but there is no mention of a return to glory following or based on his death (cf. John 12:32-34). Further, John does not interpret the Synoptic voice, "You are my Son, the Beloved; with you I am well pleased" (Mark 1:11; Matt. 3:17; cf. Luke 9:35), in the context of spectacular apocalypse but in the context of the Gethsemane scene, where Jesus, aware of his imminent death and troubled in his soul, brushes aside his own suggestion that he should pray to be saved from "this hour" (John 12:27-28). Still further — while it is extreme to assign all references to the future in the Gospel to a later redaction — its emphasis on eternal life as a present possession constitutes a radical revision of the old apocalyptic tradition. The final judgment that apocalyptic thought had associated with God's dramatic destruction and transformation of the world has been transposed into the sojourn of the Son:

> Truly, truly I say to you, he who hears my word and believes him who sent me, has eternal life; he does not come into judgment, but has passed from death to life. (John 5:24)

John has opened his readers' eyes to see that the *parousia* has already occurred, that in faith the *eschaton* has already broken in and become present.

As for Qumran and its relationship to the Fourth Gospel, the *diastasis* is greater than was once assumed. For example, in Qumran the end of all things is purely futuristic; in John the end originates in a historical person (1:14). In Qumran two messiahs are awaited in addition to the Teacher of Righteousness; in John, Jesus is the only one sent from God (5:22-23). In Qumran there is an absence of the typically Johannine Christology of the one sent to redeem (3:16). In Qumran the covenanters await salvation for themselves; in John, Jesus gives his life for the salvation of the world (12:32). In Qumran the dualism of light and darkness is always related to the Mosaic law — "righteousness" is in order to respect Torah — and in this fash-

---

56. "And it will happen after these things when the time of the appearance of the Anointed One has been fulfilled and he returns with glory, that then all who sleep in hope of him will rise" (2 [Syriac Apocalypse of] Baruch, 30:1, *The Old Testament Pseudepigrapha*, I, 631).

ion relativized. Perhaps more important, interpretations of Qumran texts concerning the violent death of the Righteous Teacher and his glorious return in advance of Jesus[57] have been corrected, with the result that no Qumran text is currently read in terms of the Teacher's crucifixion and resurrection. Finally, though actual Qumran analogies may have reached the primitive Christian community and the author of the Fourth Gospel, possibly by way of John the Baptist, to assume (with Oscar Cullmann) a Qumran influence on the Baptist and thus on Jesus as a general rule, rather than as a possibility in a given instance, is not supported by the materials.[58] Whatever contacts there were between John and Qumran, they do not require the conclusion that John passed through the fellowship of Qumran or wrote in conscious debate with its theological views.[59]

Use and Fracture of Gnosis

In his Göttingen lecture,[60] Ernst Käsemann took his stimulus from Walter Bauer's text on orthodoxy and heresy in earliest Christianity.[61] In that work Bauer says that heresy helped shape earliest church history, that it often ran ahead of orthodoxy, and that for this reason it could not be viewed as degenerative. Proceeding to his argument, Käsemann first says that III John has been neglected in the debate regarding Johannine authorship. He next reverses Bauer's opinion concerning the roles of Diotrephes and the elder, so that it reads that the elder, and not Diotrephes, represented a position antithetical to the "incipient early Catholicism" of orthodoxy. Ac-

57. See, e.g., A. Dupont-Sommer, *The Dead Sea Scrolls: A Preliminary Survey,* trans. E. Margaret Rowley (New York: Macmillan, 1952), p. 99, and John Allegro, *The Dead Sea Scrolls* (Baltimore: Penguin Books, 1956), pp. 148-149. Cf. also Dupont-Sommer's later admission that the "rapid parallel" she drew between Jesus and the Teacher was intended "to stimulate the curiosity of the reader" (*The Jewish Sect of Qumran and the Essenes,* trans. R. D. Barnett [London: Vallentine, Mitchell & Co., 1954], p. 160).

58. See Cullmann, "The 'Significance of the Qumran Texts' for Research into the Beginnings of Christianity," in *The Scrolls and the New Testament,* ed. Krister Stendahl (New York: Harper & Brothers, 1957), pp. 18-21.

59. Stöger, "Das Christusbild im johanneischen Schrifttum," pp. 159-160.

60. Käsemann, "Ketzer und Zeuge," pp. 292-311.

61. Walter Bauer, *Orthodoxy and Heresy in Earliest Christianity,* trans. The Philadelphia Seminar on Christian Origins, ed. Robert A. Kraft and Gerhard Krodel (Philadelphia: Fortress, 1971).

cordingly, the elder and author of the Johannine literature was a Christian Gnostic who dared to write a Gospel commencing with a prologue extracted from a pre-Christian hymn, perhaps from the Baptist community, altered the description of the story and message of Jesus, and in most extreme fashion inhibited the churchly doctrine of the sacraments and primitive Christian apocalyptic, reminiscent of the heretics cited in II Timothy 2:18, who offered the solution of a resurrection already occurred. Diotrephes exercised churchly disciplinary force on the presbyter and his adherents: he expelled from his community those inclined to receive the elder's emissaries. The Johannine writings thus derived from a conventicle later hereticized by the Great Church. In the sequel to his Göttingen lecture, Käsemann said that the Fourth Gospel prepared for Gnostic proclamation or was already under its influ-ence.[62] Bornkamm agreed that, however precisely it was to be defined, Gnosis underlay the Gospel, that its speech and perspective offered the evangelist a terminological instrument as well as positive, material possibilities for his statements about revelation and salvation.[63] These students of Bultmann had taken a leaf from their teacher, whose commentary on John's Gospel, together with his discussion of the relevant literature, emphasized Gnosis as its principal thought-background. Bultmann hailed the work of pioneers and proponents of the History of Religions School; but he especially welcomed the disclosure of Mandaean sources, all of which demonstrated that the Gospel was set within the history of Hellenistic-oriental syncretism, more particularly the history of Gnosis.[64] He thought it extremely likely that the source used by the evangelist for his prologue originated with a John the Baptist sect sprung from the latter's activity at the Jordan, from which derived the sect of the Mandaeans, who regarded the Baptist as the pre-existent *logos*.[65]

In his summary of the Gnostic redeemer myth, Bultmann says that, just as in John, so in the myth, the revealer is the eternal, pre-existent deity, in the beginning with the Father and sent into the world by him, equipped

62. Käsemann, *The Testament of Jesus,* pp. 66, 73, 75, etc.

63. Bornkamm, "Zur Interpretation des Johannesevangeliums," p. 22.

64. Cf. Bultmann's review of Walter Bauer's *Das Johannesevangelium* (*ThLZ* 51, 1926), in *Theologie als Kritik,* p. 146.

65. Bultmann, "Die Bedeutung der neuerschlossenen Mandäischen und Manichïschen Quellen für das Verständnis des Johannesevangeliums," in *Johannes und sein Evangelium,* ed. Karl Heinrich Rengstorf (Darmstadt: Wissenschaftliche Buchgesellschaft, 1973), pp. 458-460.

with authority by the Father and in continual unity with him. The redeemer comes into the world and gives life as the one who himself has life; he leads out of darkness into light, from the lie into the truth. He speaks the words the Father has taught him, and he does the works with which the Father charged him. He reveals himself by the "I am" as shepherd or vine; he knows his own and they know him. In the world, however, he is an alien, hated and persecuted. Just as he has come, so will he go, taking leave of his own and commending them to the Father in prayer. His departure, however, is not an eternal separation; when exalted, he will take his own on the way he has prepared. He himself is the way and the door. For the world, however, his departure is a judgment, for he is the "Man."[66]

To this "soteriological myth," says Bultmann, a cosmological myth runs parallel. The one who is sent from heaven corresponds to the heavenly primal man *(Urmensch)*, who in the arch-time descended from the heavenly into the material world, was overcome and imprisoned by it. Like the primal man, the one sent from heaven is imprisoned in the earthly world, but he is imprisoned in order to bring to souls likewise imprisoned the revelation of their origin and a return to it. His ascent is at the same time his own redemption, so that he becomes the "redeemed redeemer." The redeemer's and the soul's redemption thus spells the liberation of the primal man and an end to the earthly world originating in the imprisonment of its light fragments.

Recognizing this "mighty myth," says Bultmann, "is the first step toward the proper understanding of John's Gospel."[67] The number of scholars who seconded Bultmann's position were legion, including Erik Peterson, another teacher of Käsemann, who fixed the origin of such connections as between "light" and "life" in John's Gospel and in other Hellenistic-oriental literature in west Syrian Gnosis. According to Peterson, a mass of Gnostic material predated the origins of Mandaeanism and underlay its speculation.[68]

66. Rudolf Bultmann, "Das Johannesevangelium in der neuesten Forschung" (*ChW* 41, 1927), in *Theologie als Kritik*, p. 207.

67. Bultmann, "Die Bedeutung der neuerschlossenen Mandäischen und Manichäischen Quellen," pp. 406, 455. Cf. also his review of Dodd, *The Interpretation of the Fourth Gospel*, in *Theologie als Kritik*, p. 469; cf. also Käsemann, "Ketzer und Zeuge," pp. 292-311.

68. Erik Peterson, "Bemerkungen zur mandäischen Literatur," *Zeitschrift für neutestamentliche Wissenschaft* 25 (1936), 244, 248.

Ferdinand Christian Baur also pioneered this view. In an essay on the composition and character of John's Gospel, he says that its sole purpose was to describe the dogmatic of separation occurring through the incarnate divine *logos,* that its historical representation was merely a means to this end.[69] In his study of the Christian church he speaks of the Fourth Gospel's intimate relationship with the Gnostic circle of ideas. To Baur's mind, however, Alexandrian religious philosophy, as represented by Philo, and Gnosis — to say nothing of Christian Gnosis — were more or less of a piece, waiting for a later generation to draw subtler distinctions.[70] At any rate, Baur said that it would be contrary to all historical analogy to assume that the evangelist came to his teaching regarding the *logos* without any link to the ideas of his time. Naturally, he added, John would not have arrived at the thought of transferring the *logos*-idea to Christ had not "Christian consciousness" already made the essential decision to set Christ according to his higher status in relation to identity with God.[71]

Other features of John's Gospel have reminded its readers of Gnosis. One of the most obvious themes in John's Gospel is the Revealer's lack of disguise. The "true light which enlightens everyone," the "glory" of the Word (1:9, 14), is immediately perceptible. The Baptist sees and bears witness to Jesus. His disciples witness the revelation of his "glory" and believe in him (2:11). Faith and trust are evoked on the occasion of each of his seven signs. Jesus' identity should have been apparent to Nicodemus; it was not — but only because he did not believe the evidence of his own eyes.[72] It should have been apparent to the Jews, but it was not — and for the same reason.[73] The fact that amazement and

---

69. Baur, "Über die Composition und den Charakter des johanneischen Evangeliums," *Theologische Jahrbücher* 3 (Tübingen: Ludwig Friedrich Fues, 1844), pp. 11-25.

70. According to Emil Schürer, Adolf Hilgenfeld (1823-1907) had emphasized more strongly than Baur the link between John's Gospel and Gnosis ("Über den gegenwärtigen Stand der johanneischen Frage," p. 7).

71. Ferdinand Christian Baur, *Das Christentum und die christliche Kirche der drei ersten Jahrhunderte: Ausgewählte Werke in Einzelausgaben,* ed. Klaus Scholder (Stuttgart–Bad Canstatt: Friedrich Frommann Verlag, 1996), III, 323-325.

72. Cf. 3:12: "If I have told you about earthly things and you do not believe, how can you believe if I tell you about heavenly things?"

73. Cf. 8:42-43: "If God were your Father, you would love me, for I came from God and now I am here; I did not come on my own, but he sent me. Why do you not understand what I say?"

blood-lust share the same heart[74] only further supports the perception that Jesus' enemies disbelieve, not because his identity is obscure, but because they refuse correctly to assess the evidence.

The dualism of the Gospel has also conjured up reminiscences of Gnosis. Just as in Gnosis, John's worldview appears dualistic, illustrated by his key concepts in antithetical pairs: light and darkness, truth and lie, freedom and servitude, life and death, above and below, God and the world. Humans are thus distributed into two classes: those who are from God or from the devil, from the truth or from the world, from above or from below. This contrast between what is above and what is below is facilitated by the Gospel's symbolism. Earthly things and events are signs or symbols of the authentic and real, of the divine.

Referring to Jesus' death in John, Baur says that the evangelist conceived it solely as a Jewish deed, that the guilt fell on the Jews alone. He adds that this guilt appears all the greater the more an effort is required to overcome gentile resistance to the Jews. Hence the entire action of Pilate springs from John's intention to transfer guilt from the executor of the punishment to its real authors, to allow the bloodthirsty hatred of the Jewish people to appear in all its magnitude.[75] Years after Baur, Haenchen has said that what the Gospel's narrator has taken from the tradition has been formed in a time when the Jewish and Christian communities have already lived apart, and in which the Jews were made to represent the unbelieving world. According to Haenchen, the Jews are the real driving power in John's Gospel, and the Romans are merely an involuntary instrument of the Jewish will;[76] and Müller says that, in the dialogue between Jesus and Nicodemus, the situation of the evangelist's

---

74. Cf. 7:14-19: "About the middle of the festival Jesus went up into the temple and began to teach. The Jews were astonished at it, saying, 'How does this man have such learning, when he has never been taught?' Then Jesus answered them, 'My teaching is not mine but his who sent me. . . . Why are you looking for an opportunity to kill me?'" Hoskyns-Davey say that this "pendulum-swinging" between faith that is no faith and the frustrated desire to kill is not an invention of the Fourth Gospel, that it can be found in the contrasted reactions of wonder and suspicion in the Synoptic accounts of the Galilean ministry, such as in Mark 2:6-7, 12 (*Crucifixion-Resurrection*, pp. 162-163).

75. Baur, *Kritische Untersuchungen über die kanonischen Evangelien* (Tübingen: Verlag und Druck von Ludw. Fr. Fues, 1947), pp. 208, 215.

76. Haenchen, "Historie und Geschichte in den johanneischen Passionsberichten," pp. 66, 68, 73, 75-76.

community shines through: its witness encounters the same rejection by the Jews as did Jesus' witness.[77] If John's use of the term "Jews" *(Ioudaioi)* is allowed its widest definition (i.e., to include not only their representatives but the people themselves[78]), then John shares with the Gnostics a universally known hostility. At this point Erik Peterson simply calls to mind the God of Judaism as the demiurge in the Valentinian system.[79]

As the reader may have already inferred, contemporary scholars have more or less jettisoned the concept of a pre-Christian, Gnostic "redeemed redeemer" as a model for the New Testament portrait of Christ. Following a re-examination of the sources that Wilhelm Bousset and Richard Reitzenstein believed yielded the myth of the *anthrōpos* or *Urmensch* as cosmogonic potency and anthropological principle, Carsten Colpe demonstrates that it was at bottom a modern interpretive device. The notion of a primal man who gathers the light fragments that share his substance but are imprisoned in matter, who paves the way to their place of origin and in so doing redeems himself and is thus able to act as their liberator, was merely an inference drawn from the system. In the sources, Colpe continues, the power to redeem and the capacity for being redeemed are separate hypostases. When they are merged in the notion of a redeemer identical in substance to his "brothers," Gnosis loses its edge, because the imprisonment of the light-fragments becomes accidental, and redemption occurs with mechanical necessity. Thus, says Colpe, the myth or formula of the "redeemed redeemer" overleaps the tragic-dramatic course of the world as background for the redemptive event and allows the Gnostic prayer to become a monologue; this is true because it is identified with a level of the divine vision at which all distinctions between the deity and humankind are absorbed.

Colpe admits that the myth was a heuristically helpful device, but without evidence in the sources, it was neither hermeneutically productive nor an appropriate category.[80] Kurt Rudolph, among the last to sur-

---

77. Müller, "Zur Eigentümlichkeit des Johannesevangeliums: Das Problem des Todes Jesu," pp. 27-28.

78. Cf. 1:19; 2:18, 20; 5:10, 15-16; 6:41, 52; 7:1, 11, 13; 8:22; 10:24, 31, 33; 11:8; 13:33; 18:14.

79. Peterson, "Bemerkungen zur mandäischen Literatur," p. 246.

80. Carsten Colpe, *Die Religionsgeschichtliche Schule* (Göttingen: Vandenhoeck & Ruprecht, 1961), pp. 174, 186, 188.

render the idea of the myth (at least as one variation of Gnostic soteriology[81]), finally conceded that the critics had left the theory in tatters, that it was only when the Gnostics took over the Christian concept of the redeemer that their idea of the *salvator salvandus* — a non-Christian concept — emerged. At the same time, Rudolph insists that the notion that the Gnostic myth of redemption derived from Christian soteriology rested on outdated prejudices. Actually, he continues, the Christology and soteriology of the New Testament were born when Gnostic and Hellenistic ideas were already in the air. Gnosis thus formed part of the milieu of earliest Christianity, and on its own entered into a symbiosis with Christian ideas — in fact, helped to stamp their development.[82]

The use of the Fourth Gospel by the Gnostics is not open to question,[83] though its interpretation against the background of Gnosis has increasingly been losing support in recent years. In the matter of sources, for example, Wilckens says that attempts to separate a signs- or speech-source with Gnostic taint from the evangelist's (or redactor's) own work reflects a methodology by which scholars assign what is unacceptable to them to these sources and attribute what they can affirm to the evangelist's "correction."[84] Very early on, Käsemann identified the author of the Gospel and Johannine epistles as a "Christian Gnostic" who was concerned with the historical reality of the revelation in Jesus and thus saw in Docetic Gnosis the revelation of the Antichrist.[85] He refused Bultmann's distinction between the Gospel's pagan-Gnostic model and its editing or redaction, declaring that in such a scenario the motif of the necessity of daily forgiveness in the life of the believer *(simul justus, simul peccator)*, a motif made clear by the author for the first time in the history of the church, would have been of pagan origin.[86]

---

81. Cf. Kurt Rudolph, *Gnosis* (Göttingen: Vandenhoeck & Ruprecht, 1980), pp. 141-145.

82. Rudolph, *Gnosis und Spätantike Religionsgeschichte,* pp. 47-49, 61.

83. Cf., e.g., Ulrich Wilckens, *Das Evangelium nach Johannes: Das Neue Testament Deutsch* (Göttingen: Vandenhoeck & Ruprecht, 1998), p. 10; Hengel, *The Johannine Question,* pp. 8-9.

84. Wilckens, p. 10.

85. Käsemann, "Ketzer und Zeuge," pp. 299, 302-303, 307, 311.

86. Käsemann, p. 306.

He later reiterated his discontent concerning Bultmann's exposition of the prologue to the Gospel, saying that the pre-Christian character of the hymn was more than problematic, the assumption of an Aramaic original unreliable, and the idea of John the Baptist as its original subject a pure hypothesis.[87] Still later, Käsemann admitted to having been "seduced" *(verführt)* by Bultmann and the Marburg School to accept Richard Reitzenstein's idea of a pre-Christian, Gnostic redeemed redeemer.[88] Günther Bornkamm noted the distance between Gnosis and the Gospel of John in the evangelist's confession of the *logos* becoming flesh as opposed to being temporarily masked or veiled. This confession, Bornkamm insisted, was clearly spoken against Gnosis, and in its "offensiveness" set passages such as Romans 8:3 or I Timothy 3:16 in the shade.[89] In a review of early Christian tradition and the modern church's dismantling of it, Haenchen gave considerable space to refuting Bultmann's hypothesis regarding John's prologue as originating in sources sprung from a Baptist sect that gave birth to the Mandaeans.[90]

Nineteenth-century scholars, however, were far from assigning pure and unadulterated Gnostic influence to the Gospel of John. In fact, conceding the influence of Alexandrian religious philosophy and its affinity with the Gnostic circle of ideas, Baur insisted that the Gospel nonetheless set aside "all those multifarious ideas with which Gnostic fantasy and speculation filled up the supersensual world." It did so by holding to the simple concept of the *logos* — and combining in it everything applicable to Christian consciousness as the highest expression of its view of the person of Christ.[91] According to Baur's "Hegelian" interpretation of early Christian history, the Gospel of John represents the reconciliation of the primitive Christian conflict between Jewish Christianity and Paulinism in the face of Gnosis, Montanism, and conflicts over the Passover.[92]

Despite his assigning "gnosticizing" to John, Bultmann declares

---

87. Ernst Käsemann, "Aufbau und Anliegen des johanneischen Prologs," in *Libertas Christiana*, Friedrich Delekat zum 65. Geburtstag (Munich: Christian Kaiser Verlag, 1957), p. 86.

88. Käsemann, *Kirchliche Konflikte*, p. 17.

89. Bornkamm, "Zur Interpretation des Johannesevangeliums," p. 118.

90. Haenchen, *Johannes Evangelium*, p. 39.

91. Baur, *Das Christentum und die christliche Kirche*, III, 324, 327.

92. Baur, *Das Christentum und die christliche Kirche*, I, 23 n. 2, 24, 146, 174; see also Baur, "Über die Komposition und den Charakter des johanneischen Evangeliums," pp. 615-631.

that the cosmological motifs of the Gnostic myth are as good as ignored in John. There is no reflection on the souls of believers as pre-existing light-fragments of that first *Urmensch* who in the arch-time descended from the world of light into the darkness and was swallowed by it. There is no idea of a divine-sent redeemer who in descending and gathering the believers redeems his double, the first *Urmensch*. There is no sense of a parallelism of the redeemer with the redeemed, without which the myth is "at bottom unintelligible."[93] The absence of this idea, Bultmann continues, makes the "riddle" of the Gospel seem greater, though it is in fact clearer. Preoccupied solely with the *that* and not the *what* of the revelation, the Gospel refuses to treat the divine as given or describable, and it speaks of God in only such a way as he can be spoken of: as shattering everything human by the revelation. Bultmann never tired of reminding his readers that the Johannine Jesus declares that he shares what he has seen and heard from the Father, but that in fact he reveals nothing but *that* he is the Revealer. The conception of revelation in John is thus "radically conceived": John refuses to describe its content, so that it cannot be said of God *how* he is, but only *that* he is.[94] If the absence of what lies at the heart of the Gnostic myth, that is, the "consubstantiality" of the redeemer and the redeemed, spelled the Gospel's lack of interest in cosmology or anthropology, it also spelled a lack of interest in the fate of the individual soul. Bultmann says:

> In the sphere of that myth the chief interest is in the fate of the soul after death. There is concern as to how the soul may complete its journey to the world of light. The result is that sacraments and rights of purification play a great role. . . . Where the piety is more spiritual, there is soul-care and mysticism, of which the Gnostics . . . and the Odes of Solomon give us a view. But all this is missing in the Gospel.[95]

93. Cf. Siegfried Schulz, who says that the cosmology and description of the soul's ascent through the heavenly spheres, as well as the myth of the pre-existence of the light-sparks and their liberation, thus of the "consubstantiality" of the redeemer with the redeemed, are "totally lacking" (*Das Evangelium nach Johannes*, p. 11).

94. Cf. Bultmann's review of Hans Windisch's *Johannes und die Synoptiker* (*ThLZ* 52, 1927), in *Theologie als Kritik*, p. 177; "Die Bedeutung der neuerschlossenen Mandäischen und Manichäischen Quellen," pp. 56, 463; cf. also Bultmann's review of Dodd's *The Interpretation of the Fourth Gospel* in *Theologie als Kritik*, p. 457.

95. Bultmann, "Die Bedeutung," p. 457.

As early as 1927, Bultmann said that the Gospel of John itself is not mythology, but that it uses, with sovereign confidence, the myth's forms of expression to describe its view of the revelation of God in Jesus. The reason for such use, Bultmann said, is that the myth is at home with the idea of revelation.[96]

Regarding the Gospel's dualism, whatever its origins, it can no more be assigned to Gnosis than to Palestinian Judaism. John describes the event of Christ in the terminology of dualism, but without appropriating the Gnostic cosmology or metaphysics. That is, the contrasting pairs of light and darkness, truth and lie, freedom and servitude, life and death, the heavenly and the earthly, are not principles that represent the ultimate causes of the world. To "walk during the day" or "at night" (John 11:9-10), for example, has nothing to do with essence but with faith and obedience. The dualism of John is thus moral or historical, something Baur had already recognized. He admitted that construing the evangelist's perspective as analogous to the Gnostic did in fact facilitate an understanding of the Gospel's prologue: for just as the Gnostics separate the world from the self-subsistent, absolute God who reveals himself in a contrast of principles immanent to the world, so John fixes the contrasts between light and dark by means of the idea of the *logos* as the principle by which everything comes into being. "But," says Baur, "with this Gnostic perspective the difference between the Christian- and pagan-Gnostic views suddenly appears in the fact that the evangelist allows the contrast in principles first to come into existence in the world of men."[97]

According to Bultmann, the critic most responsible for the "gnosticizing" of the Gospel of John in the modern era, the dualism of John was not that of Gnosis but "the expression of the situation of decision in which man stands before God and his revelation."[98] Later, Bornkamm would note the Gospel's "decidedly anti-Gnostic view of faith" as reflected in its portrayal of the antitheses of light and dark, life and death, and so forth, as possibilities open to human seizure or rejection — precisely the opposite of the principal Gnostic notion of the

96. Bultmann, "Das Johannesevangelium in der neuesten Forschung" (*ChW* 41, 1927) in *Theologie als Kritik*, pp. 214-215.

97. Baur, *Kritische Untersuchungen über die kanonischen Evangelien*, p. 88.

98. Bultmann, *Exegetica: Aufsätze zur Erforschung des Neuen Testaments*, ed. Erich Dinkler (Tübingen: J. C. B. Mohr, 1967), p. 237.

heavenly origin and God-relatedness of the redeemed.[99] The myth had thus been radically "demythologized," for which reason the Gospel did not belong to "authentic Christian Gnosis."[100]

As to the Gospel's perceived anti-Semitism, the phrase "the Jews" *(hoi Ioudaioi)* occurs seventy-one times in the Gospel — and most often in a pejorative sense. The phenomenon has been variously construed. In 1914, Wilhelm Lütgert (1867-1938) said that the Gospel's reference to "the Jews" does not distinguish the people of Israel without remainder from the Christian community. On the contrary, John is able to speak of Jews who became believers (8:31; 11:45; 12:11). "The Jews," then, are those who gather in synagogue and temple, observe the rites of purification, keep the Sabbath, and celebrate the feasts; they are that segment of the people that lives according to the law, a narrow circle of the strict ones feared by the disciples and the people, and of which the Pharisees are the kernel.[101] According to another view, the controversy between Jesus and his Jewish opponents culminating in 8:44 ("you are from your father the devil . . .") is not a historical reference. As such it would be "unreal." For example, the conflicts over the Sabbath, fasting, rites of purification, and Israel's election play no role in Jesus' debate with his opponents. It is the subsequent and ultimate breach between church and synagogue that gives coloration to the Gospel and enables the evangelist to make a theological point. That is, "the Jews" serve the motif of separation between believer and unbeliever occurring at the arrival of the Revealer. The description of the Jews as sons of the devil thus contains no judgment on the Jews as empirical entity.[102] Making the point that the "theological intention" is always uppermost in John, Hengel construes John's reference to "the Jews" as a synecdoche in reverse. That is, the whole is used for the part, so that the usage "the Jews" becomes at times almost identical to "the Pharisees." As has long been perceived, Hengel concludes, the Jews are a cipher for the cosmos, the human world that is separated from God and hostile to him.[103]

99. Bornkamm, "Zur Interpretation des Johannesevangeliums," p. 119.

100. Bultmann, "Die Bedeutung," p. 404; cf. "Das Johannesevangelium in der neuesten Forschung," p. 214.

101. William Lütgert, "Die Juden im Johannesevangelium," in *Neutestamentliche Studien Georg Heinrici zu seinem 70. Geburtstag dargebracht von Fachgenossen, Freunden und Schülern* (Leipzig: J. E. Hinrichs'sche Buchhandlung, 1914), pp. 147-154.

102. Schulz, *Das Evangelium nach Johannes*, p. 12.

103. Hengel, *The Johannine Question*, pp. 118-119.

The last two interpretations may well have had Baur for their father. Noting first of all that John used *hoi Ioudaioi* of the Sanhedrists, the Pharisees, the inhabitants of Jerusalem, the crowds, and the adversaries of Jesus, the Tübingen giant says that the evangelist conceived the gospel narrative from a "higher religious or dogmatic viewpoint." That is, since he viewed the opposition of Judaism to Christianity as an already accomplished fact, he transferred it to the Gospel narrative; he thus named Jesus' enemies as "the Jews" in order to refer that opposition to its first beginnings and causes.[104] Or, as Baur says earlier (in his *History*), at no point of John's Gospel is the religious interest of the author so directly and emphatically expressed as in 19:35-37, where he makes clear that Christ is the true Passover lamb ("when they . . . saw that he was already dead, they did not break his legs"): hence he was crucified on the day the lambs were slaughtered, so that the meal he had with his disciples was not a Passover meal but one taking place on the day prior (Nisan 14). We may infer from this that the Last Supper was a celebration of the absence of Jewish or Jewish-Christian dominance.[105]

In the last analysis, a rescue of the Fourth Gospel from its perceived hostility to the Jews may depend on its detachment from authentic Christian Gnosis, with its polemic against the Old Testament and the covenant people.

Finally, in a monograph that his teacher Wilhelm Bousset supplied with corrections, Gillis Wetter says that the utterances of the Fourth Gospel were not speculatively shaped or wrung from mystical feeling, but that they sprang from the struggle with opponents of the Christian faith. He goes on to say that, though the Johannine figure of the Son of God allows no competitor (a retroaction of the Jewish messiah idea but also of historical reality), the Jesus of the Fourth Gospel nonetheless encounters us full of humility and reverence for God. This marks its distance from Hellenistic piety, which is almost always concerned with the divine but not with God. The Jesus of John does not displace the Father. The "nerve" of the figure of the Christ is thus vastly different from that of other savior figures of antiquity, for which very reason his

---

104. Baur, "Über die Composition und den Charakter des johanneischen Evangeliums," pp. 623-625.

105. Baur, *The Church History of the First Three Centuries,* I, 159-160.

death is set at the center. "Naturally," Wetter concludes, "there were gods of the mysteries who died and rose, but about none of them could we feel that they lived and walked among us in historically calculable time. . . ."[106]

Years later, a historian with no particular brief for Christian faith would conclude his review of the saviors of antiquity with this paragraph:

> At the final ordeal of death, few, even of these would-be saviour gods, have dared to put their title to the test by plunging into the icy river. And now, as we stand and gaze with our eyes fixed upon the farther shore, a single figure rises from the flood and straightway fills the whole horizon. There is the Saviour; "and the pleasure of the Lord shall prosper in his hand; he shall see of the travail of his soul and shall be satisfied."[107]

Naturally, this thought did not escape Baur. In his investigation of the canonical Gospels, he says that a comparison of John 7:37-39 and I John 5:6 will assist toward a deeper view of the evangelist's perspective. The more vitally John is seized by the meaning of a great moment, he says, the more mightily the whole content of ideas hovering before the evangelist's mind results in a concrete view in which everything is not merely figure and shape but also action and happening. And that great moment, according to Baur, is Jesus' glorification, the most important element of which is his death.[108]

> On the last day of the festival, the great day, while Jesus was standing there, he cried out, "Let anyone who is thirsty come to me, and let the one who believes in me drink. As the scripture has said, 'Out of the believer's heart shall flow rivers of living water.'" Now he said this about the Spirit, which believers in him were to receive; for as yet there was no Spirit, because Jesus was not yet glorified. (7:37-39)

---

106. Gillis P. Wetter, *Der Sohn Gottes: Eine Untersuchung über den Charakter und die Tendenz des Johannes Evangeliums* (Göttingen: Vandenhoeck & Ruprecht, 1916), pp. 171-180.

107. Arnold J. Toynbee, *A Study of History,* abridgement of vols. I-VI by D. C. Somervel (Oxford: Oxford University Press, 1946), p. 547.

108. Baur, *Das Christentum*, III, 327.

This is the one who came by water and blood, Jesus Christ, not with the water only but with the water and the blood. And the Spirit is the one that testifies, for the Spirit is the truth. (I John 5:6)

Whatever its nature, that quite concrete cross and death at which the highest peak of the revelation was reached compelled the author of the Fourth Gospel to replace his old "paradigm," a requirement that every chapter of his Gospel indicates he welcomed.

CHAPTER EIGHT

The Death of Jesus in Hebrews

The Death of Jesus

Attempts to locate the heart and core of the Epistle to the Hebrews elsewhere than in the death of Jesus fly in the face of all but unanimous scholarly opinion. There is wide agreement regarding Jesus' death as basic to the theology of the author of this Epistle. The evidence is everywhere. Having made "purification for sins" by his death, Jesus achieves session at God's right hand (Heb. 1:3-4). The certainty of Christ's sympathy toward his own rests in his assuming a humanity culminating in passion and death (2:17-18; 4:15-16). Jesus' death, followed by his exaltation, is the assurance that God will bring his people to the glory for which he created them (3:3; 5:4-5). By his death Jesus becomes fully Son of God and High Priest forever (5:8-10; 6:20; 7:11-17, 20-22, 24-28). His crucifixion guarantees the superiority of the new covenant (8:6; 9:11-14).

Only after the death of Jesus, the testator of a new covenant, can those who are "called" enter into their inheritance (9:15-18). In the earthly temple, only the high priest could enter the sanctuary through the curtain; but now Christians are able to enter the holy of holies "by the blood of Jesus" (10:19). The gifts to be poured out at the end of days are now mediated to Christ's community through his "flesh" (10:20). Entry into "Mount Zion," "the city of the living God, the heavenly Jerusalem" comes by way of the one whose blood "speaks a better word" than Abel's (12:22-24). In Jesus' death God shook everything in the created world, so that his people might enter an unshakable kingdom (12:25-28). Jesus' death yields the criterion of a life of sacrifice as having abiding significance (13:12-16, 20-21).

In the whole New Testament, Hebrews is the most sustained piece of writing on the subject of the crucifixion. The only chapter that makes oblique reference to it is chapter 11, which hints at "something better" without which the ancients would not be made "perfect apart from us" (11:39-40).

Hebrews and Judaism

Use and Fracture of the Cultic

An examination of the margins in Nestle's *Novum Testamentum Graece* quickly reveals the extent of the Epistle to the Hebrews' reference to Old Testament passages having to do with the cultus. Since the death of Jesus furnishes the author with the dominant theological content of his exposition, the cultic, or liturgical, takes on a significance absent from any other New Testament writing. In each successive chapter the author uses cultic imagery to indicate that the death of Jesus towers above the Old Testament sacrificial system. While sacrifices were made daily in Jerusalem, Christ offered a single sacrifice (9:6; 10:1, 14). While temple sacrifices had no permanent effect but required repeating, Christ's sacrifice was once for all (7:27; 9:12; 9:25-26, 28; 10:10). While the Old Testament sacrifices did not set sins aside or lead to perfection, Christ achieved an eternal redemption (9:12; 10:1, 11). While the old covenant priests offered alien blood, Christ offered his own (9:14, 25; 10:11). While the blood of goats and bulls or the ashes of a heifer cleansed in a merely earthly and bodily respect, the blood of Christ purifies the conscience from dead works (9:9-10, 13, 26). While beasts were sacrificed by Old Testament priests, Christ offered himself (7:27; 9:14). While earthly priests died, Christ remains in eternity with an unfailing priesthood (7:23-24, 28). And while the earthly high priest entered a holy of holies made with hands, Jesus entered heaven and stands before the face of God (9:11, 24) — the great High Priest seated on the right of the throne of the majesty on high (8:1; 10:12).

The advantages accruing to the author's use of cultic images are many and varied. For one thing, they facilitate an interpretation of Jesus' death by means of the atonement idea.[1] For another, the cultic in-

---

1. Note the *to hilaskesthai tas hamartias tou laou* in 2:17, which, with the possible ex-

terpretation gives breadth to the confession of Jesus as high priest, so that the purpose of his assuming humanity is "that he might be a merciful and faithful high priest in the service of God, to make *a sacrifice of atonement* for the sins of the people" (2:17). In this interpretation of Christ's death as the new Day of Atonement anchored in the new covenant (cf. Lev. 16), the cross becomes the original or antitype to which the Old Testament corresponds as type or copy. It is the "eternal redemption" (9:12) that fulfills what the prophets required in their criticism of the cult (10:5-9).[2] Furthermore, by means of cultic imagery that identifies the confession of Jesus, the great High Priest, as a confession of hope, the author applies his "therapy" to the problem of the readers' growing lack of faith in the face of the *parousia*'s delay.[3] From this use of cultic images the readers of Hebrews could have inferred that Christ's death simply inaugurated a new ecclesiastical tradition, with its priests and liturgical routines. For this reason, as Minear writes, the liturgical images must be interpreted in a radically allegorical way: each reference to an earthly temple, priesthood, or sacrifice must function as a symbol pointing beyond itself to the eternal and uncreated.[4]

Noting that the author of Hebrews "thinks more cultically" than the older traditions, Otto Michel nevertheless observes that the cultic concepts and figures do not intertwine or fit well together. For example, on the one hand, Jesus dies as a sacrifice to create the basis for his high priestly service in heaven (5:1-10; 7:1-15); on the other hand, his sacrifice is the actual liberation from guilt, sin, and death, a fulfillment no other sacrifice achieves (10:1-18). Or again, his dying is included in his high priestly office, but his actual service as high priest only begins with his exaltation. Thus, Michel concludes, the eschatological bursts or restructures the cultic motif.[5]

---

ception of Rom. 3:25 *(hon proetheto ho theos hilastērion dia tēs pisteōs),* deviates from the usual New Testament view.

2. Bertold Klappert, *Die Eschatologie des Hebräerbriefs,* Theologische Existenz Heute, No. 156 (Munich: Christian Kaiser Verlag, 1969), pp. 26, 59.

3. Cf. Heb. 6:19-20: "We have this hope, a sure and steadfast anchor of the soul, a hope that enters the inner shrine behind the curtain, where Jesus, a forerunner on our behalf, has entered, having become a high priest forever. . . ."

4. Minear, *The Golgotha Earthquake,* p. 45.

5. Cf. Otto Michel, *Der Brief an die Hebräer: Kritisch-Exegetischer Kommentar über das Neue Testament* (Göttingen: Vandenhoeck & Ruprecht, 1966), p. 74.

In his essay on Jesus' death as sacrifice, Günter Bader argues that this conflict between images naming Jesus both as sacrifice and as high priest "exhausts" the figure of sacrifice in Hebrews. He cites the French thinker Paul Ricoeur, who sees a common semantic in Jesus' speech concerning the kingdom, language that begins with taking up the tradition in its literalness, then proceeds to supersede it by intensifying its meaning, and finally concludes by destroying the original meaning. Similarly, by means of the "intentionally provoked figurative absurdity" in Hebrews, the figure of sacrifice is "thrust out of itself." That is, liberated from the host of associations in Jewish, Greek, or ancient religion, the image of sacrifice is not only made to serve the uniqueness of Jesus' death as an event that ends the archaic necessity of repetition; it also "exhausts" in the direction of speech as sacrifice — thus, toward prayer.[6]

Use and Fracture of Apocalyptic

The author's pursuit of his theme by way of the contrasts between old and new, earthly and heavenly, type and antitype, documents "an incontestable affinity with Judaism,"[7] more specifically, with Jewish apocalyptic. Descriptions of the old covenant and its institutions as *hypodeigma* (8:5; 9:23), *skia* (8:5; 10:1), *parabolē* (9:9), or *antitypos* (9:24) are in the service of a contrast between two divine dispensations, the one earthly and provisional, the other heavenly and eternal — a contrast native to apocalyptic. Such ideas as appear, for example, in Hebrews 8:5, where Moses is instructed to erect the wilderness sanctuary according to the pattern shown him "on the mountain," is common to Jewish apocalyptic writing.[8] The Epistle's Christology likewise betrays strong connections with Jewish apocalyptic, as well as with elements of a Wisdom tradition handed down in the apocalyptic tradition. For example, the "insertion" of the hymn in 1:3 transfers to Christ the honorific predi-

6. Bader, "Jesu Tod als Opfer," pp. 428-431; cf. Stephen Patterson's description of the "critique" of the culture of sacrifice in Hebrews (*Beyond the Passion,* pp. 97-98, 100-101).

7. Cf. Grässer, *Aufbruch und Verheissung: Gesammelte Aufsätze zum Hebräerbrief* (Berlin: De Gruyter, 1992), p. 31.

8. Cf. Hooker, *Not Ashamed of the Gospel,* p. 121; Strobel, *Der Brief an die Hebräer: Das Neue Testament Deutsch* (Göttingen: Vandenhoeck & Ruprecht, 1991), pp. 85-86.

cates once related to Sophia and the *logos;* the result is that Christology has entered on a new conceptuality behind which lies a thought form that emphasizes the motif of creation.[9] For more than one interpreter, Psalm 110 ("chief pillar of the Great Hallel") underlies the entire Epistle, or, as with the high-priest motif, forms the bracket encompassing all the elements gathered up into the Epistle's Christology.[10]

Reflecting on the way the Old Testament is used, Craig Koester says that the author of Hebrews does not begin with a fully developed view of Christ that he then relates to the Old Testament, but, conversely, considers the significance of Christ in light of the Old Testament. But since what God has disclosed in Christ has priority over the Old Testament word, Christ's life, death, and resurrection furnish the touchstone for understanding it. Herein lies the tension with which the author is working: he believes that the Old Testament cannot be understood apart from the crucified and exalted Christ, but he also believes that the crucified and exalted Christ cannot be understood apart from the Old Testament.[11]

If the cultic in Hebrews is burst by the temporal-eschatological motif, or "exhausted" for the sake of Jesus' death, the temporal-eschatological is in turn fractured by the eternal-vertical — and for the same reason. It is not merely that Hebrews differs from certain streams of Jewish apocalyptic by hesitating over forming historical periods or a plan of salvation; its "history" also moves toward a goal that cannot be defined within the context of this world.[12] The primitive Christian-apocalyptic expectation may still be noticeably at work, but hope of the consummation is no longer attached to an imminent return. Rather, in Christ's death the eternal has already impinged on the temporal.[13]

---

9. Michel, *Der Brief an die Hebräer,* pp. 56, 58, 61, 65, 73; cf. Craig Koester, who says that Jewish tradition had furnished the language for the identification of God's Word with the Son as occurs in Heb. 1:2 by identifying God's creative speech with his wisdom, which could be portrayed in personified form (*Hebrews,* The Anchor Bible [New York: Doubleday, 2001], p. 186); cf. also Wilckens, cited in Klappert, *Die Eschatologie des Hebräerbriefs,* p. 19.

10. Strobel, *Der Brief an die Hebräer,* p. 81; cf. Lohse, quoted in Klappert, *Die Eschatologie des Hebräerbriefs,* p. 36.

11. Koester, *Hebrews,* pp. 117, 198-199, 240.

12. Michel, *Der Brief an die Hebräer,* pp. 60, 69.

13. Cf. Hooker, *Not Ashamed of the Gospel,* p. 121.

Since the discovery of the Qumran literature, Hebrews' description of the Messiah as priest suggests the knowledge of traditions both may have possessed. The differences between them, however, are sufficient to deny to either any specific contact with the other. For this reason, it is too much to say that the author of Hebrews "corrects" the views of the Qumran community by way of the historical Jesus.[14] On the other hand, on the basis of its "vertical" or "axiological" perspective, the Epistle does represent an antithesis to any earthly-temporal priesthood. Still, whatever the relationship of Hebrews to a syncretistic Judaism of the pre-Christian period, its concept of Jesus' high priesthood after the order of Melchizedek — into the service of which everything cultic has been pressed — may have entirely different roots than any messianic doctrine of late Judaism.[15] Of greatest significance, however, is that, in contrast to the Qumran teaching of a lay messiah from the tribe of Judah and a priestly messiah from the tribe of Aaron, the Christ of Hebrews unites both messiahs in himself. Here again a great gulf is fixed between Hebrews and Qumran: while in Qumran the messiah has been halved — his suffering and dying assigned to the one, while the other (the royal or Davidic) is exempt from death — the one messianic high priest of the book of Hebrews has "appeared once for all at the end of the age to remove sin by the sacrifice of himself" (9:26).

Use and Fracture of Hellenistic Bible Exegesis

To the question regarding the origins of the author's particular use of the Old Testament, most scholars refer to his "Hellenistic" perspective, each in one way or another attempting to remove the haze enveloping the term. Philo's name perennially emerges as representative of the author's "Hellenistic" perspective. For example, in the summary to his commentary, Hans Windisch says that the most significant religious-historical connection between Hebrews and Philo concerns Christology: the Son's relationship to the Father and his relationship to the world is like that of the *logos* in Philo. Melchizedek, paralleled with

---

14. Stöger, "Die Christologie der Paulinischen und von Paulus abhängigen Briefe," p. 192.

15. Cf. Grässer, *Aufbruch und Verheissung*, pp. 37-38.

Christ, is actually identified with Philo's *logos,* just as in Hebrews the *logos* is identified as the ideal high priest. Finally, the fact that sinlessness is predicated of the Christ in Hebrews as of the *logos* of Philo is the obvious consequence of a common view; and like the Christ of Hebrews, the high priestly *logos* of Philo is prepared for intercession and aid.[16]

In Aelred Cody's investigation of the heavenly sanctuary and liturgy in Hebrews, he assigns Platonic origins to the Epistle's dualism. He says that the author of the Epistle is far less interested in the temporal, or "horizontal," than in the eternal, or "vertical": that is, he is less intent on temporal distinctions in the activity of Christ than on the timeless value of his work. In only one instance does Cody distance Hebrews from Plato: that is, with respect to their concept of time. According to Hebrews, salvation is realized by Jesus Christ, who spans the abyss between the heavenly, eternal world of reality and the cosmic, historical world of shadow. According to Plato, time is only an imitation of eternity, without beginning or end. Cody's interpretation of the Epistle is thus an extended and sustained argument on behalf of a Platonic perspective that relegates the horizontal or eschatological to a minor role.[17] Fifteen years after Cody, August Strobel would describe the "world" of Hebrews as a "Hellenistic-philosophical faith in which Platonic conceptuality gives expression to supra-earthly non-material things."[18]

Baur, whose researches the work of Cody and others easily calls to mind, interprets Hebrews as resolving rather than creating a dilemma. He assigns to the Epistle the role of mediator between Jewish- and Pauline-Christianity, saying that, though its author was in total agreement with Paul regarding Judaism's place in the evolution of Christianity, he "immediately" offers a mediation of opposites. But due to his origins, he can only offer it from the side of Judaism — in other words, from the perspective of the priesthood. Priesthood (or the "idea" of priesthood), then, becomes reality in the order of Melchizedek; and his identification with Christ is that higher thing able to mediate between opposites, combine them into a unity, and from which derives the Epis-

---

16. Hans Windisch, *Der Hebräerbrief, Die Katholischen Briefe: Handbuch zum Neuen Testament* (Tübingen: Verlag J. C. B. Mohr, 1951), pp. 121-122.

17. Aelred Cody, *Heavenly Sanctuary and Liturgy in the Epistle to the Hebrews* (St. Meinrad, IN: Grail Publications, 1960), p. 196; cf. also pp. 78, 80, 82, 91, 99, 102-103, 119-120, 131-132, 141-145, 164, 166-167, 179, 194, 196, 198, 203.

18. Strobel, *Der Brief an die Hebräer,* p. 80.

tle's constant contrast between the "copy" *(Bild)* and its "original" *(Sache).* For the author of Hebrews, says Baur, everything belonging to the sphere of Old Testament religion is a decline from the "idea," an inauthentic shape of the "true religion" through which the idea must pass to attain to its true realization.

In the final relationship, says Baur, this opposition of copy to original becomes the opposition of the earthly to the heavenly. Since the one is only a reflection of the other, reality can be achieved only in the heavenly world. Accordingly, Jesus dies on earth only in order to have the blood with which, as the great High Priest, he must enter heaven. Thus, Jewish-Christianity and Paulinism relate to each other as copy and original, earthly and heavenly worlds, as the finite and the absolute, or — since the absolute must enter into the finite in order to become what it should be — as the present and future world.[19] If the Hegelians would spend a century or two tearing at each other over the question of whether or not the "idea" could ever achieve ultimate self-realization in a given *individuum,* Baur believed — or thought the author of Hebrews believed — that it did.

Without denying the similarities between Hebrews and Hellenistic interpretation, specifically that of Philo, we can say that the differences between them are nonetheless obvious. Franz Joseph Schierse speaks for a considerable majority when he concludes that, in spite of the formal similarity, an unbridgeable chasm lies between Hebrews and Philo:

> Here [i.e. in Hebrews], revelation of the divine reality of salvation — there [i.e. in Philo] human-speculative interest in the world of ideas; here setting metaphysics within the historical movement toward the Christian Eschaton — there dissolving the Old Testament history of salvation into naturally construed philosophical categories.[20]

In other words, in Alexandrian-Philonic thought the "beyond" or "invisible" is an idea, whereas in Hebrews it is a goal given to hope.[21] Most importantly, as Windisch says in his first edition, Philo, with his thoroughgoing dualism, would never have understood the incarnation and

---

19. Baur, *The Church History of the First Three Centuries,* I, 114, 121.

20. F. J. Schierse, *Verheissung und Heilsvollendung: Zur theologischen Grundfrage des Hebräerbriefes* (Munich: Karl Zink Verlag, 1955), p. 11.

21. Cf. Michel, *An die Hebräer,* p. 52.

the sacrificial death of the divine High Priest. In Hegelian terms, his *logos* never achieves ultimate self-realization in a single individuum, can never be exhausted in the kind of appearance open to the Christ of Hebrews, but can only be volatilized in an attribute of deity, in something human or merely uttered. Philo, Windisch concludes, used the *logos* not only for his religion but also for his philosophy. For Hebrews, however, its connection with a historical human life and death is the chief thing.[22] Further, while it is true that Philo would not have denied the value of the visible world or even the regulations and institutions of Jewish life for the masses, they were only a means for the true Jew to achieve his goal: a vision of the *ho on*. For the author of Hebrews, the work of Christ involves further affirmation of historical existence by making ethical activity possible within a historical framework. As Käsemann says,

> . . . if the inspired Scripture of the canon and the homologia of the worship prove the necessity of the Son's earthly sojourn, then his example by implication proves the need of the sons' persistence on their earthly sojourn.[23]

Whether or not one argues for the horizontal-eschatological or the vertical-axiological as dominant, more than one scholar regard their combination as constituting the dilemma of the Epistle. Windisch says that the author's thought process is not "rhetorically" correct, that his "upbringing" did not furnish him the capacity for setting forth an admittedly difficult but nonetheless transparent complex of ideas in a disciplined train of thought. Michel asks how the relationship between the heavenly and earthly in Hebrews should be understood, specifically, whether the heavenly-earthly in its Platonic or Gnostic coloration still has metaphysical weight. Klappert says that the way the Alexandrian-Hellenistic and futurist-apocalyptic elements are combined constitutes the "decisive problem" in the eschatology of Hebrews. Cody himself says that the combination of perspectives is not a good fit; and Koester acknowledges that Hebrews operates with both temporal and spatial categories, yet fits neatly into neither category.[24]

---

22. Windisch, *Der Hebräerbrief*, p. 122.
23. Käsemann, *The Wandering People of God*, pp. 173-174.
24. Windisch, *Der Hebräerbrief*, p. 120; Michel, *Der Brief an die Hebräer*, p. 63;

But what if the Epistle's irritating "double-tracking" results from the author's reflection on the event of Christ himself, who "made purification for sins" and "sat down at the right hand of the Majesty on high" (1:3); who for a little while was "made lower than the angels" and now is "crowned with glory and honor" (2:9); who "was faithful to the one who appointed him" and thus is "worthy of more glory than Moses" (3:2-3); who was "tested as we are" and now "has passed through the heavens" (4:14-15); who "learned obedience through what he suffered" and has become "the source of eternal salvation for all who obey him" (5:8-9); who entered "the inner shrine behind the curtain" and has become "a high priest forever" (6:19-20); who "offered himself once for all" and now "holds his priesthood permanently" (7:24, 27) — and so forth? The first half of each sentence relates to what was done, to the earthly, the temporal, the "horizontal"; the second half relates to what is or will be, to the heavenly, the eternal, the "vertical." And since the logical sequence is from the horizontal to the vertical, no matter what the syntax (note the reversal in chapter 7), then the horizontal must be the defining element, must give to the vertical its reason for existing. This should be apparent from Hebrews 1:3 onward, for, as "someone has said somewhere," the four-member hymn of 1:3 is programmatic: the election of the Son introduces the historical process.

> He is the reflection of God's glory and the exact imprint of God's very being, and he sustains all things by his powerful word. When he had made purification for sins, he sat down at the right hand of the Majesty on high.

And since the earthly, temporal, "horizontal" is the event of Christ's death, Hebrews' use of the Old Testament, of the cultic, its homiletic, its sermonizing, its orientation to the paraenetic,[25] its epideictic approach to the committed, or its deliberative approach to those in peril of apostasy — whatever comes under the rubric of the "Alexandrian vertical" or "axiological" is made to serve the death that the author declares was not

---

Klappert, *Die Eschatologie des Hebräerbriefs,* p. 19; Cody, *Heavenly Sanctuary,* p. 145; Koester, *Hebrews,* p. 98; cf. p. 101.

25. In *Das literarische Rätsel des Hebräerbriefs* (Göttingen: Vandenhoeck & Ruprecht, 1906), p. 19, William Wrede says that, if the author had not needed the *paraenesis* then, presumably, the Scripture speculations would have been totally left out.

a ruin but an act of God, who has power over all. Thus the author hides the promise of glory and honor for his readers. And what if the polarity of the event of Christ is the explanation of the polarity of the author's conceptuality?

Entirely aside from the absence of terms used by Plato for the heavenly patterns,[26] there is no consistent contrast in Hebrews, with all its emphasis on the visible and invisible as contending powers,[27] between the material and heavenly worlds. Rather, the heavenly is united with the earthly on the basis of the historical event of Jesus' death that guarantees its benefits within historical existence. Thus the *mesitēs* in 9:15 and 12:24 ("the mediator of a new covenant") is not one who enables his own to forsake the world of phenomena for the world of *noumena,* nor an "idea" emanating from God by which one ascends to the ideal world. Terms in Hebrews 1:3 reminiscent of Alexandrian or Platonic thought, such as *apaugasma* ("reflection") and *charaktēr* ("exact imprint"), are predicated of one who came to live a historical existence and whose work of redemption occurs within the sphere of historical reality (cf. 1:3: *katharismon tōn hamartiōn poiēsamenos*). For this reason, entry into the holy place (10:19) does not occur by way of departure from the earthly reality but by way of the historical event, "the blood of Jesus."[28]

Use and Fracture of Gnosis

Ernst Käsemann was not the first to cite Gnostic texts and ideas in a religious-historical interpretation of Hebrews. For example, in the second edition (1931) of his commentary on Hebrews, Hans Windisch had cited the Odes of Solomon, the Hermetic Corpus, the Mandaean writings available to him, and the Hebrew book of Enoch, which he assigned to Jewish Gnosis. Käsemann's interpretation, however, stands out in bold relief because it is the first to press Gnostic ideas — and specifically the Gnostic redeemer-myth — into the service of a unified interpretation of the Epistle to the Hebrews. Proceeding from 3:7 to 4:13, he sets forth the motif of "the wandering people of God" toward their heavenly rest as

26. Cf. Koester, *Hebrews,* pp. 99, 195.
27. Käsemann, *The Wandering People of God,* p. 44.
28. Cf. Harrisville, "The Concept of Newness in the New Testament," pp. 251-252.

the Epistle's underlying theme, interpreting it in terms of the Gnostic idea of the soul's journey toward heaven. Next, he argues that the Epistle's view of the Son of God who leads the sons to "perfection" rests on the Gnostic *syggeneia*-doctrine of the primal-man-redeemer, who gathers the divine seeds. Finally, he declares that beneath the Epistle's concept of the high priest lies the Gnostic *anthrōpos*-myth linked to Jewish expectation of the messiah. Consequently, he says, such passages as Hebrews 2:5-9 become intelligible on the basis of the Gnostic myth according to which the one who leads to heaven at the same time returns to his home and becomes the "redeemed redeemer." Under the influence of this Gnostic doctrine, Käsemann says, an unmistakable transformation of the temporal-horizontal into the spatial-vertical occurred; or again, under the influence of the Gnostic myth of the redeemed redeemer, the time scheme in Hebrews retreats behind the diastasis of the earthly-heavenly.[29]

Käsemann's 1938 study went through three subsequent editions[30] without revision because, as he put it, contemporary discussion had only superficially dealt with it. While opposition to the "Gnostic" interpretation of Hebrews has often been general in nature, measured against a definition derived from its sources, the difference between Gnosis and Hebrews is sufficiently clear. To the question "who were we?"[31] the Gospel of Thomas replies, "Sons of the living father" — that is, of the same substance with the divine.[32] For the author of Hebrews, this essential presupposition of the mythical scheme that the "sons" share pre-existence with the Father is "intolerable to Christian procla-

---

29. Käsemann, *The Wandering People of God*, pp. 17-96, 97-18?, 183-240; cf. the review in Klappert, *Die Eschatologie des Hebräerbriefs*, p. 16. In his studies of Hebrews, Grässer virtually repeats Käsemann's interpretation, saying that Käsemann's thesis of the Gnostically prepared soil of Hebrews has been corroborated rather than refuted by current research; in fact, that in light of the discoveries of the Coptic-Gnostic texts at Nag Hammadi, the thesis has gained heightened validity (see "Die Heilsbedeutung des Todes Jesu in Hebräer 2,14-18," pp. 168-169, 172-175, 177-178, and *Aufbruch und Verheissung*, pp. 44, 46, 49.

30. In 1957, 1959, and 1961.

31. This and the following questions are formulated in the *Excerpta ex Theodoto of Clement of Alexandria*, 78, 2, trans. Robert Pierce Casey (London: Christophers, 1934), p. 89.

32. The Gospel of Thomas, II, 32, 33, 4, in *The Nag Hammadi Library in English*, p. 126.

mation," for "it is not the identity of divine nature, but the mercy of God that unites the two." To the question "what have we become?" or "where were we — where were we placed?" the Gnostic replies that the soul came forth from the divine world and fell into this world of fate, birth, and death; thus it must be reawakened to be restored. In Hebrews the diastasis between the earthly and the heavenly does not translate into abhorrence of the material world but into an opposition to "seeking from the law and the cultus on earth" what "can only be found from heaven," the righteousness in Christ.

To the question "whither do we hasten, from what are we redeemed, what is birth, and what is rebirth?" the Acts of Thomas answers: "Thou hast shown me how to seek myself and know who I was, and who and in what manner I now am, that I may again become that which I was."[33] In other words, redemption — with or without a redeemer[34] — comes with knowing "where one comes from and where he is going,"[35] that is, with the soul's recognition of its *syggeneia* with the divine. For Hebrews, "recourse to an alleged state of pre-existence in order to explain the fact of redemption is out of the question. . . . Christian proclamation is aware that salvation and guidance through Christ are attained solely in the decision of faith." The above responses are all taken from Käsemann's study.[36] He was convinced that, in an age of Hellenism dominated by the Gnostic myth, the author of Hebrews took the "risk" of adopting mythical ideas to make clear the way of Christ. The point, however, at which he drew back from the myth was Jesus' "humiliation," the historical event of his "purification for sins" (1:3), his death on the cross. From this event, recourse to an alleged state of pre-existence to explain the fact of redemption is out of the question. The Gnostic notion of the pre-existence of the soul is completely absent in

---

33. A. F. J. Klijn, *The Acts of Thomas: Introduction, Text, Commentary* (Leiden: E. J. Brill, 1962), p. 198.

34. Cf. The Second Apocalypse of James, V, 44, 55, 15 in *The Nag Hammadi Library in English,* pp. 72, 273; *The Greek Corpus Hermeticum and the Latin Aesclepius,* trans. Brian P. Copenhaver (Cambridge, UK: Cambridge University Press, 1992), I, 19 and 32, 4, 7; cf. also Carsten Colpe, *Die Religionsgeschichtliche Schule,* pp. 16, 198.

35. The Gospel of Truth, I, 16, 22, 13-15, in *The Nag Hammadi Library in English,* p. 42.

36. For the question "who were we?" see *The Wandering People of God,* pp. 151, 165; for the question "what have we become?" see pp. 59-63; and for the question "whither do we hasten, from what are we redeemed?" see p. 151.

Hebrews. A saving decree is set at the very beginning, according to which redemption occurs historically, in an actual entry into flesh and blood, and not the mere putting on of a mask. And it is this decree that guarantees the possibility of redemption attained in a decision of faith. "Only after this dismemberment," says Käsemann, "is the myth of use." Thus he concludes: "Christ stands at the end of the myth as well as at the end of the Law."[37]

Whether or not Käsemann's proposal succeeded or failed, he appears to have suffered the same fate as his teacher, Rudolf Bultmann, whose detractors often contented themselves with general and unspecified objections to the similarities he observed between a New Testament author and his religious-historical environment,[38] often paying little or no attention to his observance of the differences.

At the least, Hebrews' linkage of the "horizontal-temporal" and the "vertical-eternal," whether eschatological-apocalyptic, Hellenistic, or Gnostic, is calculated to set forth the death of Christ as the event introducing the new eon.[39] On the other hand, to the degree that it is the *death* of Christ that the author's conceptuality is made to serve, to that degree the historical or "horizontal-temporal" has taken over the "vertical-eternal." Cody, despite his Platonizing, has allowed for the takeover by acknowledging that Hebrews' dualism leaves room for a "real participation of salvation on earth"; that the installation of Christ as high priest occurs only "after his suffering"; that he enters the eternal place of God's power "through His historical humanity"; that without his passion and death "there would be no entrance into the sanctuary"; and that the immolation on Calvary has "real value, eternal value."[40] Furthermore, however vacillating in his treatment of the religious-historical problem Michel may appear, he does say that the "real truth"

37. Käsemann, *The Wandering People of God*, pp. 179, 234.
38. Otto Hofius's attempt through a study of Hebrews 3:7–4:13 (Käsemann's "beginning point") to anchor the Epistle's conceptuality in the eschatological apocalyptic thought of ancient Judaism, rather than in the Greek *anthrōpos*-myth, is the exception to prove the rule (Hofius, *Katapausis: Die Vorstellung vom endzeitlichen Ruheort im Hebräerbrief*, Wissenschaftliche Untersuchungen zum Neuen Testament [Tübingen: J. C. B. Mohr, 1970]).
39. Klappert, *Die Eschatologie des Hebräerbriefs*, p. 26; Grässer, *Aufbruch und Verheissung*, p. 67.
40. Cf. Cody, *Heavenly Sanctuary and Liturgy*, pp. 82, 102-103, 166-167, 172, 194.

beyond the Old Testament idea of covenant, with its concept of commandment and law, is linked to a history understood neither cultically nor legally, though it may be stated in cultic and legal ways. He continues that it is improbable that an ultimately philosophical premise supports the substructure of the Epistle's argument. Rather, "the eschatological truth of history and the Old Testament promise" enter the formulation of the question. Or again, he says that the Epistle's emphasis on the name "Jesus" (cf. 2:9; 3:1; 4:14; 6:20; 7:22; 10:19; 12:2; 13:12) is calculated to set forth his uniqueness and relationship to history, with the result that "the Christology of acclamations and expressions of lordship" is corrected by historical tradition.[41]

The takeover of the "vertical" by the "horizontal" in Hebrews is thus one more variation on the triumph of the particular, the death of Christ, over the universal, the author's conceptuality or "mental furniture." In the face of the impasse attaching to history-of-religions approaches, due to the inadequacy of existing categories, Koester suggests that the model for the interpretation of Hebrews be reversed, that one proceed from the particular to the universal, observing how the particular event of Christ's crucifixion and exaltation is explicated by way of various images.[42] But, as in the preceding pages of this book, my intention here is to demonstrate the element of discontinuity, the fracture of an author's language and thought by the event he was moved to describe, a situation he himself created — or of which he was victim — signaled in a paucity of speech and thought.

41. Hofius, *Katapausis,* p. 11; cf. also Michel, *Der Brief an die Hebräer,* pp. 68, 75.
42. Koester, *Hebrews,* pp. 60, 63.

CHAPTER NINE

The Death of Jesus in First Peter

The Independence of the Epistle

This little book of five chapters is singularly unlike the other New Testament writings. First of all, it contains the lone, unaccompanied — and thus challenged[1] — "seat of doctrine" for the *descensus ad inferos,* Christ's descent and proclamation to the "spirits in prison." Framed by a twofold *poreutheis* (3:19: "*he went* and made a proclamation to the spirits in prison"; 3:22: "*he has gone* into heaven"), the reference has been interpreted either as the final stage of Christ's passion or as the beginning of his exaltation, in which he heralded his victory to the disobedient contemporaries of Noah, or, as per the older exegesis, preached to the old covenant faithful.

Second, to a great extent this Epistle does not treat Christ's passion as an independent theme. It subordinates his death to ethical exhortation.[2] For example, following the summons to a holy life "in reverent

---

1. Cf. Frank Chamberlain Porter, "The Spirits in Prison: A Neglected Theory Reconsidered," *New Englander and Yale Review* (1888), 95-121.

2. Herbert Braun, *Das Leiden Christi: Eine Bibelarbeit über den 1. Petrusbrief,* Theologische Existenz Heute, vol. 69 (Munich: Christian Kaiser Verlag, 1940), p. 19. See also Rudolf Bultmann, "Bekenntnis- und Liedfragmente im ersten Petrusbrief," *Coniectanea Neotestamentica* XI (Lund: C. W. K. Gleerup, 1947), p. 3. In his *Theology of the New Testament,* Bultmann notes that this Epistle falls short of the Pauline idea in its idea of the suffering Christ as model (II, 146). Cf. also Morna D. Hooker, *Jesus and the Servant,* pp. 151-152; Paul Achtemeier, *I Peter,* Hermeneia (Minneapolis: Fortress, 1996), p. 37.

fear," the author reminds his readers of their ransom through "the precious blood of Christ like that of a lamb without defect or blemish" (1:15-19). In chapter 2, the passion of Christ serves as model or example:

> . . . if you endure when you do right and suffer for it, you have God's approval. For to this you have been called, because Christ also suffered for you, leaving you an example, so that you should follow in his steps. (2:20b-21)

In chapter 3, writing that "it is better to suffer for doing good," the author refers to Christ's having "suffered for sins once for all, the righteous for the unrighteous" (3:17-18). In his response to Bernhard Weiss (1827-1918) concerning the dating of the epistle, F. C. Baur says that the Pauline view of Christ's death hovered before the author, though he did not intend to treat it specifically, but rather weakened it by making moral use of it.[3]

There are instances, however, in which moral use is not made of the death of Christ, but in which the motif of his suffering as model is crisscrossed by the tradition. For example, if I Peter 2:21 suggests that, like Christ, slaves may also suffer vicariously, verse 24 totally excludes that idea:

> He himself bore our sins in his body on the cross, so that, free from sins, we might live for righteousness; by his wounds you have been healed.

Or again, in 3:18 it is the *unique* suffering of Christ that serves as model. Moreover, the performance of that for which Christ serves as model is not left to the spontaneity of the Christian, since it was "to this" that the readers were "called" (2:21).[4] Therefore, if, as Paul Achtemeier says and Ralph Martin echoes,[5] the "controlling metaphor" throughout I Peter is

---

3. Baur, "Der erste petrinische Brief, mit besonderer Beziehung auf das Werk . . . von Lic. Dr. Bernh. Weiss," *Theologische Jahrbücher* 15 (1856), 235.

4. See Braun, *Das Leiden Christi*, p. 34, and Wolfgang Schrage, *Der Erste Petrusbrief: Die "Katholischen" Briefe* [Horst Balz und Wolfgang Schrage] (Göttingen: Vandenhoeck & Ruprecht, 1973), p. 93.

5. Achtemeier, "Newborn Babes and Living Stones: Literal and Figurative in 1 Peter," in *To Touch the Text: Biblical and Related Studies in Honor of Joseph A. Fitzmyer,* ed. M. P. Horgan and Paul J. Kobelski (New York: Crossroad, 1989), pp. 229-231, 235-236;

that of the new people of God, a metaphor prompting the author to construe Christ as the model for Christian suffering, that people of God is nonetheless "constituted" by the Christ who suffered and rose.[6]

The independence of the passion theme is further challenged by its apparently indissoluble link to the resurrection, which is reflected, for example, in 1:20-21 and 2:24-25. Of the latter passage, Herbert Braun (1903-1991) says: "How could a dead person exercise the office of shepherd and bishop?" He adds that the two events can be neither materially nor temporally separated from their goal.[7] Similarly, in opposition to the now-abandoned view of the Epistle as an adaptation of early baptismal material, Wolfgang Schrage says that its readers are referred with particular emphasis to the suffering and tested Christ, to the eschatological glory and to baptism, all of which gives central significance to the eschatological hope.[8] But if the situation of the community that the Epistle reflects is that of a period of hostility and antagonism, however sporadic,[9] a situation that prompts the author to take up the metaphor of the people of God and for this reason to refer to Christ as model, then Christ's passion does in fact "play a more developed role in the argument of the letter."[10]

Third, the First Epistle of Peter distances itself from the New Testament collection by the author's frequent hermeneutical "move" from Scripture to the event of Christ's passion in place of the customary move from the event to Scripture. For example, the application of the oracle in 1:24-25a ("All flesh is like grass . . . but the word of the Lord endures forever"), through declaring that "this [NRSV: 'that'] is the word which was announced to you" (1:25b); the use of Psalm 34 in 2:3 or 3:13-

---

Ralph P. Martin, *The Theology of Jude, I Peter, and 2 Peter: New Testament Theology* (Cambridge, UK: Cambridge University Press, 1994), p. 100.

6. Paul Achtemeier, "Newborn Babes and Living Stones," p. 229.

7. Braun, *Das Leiden Christi*, pp. 27-30; see also Martin, *The Theology of Jude, I Peter, and 2 Peter*, p. 107.

8. Wolfgang Schrage, *Der Erste Petrusbrief*, p. 64.

9. For a brief synopsis of scholarship regarding the Epistle's situation in life, see Achtemeier, "Newborn Babes and Living Stones," pp. 210-211; cf. also C. F. D. Moule, who suggests that the author released two forms of the Epistle, one for those not yet under duress (1:1–4:11 and 5:12-14), and the other, terser and swifter, for those who were undergoing "private" persecutions or pogroms (1:1–2:10; 4:12–5:14) ("The Nature and Purpose of I Peter," *New Testament Studies* 3 [1956-1957], 7-8).

10. Achtemeier, "Newborn Babes and Living Stones," p. 229.

17; the use of Isaiah 8:12-13 in 3:14-15 to expand the application of the Psalm; and the Christological application of Isaiah 11:2 in 4:14 — all these appear to reflect the move from Scripture to event.

Use and Fracture of the Old Testament and Judaism

The epistle "teems" with Old Testament references. William Schutter locates forty-six quotations and allusions, apart from iterative allusions, which would increase the total. He adds that "homiletic midrash" is the most plausible influence behind the Epistle's literary structure.[11]

Wherever the Old Testament is extensively used, an introductory formula appears indicating that the passage is distinguished qualitatively from other sources. The first appears in 1:16 ("for it is written") and introduces a quotation from the Septuagint version of Leviticus 19:2, part of the so-called Holiness Code in the priestly source of the Pentateuch: "You shall be holy for I am holy." The second appears in 1:24-25 ("for"), and with slight changes introduces the Septuagint version of Isaiah 40:8: "All flesh is like grass. . . ."[12] The third appears in 2:6-8 (v. 6: "for it stands in Scripture"; v. 8: "and"), and introduces a combination of texts in part drawn from the Septuagint version of Isaiah 28 (v. 16b; cf. also Ps. 34:5; Ps. 118:22, and Isaiah 8:14): "See, I am laying in Zion a stone. . . ." The fourth formula occurs in 3:10-11 (v. 10: "for"; v. 11: "and"), and with slight alterations introduces a quotation from the Septuagint version of Psalm 34:12-16: "Those who desire life and desire to see good days, let them keep their tongues from evil." The Old Testament scriptures as a whole are broadly represented in the Epistle, though the heaviest concentration is on Psalms and Isaiah.[13] Wilhelm

---

11. Schutter, *Hermeneutic and Composition in I Peter*, p. 43.

12. Other references with Septuagint parallels occur in 1:3 (Ps. 33:2); 2:3 (Ps. 34:8); 2:9 (Isa. 43:20-21; cf. Ex. 19:6; 23:22); 3:10-13 (Ps. 34:12-16), and 5:5 (Ps. 34:18; cf. Prov. 3:34).

13. In addition, Windisch calls attention to the use of Ex. 12:5 in 1:19; Leon Morris notes the use of Ex. 24 in 1:2, 18-19, and of Ex. 19:5 in 2:9; Wolfgang Schrage points to the use in 1:18-19 of Ex. 12:5, with its reference to the Passover lamb rather than to the Servant in Isa. 53:7; Gerhard Friedrich notes the use of Ex. 24:4-8 in 1:2; and Krodel calls attention to the use of Ex. 19:6 in 2:9, and in 1:19 to the use of Ex. 24:5-8, with its reference to the blood of the covenant rather than to the Passover lamb. Cf. also Hans Windisch, *Die Katholischen Briefe,* Handbuch zum Neuen Testament (Tübingen: Verlag J. C. B.

Bornemann (1858-1946) says that the sequence of the argument in I Peter is identical to that of Psalm 33(34), and concludes that the similarities between the passages are sufficient to assume a literary connection.[14]

Chapter 2 makes extensive use of the Fourth Servant Song in Deutero-Isaiah as commentary on Christ's passion. References to Christ's sinlessness, his refusal to return abuse, his bearing of sins, and the healing through his wounds, together with the reference to straying sheep, are paralleled in Isaiah 53:4-7, 9. If Bornemann is convinced that the Epistle's sequence is dictated by Psalm 33(34), others are convinced that the historical events of Christ's passion are blended with the portrait of the Servant in Deutero-Isaiah.[15] Whatever "demolition" the traditional figure of the Servant-Messiah may have suffered with the other New Testament authors, I Peter, says Hooker, is the earliest definitive proof for the full identification of Jesus with the Servant in all its Christological significance.[16] The author's dependence on Old Testament texts obviously reflects more than the mere desire to illustrate an argument. A theological motive is at work: the concern to indicate that the God who redeemed the Old Testament covenant people and the God who redeems Christians is one and the same.

From the observation of the Epistle's dependence on the Old Testament, it is only a short step to assuming its relationship to the variegated Jewish hermeneutical tradition. The exhortation in 1:7 to remain steadfast in the face of suffering has its context in the Jewish apocalyptic idea of the "footsteps of the Messiah" immediately preceding the end (cf. 4:5, 13; 5:4, 10-11 and Dan. 12:1 or 4 Ezra 13:16-19). The dual reference to

---

Mohr, 1951), p. 57; Morris, *The Apostolic Preaching of the Cross* (London: Tyndale Press, 1955), pp. 101, 57; Schrage, *Der erste Petrusbrief,* p. 77; Friedrich, *Die Verkündigung des Todes Jesu im Neuen Testament,* p. 56; Gerhard Krodel, *I Peter, The General Letters,* Proclamation Commentaries (Minneapolis: Fortress, 1995), pp. 70, 81. In addition to possible allusions (cf. 1:7, 13; 2:17; 3:6, and 4:8), the Epistle contains two direct quotations from the Septuagint version of Proverbs (4:18b from Prov. 11:31, and 5:5 from Prov. 3:34).

14. W. Bornemann, "Der erste Petrusbrief — eine Taufrede des Silvanus?" *Zeitschrift für die Neutestamentliche Wissenschaft* 19 (1919), 146-149.

15. Cf. Braun, *Das Leiden Christi,* pp. 24, 25, 33; Windisch, *Die Katholischen Briefe,* pp. 65-66; Delling, *Der Kreuzestod Jesu in der urchristlichen Verkundigung,* p. 38; Schrage, *Der erste Petrusbrief,* p. 77; Schutter, *Hermeneutic and Composition in I Peter,* p. 140; Martin, *The Theology of Jude, I Peter, and 2 Peter,* pp. 105-106, 110, 126; Johnson, *The Real Jesus,* p. 165.

16. Cf. Hooker, *Jesus and the Servant,* pp. 17, 124-125, 127.

Christ in 1:20 — as "destined before the foundation of the world" and "revealed at the end of the ages" — is reminiscent of the figure of the "Son of the Most High" in the pseudepigraphical Odes of Solomon.[17] The reference in 2:23 to Christ's refusal to return abuse or to threaten when he suffered obviously moved the translator of the Odes to make "Christ Speaks" the heading for chapter 31.[18] The creedal tradition that interprets Christ's death as a vicarious representation in 3:18 may be anticipated in the apocryphal Maccabees.[19] The special attention given women's coiffure and apparel in 3:3 is suggestive of Hellenistic practices that the Isaiah Targum promises will be recompensed by the ruin of Jerusalem.[20] In 4:18, the contrast between the righteous and the ungodly, absent any shading in between, is characteristic of Wisdom and apocalyptic thought.[21]

Most striking is the anticipation of the *descensus* in Ethiopic Enoch 6–16, whose subject went down to the netherworld to announce to the fallen angels that they could hope for neither peace nor forgiveness:

17. The Odes of Solomon 41:13-15: "The Son of the Most High appeared in the perfection of his Father. And light dawned from the Word that was before time in him. The Messiah in truth is one. And he was known before the foundations of the world" (*The Old Testament Pseudepigrapha,* II, 770). The same motif occurs earlier in the Wisdom literature, in Proverbs 8:23 and Sirach 24:9; cf. Windisch, *Die Katholischen Briefe,* p. 57; cf. also Bultmann, "Bekenntnis- und Liedfragmente im ersten Petrusbrief," p. 41.

18. The Odes of Solomon 31:10-11: "I endured and held my peace and was silent, that I might not be disturbed by them. But I stood undisturbed like a solid rock which is continuously pounded by columns of waves and endures" (*The Old Testament Pseudepigrapha,* II, 763).

19. II Macc. 7:37-38: "I, like my brothers, give up body and life for the laws of our ancestors, appealing to God to show mercy soon to our nation and by trials and plagues to make you confess that he alone is God, and through me and my brothers to bring to an end the wrath of the Almighty" (*The New Oxford Annotated Bible,* ed. Bruce M. Metzger and Roland E. Murphy [New York: Oxford University Press, 1989], pp. 242-243; cf. also IV Macc. 6:28-29 in *The Old Testament Pseudepigrapha,* II, 552.

20. 3:16-24: "Because the daughters of Zion are haughty, they walk with uplifted neck and walk ogling with their eyes and with ringed locks of hair and inciting with their feet. . . . In that time the Lord will take away the finery of the sandals, and the headbands . . . and it shall come to pass that the place where they used perfumes will melt away" (Bruce D. Chilton, *The Isaiah Targum, The Aramaic Bible,* Vol. II [Wilmington, Del.: Michael Glazier, Inc., 1987], p. 11).

21. Cf., e.g., Prov. 11:31: "If the righteous are repaid on earth, how much more the wicked and the sinner!"

At that moment the Watchers were calling me. And they said to me, "Enoch, scribe of righteousness, go and make known to the Watchers of heaven who have abandoned the high heaven, the holy eternal place, and have defiled themselves with women. . . . They have defiled themselves with great defilement upon the earth; neither will there be peace unto them nor the forgiveness of sin."[22]

The suggestion that there is "a mass of supporting evidence" in favor of the Epistle's *pesher*-like hermeneutic as it was used at Qumran — and thus the assumption of a "stream" from the Dead Sea community to early Christianity in which I Peter shared — has been challenged.[23] Nevertheless, the formulae used by Qumran to introduce Old Testament quotations are often the exact Semitic equivalent of those of the New Testament, thus revealing a reverence among both groups for the Old Testament as the Word of God.[24] Furthermore, both reflect similarity in their use of the Old Testament, for example, in such practices as the linking of verses in a *haraz* or *catena*.[25]

However frequent the author's move from Scripture to event, that is, from the Old Testament as prefiguring the event of Christ to the event itself, at strategic points in the Epistle the move is reversed. Let the Christological hymns and the verses surrounding them serve as evidence.

In the first "Christ-hymn" (1:17-21), Isaiah's statement about the "lamb" that was led to the slaughter and was silent before his shearers (Isaiah 53:7) is not a sufficient model for the "lamb without defect or blemish." It does not reach back far enough to prefigure a lamb "destined before the foundation of the world."[26] Furthermore, the exegesis of Isaiah 40 in the admonition following the hymn (1:22-25) indicates that the Christians' redemption does not simply root in Christ's suffer-

22. I Enoch 12:3-5, *The Old Testament Pseudepigrapha,* I, 19.

23. Cf. Schutter, *Hermeneutic and Composition in I Peter,* pp. 110, 122, 138, 166; Achtemeier, *I Peter,* p. 13. Fitzmyer argues that the devices used by Qumran and the New Testament in referring to the Old Testament were not exclusive to the *pesharim;* cf. Joseph Fitzmyer, "The Use of Explicit Old Testament Quotations in Qumran Literature and in the New Testament," *New Testament Studies* 7 (October 1960), 331.

24. Cf. Fitzmyer's discussion of the parallels, pp. 300, 333.

25. Schutter (in *Hermeneutic and Composition in I Peter,* p. 87) finds similarities between the *catena* in I Peter 2:6-8 and 4Qtestimony, between *florilegia* in I Peter 2:3-10 and 4Qflor, 11Qmelch; cf. Achtemeier, *I Peter,* p. 13 n. 121.

26. Cf. Braun, *Das Leiden Christi,* p. 31.

ing but rather *together with* his suffering — in the decree of the God who allowed him to be "revealed at the end of the ages."

Prior to the second "Christ-hymn" (2:21-25), the complex of Old Testament materials in 2:4-10 moves from the event of the readers' hardship and the miracle of their faith to the image of the stone in Isaiah 28:16. The hymn itself blends the historical events of Christ's passion with phrases from Isaiah 53, but does not distort them to agree with it. On the contrary, the hymn interprets the phrases in the light of the passion[27] — to the point that it reverses the movement in the Isaiah text. Now the action of the Servant can be interpreted as preceding its benefits. The Isaiah "commentary" has thus undergone "rearrangement": it has been warped to the event of Christ's passion.[28] It has also undergone supplementation. As Gerhard Krodel observes, in three moves the author links the tradition of the Isaian Servant to the undeserved suffering of slaves. In 2:21, he substitutes "suffered" for "died" and "you" for "us," then adds, "leaving you an example that you should follow in his steps," and in verse 24 adds, "by his wound (singular) you have been healed."[29] In addition, the author abbreviates "all we like sheep have gone astray" to "you were like straying sheep" (Nestle text), and furnishes the statement with its opposite: "But now you have returned to the shepherd and guardian of your souls."[30] Finally, the use of this song as a model for human suffering represents a departure from a later, customary use of the passage in the interpretation of Christ's death.[31]

If the third "Christ-hymn" (3:18-22) is, in fact, reminiscent of the first Servant Song (Isa. 42), its subject is no longer Israel, the covenant people, but Christ; furthermore, the action is no longer projected into the future (Isa. 42:7: "to open the eyes that are blind, to bring out the prisoners from the dungeon, from the prison those who sit in darkness") but is rather "a proclamation to the spirits" that has already taken place. If, as Baur says, "hope is supposed to be the peculiar expression of the Petrine individuality," it has scarcely left its trace here.[32] Lastly, as

27. Hooker, *Jesus and the Servant*, p. 125.
28. Schutter's statement in *Hermeneutic and Composition in I Peter*, p. 140.
29. Krodel, *I Peter*, p. 74.
30. Braun, *Das Leiden Christi*, p. 33.
31. Martin, *The Theology of Jude, I Peter, and 2 Peter*, p. 131.
32. Baur, "Der erste petrinische Brief," p. 213. On the other hand, cf. Schrage, *Der erste Petrusbrief*, p. 64.

with the two preceding, this hymn is pressed into the service of exhortation. Consequently, Schutter's statement concerning the author's use of the Fourth Servant Song, that it is "the most elaborate reorganization or rewriting of Isaiah 53 . . . that survives from the early Church," could just as well be said of his use of the first Song here. The author's hermeneutic is thus not a wholesale move from Old Testament Scripture to the historical event of Christ's passion. In fact, whenever such a move does appear to occur, it is necessary to recall that the writer, like the other New Testament authors, is immersed in the fulfillment-theme, a theme ultimately dominated by the move from event to Scripture.[33] Furthermore, the biblical author's insistence on that event as relevant to the present experience of divine forgiveness all the more inhibits the Old Testament's functioning as "proof text."[34] Rather, the move from event to Scripture renders the reading of the Old Testament a tour de force — and thus spells fracture.

Despite a similarity in their use of it, Qumran and I Peter read the Old Testament in a way that relegates their similarity to the periphery. According to Qumran, the Teacher of Righteousness and his followers still await deliverance; for the author of I Peter, on the other hand, the Deliverer has already come. For example, the *pesher* in IQpHab 8 on Habakkuk 2:4 ("the righteous live by their faith") opens with these words:

> Its interpretation concerns all those who observe the Torah in the House of Judah, *whom God will save* from the house of judgment on account of their tribulation and their fidelity to the Righteous Teacher.[35]

Whatever the nature of its messianic speculations, Qumran's hope is not yet fulfilled. On the other hand, I Peter 1:20 reads: "He was destined before the foundation of the world, but *was revealed* at the end of the ages for your sake." Whatever the similarity in dependence on the Old Testament or in exegetical procedure, this contrast between anticipation in the one community and realization in the other fixes a gulf between them.

---

33. Schutter, *Hermeneutic and Composition in I Peter,* pp. 143, 173-175.

34. Cf. Hooker, *Jesus and the Servant,* pp. 125, 127.

35. *The Dead Sea Scrolls, Hebrew, Aramaic, and Greek Texts with English Translations,* ed. James H. Charlesworth et al. (Tübingen: Mohr Siebeck, 2002), Vol. 6b, 175 (italics mine).

Further, if in fact there was a stream of theological thought that flowed from Qumran to early Christianity — and in which I Peter also shared — nevertheless, as Achtemeier says, the outcome of that stream regarding the relationship of the faithful to society is markedly different in the one and the other instance. Whereas the Qumran community effected virtually a total withdrawal from society, for our author the "exiles" should continue to live in society and conform to its laws provided they do not compromise their commitment to Christ.[36]

Hellenization and Its Fracture

Preoccupation with Greco-Roman parallels to I Peter is no less vigorous than that with Old Testament, Jewish parallels. According to Baur, the question of Pliny the Younger (62-113 C.E.) to the emperor Trajan (53?-117 C.E.)[37] furnished the clue to the time of the letter's composition. Referring to the author's injunction that his readers keep themselves from whatever might suggest that being a Christian involved moral reproach (2:18-20), he asked:

> From what other standpoint could this occur than from that of the state, and what earlier datum do we have for this idea of Christianity than the report of Pliny?

Consequently, the author's summons and Pliny's question to Trajan conjoined to indicate the time of the letter's composition.[38] It was a time, Baur says, during which the difference between pagan and Christian morality had taken on more public character, thus one in which Christians began to appear as a markedly different society. But it was also a time when the original opposition between groups in the Christian community had been so weakened that what was common or mediating was held to, thus creating the possibility for the emergence of a "catholic church."

36. Achtemeier, *I Peter,* p. 13.

37. "Whether the mere performance of Christianity, albeit without crimes, or only the crimes associated therewith are punishable . . ." (Pliny, *Letters,* trans. Wm. Melmoth [Cambridge, MA: Harvard University Press, 1963], II, 401).

38. Baur, "Der erste petrinische Brief," pp. 213, 221-224.

In his commentary on I Peter, E. G. Selwyn (1885-1959) refers to the writer's "Aeschylean use of compounds," the "Euripidean tenderness" of his words, the steady strain of typical Greek "moderation" throughout, and to the element of "Socratic irony" in the author's reference to Christ's passion (2:21-25) and his own relationship to it (5:1). Selwyn appends to his commentary a classical index containing three entire pages of Greek parallels.[39] Contemporaneous sourcebooks on Greek and Roman parallels contain numerous references to I Peter.[40]

In a 1977 essay on the tables of duties in the New Testament, Eduard Schweizer says that, despite their Christian development, with respect to form and content they reflect a Hellenistic-Stoic ethic with its concept of "unwritten laws" — and as mediated by Hellenistic Judaism. Under the title "Paganization of the *Haustafeln*," Schweizer goes on to note the danger involved in the appropriation of the Hellenistic model. For example, he believes that the table of duties in 2:18-25 came perilously close to assuming a divinely decreed hierarchical order of master and slave.[41] In an article entitled "Hellenization/Acculturation in I Peter," David Balch echoes Schweizer's argument regarding the danger of "paganization," noting that its acculturation of the values of Hellenistic society placed the Petrine community in tension with Jewish tradition as well as with the early Jesus movement.[42]

In his *Hauptprobleme der Gnosis*,[43] Wilhelm Bousset discourses on the religious-historical background of the *descensus* passage. Noting its

---

39. E. G. Selwyn, *The First Epistle of St. Peter,* pp. 26, 499-501.

40. Cf., e.g., the parallels to I Peter in Aeschylus cited by Windisch, *Die Katholischen Briefe,* p. 9; the parallels in Plutarch cited by Heinz-Dieter Betz, *Plutarch's Ethical Writings and Early Christian Literature* (Leiden: E. J. Brill, 1978), p. 41; and the parallels in the Greek writers Dio Chrysostom, Pseudo-Isocrates, Hierocles, Plutarch, Lucian, and the Pythagoreans, cited by Abraham H. Malherbe, *Moral Exhortation: A Greco-Roman Sourcebook* (Philadelphia: Westminster, 1986), pp. 42, 82, 88, 93, 107, 124-125, 136; and in the Roman writers Seneca and Musonius, pp. 62, 64, 152.

41. Eduard Schweizer, "Die Weltlichkeit des Neuen Testaments: die Haustafeln," in *Beiträge zur Alttestamentlichen Theologie: Festschrift für Walther Zimmerli,* ed. Herbert Donner, Robert Hanhart and Rudolf Smend (Göttingen: Vandenhoeck & Ruprecht, 1977), pp. 401-406, 409-410, 412-413.

42. David L. Balch, "Hellenization/Acculturation in I Peter," in *Perspectives on First Peter,* ed. Charles H. Talbert (Macon: Mercer University Press, 1986), pp. 81-82, 87, 93-94, 96-101.

43. Göttingen: Vandenhoeck & Ruprecht, 1907.

uniqueness in the description of the purpose of Jesus' descent as "proclamation to the spirits in prison," he adds that its original meaning can no longer be arrived at. In the *descensus* passage Bousset finds direct influence of the myth of the redeemer-god who makes his descent to the underworld to conquer the demonic powers. This connection alone, he argues, explains how the idea could appear so early in the New Testament age. As to the means of its entry, Bousset suggests Jewish apocalyptic, and in evidence he cites a Latin fragment among the additions to Sirach, as well as the fantasy of Enoch in which the patriarch is sent to proclaim the punitive judgment of God to the fallen angels.[44] Concerning the time of the myth's entry, Bousset says that it may have occurred when Christianity was no longer at risk from paganism, when such features could be transferred to the person of Christ without coming into dangerous proximity to the heathen-mythological world.[45]

The differences between I Peter and the "common ethic" are often noted. In an essay on I Peter 1:18, W. C. van Unnik (1910-1978) rings the changes on a term used by the author to describe the kind of life from which his readers have now been set free: "You know that you were ransomed from the futile ways inherited from your ancestors *(patroparadotos)*." When combined with the adjective "futile" *(mataia),* this term — with obvious religious connotations and denoting what is venerable or held in high esteem — is altered to its opposite, resulting in a characterization of paganism as null and void. Van Unnik suggests that the author of I Peter may have been the first Christian to apply the epithet to describe his readers' former religion and way of life as worthless. The author's critique is thus unique, but it is used in a significant connection — that of the redemption wrought by Jesus Christ.[46] Regarding the admonition to submit to earthly authority in 2:18-25, Krodel says that this submission is not conceived as yielded through compulsion, but rather "for the Lord's sake . . . as free people" (2:13, 16). The same thought underlies the admonition that wives submit to their husbands'

---

44. Sirach 24:32: "I will go through all the regions deep beneath the earth, and will visit all those who are asleep, and will illumine all who hope in the Lord"; see also Enoch, chaps. 12ff., in Bousset, *Hauptprobleme der Gnosis,* pp. 256-257, n. 1.

45. Bousset, p. 257.

46. W. C. van Unnik, "The Critique of Paganism in I Peter 1:18," *Neotestamentica et Semitica,* Studies in Honor of Matthew Black, ed. E. Earle Ellis and Max Wilcox (Edinburgh: T&T Clark, 1969), pp. 130, 140-141.

authority in 3:1-7, whereas in popular Greek ethics the submission of the wife to her husband meant that the husband should dominate his wife, even to the point of requiring that she worship only his gods.[47]

Despite the similarity that Eduard Schweizer observes between the form of the *paraenesis* in the *Haustafel* of I Peter and the ethics mediated by Hellenistic Judaism, he is still at pains to note the differences. He says, for example, that I Peter never teaches deification of the cosmos, never suggests a link between God and nature or human reason, never gives self-fulfillment or private welfare central place, and nowhere lists God as the first member in a table of duties. What is more drastic, says Schweizer, is that the contrast between masters and slaves is viewed simply as the form of a service relationship that exists in this world and in which the one or the other must prove his worth. This attention to the other who is not an object but a subject gives to the *Haustafeln* their peculiar stamp, and it distances them from the Stoics, who summon to freedom from all-too-intimate relationships. Thus, since everything is subordinated to the will of the Lord and directed to the welfare of the other, I Peter sanctions neither the old nor a revolutionary order.[48] According to Schweizer, this singularity attaching to the *Haustafel* ethics in I Peter is rooted in the knowledge of the teaching and activity of Jesus, especially his dying and rising again: "Not only the greatness of a life in service and submission, but also a link to the other who needs me, is rooted in it, just as is the entire nonenthusiastic view of earthly-human affairs."[49] Again, David Balch concurs: he says that in I Peter the basis of the ethical exhortations is Christological, that "the key identity symbol was a *mythos* not an *ethos,* a sacred story, not a domestic political institution." Balch concludes his essay with the statement that, just as Israel learned to live without priests or kings, the church has learned to live without emperors and slaves or the Roman form of marriage while still maintaining its identity through re-

---

47. Krodel, *I Peter,* pp. 76-77. A relevant passage in Plutarch to which Krodel points reads: "A wife ought not to make friends of her own, but to enjoy her husband's friends in common with him. The gods are the first and most important friends, wherefore it is becoming for a wife to worship and to know only the gods that her husband believes in . . ." (*Plutarch's Moralia,* trans. Frank Cole Babbitt [Cambridge, MA: Harvard University Press, 1971], II, 19, 310-311).

48. Schweizer, "Die Weltlichkeit des Neuen Testaments: die Haustafeln," pp. 402-404, 406, 412.

49. Schweizer, p. 405.

telling the story of Jesus' death and resurrection.[50] The cross spells discontinuity — in this instance, the fracture of "the common ethic."

Gnosis and Its Fracture

Commenting on the hymn in 3:18-19, with its reference to Christ as "put to death in the flesh, but made alive in the spirit," Kurt Rudolph interprets the verse to read that Christ died "fleshly" but that the "spirit Christ," the divine power as such, could not "suffer." His "flesh" or "body" was only the outer covering that could not touch his real, redemptive nature. The idea is not that the "flesh" merely *appeared* to suffer, but that the suffering affected only his body, not his spirit. In this form, Rudolph continues, the verse is merely a variation on the two-natures doctrine; he cites Harnack (1851-1930) to the effect that second-century Christianity often took no offense at Gnostic Docetism. In fact, since this spirit-body dualism threads throughout all of early Christian literature,[51] it is difficult to distinguish it from "genuine docetism" as the heresiologues understood it.[52]

Characteristically, Bultmann says that the Epistle reflects the Gnostic view of salvation as a cosmic work. This feature, he adds, distinguishes its perspective from the older, primitive Christian view originating in Jewish apocalyptic.[53] Windisch agrees that this first appearance of the "myth of Christ's descent into hell" was "certainly" an originally reworked piece of ancient redeemer-mythology transferred to Jesus. As Schrage would suggest twenty years later, Windisch describes it as a variation on the myth of the sun.[54] While Bultmann identifies "the spirits" of 3:19-20, in harmony with the myth, as the souls of the dead who had been hindered in their ascent to the heavenly world and taken captive by the hostile spirit-powers dwelling between heaven

---

50. Balch, "Hellenization/Acculturation in I Peter," pp. 100-101.

51. Cf. pp. 36-39.

52. Kurt Rudolph, *Gnosis und Spätantike Religionsgeschichte,* p. 268. Cf. also Adolf von Harnack, *Lehrbuch der Dogmengeschichte* (Darmstadt: Wissenschaftliche Buchgesellschaft, 1964), I, 212-215.

53. Bultmann, "Bekenntnis- und Liedfragmente im ersten Petrusbrief," p. 7.

54. Windisch, *Die Katholischen Briefe,* pp. 71-72; cf. Schrage, *Der Erste Petrusbrief,* p. 104.

and earth,[55] Windisch registers the uniqueness of the Redeemer's activity in the underworld as limited to proclamation, and he identifies its hearers with the fallen angels of Ethiopic Enoch or with the contemporaries of Noah in the "Haggadah" of Jude 8. At play here, says Windisch, was a Gnostic, anti-Jewish, and anti-Jewish-Christian tendency that emphasized that the Christian Redeemer drew to himself people rejected in the Old Testament. For this reason, he concludes, the notion that the apostle Peter could have introduced this Gnostic myth into Christian doctrine was unbelievable.[56]

Braun's question is this: "Does the author want to say that Christ suffered only in his flesh, and only in his flesh suffered death? Is the connection of the resurrection with the spirit in 3:18 perhaps supposed to mean that according to his human nature he suffered and died, but that according to his divine nature he was alive?"[57] Schrage's suggestion is that "perhaps" the author distinguishes between making alive in the spirit without a body *and* bodily resurrection, or perhaps the author divides the resurrection into the descent *and* the ascension. To this question and suggestion — in other words, to the question of the little Christ-hymn's (thus of the Epistle's) essentially Gnostic character — let the century-old word of the *religionsgeschichtlich* pioneer supply the response. I Peter 3:18-19, Wilhelm Bousset wrote in 1907, testifies to Christian reserve toward the authentically mythological figures of the "fantasy." No more than the fact of the descent itself is appropriated, and for this reason: earliest Christianity needed it to answer the question concerning what happened to Jesus between his crucifixion and resurrection. Only subsequently was the Gnostic redeemer-figure connected with the figure of the historical Jesus Christ.[58] In fact, wherever the mythology dominates and the redeemer is not identified with the historical Jesus Christ, redemption is set in the arch-time. Pagan Gnosis thus knows no real descent into hell, since the nether world is this earth on which the redeemer makes his sojourn. The reason for this is clear: the Gnostic systems were not able to take into themselves the full and

---

55. Bultmann, "Bekenntnis und Liedfragmente im ersten Petrusbrief," p. 5.

56. Windisch, *Die katholischen Briefe,* pp. 72-73.

57. Braun, *Das Leiden Christi,* p. 26.

58. Not even in their pre-Christian period, says Schrage, were the Epistle's gentile readers influenced by the speech- and thought-world of the ancient mystery religions (*Der erste Petrusbrief,* p. 62).

true shape of Jesus the Redeemer. The death of Christ stuck in the craw of Gnosticism. And as for the so-called Christian Gnosis, only incidentally and secondarily does it suggest that the coming of the Christ occurred for believers' salvation. Bousset concludes:

> After all our observation, we may assert that the redemptive myth or myths of the Gnostic religion are not first derived from the circle of ideas within the Christian religion, but were present beforehand and only synthetically combined with this circle of ideas. In Gnosis, then, alien mythical redeemer figures are subsequently and synthetically identified with the figure of Christ.[59]

The operative term is "synthetically" *(künstlich),* for if, as no one cares to deny, the mythology of Gnosis ran ahead of Christianity, its attachment to Christianity in terms of the message of a historical redemption ran far behind it. While Bultmann sets the couplet "put to death in the flesh, but made alive in the spirit" as the master theme in I Peter (which, incidentally, may have served as the basis for the six-line hymn in I Timothy 3:16: "He was revealed in flesh, vindicated in spirit, seen by angels, proclaimed among Gentiles, believed in throughout the world, taken up in glory"), he once more assents to discontinuity because — however described, as "Christus Victor" or otherwise — the couplet affirms a Christology that makes the way to glory conditional on suffering and death.

Christian Sources and Their Fracture

The Epistle of I Peter has appropriated much traditional material, including doxologies, creedal formulae, hymn fragments, and Jesus-tradition. Thus the reference to Christ in I Peter 1:20 as "destined before the foundation of the world" and "revealed at the end of the ages" appears to derive from early tradition, to which the author then appends his own words ("for your sake"), together with the fragment of a creedal formula ("have come to trust in God, who raised him from the dead" [1:21]). Selwyn says of 2:6-10 that the hypothesis of the *periechei* ("it

---

59. Cf. Bousset, *Hauptprobleme der Gnosis,* pp. 238-239, 242, 256, 259, 276.

stands in Scripture") as originally belonging to a hymn solved so many problems as to be almost certain. More probably, the verses that follow (2:18-24) suggest an origin in early hymnody or confession, perhaps even in Gospel passion narrative.[60] As for 3:18-22, there is little doubt that it cites an early tradition that explicated the meaning of Christ's death.

Whether or not it reflects a rudimentary version of the more elaborated Christological saga in I Timothy 3:16, its similarity to that passage, with its flesh-spirit antithesis, suggests an origin in a tradition that combined the interpretation of Christ's death as atoning sacrifice with its interpretation as vicarious representation. In sum, contemporary interpretation tends to support the hypothesis of three Christ-hymns (1:17-21; 2:21-25, and 3:18-22).[61]

One of the oddest features concerning the question of Christian sources attaches to the now dimly remembered dispute between Baur and Bernhard Weiss.[62] The question of the Epistle's date of composition furnished the occasion. In 1855, Weiss had written that this Epistle could only have been written when the gentile-Christian element had not yet gained ascendancy through Paul's activity, that is, prior to the apostle's third missionary journey. According to Weiss, the gentile-Christians, initiated in the primitive community "ahead of time" *(vor der Zeit)*, formed only a vanishing and inconsiderable part of it. Consequently, the apostle Peter, as author of this Epistle, could not possibly have read Paul; in fact, the reverse was true: Paul had made use of Peter.

A year after Weiss's pronouncement, Baur responded that what might reflect an early stage of doctrinal development could just as easily reflect a period in which the original opposition of the various lines in earliest Christianity had been so weakened that what was common and mediating was affirmed, thus preparing the way for the emerging catholic church. During this period the Christians were no longer a shy, self-

---

60. Selwyn says the *verba Christi* reflected in the Epistle are predominantly Matthaean, and Krodel says that what the author knows is the Synoptic Sayings tradition (cf. *The First Epistle of St. Peter*, pp. 17, 24); Martin says that the verses represent a kind of early Christology that quickly dropped from developing Christian thought (*The Theology of Jude, I Peter, and 2 Peter*, p. 94). Cf. Krodel, *I Peter*, p. 65.

61. Windisch, *Die Katholischen Briefe*, pp. 56, 65, 70.

62. Note, for example, Achtemeier's reference to a critique of Weiss's position dating almost twenty years later than that of Baur (Achtemeier, *I Peter*, p. 15, n. 138).

engrossed, and self-contained sect; instead, they were an independently emerging society eager to win public opinion. Consequently, the author — who was *not* the apostle Peter — had in fact read Paul, and the proof lay in the Epistle's doctrine of the death of Christ (4:1), in its making Paul's companion Silvanus the transmitter of the letter (5:12), and in its holding to the principle of the universal scope of Christianity — thus the integrity of gentile Christianity, free from the law, alongside Jewish Christianity. What had vanished were the earlier and peculiarly Jewish-Christian requirements, and what remained indicated that everything around which Jewish- and gentile-Christians wished to unite had already been intended by the two apostles themselves, the point at which Acts takes up its position.[63] "Is it possible," Baur asked, "to conceive a clear connection of ideas without supplementing the unmotivated statements from the Pauline context?" In the years that followed, more than one author took note with Baur of the Epistle's omission of the problem of synagogue and church, of the status and future of old Israel, of Torah observance, or of the apostles' decrees (Acts 15:23-29).[64] And more than one author said that the "theological proximity" affecting even the Epistle's terminology is possible only within the reach of Pauline ideas, a fact that explains its connection with the Deutero-Paulines.[65]

Current discussion of Christian sources used in the Epistle is more or less a reprise of Baur's argument. That is, aside from noting the letter's framework as a convention originally coined by Paul, the bulk of scholarship concentrates on I Peter as reflecting a period in which the questions passionately debated in Paul's time no longer play a role.[66] In an extended essay on the relationship between I Peter and the Pauline tradition, Jens Herzer says that, while I Peter takes up early Christian

63. Baur, "Der erste petrinische Brief," pp. 198-199, 203, 213, 221, 233, 236; cf. also *Die Christliche Kirche in den drei ersten Jahrhunderten*, I, 123-125, 205-206, 208, 235.

64. Cf., e.g., Krodel, *I Peter*, p. 66; on the other hand, cf. Achtemeier (*I Peter*, p. 37), who says that the Christology of the Epistle offers ambiguous evidence for the attempt to determine whether it belongs to a time contemporary with or subsequent to that of Simon Peter.

65. Schrage, *Der erste Petrusbrief*, p. 59. Along with the *descensus* in 3:19, Bultmann traces Ephesians 4:7-10 to the Gnostic redeemer myth ("Bekenntnis- und Liedfragmente im ersten Petrusbrief," p. 5).

66. Cf. Bultmann, "Bekenntnis und Liedfragmenteim ersten Petrusbrief," pp. 7-8; Delling, *Der Kreuzestod Jesu in der urchristlichen Verkündigung*, p. 55; Schrage, *Der erste Petrusbrief*, p. 60; Krodel, *I Peter*, pp. 64-65; Achtemeier, *I Peter*, p. 19.

tradition regarding Christ's saving work in direct reference to Isaiah 52–53, Paul prefers other concepts for describing it and inserts the ransom motif only where he can allow it as already known. He continues that I Peter's division of the event of deliverance and the reception of salvation into present and future is without parallel in the *Corpus Paulinum* — that, conversely, the Pauline emphasis on the completed atonement and deliverance still to occur is not found in I Peter. He further notes that the Epistle's unfolding of the Deutero-Isaianic motif of the sacrificial lamb in its description of the saving work of God has no correspondence in Paul. Herzer concludes that these differences in contextualization speak for a level of tradition in which Pauline terms and ideas were reshaped, independent of their Pauline origin. I Peter is thus an independent witness to early Christian tradition alongside Paul and his school.[67]

Thus, whatever language or conceptuality may be urged as supplying the mental furniture of the author of I Peter — whether "orthodox" or sectarian Judaism, Gnosis, Hellenistic thought, or Christian tradition — it has all undergone qualification, and at the same place where the others under review encountered fracture: at the cross of Jesus of Nazareth, confessed as Son of God and Savior.

---

67. Jens Herzer, *Petrus oder Paulus? Studien über das Verhältnis des Ersten Petrusbriefes zur paulinischen Tradition* (Tübingen: Mohr Siebeck, 1998), pp. 133-134, 142.

Conclusion

For the authors of the New Testament, the death of Jesus of Nazareth was the "anomaly" that threatened allegiance to whatever language- and thought-forms they may have inherited, and that required a new model, or "paradigm," by which to see themselves, to see others, and to see God.

With respect to the Old Testament and its theology, our authors' "hermeneutical move" begins with the event of Jesus' death and from there harks back to the biblical text. In Paul's debate with the synagogue, he declares that only from the perspective of that event does the Old Testament become intelligible. Remarking that Moses had veiled his face to keep the Israelites from noting its waning brilliance and thus concluding that his leadership was at an end, he adds:

> To this very day, when they hear the reading of the old covenant, that same veil is still there, since only in Christ is it set aside. Indeed, to this very day whenever Moses is read, a veil lies over their minds; but when one turns to the Lord, the veil is removed. (II Cor. 3:15-16)

Obviously, this move denotes a wrenching of the biblical text insofar as it is the event of Jesus' death that creates the history of salvation and refers the Christian community to the Old Testament for an interpretation of its faith. Prophecy is thus rendered *from* Christ and not *toward* him. Methodologically speaking, this move was not of Christian origin. The community of Qumran, for example, could take a contemporary event for its point of departure and, like the Christian community, discover the Old Testament anew. What was new in the Christian community was its exclusive reference to the sufferings and death of Jesus of Nazareth as the point of hermeneutical departure. Thus, as Hans Weder says, by virtue of its relationship to the cross, a truth was attached to the biblical word that it did not initially possess.[1] This attachment renders the relationship between cross and Scripture more than dialectical; rather, the relationship is *diastatic*. The fulfillment does not automatically follow from the promise; for the promise cannot be what it is, cannot emerge as promise, without first being shattered, or fractured. "Scripture fulfillment" is thus too facile an expression for New Testament interpretation of the event of Christ. In fact, there would never have been a "scandal" if that event had been seen as making one, two, or even three Old Testament predictions come true. As the old rabbi said, "When God says one thing, I hear two." Nothing in Paul's method distanced it from that of his contemporaries. It was the incessant emphasis on the singular occurrence of the crucifixion of one lone victim and the submission to it of all the language and conceptuality adhering to Israel's hope that fixed the gulf.

As for apocalyptic, the first and primary variation on the Good News may well have had its home in white-hot expectancy. And, despite Käsemann's denial, Jesus himself may have been an apocalypticist. Why else would his community have interpreted his person and mission within its thought-forms? For one thing, the period in which he lived was aflame with apocalyptic expectation: the revolt of Judas of Galilee (4 B.C.E.), urging comparison with Jesus' own appearance (cf. Acts 5:37); the anti-Semitic measures of Tiberius Caesar; the revolt of 66-70 C.E., or of Bar Kochba in 132-135 C.E. — some if not all were driven by apocalyptic reckonings and furnished the larger context of Jesus' life and work. The question is whether or not Jesus could have avoided conceiving his person and mission within such a framework, whether or not he awaited the visible manifestation of God — and all the more as his own death came into view. His terror in the garden, that contest of wills ending in "yet, not what I want, but what you want," cannot have been written merely to adjust the Jesus story to the readers' plight. The fracture of what had evolved into that first and primary variation occurred with its harnessing to the crucifixion. Let Matthew 27 ("the earth shook . . . the rocks were split . . . tombs

---

1. Weder, *Das Kreuz Jesu* (Göttingen: Vandenhoeck & Ruprecht, 1981), p. 145.

also were opened . . . many bodies of the saints who had fallen asleep were raised") stand in evidence. And as for Jesus, what could his cry "My God, my God, why have you forsaken me?" have meant but the fracture of expectation? It is too much to say with Schweitzer that Jesus intended to compel the kingdom to come by his death; but it is not too much to say with Bultmann that, *this side of the resurrection*, "we may not veil from ourselves the possibility that he suffered a collapse."[2]

Regarding the Stoa, however similar its *peristasen* to the tables of duties or enumerations of destiny's "strokes" in the New Testament; however similar its call to nonengagement, to steadfastness in face of calamity; and however suggestive its idea of the body and its members — it, too, suffered fracture. And what lay at its core, its everlasting preoccupation with the self, its "nonengagement" without limits, its capacity for overcoming evil in an autosuggestive feat of the will, its need of the other only for the other's applause after having scaled some moral height, and, to whatever that self belonged, in whatever it inhered as an indigenous thing, a thing given with nature — this all had to give way before the message of the cross.

Gnosis, with its innumerable "denominations," each with its own cosmogony, anthropology, and soteriology, with its flood of charismatic leaders, its geniuses and prophetesses, its libraries of gospels and acts, came near to engulfing the nascent Christian fellowship and moved that fellowship to protective measures against what threatened its own origins and goals. Gnosis has left its traces everywhere, and it still attracts an elite core that is ready to lead the hordes to some glorious future. But in the end, Gnosis and the "word of the cross" are incommensurables, requiring removal of the one or the other: for while the one emphasizes the human's oneness in essence with deity, the other flatly denies it.

That notion of the human as divine did not originate with Stoicism or Gnosis. However casual the parentage, the idea had its origin with the Greeks. For Socrates and for Plato, the nature of knowing was hidden in the soul; the striving for truth was nothing but the unfolding of the soul and its own content.[3] Hence, righteousness was innate, an in-

---

2. Rudolf Bultmann, "The Primitive Christian Kerygma and the Historical Jesus," in *The Historical Jesus and the Kerygmatic Christ,* trans. and ed. Carl E. Braaten and Roy A. Harrisville (Nashville: Abingdon Press, 1964), p. 24.

3. Plato, "The Meno," 86B: "If the truth about reality is always in our soul . . ."

ner condition of soul by which each of its parts performed its function and helped to create a unity and stave off whatever threatened disunity.[4] It was the genuine and true *physis* of the soul — lodged and borne in the soul — for which reason none could willingly deceive himself or choose evil.[5] Only *technē* was needed: a proper directing of the soul toward what was innate to it, a directing toward what was already there, toward deity.

Our New Testament authors could never have reconciled themselves to this total orientation to the self, because they had come to embrace an event that occurred completely independent of the self, with neither origin nor goal in the self, with the self unasked, unsolicited, and for this reason in opposition to the self — an action whose initiative lay solely with God. This was the "peculiarly new symbol."

Not even pre-Pauline, pre-Synoptic, pre-Johannine Christian material could avoid fracture. In response to the alleged anti-Semitism of a recent biblically based film on the passion, two scholars — one Christian and one Jewish — said that the Bible is "hardly an exact transcript of what happened, but a multi-layered document, evolving over time."[6] The latter part of that sentence is relevant to our discussion. If, for example, in one layer beneath the Philippians hymn the move toward the stage of Christ's exaltation was too sudden, it was "depotentiated" with a tiny insertion: ". . . and became obedient to the point of death — even death on a cross" (Phil. 2:8b). Or, if in Mark's sources, Jesus "doth bestride the narrow world like a Colossus," that portrait is altered almost to the point of being defaced by the constant of the death-motif. Or again, whether or not Matthew represents a voice no longer heard in all its gentile alarm, that part of his Gospel that sets him off from the oth-

---

(*Protagoras and Meno,* trans. W. K. C. Guthrie [Harmondsworth: Penguin Books, 1970], p. 139).

4. Plato, "The Republic," 443D: "Justice . . . is not a matter of external behavior, but of the inward self . . ." (*The Republic of Plato,* trans. Francis Macdonald Cornford [Oxford: Oxford University Press, 1971], p. 141).

5. Plato, "Protagoras," 345D: ". . . no wise man believes anyone sins willingly or willingly perpetrates any evil or base act"; 358C: "No one willingly goes to meet evil or what he thinks to be evil. To make for what one believes to be evil, instead of making for the good, is not, it seems, in human nature" (Plato, *Protagoras and Meno,* pp. 80, 95-96).

6. Calvin Roetzel, Barry D. Cytron, "'The Passion' Represents a Teachable Moment," *St. Paul Pioneer Press,* February 19, 2004.

ers — with its almost exclusively apocalyptic cast — is bent, warped, and adapted to the event of the cross.

For each New Testament author, the death of Jesus of Nazareth, God's Son, made Lord by virtue of his obedience unto death, "even death on a cross," was the crisis, the "anomaly" that effected a revolution in thought, mind, and soul, a revolution through which he had come to see himself, others, and the world. Now, with whatever "paradigm," whatever theory, value, or technique, with whatever language, conceptuality, way of viewing reality, or looking at the world the New Testament writers came to their encounter with the gospel of Jesus Christ, the death of Jesus forced them to a drastic revision. The "fracture" of language and conceptuality, the "depotentiation" in Paul, in the Gospel writers, in Hebrews, and in I Peter, attests to the discontinuity between the deed of the cross and the old constellations of theory and practice — all of it a reflex of the divine initiative in sending Jesus to his cross. Put positively, with each author, faith in the death of Jesus Christ as the event in which God acted decisively and ultimately for the salvation of the world is not only implicit "in, with, and under" whatever language- or thought-spheres that author draws on to interpret it; the cross is the *criterion* for their use.[7] These spheres lose their independence, and whatever views of reality they once contained are now warped, twisted, and bent to serve the central model.

True, the death of Jesus has its analogies in the crucifixions of thousands in the Roman empire; true, Jesus could become just one more of the dying and rising savior gods parading throughout antiquity; and true, Christians might not look to him for a way of life but for salvation and thus prefer their Christ crucified. Nevertheless, the passion stories themselves, which are, not arguably but demonstrably, the oldest shape of the gospel narrative, render improbable if not impossible that reversal of cause and effect that assigns to Jesus' "countercultural lifestyle" rather than to his *death* the status of heart and core of Christian witness and faith.[8]

Obviously, what the cross of Christ intends with respect to content is not the same everywhere. A self-conscious theology of the cross may be "an extreme theology."[9] The new model, or matrix, symbol of the indigest-

---

7. Cf. Jürgen Becker, "Die neutestamentliche Rede vom Sühnetod Jesu," p. 48.

8. Cf. Patterson, *Beyond the Passion,* pp. 43, 79, 117, 127-130.

9. Ulrich Luz, "*Theologia crucis* als Mitte der Theologie im Neuen Testament," p. 117.

ibility of human tragedy and the sign of God's own life, made a single or indivisible view impossible. To induce fracture was its reason for being:

> For since, in the wisdom of God, the world did not know God through wisdom, it pleased God through the folly of what we preach to save those who believe. . . . Christ crucified, a stumbling block to Jews and folly to Gentiles, but to those who are called, both Jews and Greeks, Christ the power of God and the wisdom of God. (I Cor. 1:21-24)

So it was inevitable that the event of Christ's death should attract a host of metaphors, mixed or otherwise, for its description. With a slight revision of one scholar's reply to the question of whether or not the metaphors of Christ's work in the New Testament imply a "metanarrative" in which each finds its place, the metanarrative to which each New Testament author contributes is none other than the story of the passion itself.[10]

Once more, that cross signaled an activity for which God and God alone had the initiative. And *there,* finally, lay the "scandal" or the "foolishness," because the declaration that "while we were still weak" — or "while we still were sinners," or "while we were enemies" — Christ "died for the ungodly" (Rom. 5:6-8) ruled out, by implication, anything human, whether in preparation for, preamble to, or in execution of the deed. Protagoras said that "man is the measure of all things," and Plato altered his maxim to read that "God is the measure of all things," but that God was what anyone could become. And there lay the legitimacy for that construct of the "redeemed redeemer," who allegedly sat for the portrait of the Christ. And there lay justification for merging the power to redeem with the capacity for being redeemed, whether or not it would take the "edge" from Gnosis and render its prayer a monologue.[11] The Gnostic's prayer was in fact a monologue, the result of an idea of redemption as monological.

It has been said that it would not have been to the advantage of the earliest Christian community tactically to counter massive disbelief with massive miracle, that is, by announcing Jesus' resurrection, especially when Jews and pagans alike were ready to affirm resurrection or

---

10. Lee C. Camp, "The Cross in Christendom: Constantinianism and the Doctrine of the Atonement, or Understanding Jesus' Cross when 'Everybody's Doing It,'" *Restoration Quarterly* 40, No. 2 (1998), 101-102.

11. Colpe, *Die Religionsgeschichtliche Schule,* pp. 174, 186, 188.

immortality. That lay at the heart of their conceptuality; what they could not believe was that a messiah or *kyrios* could die. Some believed with the Wisdom of Solomon that the righteous would "shine forth and run like sparks through the stubble . . . would govern nations and rule over peoples."[12] Or they believed with Jubilees that the Lord would heal his servants and drive out their adversaries, that they would rejoice forever and ever and would see all their curses on their enemies fulfilled.[13] In the Mishna, heart and soul of that codification of "oral Torah" (called the Talmud) that was given shape two to four centuries after Christ, the posterity of those who agreed to Jesus' death confessed that humility leads to the shunning of sin, the shunning of sin to saintliness, saintliness to the Holy Spirit, and the Holy Spirit to the resurrection of the dead.[14] They believed that whoever says there is no resurrection has no share in the world to come.[15] And a pagan Phoenician could hymn an Egyptian prince whom Zeus would lead to Olympus:

> Thou didst perish by a pestilence that devastated all the land, before thou couldst grasp in thy young hand the scepter of thy fathers. Yet night did not receive thee from night; for such princes are not led by Hades to his house, but by Zeus to Olympus.[16]

12. "In the time of their visitation they will shine forth, and will run like sparks through the stubble. They will govern nations and rule over peoples, and the Lord will reign over them forever. Those who trust in him will understand truth, and the faithful will abide with him in love, because grace and mercy are upon his holy ones, and he watches over his elect" (Wisdom of Solomon 3:7-9, *The New Oxford Annotated Bible with the Apocryphal/Deuterocanonical Books,* ed. Bruce M. Metzger and Roland E. Murphy (New York: Oxford University Press, 1991), p. 60.

13. "And then the Lord will heal his servants, and they will rise up and see great peace. And they will drive out their enemies, and the righteous ones will see and give praise, and rejoice forever and ever with joy; and they will see all of their judgments and all of their curses among their enemies" (Jubilees 23:30, *The Old Testament Pseudepigrapha* II, 102).

14. Soṭah 9:15, *The Mishnah,* trans. Herbert Danby (London: Oxford University Press, 1964), pp. 306-307.

15. "And these are they that have no share in the world to come: he that says that there is no resurrection of the dead prescribed in the Law, and [he that says] that the Law is not from Heaven, and an Epicurean" (Sanhedrin 10:1, *The Mishnah,* p. 397).

16. Antipater of Sidon (ca. 125 B.C.E.), Book VII, Epigram 241, *The Greek Anthology,* trans. W. R. Paton (Cambridge, MA: Harvard University Press, 1970), II, 135-136.

Concentration on the cross could not long endure; the cross needed overcoming in a synthesis. That endless hammering away at the Son, who not only worked his own ruin but the ruin of the Father who arranged his death, . . . so that from then on, apart from that one act of obedience, not a soul would ever know whether or not it was praying to God or to itself — that needed domesticating. That turning of the story of the creation on its head, making the serpent whom the Creator had cursed a symbol of life, of God, needed attenuating through extension. That single, solitary event of Jesus' death needed parceling out over two thousand years, so that what was once said of Christ could now be said of his devotees, so that the line "cursed is everyone who hangs on a tree" could be exchanged for "led on their way by this triumphant sign, the hosts of God in conqu'ring ranks combine."

Long ago, Immanuel Kant saw the truth of it — and perhaps clearer than any other. In *Religion Within the Boundaries of Mere Reason,* he said that, if there were such a faith that could improve "the whole human being radically," then it would have to be regarded as imparted and inspired directly by heaven, and "everything, the moral constitution of humankind included, would then be reduced to an unconditional decree of God: 'He hath mercy on whom he will, and whom he will he hardeneth,' and this, taken according to the letter, is the *salto mortale* of human reason."[17] Precisely such a religion and such an unconditioned decree, spelling the death of every human attempt at constructing a single view of life, of reality — whether baptized by the Christian community or not — lies at the heart of the biblical witness. That death of a system that Kant implied must follow, should there be such a religion as could remake a person altogether, is precisely what occurred with the New Testament authors. Each came with a worldview that he shared with thousands of his contemporaries, and for each the cross meant the abandonment of that view. Not that he exchanged the language- and thought-forms of his time for ecstatic gibberish: many of the words peculiar to the New Testament are compounds of words the entire world already knew. Rather, the writers' abandonment of that worldview meant that they now abstracted those forms and that language from whatever schemes or systems they

17. Immanuel Kant, "Religion within the Boundaries of Mere Reason," in *Religion and Rational Theology,* trans. Allen W. Wood, George Di Giovanni (Cambridge, UK: Cambridge University Press, 1996), p. 151.

once served and by sheer force made them fit the gospel of the cross. The Son of God was going forth to war in a chariot whose car had been carved for Dionysus, whose wheels had been fashioned for Zeno of Citium, and which was drawn by horses sired by Jewish apocalyptic. From any rational or systematic point of view, the result could only be a motley, a linsey-woolsey, a hodgepodge of thought. The evidence lies on every page of the New Testament, and all the attempts to fly in the face of that fracture of thought that the earliest community believed it had suffered by God's own hand — in the interest of some view, some "theology" — have not succeeded in erasing it.

Despite attempts at eliminating its turbulence, the cross denotes an activity that defies repression, perhaps even expression. For Walter Benjamin (1892-1940), celebrated Jewish philosopher and critic, the reprint of Grünewald's *Crucifixion*[18] that hung on his study wall for years represented the *Ausdruckslose,* a thing beyond telling, out of the reach of words.[19] The cross refuses assimilation but takes captive every serious thought or reflection paid to earth or heaven. And its initiative is with the One who warps and twists the present to his future, not only with those who come near or believe him, but with everything and everyone destined one day to acknowledge, in the words of that great beast of the musical jungle, that "earth may vanish, heaven may sever, God is God forever!"[20]

18. The central panel of Matthias Grünewald's (Mathis Gothardt, 1606-1688) retable for the altar at Isenheim, Germany.

19. Gershom Scholem, *The Story of a Friendship,* trans. Harry Zohn (Philadelphia: The Jewish Publication Society of America, 1981), p. 37.

20. J. S. Bach, "Jesu Meine Freude," Movement V, BWV 227.

Index of Names

Index of Scripture and
Other Ancient Literature